Teaching Performance Expectations for Educating English Learners

María V. Balderrama
California State University, San Bernardino

Lynne T. Díaz-Rico
California State University, San Bernardino

PEARSON
AB

Boston   New York   San Francisco
Mexico City   Montreal   Toronto   London   Madrid   Munich   Paris
Hong Kong   Singapore   Tokyo   Cape Town   Sydney

Senior Editor: *Aurora Martínez Ramos*
Series Editorial Assistant: *Mekea Harvey*
Senior Marketing Manager: *Krista Clark*
Editorial Production Service: *Omegatype Typography, Inc.*
Composition and Manufacturing Buyer: *Andrew Turso*
Electronic Composition: *Omegatype Typography, Inc.*
Photo Researcher: *Omegatype Typography, Inc.*
Cover Administrator: *Joel Gendron*

For related titles and support materials, visit our online catalog at www.ablongman.com.

Between the time Website information is gathered and then published, it is not unusual for some sites to have closed. Also, the transcription of URLs can result in typographical errors. The publisher would appreciate notification where these errors occur so that they may be corrected in subsequent editions.

Library of Congress Cataloging-in-Publication Data

Balderrama, María V.
    Teaching performance expectations for educating English learners / María V. Balderrama, Lynne T. Díaz-Rico
        p. cm.
    Includes bibliographical references and index.
    ISBN 0-205-42219-5 (pbk.)
    1. English language—Study and teaching—Foreign speakers.   2. English teachers—Training of.   I. Díaz-Rico, Lynne T.   II. Title.

PE1128.A2B297 2006
428'.0071—dc22

2005050979

Printed in the United States of America

10 9 8 7 6 5 4 3 2 1   10   09   08   07   06   05

Photo Credits

p. 1, Ken Karp/Prentice Hall School Division; p. 19, Mark Richards/PhotoEdit; p. 40, Robert Harbison; p. 77, Courtesy of María V. Balderrama; p. 105, Bob Daemmrich/PhotoEdit; p. 139, Courtesy of María V. Balderrama; p. 160, Robert Harbison; p. 196, T. Lindfors/ Lindfors Photography; p. 240, Ken Karp/Prentice Hall School Division; p. 276, Pearson Learning Photo Studio/David Mager; p. 291, Robert Harbison; p. 309, T. Lindfors/Lindfors Photography

To Elizabeth G. Cohen, my mentor, who taught me the importance of teaching with integrity. —MVB

To Phillip, Voltaire, Daniel, and Eva: Thank you for your love and care. To Sondra, Simon, Ian, and Liana: Love to my extended family. To my students, who work so hard as learners and as teachers: Thank you for your devotion to the success of English learners. To my colleagues: Thank you for making the education of English learners a worthy profession. —LTD-R

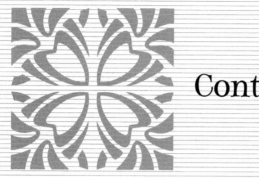

Contents

part I *Expectations for Teaching Performance*

part IV *Planning Standards-Based Instruction*

6 Integrity in Designing and Planning Instruction for English Learners   139

part   **V**   *Instructional Applications*

7   Promoting Academic Achievement of English Learners   160

part VI *Assessment and Accountability for Students*

10 The Assessment of English Learners   276

part VII   *Assessment and Accountability for Teachers*

List of Tables, Figures, and Boxes

Tables

Preface

About 18 percent of the 300 million residents of the United States report that they do not speak English at home. Among the children in this population who are in school, many are not proficient in English. In the past, many teachers were not well prepared to provide instruction for English learners, but the standards-based education movement has raised the bar for teachers. Teaching standards are now available that specify the expectations that govern teaching practices for English learners so they receive English-language development and access to academic content.

This book addresses the **Teaching Performance Expectations (TPEs)** for English language learners that have been established by the California Commission on Teacher Credentialing. Each of the sixteen expectations is embodied in one of the Chapters 3 through 11.

The organization of these chapters follows the cycle of foundations, planning, application, and assessment (see Figure 2.2, page 34) that is used to display the four parts of teaching: *Foundations* consist of pedagogical knowledge, theories of learning and language acquisition, and knowledge about the learner; *planning* consists of teacher planning in light of state and local standards and informed by professional development. This knowledge and planning is applied to three areas of education *application:* academic development, English-language development, and primary-language development. Last, *assessment* consists of teacher-made tests, standardized assessment, and accountability to community and family members and others with a stake in educational outcomes.

The most exciting aspect of the teacher's role in educating English learners is that this vocation can be performed with integrity (see Figure 2.1, page 21). The role demands a high level of professional knowledge and skill, as well as moral courage, because it involves expertise in content, high academic expectations for students, a flexible intercultural repertoire, clarity of vision, professional ethics, and, what is perhaps most important, willingness to be fully human. These aspects are explored in Chapter 2.

A note about terminology is in order—the term **English learner** denotes students whose first language is not English and who are engaged in the process of learning English. This term is shortened from the slightly redundant term *English-language learner,* which has unfortunately given rise to the acronym ELL. The older terms *non-English proficient* (NEP), *limited-English proficient* (LEP), and *fluent-English proficient* (FEP) are no longer widely used. However, when sources are cited using the older terms, the original text is preserved.

A last note about grade levels: Pedagogical examples are distributed over grade levels kindergarten through high school, but many basic principles hold true for grades K–12.

Readers are asked to evaluate the knowledge base that is presented with their own grade-level specialty in mind.

Acknowledgments

Muchísimas gracias a todos los que nos dieron apoyo y cariño durante le escritura de este libro. Gracias to our colleagues who shared their experiences and expertise. The teachers and students with whom we have worked have given us insights and examples. In addition to those who gave so much of their time, expertise, and support for this book, we would like to thank the staff of the California Commission on Teacher Credentialing for their work in designing California's 2042 credential. We continue to thank our teacher education students at CSUSB who have enriched our understanding of the teaching–learning process as it relates to second-language learners.

To all those who have provided linguistic and cultural support not only to English learners, but also to those who have struggled to acquire a second language and adapt to a new culture, we salute you. We also thank Aurora Martínez and the editorial staff at Allyn and Bacon for their efforts. Finally, we would like to thank the following reviewers: Barbara Hruska, University of Tampa; Rosalinda Quintanar, San Jose State University; Rebecca G. Stewart, Dominican University of California; and Kathyrn Z. Weed, California State University, San Bernardino.

1 Professional Preparation to Teach English Learners

Increasing numbers of English learners attend high schools in the United States.

expectation

■ The prospective teacher is able to describe the roles of the educator in the classroom, school, community, and profession; is able to consult with other colleagues and share expertise and research about teaching English learners; exhibits motivation to contribute time and expertise to professional organizations. *(Adapted from Element L of the Required Elements for Teaching Performance for the Advanced Teaching English Learners course of the Clear [Second-Tier] California Teaching Credential. Reprinted by permission of the California Commission on Teacher Credentialing.)*

Many elementary and secondary classrooms at the beginning of the twenty-first century have a diverse look. Many towns and cities in the United States have a multicultural history, with residents whose heritage could be traced both to Native Americans and to immigrants from many parts of the world. Continuing this tradition of diversity are modern-day immigrants, who bring to the United States their deepest and highest desires, dreams, and ideals, just as people did in the past. Contemporary pedagogy, however, differs from that offered in classrooms of yesteryear. Teachers are adapting instruction to meet the specific needs of culturally and linguistically diverse (CLD) students, especially English learners, using **English-language development (ELD)** techniques. (See the glossary for a definition of this and other terms, and Table 1.1 for a set of useful acronyms in this field.) Skilled teachers now are able to include English learners as they ensure that all students have access to an excellent education.

Language learning is a complex, dynamic process that forms the foundation for academic skills. Perhaps the most important result of current research is widespread acknowledgment of the value of bilingualism. In countries all over the world, competence in more than one language is the norm, not the exception. Students who come to school already speaking a home language other than English have the potential to become bilingual if schooling could preserve and augment their **native-language** proficiency.

Because a growing number of classrooms across the United States have English learners, Teaching English to Speakers of Other Languages (TESOL) educators are in increasing demand. Many mainstream teachers—even those who do not define themselves as TESOL or bilingual educators—need English-language development (ELD) strategies to teach their students.

This chapter offers an overview of the demographics of English-language learners. In the past, students who did not speak English were called *limited English proficient* (LEP). Many educators, however, object to the term because it has a negative connotation, focusing on what students cannot do, and it "fails to dignify the effort they are making to become proficient" (Fields, 1997, p. 5).

This book uses the term *English learner* to mean "students whose first (primary, native, heritage) language is not English and who are learning English at school." (See Table 1.1.) But who are English learners?

English Learners in U.S. Schools

English learners in U.S. elementary and secondary schools need English-language development in addition to academics. Many have educational experiences and literacy skills in their native language, whereas others may have had little or no previous schooling and are unable to read and write or perform academically at grade level in their first language. Aside from their developing English skills, English learners possess the same range of skills and educational needs as any other students, with academic abilities across a wide range and with unique interests and talents.

Schooling: An Academic and Linguistic Challenge

English learners must learn the same academic content as English-speaking students, but at the same time they must acquire a new language, which is an intellectually demanding and time-consuming task. In school, academic English is employed by teachers and used in textbooks, increasing the difficulty of comprehension as students advance in grade level. At the same time, English learners who are immigrants must adjust to a new culture, as well as integrate socially into the life of the school.

table 1.1 Useful Acronyms in the Profession of Teaching English Learners

Acronym	Meaning
BSM	Bilingual syntax measure
CCR	Coordinated compliance review
CELDT	California English Language Development Test
CUM	Cumulative education file
ELAC	English language advisory committee
ELD	English-language development
ELL	English-language learner
ESL	English as a second language
FEP	Fluent English proficient
LAT	Language assessment team
LEP	Limited English proficient
NABE	National Association for Bilingual Education
NEP	Non-English proficient
PAC	Parental advisory committee
PTA	Parent–teacher association
PEW	Parent exemption waiver
QRC	Quality review criteria
RSP	Resource specialist program
SABE/2	Spanish assessment of basic education (secondary)
SDAIE	Specially designed academic instruction in English
SIP	School improvement plan
SOLOM	Student oral language observation matrix
SLS	Speech language specialist
SST	School study team
TESOL	Teachers of English to Speakers of Other Languages
TPA	Teaching performance assessment
TPE	Teaching performance expectation

Source: Adapted from Rose (2001).

The United States has laws and judicial rulings that govern the process of educating English learners (see Chapter 9). In 1974 the Supreme Court ruled in *Lau v. Nichols* that school districts must provide special services to English learners, including language-instruction programs that allow them to progress academically while they are acquiring English-language skills—that is, educational programs must feature both academic content and English-language development components. School district programs vary in design depending on the composition of the student population, available language resources, and social and contextual factors.

English Learners and the No Child Left Behind Act

In 2001 the Elementary and Secondary Education Act (ESEA) was reauthorized and renamed the No Child Left Behind (NCLB) Act. Funding for English learners is contingent on states providing evidence that

[C]hildren who are limited English proficient, including immigrant children and youth, attain English proficiency, develop high levels of academic attainment in English, and meet the same challenging State academic content and student academic achievement standards as all children are expected to meet. (NCLB, 2001)

Under pressure to provide this accountability, however, states must test English learners—even those in the earliest stage of language acquisition. This has proved to be a burden for these learners.

The goal that each student master the same set of designated and standardized academic knowledge may seem a noble ideal. In actuality, it is carried out in school systems in which the resources to accomplish equality are not available, and where students entering the school at the beginning stages of learning English are held to the same academic standards as native English speakers. The problem remains as to how these standards can be implemented in a manner that does not further disadvantage, or punish, English learners.

The scramble to respond to the terrorist attack on the United States on September 11, 2001, caused a federal reassessment of second-language study programs in U.S. schools. The federal government has made funds available under the Foreign Language Assistance Program for foreign-language study in elementary and secondary schools. Among bilingual program models, two-way (or dual) immersion has been chosen as the premier models because of the opportunity such programs offer to both language-majority and language-minority students to become proficient in two languages.

The education of students whose home language is not English has been a challenge since the early days of North American colonization, and many kinds of educational programs have addressed the complicated balancing act required to preserve first-language skills, teach English, and deliver grade-level content to all students, regardless of their English skills. The following is an overview of the current thinking on the topic of English learners and a rich repertoire of educational solutions in response to the challenges raised.

Demographics of English Learners in the United States

The National Clearinghouse for English Language Acquisition and Language Instruction Educational Programs (NCELA, 2003) put the number of English learners (K–12) in the United States at 4.7 million for 2001–2002. To the 2000 U.S. Census question, "Do you speak English less than 'very well'?" 8.1 percent of the population answered yes. Based on a population of 280 million people, this means that almost 23 million people in the United States report that they *do not* speak English well.

The number of people who do not speak English well is highly correlated with racial and ethnic diversity; therefore it is not surprising that increased immigration from Mexico, Central and South America, and Asia has resulted in one-third of the U.S. school population being non-white (Marlowe & Page, 1999).

Throughout the United States, 47 million people (18 percent of the population) speak a language other than English at home (U.S. Census Bureau, 2001b). This number is up from 14 percent in 1990 and 11 percent in 1980. States vary in this percentage, with California leading at 40 percent, followed by New Mexico at 36 percent, and Texas at 32 percent. Detailed population maps are available detailing when and where immigration has occurred within the continental United States (Swerdlow, 2001).

English Learners: Geographic Distribution

Although the largest percentage of non–English speakers (37 percent) lives in the West, English learners and their families are increasingly living in the Midwest (9 percent) and the South (15 percent). The states with the most growth in English learners from 1992 to 2002 are in the South, Midwest, and West (Oregon, Idaho, and Nevada). In Colorado, for example, the number of language-minority students rose 86 percent between 1992 and 1993 and between 1996 and 1997; not all were Spanish speakers (up 118 percent)—Russian speakers increased by 95 percent and Hmong by 135 percent (Mirich, 1998).

California had the largest percentage of non-English-language speakers. Table 1.2 lists the states in which the percentage of English learners is highest compared to total learners. Eight states had over 1 million non-English-language speakers in 2000, led by California, with more than twice the number of any other state (see Table 1.3).

The largest percentage increase from 1990 to 2000 occurred in Nevada, where the number increased by 193 percent. In California, English learners increased 44 percent in the decade 1992 to 2002.

Los Angeles Unified School District leads all other school districts in the number of English learners (299,232 in 2002–2003), number of languages spoken (56), and percent of total enrollment that is made up of English learners (40 percent) (see Table 1.4).

According to Samway and McKeon (1999), in 1993 to 1994, cities in California constituted 12 of the top 20 U.S. cities in number of English learners, with 56 percent of all U.S. English learners in the largest urban districts. The three largest cities in Texas had a total of 11 percent of the nation's English learners.

In 2004, California, with a school enrollment of approximately 1.6 million English learners, led the states in need for English-as-a-second-language (ESL) services at the K–12 level (California Department of Education [CDE], 2004b). Services were delivered in California for students of 56 primary languages, including Khmu, Albanian, Marshallese, and

table 1.2 States with Highest Percentage of English Learners

State	English Learners as Percentage of All Learners
California	39
New Mexico	37
Texas	31
New York	28
Hawaii	27
Arizona	26
New Jersey	26

Source: U.S. Census Bureau (2003).

table 1.3 States with Highest Number of English Learners

State	English Learners (in millions)
California	12.4
Texas	6.0
New York	5.0
Florida	3.5
Illinois	2.2
New Jersey	2.0
Arizona	1.2
Massachusetts	1.1

Source: U.S. Census Bureau (2003).

table 1.4   **School Districts with Highest Number of English Learners**

State	English Learners	Percentage of Total Enrollment
Los Angeles Unified	311,958	43
New York City, NY	180,440	17
Miami-Dade, Florida	66,719	18
Chicago, IL	57,767	13
Houston, TX	56,738	27
Dallas, TX	53,053	33
San Diego, CA	39,491	28
Santa Ana, CA	39,392	65
Long Beach, CA	34,132	36
Clark Co., NV	32,430	14

Source: Adapted from www.ncela.gwu.edu/expert/faq/02districts.htm

Chamorro, with the largest number of students speaking Spanish (84.3 percent) (Office of English Language Acquisition [Language Enhancement, and Academic Achievement for Limited English Proficient Students] [OELA], 2004). Of these, about 181,000 were Spanish speakers.

Spanish-Speaking English Learners

The majority of English learners in the United States are Spanish-speaking (28.1 million); this represents an increase of 62 percent over the decade 1990 to 2000. In 2000, 32.8 million Latinos resided in the United States, constituting 12 percent of the total U.S. population (the terms *Hispanic* and *Latino* are used interchangeably in the 2000 census reports). Table 1.5 presents the regional origin of Spanish speakers. The Spanish-speaking population is not

table 1.5   **Region of Origin for Hispanics/Latinos in the United States**

Region of Origin	Percent of Total Hispanics/Latinos
Mexico (meaning either from Mexico or of Mexican American origin)	66.1
Central or South America	14.5
Puerto Rico	9.0
Cuba (meaning either from Cuba or of Cuban American origin)	4.0
Other Hispanic/Latino	6.4

Source: U.S. Census Bureau (2000).

table 1.6   Regional Distribution of Hispanics/Latinos in the United States by Region of Origin

Region of Origin	Percent by Geographic Area of U.S.
Mexico (meaning either from Mexico or of Mexican American origin)	West: 56.8 South: 32.6
Central or South America	Northeast: 32.3 South: 34.6 West: 28.2
Puerto Rico	Northeast: 63.9
Cuba (meaning either from Cuba or of Cuban American origin)	South: 80.1

Source: U.S. Census Bureau (2001a).

evenly distributed across the United States. Table 1.6 shows the distribution of the various Spanish-speaking populations. Latinos make up more than 30 percent of the population of New York City (Wallraff, 2000) and 39.5 percent of the population of California.

Nearly half of all Latinos live in a central city within a metropolitan area (46.4 percent). Moreover, many Spanish speakers are poor. In 1999, 22.8 percent of all Latinos were living in poverty (compared to 7.7 percent of non-Latino whites). In addition, Latino children under age 18 were more likely than non-Latino white children to be living in poverty (30.3 percent versus 9.4 percent) (U.S. Census Bureau, 2001a).

Asian/Pacific English Learners

The second largest non-English-speaking population comprises Asians and Pacific Islanders. In March 1999, the Asian and Pacific Islander population in the United States numbered 10.1 million, constituting 4.0 percent of the population. (*Asian* refers to those having origins in any of the original peoples of the Far East, Southeast Asia, or the Indian subcontinent including Cambodia, China, India, Japan, Korea, Malaysia, Pakistan, the Philippine Islands, Thailand, and Vietnam. *Pacific Islander* refers to those having origins in any of the original peoples of Hawaii, Guam, Samoa, or other Pacific islands.)

Like Spanish speakers, the Asian and Pacific Islander population lives in metropolitan areas (nearly 96 percent), with 45 percent living in central cities, double the proportion for non-Hispanic whites (22 percent) (U.S. Census Bureau, 2001b). Approximately 2.4 percent Asians are Chinese speakers, about 2.0 million speakers of Chinese (Mandarin). Four out of five respondents report that they prefer to speak Chinese at home (Wallraff, 2000).

By and large, then, in the United States, those who educate English learners are more likely to find employment in California, New Mexico, New York, or Texas, in central city schools, serving Hispanics or Asian/Pacific Islanders. Aside from this employment likelihood, demographics indicate that services for English learners are needed in every state and large city.

The education of English learners in the United States is deeply connected to urban education, and urban education is closely connected with school failure. This is a part of the "Third Worldization" of North America (Macedo & Freire, 1998, p. ix), in which high levels of poverty, violence, homelessness, and human misery increasingly characterize the inner cities of the United States. The education of English learners is closely tied to the endemic problems of urban poverty; for example, despite the myth of Asians as some sort of monolithic "model minority," between 30 percent and 54.5 percent of Vietnamese, Native Hawaiians/Pacific Islanders, Laotians, and Cambodians live in poverty (Asian Pacific Fund, 2003).

To educate these students, resources are badly needed; however, school districts with large numbers of poor children often lack books and supplies, and teachers often lack training and experience. Thus English learners frequently attend underfunded and poorly equipped schools.

Putting Faces to Demographics

English learners in the United States present a kaleidoscope of faces, languages, and cultures:

Ahmad, twelfth grade, refugee from Afghanistan, living in Oakland, California . . .

Lukas, eighth grade, adoptee from Romania, living in Kansas City, Missouri . . .

Vivian, third grade, second-generation Mexican American living in Yuma, Arizona, whose parents speak no English . . .

Mohammed, sixth grade, immigrant from Somalia, living in Lewiston, Maine . . .

Hae Lim, second grade, visitor from Pusan, Korea, "temporarily" living with an aunt in Torrance, California . . .

Wu Liang, kindergarten, attending a neighborhood school in Amherst, Massachusetts, while his mother is an international student at a nearby university . . .

Trang, tenth grade, living in inner-city San José, whose parents speak Vietnamese but who has lived in the United States since he was 2 years old . . .

Adolfo, fourth grade, a Mixtec Indian from Oaxaca State in Mexico, speaks Spanish as a second language and is learning English as a third language.

Juan Ramon, second grade, whose mother recently moved from San Juan, Puerto Rico, to live with relatives in Teaneck, New Jersey, has been educated to date only in Spanish. . . .

Some of these students may be offered primary-language instruction as a part of the school curriculum, but those students whose language is represented by few other students in the school district face structured English immersion, with little support in their native language.

English Learners with Learning Challenges

Some English learners are not only experiencing a process of acquiring a second language but also facing academic learning challenges—learning disabilities, culture shock, or language-acquisition difficulties. The following vignettes represent a sample of these students and their learning situations.

Mrs. Morgan, a third-grade teacher, is struggling with Adam. His family emigrated from a small town in Serbia after requesting political asylum in the United States during the conflicts in the Balkan region in the 1990s. They settled in a rural area where Adam's father works as a farm laborer. Adam shows little interest in school, and his English has shown little sign of improvement since first grade.

Aggrey comes from a family that emigrated from Tanzania when her father came to the United States to take a teaching position in an urban university. Her parents speak their tribal dialect at home with her and English outside the home. Aggrey is extremely shy and seldom speaks at school; during kindergarten she was assigned to a pull-out ESL class because her teacher did not think she spoke English, but midway through kindergarten her parents protested this placement, and she was instead sent to a speech-language therapist to improve her speaking fluency.

Marta, a second-generation Puerto Rican living in Connecticut, is in second grade, and her teacher is wondering if Marta has a memory problem. She did not attend kindergarten, and in first grade the instruction was primarily in Spanish. In second grade, the class is taught in English. Now that Marta is being asked to learn to read in English, she doesn't seem to remember words she has read before. When she reads aloud, she can sound out words adequately but has little comprehension of their meaning.

Pedro's parents emigrated from Guatemala and settled in a rural area in the school district. The family speaks Mayan, and Spanish is their second language. Pedro has attended school only intermittently and never learned to read. During the year, he has made little academic progress. Tutoring is not available in his native language.

The parents of Takeshi, a high school sophomore, asked the local high school to place him in the highest academic track during the period that his family will live in the United States. His father is a manager in a Japanese-owned company with a branch office in town. The counselor lined up placement in the high school's ESL program, but Takeshi's parents refused the placement, claiming his English is good enough to warrant placement in a regular English program. On an entry placement test, his math scores were high, but his English scores were not.

Kemal is a native of Turkey. He has just immigrated with his parents to a small town in which his uncle runs a jewelry store. He was taught to read in Turkish, but now that he does not have access to Turkish reading instruction, he is falling behind in the fourth grade. Kemal attends a resource program in reading, but the resource teacher sees that problems that show up in English (limited oral language and vocabulary, difficulties with writing, and poor comprehension) limit his progress.

Ny is in eighth grade. Her family lives in a rural area in central California. Her parents speak to her sister and her in English. However, because they work, they leave Ny for long periods with her grandmother, who speaks only Hmong. Ny acts like a dual personality. Outside of class, she demonstrates a quick intelligence that comes out when she interacts with other girls in her social group. In class, however, her performance is uneven; she does not volunteer and does not complete work.

Like their counterparts who are native English speakers, English learners may require special services, including referral to gifted-and-talented programs, resource specialists, reading-resource programs, counseling, or tutoring.

Other Challenges Facing English Learners

Complications of Gender, Culture, and Language.   Although almost all parents voice high aspirations for their children's academic achievement, some families simply are unable or unwilling to dedicate time each evening for students to complete school assignments. Many young people find themselves working long hours outside the home to help support the family or taking care of siblings while parents work double shifts. Adding to this difficulty are perceptions of gender roles on the part of some immigrant families that favor the academic success of sons over daughters. Teachers in the United States who espouse equality of opportunity for women may find opposition from the families. This issue may be more acute as high school students contemplate attending college.

Other issues have emerged as immigrants enter U.S. schools from ever-more diverse cultures. A young Sikh student is sent home from school for wearing a ritual knife. Many Pakistani girls are forbidden by families to wear physical education attire that reveals bare legs. A male exchange student from Saudi Arabia refuses to work in a mixed-gender cooperative learning group in the classroom. A parent who just adopted a child from Kazakhstan demands primary-language services from the local elementary school. Issues of language and culture complicate schooling for English learners—and provisions of the U.S. Constitution protect individuals from discrimination as these issues are resolved.

Overreferral to Special Education.   Referrals and placements in special education have been disproportionate for culturally and linguistically different students (Cummins, 1984; Rodríguez, Prieto, & Rueda, 1984), often because of inadequate assessment, poor school progress, academic or cognitive difficulties, or special learning problems (Malavé, 1991). Biased assessment can result in negative evaluation of English learners (Rueda, 1987; Valenzuela & Baca, 2004).

Dropping Out of School.   An unfortunate and direct result of being schooled in an unfamiliar language is that some students begin falling behind their expected grade levels almost immediately on entering school. In 1995, of the 13.7 percent of children who spoke a language other than English in the home, 10 percent were retained at least one grade. And, as the Department of Commerce warns, students who repeat at least one grade are more likely to drop out of school.

Meaningful dropout statistics are difficult to gather because many students disappear from the school system between ninth and tenth grade and thus never enter high school and are not counted as dropouts. There are many English learners among the 50 percent yearly dropout population of the Boston public school system, or the 70 percent dropout population in New York City public schools. Poverty and high transient rates together create social and economic pressures that "pull" students away from secondary education; institutional racism and lack of supportive programs create "push" factors, driving students away from school success.

Difficulties in Higher Education and Management.   In 1998, of the 65 percent of high school graduates who attended college, 53 percent were white and only 5 percent were of Latino origin (National Center for Education Statistics [NCES], 2003b). Only about one in six Latinos who attend college ultimately graduates (Thernstrom & Thernstrom, 2003). In addition, Latinos represent only a small number of faculty members and administrators in higher education; they hold 2.5 percent of such positions (U.S. Department of Education, 1998).

Low educational levels have resulted in poor subsequent incomes and a lower likelihood of high-prestige occupations. Whether due to English-language limitations or other structural problems in society, Latino men hold only 0.7 percent of top management positions in U.S. society and Latinas only 0.1 percent (Cockcroft, 1995).

Access to Core Curricula.   No matter what educational program is designed for English learners, access to the core curriculum is essential. This means that language-development activities cannot stand in the way of other academic subjects. A student who is pulled out of the class to receive ESL services, for example, cannot miss social studies class. Meeting the needs of English learners with SDAIE instruction (a "sheltered" math class, for example) is a challenge for schools—a challenge that must be addressed (see Chapter 5).

Issues of race and class are compounded by issues of language in U.S. schools. For example, compared to whites, Latino students are less likely to be placed in education tracks with rigorous curricula that prepare them for college (Haycock, Jerald, & Huang, 2001). Only one in five eighth-grade Latino students takes algebra, compared to one in four whites (The Education Trust, 1998). Among 17-year-olds, only 8 percent of Hispanics have taken precalculus or calculus, compared with 15 percent of whites (National Center for Education Statistics [NCES], 2000).

Little Support for the First Language.   In many countries, students begin to study second or foreign languages in upper elementary school. Foreign Language in the Elementary School (FLES) is an academic subject in the United States in elite schools (private schools in New York and Washington, D.C., for example), where French (or, less commonly, Japanese) is offered, as well as in privileged environments such as the wealthy suburbs of New York, Boston, San Francisco, and Minneapolis and in university towns such as Chapel Hill (North Carolina) and Austin (Texas).

Yet the urban school districts that do not support maintenance programs in heritage languages are causing students to lose the very language resources that are difficult to reestablish as foreign languages at the high school level. Access to the core curriculum is the right of all learners—and in the case of English learners, that core curriculum should include language classes in the heritage as well as perhaps a third language.

The issues just outlined offer some examples of the complexity involved in educating students of diverse primary languages and cultures. The current emphasis on standards heightens the tensions inherent in such a project. On the one hand, students have a right to a high standard of rich, challenging instruction no matter what linguistic and cultural resources they bring to schooling. On the other hand, the emphasis on high standards must be matched with allocation of funds so that teachers are given the resources they need to accomplish these lofty goals.

A Critical Perspective

This book takes a critical perspective on the education of English learners—one that looks at dual-language proficiency and language policy as part of broader issues of social equity and social justice. Teachers with a critical perspective look within, around, and beyond educational issues; ask probing questions about the role of educators in the struggle to attain fairness, justice, equity, and equal opportunity in the world; and work toward social equity and justice as a part of their role as language educators.

Challenges for Teachers

One of the major challenges for those who teach English learners is to motivate them to achieve the highest possible level of proficiency. In this process, teachers of English work to create a classroom environment characterized by equal opportunity and a democratic process so that English learning represents a positive experience for English learners.

A second challenge for teachers of English learners is to respect the native language and the rights of its speakers. Teachers who make sincere attempts to learn the languages of their students and build English on students' prior language expertise serve as intercultural and interlingual educators. Chapter 11 examines ways in which educators can involve the broader heritage-language community in English learning.

Teaching for Social Justice

Critical educators are those who teach with integrity (see Chapter 2). Their passion for teaching and learning fosters within their students the capacity for joyful lifelong learning, a sense of respect for and pride in their own cultures, and a sense of curiosity regarding human diversity. Colleagues can undertake together the task of achieving social justice: equal access to, and opportunity for, quality education for all students. Critical educators advocate an inclusive society in which language, literacy, and culture are integrated with respect and not compromised in any way.

The Professional Preparation of Teachers to Educate English Learners

Bilingual teachers with bilingual certification who can deliver primary-language education K–6 should be hired in school districts that support bilingual education in recognition of the fact that these teachers have additional preparation in delivering English-language development (ELD) instruction along with primary-language instruction in literacy and in content areas. In states where **structured English immersion (SEI)** (content delivery in English without support for primary-language literacy) is the specified model for English learners, teachers who use specially designed academic instruction in English (SDAIE) strategies (see Chapter 5) in addition to ELD may have an add-on certification or training in ELD.

The United States is expected to need from two to four million teachers by 2010 (Chan, 2004). The teacher shortage is particularly acute in urban areas, where 40 to 50 percent of English learners are found. Almost half of new teachers leave the profession after five years, and the rate is even higher in low-income communities (National Commission on Teaching and America's Future, 2002). Districts are setting aside funds for training, raising starting salaries for teachers, and recruiting teachers for bilingual education. The employability outlook has never been better for teachers who specialize in teaching English learners.

Career Preparation for Teachers

To prepare for teaching English learners, an individual can pursue various levels of precareer preparation, from BA programs to 12-hour certificate or endorsement programs, to post–BA teacher credential programs, to MA programs that may or may not include teacher certification. The Website of the organization Teaching English to Speakers of Other Languages (TESOL, Inc. [www.tesol.org]) has a link (www.tesol.org/careers/seekers-faq1.html#2) that may help to distinguish these programs and levels of career training. Despite the widely varying career ladders available to educators, the demand for English-language teaching professionals has steadily grown, not only in the United States but also throughout the world. In all parts of the world, at all times of the day, someone is teaching or studying English.

States vary in their professional requirements for teachers of English learners. For example, effective in school year 2004–05, Pennsylvania requires not only that teachers have the Pennsylvania Level I or Level II certificate, but also that all ESL teachers hold the Program Specialist-ESL certificate. In Texas, teachers holding bilingual generalist or supplemental credentials (early childhood–grade 4 or grades 4–8) can teach in ESL programs at those grade levels. In Florida, credentialed teachers can qualify for an endorsement or specialization with 15 semester hours of work in the areas of methods of teaching English to speakers of other languages (ESOL), ESOL curriculum and materials development, crosscultural communication and understanding, and testing and evaluation of ESOL learners, or have an undergraduate or graduate degree in ESOL. The Website www.ncela.gwu.edu/policy/states/index.htm offers a complete listing of requirements for teaching English learners by state.

The field of teaching English learners is equally open to those whose native language is English and those who are non-native speakers (see Brutt-Griffler & Samimy, 1999). TESOL's Nonnative English Speakers in TESOL (NNEST) Caucus (http://nnest.moussu.net) can provide more information about this topic.

The Internet can help to provide a broad picture of the possibilities available to those who specialize in teaching English learners. Bilingual and ESL educators in the United States might enjoy the Bilingual ESL Network (www.csun.edu/~hcedu013/eslbil.html). The Center for Research on Education, Diversity, and Excellence offers a range of resources, including research articles and teaching guides (www-rcf.usc.edu/~cmmr/crede.html). The Center for Multilingual Multicultural Research offers links to scholarships and teacher training programs (www.usc.edu/dept/education/CMMR).

Professional Organizations for Teachers

Teachers of English learners choose as their major professional affiliation such organizations as the National Association for Bilingual Education (NABE, www.nabe.org), Teachers of

English to Speakers of Other Languages (TESOL, Inc., www.tesol.org), National Council of Teachers of English (NCTE, www.ncte.org), International Reading Association (IRA, www.ira.org), or state, regional, or local affiliates of these organizations. These organizations increasingly include a focus on English learners in their publications and conference sessions. However, NABE and TESOL are the only U.S.-based professional organizations with the teaching of English learners as their central mission.

Information about Teaching English Learners

The professional information available from the National Clearinghouse for English Language Acquisition (www.ncela.gwu.edu) includes an archive of newsletters, a conference calendar, links to scholarly journals, statistics about English learners, and resources for heritage languages. For Tagalog (Filipino), for example, NCELA's website offers links to Tagalog curriculum materials, multilingual books in Tagalog, lists of language and cultural resources, Web resources and organizations, and a listing of colleges and universities in North America that teach Tagalog.

For ELD teaching, Dave's ESL Cafe (www.eslcafe.com) is a popular site for English learning, featuring chatrooms, an online bookstore, job listings, and sections on slang, idioms, and other language-teaching tips. The site also includes 3,020 links to other topics such as flash cards, multicultural issues, lesson plans, and online help.

The Internet TESL Journal (http://iteslj.org) connects to 3,500 additional links of interest to ESL/EFL students and teachers. Englishtown (www.englishtown.com) is an EFL site for Portuguese educators. Boot up, click, and enjoy the international flavor of the profession of teaching English learners.

Helpful links to bilingual education include a collection of Websites from Dr. Martin Levine (www.csun.edu/~hcedu013/eslbil.html). Here teachers can find where to buy bilingual books for children, bilingual lesson plans K–3, Internet sites in Spanish, and a trilingual tour of Mexico, among other resources. Spanish-language Web resources for lesson planning and instruction are featured at the Enlaces Bilingües Para Niños y Maestros site (http://members.tripod.com/~hamminkj/bilingue.html).

The Website JALT Bilingualism SIG Website Map (www.kagawa-jc.ac.jp/~steve_mc/jaltbsig/index.html) is a product of the Japan Association for Language Teaching. The articles on raising children bilingually are especially informative. This site, along with other Internet resources, raises awareness that issues of bilingualism and English teaching apply worldwide. English-language development within the context of the United States is only one part of a much larger picture.

Teaching Performance Assessment: Focusing on the English Learner

Standards-based learning and outcomes assessment are two major areas of focus in preparing today's teachers. Under the aegis of the 2001 No Child Left Behind Act, teachers are required to document that they have subject area competence in the areas to which they are assigned. This competence has increasingly been measured in the form of outcomes measures for teacher education programs.

box 1.1

The California Standards for the Teaching Profession (CSTP): Summary

CSTP One	Engaging and supporting all students in learning
CSTP Two	Creating and maintaining effective environments for student learning
CSTP Three	Understanding and organizing subject matter for student learning
CSTP Four	Planning instruction and designing learning experiences for all students
CSTP Five	Assessing student learning
CSTP Six	Developing as a professional educator

Source: California Commission on Teacher Credentialing (1997). Reprinted with permission.

State teaching commissions such as the California Commission on Teacher Credentialing (CCTC) are increasingly specific in their expectations for teachers' performance. The California Standards for the Teaching Profession (CSTP) have been legislated as a standardized set of expectations about the expertise that is required of beginning teachers (CCTC and California Department of Education, 1997). The six standards cover broad domains of teaching (see Box 1.1) and are each further divided into indicators to demonstrate the facets of each standard (see Box 1.2).

More recently in California, Senate Bill 2042 (2002) legislated that the California Level I teaching credential be issued after the candidate has demonstrated a level of expertise that is documented by the Teaching Performance Assessment (TPA). This assessment comprises four tasks, each of which corresponds to a teaching situation. The expertise of the candidate is measured across the six domains of the CSTP by these four tasks. Each task challenges the prospective teacher to design instruction not only to meet the needs of the class as a whole, but also to modify instruction to address the needs of two "focus students," one of whom must be an English learner.

California's Teaching Performance Assessment is matched by a set of Teaching Performance Expectations (TPEs). As a part of these TPEs, Element 7 comprises a set of 16 expectations about the skills and knowledge base that teachers need in order to adapt instruction to meet the needs of English learners (see Box 1.3). This book is organized to match each element of these expectations with explicit information designed to prepare prospective teachers for success on the Teaching Performance Assessment.

Based on these requirements, the specific adaptation of instruction for English learners is an integral part of teacher preparation. This book addresses the instructional needs of the English learner, offering strategies and techniques necessary to prepare teachers and other professionals to teach English learners from many language, racial, and cultural backgrounds. With this preparation, the ELD teacher is equipped with the tools necessary for fully competent professional performance.

An Award-Winning ELD Teacher

One sign that ELD instruction is an integral part of the fabric of teaching is the fact that the 2004 National Teacher of the Year is an ESL teacher at Davisville Middle School in North Kingstown, Rhode Island. Kathy Mellor has been at the forefront of designing and

box 1.2 The California Standards for the Teaching Profession (CSTP): Detail

CSTP One: Engaging and supporting all students in learning

1.1 Connecting students' prior knowledge, life experience, and interests with learning goals
1.2 Using a variety of instructional strategies and resources to respond to students' diverse needs
1.3 Facilitating learning experiences that promote autonomy, interaction, and choice
1.4 Engaging students in problem solving, critical thinking, and other activities that make subject matter meaningful
1.5 Promoting self-directed, reflective learning for all students

CSTP Two: Creating and maintaining effective environments for student learning

2.1 Creating a physical environment that engages all students
2.2 Establishing a climate of fairness and respect
2.3 Promoting social development and group responsibility
2.4 Establishing and maintaining standards for group behavior
2.5 Planning and implementing classroom procedures and routines that support student learning
2.6 Using instructional time effectively

CSTP Three: Understanding and organizing subject matter for student learning

3.1 Demonstrating knowledge of subject matter content and student development
3.2 Organizing curriculum to support student understanding of subject matter
3.3 Interrelating ideas and information within and across subject matter areas
3.4 Developing student understanding through instructional strategies that are appropriate to the subject matter
3.5 Using materials, resources, and technologies to make subject matter accessible to students

CSTP Four: Planning instruction and designing learning experiences for all students

4.1 Drawing on and valuing students' backgrounds, interests, and developmental learning needs
4.2 Establishing and articulating goals for student learning
4.3 Developing and sequencing instructional activities and materials for student learning
4.4 Designing short-term and long-term plans to foster student learning
4.5 Modifying instructional plans to adjust for student needs

CSTP Five: Assessing student learning

5.1 Establishing and communicating learning goals for all students
5.2 Collecting and using multiple sources of information to assess student learning
5.3 Involving and guiding all students in assessing their own learning
5.4 Using the results of assessments to guide instruction
5.5 Communicating with students, families, and other audiences about student progress

box 1.2

(Continued)

CSTP Six: Developing as a professional educator

6.1 Reflecting on teaching practice and planning professional development
6.2 Establishing professional goals and pursuing opportunities to grow professionally
6.3 Working with communities to improve professional practice
6.4 Working with families to improve professional practice
6.5 Working with colleagues to improve professional practice

Source: California Commission on Teacher Credentialing (1997). Reprinted with permission.

box 1.3

Teaching Performance Expectations Matched to California Standards for the Teaching Profession

California Standards for the Teaching Profession	Teaching Performance Expectations
Engaging and supporting all students in learning	1. Specific pedagogical skills for subject matter instruction (multiple subject and single subject)
Creating and maintaining effective environments for student learning	2. Monitoring student learning during learning
	3. Interpreting and using assessments
Understanding and organizing subject matter for student learning	4. Making content accessible
	5. Student engagement
	6. Developmentally appropriate teaching practices (K–3, 4–8, 9–12)
	7. Teaching English learners
Planning instruction and designing learning experiences for all students	8. Learning about students
	9. Instructional planning
Assessing student learning	10. Instructional time
	11. Social environment
Developing as a professional educator	12. Professional, legal, and ethical obligations
	13. Professional growth

Source: California Commission on Teacher Credentialing. Copyright ©2003. Reprinted with permission.

implementing the school district's ELD program. The instructional program Mellor designed combines language and literacy instruction with support in the content area subjects. Applying the Rhode Island English language arts standards, the curriculum takes the students through five proficiency levels before they exit the program and are ready to achieve alongside their native-English-speaking peers (online at www.ccsso.org/Whats_New/Press_Releases/4561.cfm).

Those who teach English learners work within a variety of cultural, linguistic, and socioeconomic contexts. They honor the diversity in culture, language, social class, and talents that makes their students unique. There is no end to the intellectual and pedagogical challenges of teaching in a language-acquisition classroom or to the rich opportunities for personal and professional growth. Those who offer cultural understanding receive it; those who offer language exchange expand their language skills; those who offer empathy grow as human beings. No other teaching profession offers such possibilities for intercultural communication, literacy development, creative instruction, reflective social praxis, and just plain hard work!

Using this text, prospective teachers undergoing education that culminates in California's Teaching Performance Assessment can prepare for a successful assessment experience. Current teachers can use the Teacher Performance Expectations addressed in this text to update their expertise in teaching English learners. The Teacher Performance Expectations for Element 7 are featured at the beginning of each chapter.

2 Teaching with Integrity

Teachers with integrity collaborate and exchange to create a high-quality academic environment.

Teachers, as intellectual workers, are not technocrats whose job it is to deliver information. Teachers are knowledge professionals with cultural expertise. As such, the true role of teachers is to keep students together with the community, to help them attain the wisdom and skills the whole community needs in order to live. Without an ethical foundation, knowledge is without purpose and skill is without soul. Without an ethical foundation, teachers run the risk of undermining democratic principles while actively perpetrating and practicing oppressive pedagogy that privileges some students and disempowers others. The teaching enterprise requires an ethical map, with integrity as its compass.

This chapter proposes a model of "teaching with integrity" whereby teachers of English learners teach academic content and English-language development while upholding high professional standards. Given the complexity of educating English learners (see Chapter 1), this book (and model) proposes that teaching English learners should be situated within a context that is humane, academically challenging, grounded in academic knowledge, and ethical, and that upholds intercultural relationships and promotes educational equity. That is, teacher expertise in its various forms, including planning, application, and assessment and application, flourishes in a context in which optimal conditions for learning are created and maintained without compromising the integrity of teaching and learning.

In this chapter, the teaching with integrity model is introduced, including its various elements. Second, the process of instruction for English learners is examined within the framework of teaching with integrity. This instructional process is cyclic and includes those professional skills such as knowledge about the learner; knowledge of academic content and language development; pedagogical skills; the ability to plan; the ability to teach academic content, English-language development, and bilingual education; and knowledge of assessment, including accountability to community and families. Also, a critical stance is featured, by which the teacher reflects, monitors, critiques, and improves instruction and pursues professional development as a means to improve the world of the classroom and society at large.

What Is Teaching with Integrity?

Teaching with integrity means wholeness in all that teachers do. This implies a genuine vision of social justice in the classroom. Designing a curriculum that is inclusive of all students and their needs, creating authentic opportunities for all to make academic gains, and implementing teaching practices that facilitate critical thinking and benefit all students are ways that teachers evidence integrity.

In a postmodern society, teaching with integrity is complex. Teachers with integrity are fully educated for the roles they undertake. They are able to sustain their humanity in the face of potentially dehumanizing forces that would reduce teaching and learning to mechanical enterprises, devoid of intrinsic interest and personal investment (Bartolomé, 1994; Freire, 1970; Giroux, 1988).

Teachers with integrity are able to inspire students to achieve a high level of educational success, because they are experts possessing content and pedagogical knowledge. They are familiar with the culture of their students to the extent that they are able to communicate effectively with parents and community members, and are able to help students cultivate focused learning habits that are compatible with their cultures (Gallegos-Nava, 2001; Freire, 1970). Teachers with integrity have achieved clarity of vision so that they are able to identify social and political issues that affect classroom instruction (Bartolomé & Balderrama, 2001).

Last, teachers with integrity approach their work ethically and with critical contemplation, aware of its interconnectedness to the wider social context. This is similar to Freire's (1970) concept of praxis, whereby action and reflection on the world are integrated with acts that change the world. Such praxis incorporates elements of Díaz-Rico's (2004) cycle of stance, whereby teachers take a stance and then reflect on the consequences, critically checking for improvement and connections to change the world. Figure 2.1 shows the teaching with integrity model, and Table 2.1 presents the six components of teaching with integrity guided by critical contemplation.

table 2.1 Teaching with Integrity: Components

Component	Definition
Willingness to be fully human	Teachers who fully actualize their humanity
High academic expectations for students	Commitment to the idea that students will achieve academic success
Expertise in content	Teachers who are fully qualified in the areas they will instruct
Professional ethics	Willingness to uphold the morals of the profession of teaching
Intercultural repertoire	The ability to communicate effectively with people from other cultures
Clarity of vision	Ability to sustain political and ideological insight about the process of schooling and their role as teachers

Willingness to Be Fully Human

The most urgent component of teaching with integrity is the need for teachers to fully actualize their humanity. Martin Buber (1991) expressed this as achieving an "I–Thou" relationship in which the sacred inner core of spirit is shared between two human beings. This is partially fulfilled when the teacher deeply believes—and communicates—the sense that teachers and students have equal civil rights in the classroom as well as parity as fellow human beings.

Being fully human requires a deep commitment to overcoming such inequities as white supremacy—the culturally ingrained notion that having white skin means that one is entitled to dominate, to speak more often, to exert leadership, and to set the tone, language, and pacing of every interaction. To participate without having to dominate, to listen rather than speak, to enjoy fellowship rather than exercise leadership, and to allow the rhythms of others to guide interaction—these are the joys of humanity that sustain those who do not always have to dominate.

figure 2.1 The Teaching with Integrity Model

table 2.2   Components of Intersubjectivity

Component	Definition	Example
Mutual respect	Two-way equality and honor such as mutual paying attention during speaking	José is sharing with the listening teacher the news about the birth of a litter of kittens.
Shared activity	Co-participation in learning tasks	Mrs. Alvin is painting the grapevines in the scenery for the class play about César Chávez while Jessica and Rafael paint the grapes.
Nonverbal immediacy	Shared emotional presence as evinced by body language	For the sake of confidentiality, Mr. Torres leans in as Rene tells him that his coat zipper is stuck.
Intergaze	Looking at one another when communicating according to cultural norms	Raymond looks to the side while telling Mrs. Crede about his sister's graduation, glancing up at her only occasionally. This is Navajo narration style.
Shared pacing	Coordinated timing of speech, actions, and gestures	José adds to Mr. Wright's teaching by inserting comments skillfully, overlapping, and taking full advantage of pauses. He is commended for his contributions.
Shared space	Intersecting personal space in a mutually nonthreatening way	Mr. Vivaldi stands so close to Arturo that they can "smell lunch." Because both are from Mediterranean cultures, they are OK with close interpersonal space.
Cultural commonplaces	Mutual enjoyment of jokes, folk sayings, and community memories	Mrs. Costa reminds Esmeralda to volunteer for an easy classroom chore before harder tasks come up: "Mejor mal que sabe que mal que no sabe." (Better the bad that you know than the bad that you don't know.")

One way of looking at the humanity of teaching is to examine the ways in which teachers and students mutually socialize one another in classroom interaction. Cole (2003) has called this *intersubjectivity*—the co-creation of joint activity. Intersubjectivity in the classroom has at least seven components. Table 2.2 presents these components accompanied by examples.

Intersubjectivity is not to be equated with role confusion, in which the teacher encourages the students to be a "buddy" or call the teacher by his or her first name—a model that almost inevitably leads to what psychologists call "issues of fuzzy boundaries"—but rather is a deep-seated conviction that students must have equal opportunity to succeed and create a life of value. A fully actualized human being is able to apologize when wrong, seek peer help when unsure, and grow and learn alongside students.

Compassion also grounds an individual's willingness to be human. Compassion is informed by understanding the history of historically subordinated cultural, linguistic, and racial groups, and moves beyond blaming the victim or enacting the omnipotent role of deciding who are "better" human beings in classrooms and who thus deserve the rewards. Teachers with integrity have compassion and empathy at their core because they are conscious of others' misfortunes and distress and actively desire to alleviate such hardships.

High Academic Expectations for Students

Part of the art of teaching is nuturing a deep commitment to the idea that all students can achieve academic success. Teacher expectations communicate continuous, day-to-day assessment of students' worth and capabilities (Rist, 1970). This assessment operates as a cycle of teacher–student mutual perceptions and can be divided into three areas: how these perceptions are formed by the teachers and students, how these are communicated by teacher to students, and how students respond. Recognizing, addressing, and understanding these expectations and how they operate is therefore an integral part of examining the role of a teacher's integrity toward English learners.

Jussim (1986) offered a general framework for the operation of expectancy effects: Teachers develop expectations, teachers treat students differently depending on their expectations, and students react to this different treatment in ways that confirm the expectations. According to Jussim, teachers first form expectations about students based on *prejudgments* (inferences based on a student's reputation, information in cumulative files, experience with older siblings, or anecdotes from other teachers); **stereotypes** (racial and cultural typologies that are applied to individuals): *scores from placement or standardized tests; observations of a student's classroom performance;* and *naive predictions and fallacies,* such as exaggerating the significance of a few examples of behavior. Together, these factors create an image in a teacher's mind about the possible success or failure of a student.

Cohen's extensive research in cooperative group work (1994) has found that teacher expectations play a critical role in how well students participate and perform in group activities. For example, Cohen found that high-status students are generally expected by teachers to do well on new intellectual tasks, whereas low-status students are expected to perform poorly on these same tasks.

> When the teacher assigns a group work task, general expectations come into play and produce a self-fulfilling prophecy in which the high-status students talk more and become more influential than the low-status students. The net result of the interaction is that the low-status students are once again seen as incompetent. (Cohen, 1994, p. 117)

Teachers with flexible expectations readily revise their impressions when direct information about student achievement is available (Brophy, 1983). In this way, teachers' critical contemplation can resist perpetuating a cycle of low expectations for low-status students.

The social context of the learning environment also influences teachers' expectations. Students who are tracked into classes with low-ability peers may be systematically denied access to "high-status" knowledge, which includes the academic skills, content, attitudes, and experiences that are inculcated in well-educated members of society. Teachers tend to try to exert more control over discourse in low-track classes, whereas they expand feedback and positive attention for students in high-ability tracks, reduce the frequency of teacher-directed lessons, and provide opportunity for more peer interaction and support.

Minority-group students could be victims of well-meaning pity from teachers who ease up on requirements so students will experience success and feel good about themselves. But this communication, however well meaning, may also transmit the message, "You don't have the ability to do this, so I will overlook your failure." This targeting of minority-group members for pity, praise in the event of failure, or unsolicited help may cause the internalization of low self-esteem (Graham, 1991) and is a subtle form of racial discrimination that detracts from academic motivation and achievement. Rather than pitying or excusing students who need additional academic support, teachers can teach them how to learn and hold them accountable to high standards of performance.

Differences in the cultures of the teacher and the student may cause miscommunication of expectations. Language and word choice are other factors making intercultural communication challenging. Words that may seem harmless in one context may have a subculture connotation; teachers have to be equally careful both to use appropriate terms of address and reference when communicating with students and to be aware of terms that are used in the classroom that might have an incendiary effect.

Expecting high achievement from English learners and communicating these expectations require specific educational programs that draw attention to the hidden curriculum of the school, the quality of dialogue between teachers and students, diverse learning styles, the use of the community as a resource, and a commitment to democratic ideals in the classroom (Gollnick & Chinn, 2001).

The fact that students do not speak English as a native language should not be an excuse to lower expectations for academic achievement. In the secondary school setting, it is particularly important not to expect too little of recently arrived adolescents because it is perceived that "it is too late for them to acquire English." Instruction that promotes equity and equal opportunity for all to achieve establishes the possibility that all will do so. This is an integral part of teaching with integrity.

Expertise in Content

The No Child Left Behind federal education legislation (2001) specifically requires schools to employ teachers who are fully qualified in the areas they will instruct. "Fully qualified" means that teachers must have three kinds of expertise. The first is *content area knowledge*. Science teachers, for example, must demonstrate knowledge about the theories and facts of the science they teach. The second kind of expertise is *content-specific pedagogy*. Again, using science education as an example, this means that a chemistry teacher is able to use appropriate laboratory equipment to teach science. A third kind of expertise is *general pedagogy*. A teacher must be able to deploy specific teaching strategies such as the use of cooperative learning groups, graphic organizers, specially designed academic instruction in English (SDAIE), explicit use of learning strategies, questioning strategies, positive/authentic discipline, and so forth to meet the needs of all students (see Chapter 5).

Two areas of a teacher's content expertise related specifically to English learners that are not often required but that should be are the following: (1) theories and pedagogy relevant to teaching English learners academic literacy and (2) some degree of proficiency in the primary language of their students. Given the existing linguistic diversity prevalent in classrooms, these two areas of expertise are central to the implementation of content knowledge.

Because language is the oil that greases the wheels of teaching, it is imperative that teachers are able to understand fundamental principles about second-language acquisition and can communicate, to some degree, with those students acquiring English. Thus, in order for teachers to be fully qualified as required by the No Child Left Behind legislation, they must dedicate themselves to acquiring at least a basic linguistic competency in the languages that students speak.

Furthermore, the convenient and widely accepted mythology in the United States that a person can be well educated and remain monolingual is questionable, certainly with regard to being a "fully qualified" teacher. The Latino population has become the largest minority in the United States, and educators who are able to augment their teaching using both second-language acquisition principles and Spanish-language skills are increasingly needed. Teachers with linguistic competence are able to enhance the stature of the U.S. educational system in the eyes of the world because U.S. citizens will no longer be viewed by linguistically multicompetent world citizens as linguistically handicapped by monolingualism.

Professional Ethics

Inherent in the teaching process is a major responsibility to teach ethically. The educator with ethics upholds the morals of the profession of teaching, which includes believing in the good and dignity of each human being and recognizing the supreme importance of democratic principles (National Education Association, *Code of Ethics of the Education Profession*, 1975). Teachers with integrity are educators with ethics who recognize the import of professional conduct and are willing to accept a role in protecting the freedom to teach and learn and who work toward providing equal educational opportunity for all. The Code of Ethics of the education profession, presented in Box 2.1, specifies those standards of conduct to which educators with integrity aspire.

Intercultural Repertoire

The ability to communicate effectively with people from other cultures is the hallmark of the intercultural educator. According to Smith, Paige, and Steglitz (1998), a person with an *intercultural perspective* has incorporated a set of eight elements into his or her repertoire that facilitate, and form the foundation for, **intercultural communication.** These elements are complex and subtle yet represent a clear and useful body of knowledge, skills, and dispositions that educators need to function professionally in a diverse society.

These eight elements are here condensed into three central elements of an intercultural perspective. First is the disposition on the part of an educator to engage in face-to-face interactive communication that shows sensitivity to the different and equally valid ways in which individuals construct their social reality, involves the whole person in a compassionate manner, and takes into consideration the social context of the communication. The intercultural educator also recognizes that the ability to engage in intercultural communication is developmental; educators must work on themselves in order to progress from ethnocentric to ethnorelative views. An individual's own culture provides tools to interpret reality only one way; intercultural educators must work to move beyond this limitation. This involves examining many aspects of life: cognitive, behavioral, and affective. The three central elements of an intercultural perspective are more fully described in Table 2.3.

Clarity of Vision

The focus of teaching, however, should be on more than high achievement and intercultural communication. Intellectual teachers pose many "why" questions, particularly around areas related to school achievement and failure. Why do certain students achieve whereas others fail academically? Why is there disproportionate academic failure between groups of

Principles of the Code of Ethics of the Education Profession

Principle I: Commitment to the Student

The educator strives to help each student realize his or her potential as a worthy and effective member of society. The educator therefore works to stimulate the spirit of inquiry, the acquisition of knowledge and understanding, and the thoughtful formulation of worthy goals.

In fulfillment of the obligation to the student, the educator—

1. Shall not unreasonably restrain the student from the independent action in the pursuit of learning.
2. Shall not unreasonably deny the student access to varying points of view.
3. Shall not deliberately suppress or distort subject matter relevant to the student's progress.
4. Shall make reasonable effort to protect the student from conditions harmful to learning or to health and safety.
5. Shall not intentionally expose the student to embarrassment or disparagement.
6. Shall not on the basis of race, color, creed, sex, national origin, marital status, political or religious beliefs, family, social or cultural background, or sexual orientations, unfairly—
   a. Exclude any student participation in any program.
   b. Deny benefits to any student.
   c. Grant any advantage to any student.
7. Shall not use professional relationships with students for private advantage.
8. Shall not disclose information about students obtained in the course of professional service, unless disclosure serves a compelling professional purpose or is required by law.

Principle II: Commitment to the Profession

The education profession is vested by the public with a trust and responsibility requiring the highest ideals of professional service.

In the belief that the quality of the services of the education profession directly influences the nation and its citizens, the educator shall exert every effort to raise professional standards, to promote a climate that encourages the exercise of professional judgment, to achieve conditions that attract persons worthy of the trust to careers in education, and to assist in preventing the practice of the profession by unqualified persons.

In fulfillment of the obligation to the profession, the educator—

1. Shall not in any application for a professional position deliberately make a false statement or fail to disclose a material fact related to competency and qualifications.
2. Shall not misrepresent his/her professional qualifications.
3. Shall not assist any entry into the profession of a person known to be unqualified in respect to character, education, or other relevant attribute.
4. Shall not knowingly make a false statement concerning the qualifications of a candidate for a professional position.
5. Shall not assist a non-educator in the unauthorized practice of teaching.
6. Shall not disclose information about colleagues obtained in the course of professional service unless disclosure serves a compelling professional purpose or is required by law.
7. Shall not knowingly make false or malicious statements about a colleague.
8. Shall not accept any gratuity, gift, or favor that might impair or appear to influence professional decisions or action.

Source: National Education Association (1975).

table 2.3   Elements of an Intercultural Perspective

Element	Definition
Face-to-face interactive intercultural communication	An intercultural communicator is able to carry out direct, conscious interaction with individuals from different cultural backgrounds. This involves continuous, multidirectional feedback by individuals who are using cultural and linguistic codes that lead to differences in their communicative behaviors, perceptions, institutions, basic assumptions about the world, and underlying value systems. This communication necessitates sensitivity, alertness, and openness to the possibility of breakdown of meaning.
Holistic, humanistic communication	Moment-by-moment interaction between individuals is based on the recognition that cultural behaviors, patterns, beliefs, values, and institutions form a rational and coherent whole, a "cultural map" based on cognitive schemata. Humans exist within cultural frameworks internalized within individuals in a dynamic, ever-changing manner. Educators need to employ respect and compassion, and understand the limits of their own knowledge, skills, and interpretations.
Consideration for social context	It is important to understand the influence of the external environment and its impact on learning and cultural styles. Human interaction is given meaning by the time, place, and participants within the occurrence. Intercultural communicators are sensitive to the environment that surrounds discourse.

Source: Adapted from Smith, Paige, and Steglitz (1998).

students, particularly between majority whites and African Americans, Latinos, English learners, and low-income students, for example? Why do those with European American origin, or those who are white, monolingual-English-speaking students, especially those who come from high-income groups, succeed disproportionately? Thinking teachers interrogate those processes that affect their teaching and professional performance, and, in turn, achieve political and ideological insight into the process of schooling and their role as teachers. Bartolomé and Balderrama (2001) define more precisely the term *political clarity*:

> Political clarity is . . . the process by which individuals achieve a deepening awareness of the sociopolitical and economic realities that shape their lives and their capacity to transform their lives. It also refers to the process by which individuals come to understand better the possible linkages between macro-level political, economic, and social variables, and subordinated groups' academic performance at the micro-level classroom. (p. 48)

This political clarity is important if teachers are to act with power and facilitate student empowerment. First and foremost, teachers function as more conscious and conscientious professionals when they understand the larger social and political forces that affect their professional lives. For example, there is a tendency to depoliticize the school curriculum; teachers often buy into the myth that teaching is a neutral activity far removed from large social contextual and economic issues.

> To teach is to have a political agenda. We don't have a choice about whether to take control of that agenda so that we can support and challenge students as learners and as human beings; ... our goal ... is to open up new possibilities in their lives. (Short, 2001, p. 191)

McLaren (1987) suggested that everyday life in school is itself ideological, with school rituals being part of a historical–cultural existence that is inherently political. For example, excusing all students from academic classes to attend a football pep rally is inherently political, if one understands that football in the United States is a male-dominated sport, often excludes English learners, and does not promote scholarship in mathematics or science. With this understanding, teachers can confront social and political forces that undermine educational success, particularly for low-status student groups such as English learners.

Second, this political clarity, guided by critical contemplation, encourages teachers to understand their role in perpetuating cycles of disempowerment for groups such as English learners. For example, Brantlinger (1994) found in her study of adolescents that teachers are perceived "... not only as members of a social class but also as personifications of the institution of school—and school, for low-income adolescents, was an institution that did not work well for them" (p. 107).

The concept of political clarity suggests that teachers acknowledge themselves as members of a social class, race, or gender whose perceptions of specific groups, such as English learners, are influenced by their worldviews, mythology, and preconceptions. Thus teachers' intercultural repertoire should be extended to include not only their own feelings toward members of different social groups but also their understanding of historical–cultural ways that influence students' behavior, sense of identity, and academic performance. Delving beneath the surface of students' behavior helps a monolingual European-American female teacher, for example, understand why low-status students may initially resist her authority and legitimacy as a teacher.

Finally, political clarity can help teachers act together as professionals to affect the larger social and political context in which they work. Teachers can act together to question and interrupt unfair and unjust practices in their individual classrooms as well as their schools. Unfortunately, teachers have a tradition of working in isolation, and this is particularly true in secondary settings. By working alone, teachers tend to suffer from disempowerment because they have few opportunities to work collegially to address common concerns. However, when teachers remove the barriers of isolation, they can compare notes about their collective experiences. They may begin to see that individual concerns are not chance occurrences but are instead related to wider social issues.

This collegial interaction lends political clarity to teachers' daily teaching realities and allows them to see that their concerns are not necessarily classroom or subject specific but rather part of an overall systemic process of unequal power relationships. Moreover, as educational professionals, teachers and administrators are best qualified to work with legislators to make educational policy that advances the possibility of educational equity, and they should make every effort to do so.

As suggested, teachers must be aware that they do not teach in a vacuum, but that instead their work is interconnected to broader social processes that affect their teaching.

Such processes include ideology, hegemony, meritocracy, and institutional and linguistic racism. Following is a discussion of these processes and their impact on teaching and schooling.

Ideology. What are the ideas that underlie teachers' acceptance of the notion that some students will succeed academically whereas others will fail? What belief system inspires dubious explanations as to why English learners have disproportionately high levels of academic failure? How do educators explain institutionalized linguistic racism, for example? How do teachers explain the fact that multilingualism is facilitated for the privileged but not encouraged for those students who come from lower socioeconomic backgrounds? The answers a teacher provides for these questions reflect his or her ideology, which includes a set of explanations to support that ideological position. Individuals and societies have **ideologies,** political belief systems that explain and rationalize the existing social order. This is where political clarity becomes essential for teachers.

Examining and questioning schooling practices thus involves acts of political and ideological clarity. We must question the belief system at the macro or societal level that is used to explain social and economic inequalities, because this ideology affects our teaching and schooling practices at the level of micro interactions of daily classroom life.

Hegemony. What is hegemony? How are schools, and teachers, responsible for participating in dispersing or furthering hegemonic processes, and how is hegemony connected to teaching and, furthermore, teaching with integrity?

All societies in the world have a system of social stratification, although they vary in degree of stratification. Social stratification means that the social system is hierarchically arranged and that some groups have more or less access to power, resources, and even perceived social worth. The United States, as a complex society, is stratified, and its social stratification processes are influenced by class, race, occupation, income, and level of education, as well as by gender, age, region of residence, and, in some cases, national origin and level of English-language proficiency.

In short, social stratification corresponds to social inequality. At the core of this inequality is disproportionate power and relationships. Social institutions such as schools play major roles in maintaining and perpetuating social processes important to that society. Berman (1984) suggested that schools are the most visible area in which capitalist hegemony is disseminated to a captive audience. Thus teachers with clarity look critically beyond the surface of societal processes, and they ask questions about their role in these processes.

The concept of **hegemony** is derived from the writing of Italian theorist Antonio Gramsci (1971). *Hegemony* is defined by Leistyna, Woodrum, and Sherblom (1996) as the way in which certain groups manage to dominate others and how people in positions of privilege maintain these positions with the consensual support and approval of the disempowered.

Analysts look to the concept of hegemony as they attempt to answer this question: If exploitation of people occurs in a society, why is there no revolt or opposition? Why do disempowered and oppressed people go along with an ideology that is against their interests and keeps them relegated to lower social status and poor economic conditions? What are the social and psychological processes that cause those being exploited to comply with the exploitation without protest?

Gramsci (1971) addressed this question by suggesting that a key way in which hegemony operates is in the creation of social systems (schools and classrooms, for instance) that marginalize certain social groups and relegate their members to subordinate roles. This subordination is rationalized, explained, and accepted as essential to maintaining order (Sim & Van Loon, 2005). In other words, schools perpetuate processes by which students and teachers come to accept that there will always be a ranking of students, some on top, some on the bottom, and that this is necessary for society to work. Everyone accepts, unquestioningly, "that's just the way it is."

By accepting this order, neither teachers nor students pose the question of why some economic, ethnic, cultural, or linguistic groups do better in school than others and why these patterns of academic failure perpetuate themselves. Schooling practices are unexamined, with teachers believing that hierarchical ranking is part of the schooling tradition—"business as usual," "that's just the way it will always be"—and by not questioning their practices, they are, to use a colloquial expression, "going along with the program."

Myths and stereotypes play central roles in establishing and perpetuating hegemony. Endemic to modern U.S. society are stereotypical beliefs (so-called folk wisdom) about cultural and linguistic disadvantage, cultural mismatch, or lack of positive parental values as a cause of low achievement on the part of minority students. With these beliefs serving as cognitive "shortcuts," teachers can justify the academic failure of certain students while distancing themselves or their institutions from complicity in this failure.

One beginning teacher admitted that 70 percent of the students in her sixth-period high school English class were failing. She did not say, "I have failed 70 percent of my students," or "Because of academic tracking, 70 percent of students who cannot meet current standards of performance in English were placed in one class." When we admit that grading and tracking practices are partly to blame for students' failures, we avoid solely blaming the students. (LTD-R)

Hegemonic beliefs and practices are internalized by students and act as invisible barriers or governors of behavior. These are deeply entrenched in the social and psychological fabric of U.S. belief systems and manifest themselves in complex ways. An example of internalization is the acceptance of being relegated to subordinate social and academic roles within a school.

I recall substituting at a "low track" social studies high school classroom in southern California. This class was primarily made up of Mexican American youth. Soon after students entered the room, they were proudly telling the substitute teacher that this was the "dummies' social studies class" and that their teacher was "cool" because he did not expect too much, and they had fun just talking and telling jokes. Hegemony worked for them to the extent that they affirmed their subordination. (MVB)

Language is an incredibly powerful hegemonic device, intimately connected to social position. For example, hegemonic beliefs about second-language acquisition in the United

States privileges French above Spanish as a preferred foreign language of study; favors European accents over African accents in the speaking of French, as in the case of French-speaking Haitian students; favors western European tourist destinations over those in eastern Europe as places where foreign languages can be experienced; privileges high school students over elementary school students as second-language learners; and stigmatizes non-native speakers of English in the role of English teachers as opposed to native speakers of English.

At every opportunity, teachers with integrity oppose attitudes based on hegemonic ideas or folk beliefs, upholding professional practices that are substantiated by research or infused with clarity of vision about the all-too-hidden processes that perpetuate unequal power relations and inequality.

Meritocracy. A third aspect of clarity of vision involves a fair examination of the issue of **meritocracy.** The merit system is a strong ideological construct, particularly in schooling and teaching practices, and it becomes imperative for teachers with integrity to examine in depth the implications of meritocracy. Although there are numerous class myths perpetuated by the power elite to dismiss inequity, the myth of meritocracy is one of the most central to schools and teachers.

The myth of meritocracy is often expressed by the cliché "the cream rises to the top." This myth maintains that those who succeed in school and society are gaining the rewards of what they have "earned." This myth proposes that a student merely needs ability, willpower, and academic achievement for economic success to follow. More important, the myth of meritocracy rests on the assumptions that all schools are created equal and provide even "playing fields," and that all students have equal access and opportunity to quality education. These assumptions fall short when tracking policies in schools place 90 percent of white students on college preparatory tracks and relegate the majority of African American and Latino students to the lowest academic tracks.

The myth of meritocracy is one of the oldest and most enduring falsehoods in the practices of schools and teaching, as teachers embrace the belief that the individual deserving of success will attain it merely by working hard and thus be meritorious. This ignores the inequities of socioeconomic context and denies the role of background factors such as class and race.

As Bell (1977) explains, most people believe that meritocracy is an improvement over traditional means of advancement, in which to be rich and well connected socially was the avenue to success. However ideal the notion of meritocracy seems, in reality standards of achievement usually systematically favor the rich and socially well-connected—those who both determine the standards and can also afford to position themselves and their progeny to achieve success. Thus a system based on meritocracy is often indistinguishable from a system designed to favor a narrow elite.

Meritocracy as a way of filling positions of power in a capitalist economy is most often used to certify professionals, the doctors, lawyers, and knowledge workers who populate the offices and classrooms of the United States. Despite the right-wing outcry against quota systems to admit a given number of minorities to the colleges and training centers for this professional class, the whole enterprise functions as a robust tacit quota system that admits a consistently tiny percentage of the nonelite.

The safety valve of this rather rigid system lies within capitalism itself—now and then, working outside the confines of a meritocracy, a genius comes along and makes millions of dollars selling pet rocks, hula hoops, or hip-hop, and thus gives hope to the disenfranchised masses. The graceful solution—short of a drastic reordering of socioeconomic and scholastic resources—is to sincerely believe that every student is a potential scholar and then work to make that happen.

Those who dare teach with integrity deconstruct and debunk the myths that falsely explain success as due solely to merit. Teachers who lack clarity blame their students for their inability to attain success and explain failure by ignoring the sociocultural context in which schooling and teaching take place.

Institutional Racism.   A key area in which clarity of vision is a necessity is in the opposition to **institutional racism,** one of the key institutional practices that support hegemonic practices. Teachers do not have to look far to encounter educational practices that are imbued with racial, ethnic, and class privilege. U.S. society has had only forty years to recover from apartheid—not a long time in the life span of cultures. David Reid (1992) captures the ubiquity of the practices based on race and class privilege:

> We are all caught up on the continuum of racism. The only viable position is an anti-racist one which acknowledges the ideological influences and recognizes that everyone in one way or another is involved in discriminatory structures, and needs to take a stand against racism to dismantle both racist structures and racist attitudes. (p. 16)

How do we identify institutional racism? One way is to profile the racial and ethnic composition of a school staff, of academic "tracks," and of school activities. Box 2.2 features questions to ask to identify institutionally racist practices (see also Chapter 3).

Ways to counteract institutional racism are for teachers of English learners to act informally to recruit teachers from underrepresented minorities as colleagues, to monitor the

---

box 2.2

Questions to Ask to Identify Institutionally Racist Practices

- Do the racial demographics of the teaching staff match those of the students?
- As English learners come to school, do they meet only maintenance personnel and cafeteria workers who speak their language?
- Does the school offer English learners equal access to an academic curriculum, including classes for the gifted and talented?
- Does the school provide equality in resources to support and enrich learning for all students?
- Do school clubs recruit effectively from all races and cultures of the student body, or are English learners segregated into "culture" clubs while native speakers of English staff the more high-status activities such as the school yearbook, newspaper, and student leadership clubs?
- Are parents provided equal opportunities for involvement in school-level activities, or is the only parent organization available designed for middle-class parents who are English literate and have flexible work schedules that enable them to participate in school functions and fundraisers during the school day?

academic quality of life available to English learners, to volunteer to organize clubs that can effectively recruit English learners, and to involve parents and the community in cooperative endeavors.

Does this advocacy demand clarity of vision? It does—and it leads to further clarity. Vision, like other forms of power, has to be used continuously to operate well. Teaching with integrity means being actively antiracist and working collectively with other colleagues and community members to name and oppose institutionalized practices that dehumanize and disempower people based on their racial background.

Linguistic Racism.   Many social scientists have observed that discrimination based on language is taking the place of discrimination once based exclusively on race. For instance, each day millions of Americans are denied the right to speak in their own words. Remarkably, civil rights advocates still do not identify and condemn this silencing. Santa Ana (2004) suggests that this **linguistic racism** is most evident in schools, where the largest silenced group is the millions of American schoolchildren who do not speak English. He states that although racism based on skin color has been publicly discredited, the linguistic reflection of colonialism—linguistic discrimination—remains largely unexamined by most people in the United States.

Teachers with integrity oppose any act that systematically silences students or punishes them for speaking their native or home language. Teachers in California, Arizona, and Massachusetts, for example, must be particularly mindful about what they are asked to do with regard to their English learners, because these states have passed legislation that denies children whose home language is not English the use of that home or primary language for instruction.

Clarity of vision includes being educated and knowledgeable about the intricacies of these laws, and working with parents and communities to counteract acts of linguistic racism. Also, practicing critical contemplation will allow teachers to see how social policy is connected to legislated instructional practices that discriminate and promote linguistic racism.

Teaching with Integrity and the Process of Instruction for English Learners

Teaching English learners is a complex process, grounded in integrity, within an instructional framework that is pedagogically sound. The planning and delivery of instruction is cyclic, consisting of four elements: *foundations, planning, application,* and *assessment* (see Figure 2.2). This section describes each of these four main parts and explains how they frame the process of instruction for English learners that is examined in this book. The teaching with integrity model provides a theoretical framework for pedagogical decision making on a daily basis, and the cycle of instruction discussed below is what drives the delivery of instruction for English learners.

The Foundations of Instruction

Knowledge about the Learner.   Most teachers specialize in certain types of learners. For example, primary school teachers have specialized age-related understandings and techniques relevant to their learners that differ from those of high school teachers. These include

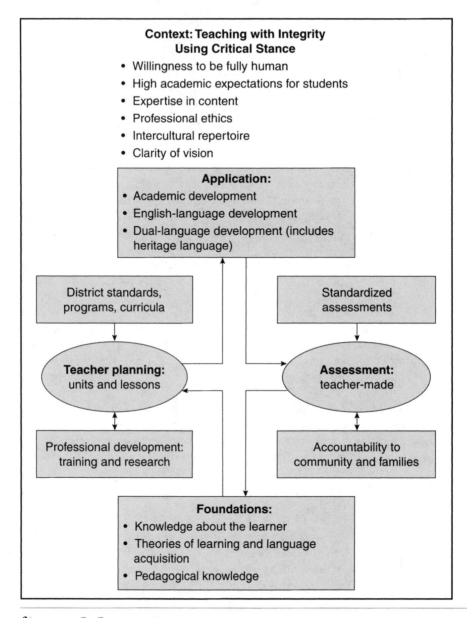

**Context: Teaching with Integrity
Using Critical Stance**
- Willingness to be fully human
- High academic expectations for students
- Expertise in content
- Professional ethics
- Intercultural repertoire
- Clarity of vision

Application:
- Academic development
- English-language development
- Dual-language development (includes heritage language)

District standards, programs, curricula

Standardized assessments

Teacher planning: units and lessons

Assessment: teacher-made

Professional development: training and research

Accountability to community and families

Foundations:
- Knowledge about the learner
- Theories of learning and language acquisition
- Pedagogical knowledge

figure 2.2   **The Process of Instruction for English Learners: A Cycle of Foundations, Applications, Planning, and Assessment**

the ability to present information at specific rates, levels of abstraction, and levels of learner activity.

Regarding ethnic background, teachers who are experienced in educating students from certain ethnic subcultures in the United States know the unique characteristics of their learners. For example, in communities such as New York City, with its high population of both Puerto Rican New Yorkers and immigrants from the Dominican Republic, experienced teachers can usually differentiate students of the two ethnicities on sight, whereas a teacher with the same number of years of teaching experience in Idaho Falls, for instance, would be unable to make this distinction as rapidly. The same would be true of teachers at Sherman Indian School in Riverside, California, a boarding school that educates Native Americans from all over the Southwest. A teacher there would easily differentiate a Ute from a Navajo youth, again based on knowledge about the learner.

Another example of knowledge about the learner is the stage of second-language ac-quisition. An English learner at the beginning stage has quite different capabilities from those of a learner in the stage of intermediate fluency, requiring distinct modifications of communication input from the teacher, and is capable of distinct modalities of verbal and written output. The ability to assess the learner's second-language learning level and to modify instruction accordingly is a specialized part of the knowledge base of the teacher of English learners. Knowledge about the learner is featured in Chapter 3.

When planning for instructional delivery, the teacher draws on three basic kinds of foundations: knowledge about how to teach students of a given age, learning style, language-acquisition stage, and so on; knowledge about how learning takes place (both learning in general and language learning); and pedagogical knowledge.

Knowledge about Learning and Language Acquisition.   Educational psychology and so-cial foundations of learning are disciplines that include not only philosophies of learning (traditional versus progressive, for example) and theories of learning (e.g., cognitive, be-havioral, constructivist, humanistic) but also the understanding of how theory informs practice. Chapter 4 addresses theories of learning and language acquisition.

Theories of learning are also applied to the specific domain of language acquisition. Second-language acquisition shares some of the characteristics of learning in general. Also, some characteristics of first-language learning are shared in that language use differs from cognition in general; it is a modularized subsystem with its own dedicated means of brain processing. Therefore second-language learning has its own specialized methodologies and practices that differ from other types of learning principles and practices.

Pedagogical Knowledge.   Knowing how to teach consists of knowing those concepts that are broadly relevant across all instructional contexts: how to manage a classroom, discipline students, use dialogic discourse, group students cooperatively, and so forth. Although this knowledge can be learned in the context of the classroom if a new teacher is apprenticed to an experienced teacher, specialized classes in these skills are part of every high-quality teacher education curriculum. Pedagogy is addressed in Chapter 5.

Teacher Planning

Effective instructional application is preceded by thoughtful planning. Admittedly, planning is labor intensive, requiring much of a teacher's time. However, lesson plans are more than instructional road maps, because plans allow teachers to reflect and contemplate on their instruction by looking back on the paths designed and taken and to use this reflection to guide instructional application. Increasingly, lesson plan objectives are focused by standards (local and state) while leaving room for teachers to use their professional knowledge to design lessons that are creative and engage students in learning.

Standards, Programs, and Curricula.   Teachers are responsible to a variety of authorities for the delivery of instructional content. The U.S. Constitution gives states the statutory authority to mandate curriculum in the form of state-adopted curricular frameworks that divide content learning into grade-level-appropriate goals and objectives. These are usually aligned with the goals determined by national professional organizations such as the National Council of Teachers of English. Such unified frameworks eliminate redundancy and ensure content that builds on prior learning. School districts, in turn, usually publish and circulate the local goals and objectives for each grade derived from similar state documents. These are the basis of the teacher's yearly, monthly, weekly, and daily plans.

Textbook publishers are very aware of these state-mandated goals and objectives and incorporate them into their texts (at least they do if they want to sell books in the lucrative markets of California and Texas, for example). Teachers who follow the required textbooks page for page usually have no problem covering the required curriculum.

However, following the "recipe" without modifications in the instructional application may result in lessons that fail to address fully the teaching context and that overlook specific needs of individual students.

Professional Development.   Ongoing training in how to deliver curriculum and deploy innovative teaching methods takes place for the corps of practicing teachers by means of professional development activities that teachers attend either on a voluntary or required a basis. These activities are offered by the school districts; by national, state, or local professional conferences; or by local universities in the form of credit-bearing or non-credit-bearing institutes or courses. In addition, beginning teachers can be matched with mentor teachers in structured ways, such as beginning teacher support programs, or in more informal ways, such as grade-level teacher planning groups or buddy- (paired-) teacher arrangements. These professional development activities are an effective way to rejuvenate teaching by learning ways to incorporate innovations and relevant practices into the teaching of academic content.

The Instructional Design Process.   As teachers plan, then, they pull together standards documents, district lists of curricular goals, teacher's manuals, student textbooks, student workbooks, lists of recommended and required core literature books, handouts from training experiences, and other assets and resources as they lay out their yearly, monthly, weekly, and daily plans. Some school-site authorities require written daily lesson plans of beginning teachers, but detailed written plans over and above a weekly planning grid are rarely mandated for experienced teachers. On close inspection, these plans often appear as time schedules with textbook-based activities penciled in distinct time slots.

Three major items are missing from this activity or schedule approach to instructional planning. The first is the statement of the performance goal for the activity—what is to be accomplished in a measurable way as a result of instruction. The second is an explicit link to content standards. A good instructional plan cites the relevant standard and makes a direct connection between the performance goal and the standards. The third frequent omission is explicit attention to ELD standards—language objectives in the lesson that are phrased in terms of the progress the student will make in mastering the given ELD standards. This is the hallmark of solid planning. These aspects are addressed in Chapter 6.

Instructional Application

Instruction is applied in three areas: academic development, or subjects in the content areas; English-language development; and primary-language development. The last two are, in fact, content areas, but they are distinguished for separate attention in Figure 2.2 because of their salience for English learners.

Academic Development. The content areas—reading/language arts, mathematics, science, social studies, foreign languages, visual/performing arts, music, and physical education—each have their distinct content standards derived from professional organizations and state mandates. In turn, the first objective in planning is the academic objective. However, it is not uncommon to see instructional plans with more than one academic objective to accomplish the work of teaching to relevant content standards.

The second objective—the **learning-strategy objective**—places the lesson squarely within the cognitive paradigm. The learner is not simply acquiring knowledge—as stipulated by the content objective—but is acquiring knowledge of the "operating system"—the human mind. For example, in the case of physical education, a content objective might be to learn the rules of softball (a knowledge objective) or the skills of throwing the ball quickly in the infield (a skill objective). However, in addition to these content objectives, the teacher may add a learning-strategy objective: to learn to warm up the muscles before beginning to exercise. This learning-strategy objective is broadly applicable to learning in any sport and, once learned, becomes a part of the strategic repertoire for physical education of all kinds.

Chamot and O'Malley (1994) describe the importance of learning-strategy objectives in planning to teach English learners. Most lesson plan templates or formats do not require a learning-strategy objective, and teachers often confuse a learning objective with what students are to learn, the content objective. Note that content and learning-strategy objectives are distinct and result in different outcomes. Chapter 7 explicates academic instruction.

English-Language Development. Every content lesson has a third objective, the English-language development (ELD) objective. In a well-managed program for English learners, this objective is stipulated by an ELD framework. In California the ELD framework provides language objectives along the four dimensions of language: speaking, listening, reading, and writing. It is also matched to the English language arts (ELA) framework category for category, so the transition is seamless between the ELD and ELA frameworks when the student makes the transition from the status of English learner to full participator in the mainstream classroom. This progress, in California, is measured by the California English Language Development Test (CELDT).

The ELD objective is closely matched to the content objective because the language features of the lesson support content instruction. For example, if the lesson content involves reading a chapter of the story *Charlotte's Web,* the ELD objective for beginning English learners might be to ask and answer simple questions (speaking/listening). As the students pose questions to one another—perhaps relating to story comprehension—the teacher circulates to observe their speaking and listening behaviors, gathering evidence that the learners have progressed to the required level. In a well-documented system, the teacher then checks that box on each individual's ELD record to chart the evidence of progress. Chapter 8 addresses ELD instruction.

Primary-Language Development.   Because foreign language is—or should be—an integral part of the content area instruction of any academic program, it is perhaps misleading to single it out as a separate instructional application. Because in the United States foreign-language instruction is often overlooked (or, in the case of heritage-language instruction, often suppressed), it is separated in Figure 2.2 as a distinct focus and an integral element of dual-language development. Chapter 9 addresses in detail the scientific and political issues surrounding foreign/heritage-language instruction. It is sufficient to underscore here that development of the primary/heritage language is a vital and integral part of any well-designed instructional process.

Assessment of Instruction

The last part of the cycle represented in Figure 2.2 is assessment. Because planning and delivering instruction is a circular process, the last is also paradoxically the first. Assessment is built on the teacher's determination of the learner's needs, the theoretical possibilities of the learning environment, and the goals of instruction applied to the content and language-development tasks. Performance-based assessment asks first the question, "What is required of the learner to provide evidence that learning has taken place?" With a tangible goal in mind, the evidence of learning, the teacher builds the lesson so the learner will be capable of providing this evidence. In this manner, assessment and planning are ultimately linked.

Teacher-Made Assessments.   A key role of the teacher is to design assessments that are "built in" to instruction. In other words, the assessment is not a decontextualized "add-on" to the lesson, but rather a goal and feature of instruction from the beginning. For example, a *preliminary formative assessment* takes place as the teacher provides direct instruction (often called "checking for understanding"). *Continued formative assessment* takes place as the learner moves to supervised and independent practice (often called "monitoring"). *Summative assessment* takes place as the teacher sets up situations that check to see if the learning has been accomplished and provides documentation of this accomplishment. These assessments are most effective if the teacher designs instruction and assessment together. The assessment then comprises authentic documentation that arises from the lesson activities.

Standardized Assessments.   Some assessments, however, are mandated by governing authorities and do not match instruction as closely as the teacher-made assessments that accompany instruction. Although these standardized assessments are supposed to be keyed to the development levels of the students in the age range tested, by their very nature they are normative tests designed so that learners' scores are displayed to form a bell-shaped curve. In contrast to the lesson assessments described previously, in which the teacher designs instruction to bring all learners to completion on the goal, the standardized test is set up so that some learners will succeed beyond all average expectation (the upper end of the bell curve) and other learners of the same age or grade will fail miserably (the lower end of the bell curve).

Unfortunately, these tests do not measure academic knowledge or progress achievement as much as they measure ability, as confounded by prior ability in English, the language of the standardized assessment. Therefore, unless *tested and taught* in their primary language, English learners too often constitute the group of those who score poorly. "Teaching to the test" only frustrates the learners at the lower end of the scale because no amount of last-minute test-prep activity can bring a second-language learner up to native speaker ability in a second language. Only time spent in a balanced bilingual program can accomplish this.

Accountability.   Standardized tests are only a part of the accountability that schools must show in response to the community's trust that the task of educating children is done well. Grades are the primary indicator of progress and achievement. Parents, who are the first and most important monitors of educational excellence, depend on grades to monitor their children's learning. If the parents and teachers do not cooperate on a home–school intervention to raise grades, the child's academic potential is compromised. However, if the parents are too trusting of a poor school, grades are a misleading indicator of learning.

High grades in a mediocre school do not add up to educational excellence but rather to educational mediocrity—the dark side of the myth of meritocracy. Many a student in a California high school, for example, has received a 4.0—all A's—only to find that a 4.6 grade must be attained to be competitive for admission to the University of California, Berkeley, the flagship campus for the UC system. How can this happen, the parents ask? The answer: Those high schools offering Advanced Placement courses score the A in an Advanced Placement course as a 5.0, not a 4.0. A school in a rural or inner-city area that does not offer Advanced Placement courses dooms an otherwise high achiever to a noncompetitive GPA on completion. Remedying this inequity is part of the real world of accountability—ensuring equal opportunity to achieve.

Conclusion: Teaching with Integrity and the Process of Instruction

As suggested earlier, teaching English learners is a challenging and complex task requiring both integrity in teaching and pedagogical skills and knowledge along various dimensions of instruction. The teaching with integrity model provides the theoretical framework for an academic context that is humane, student-centered, and equitable.

The process of instruction model represented in Figure 2.2 is a depiction of the complexity of instructional planning and delivery. Because of its complexity, those who approach the complicated task of teaching English learners and who are dedicated to excellence must be persons of high integrity to ensure that no phase of excellence is undermined by low standards, lack of pedagogical expertise, or poor professional behavior. Both models suggest that those who dare teach English learners must be cognizant that this endeavor be viewed as a career commitment grounded in integrity, with the futures of English learners hanging in the balance.

3

Knowledge about the Learner

What's in a name? Names represent cultural pride and self-esteem.

expectation

■ The prospective teacher can draw upon information about students' backgrounds and prior learning, including students' assessed levels of literacy in English and their first languages, as well as their proficiency in English, to provide instruction differentiated to students' language abilities. *(Element 7.5 of the California Teaching Performance Expectations. Reprinted by permission of the California Commission on Teacher Credentialing.)*

Learning about the Learner to Adapt Instruction

English learners come in all shapes, sizes, and language-acquisition stages. The foremost responsibility of the teacher of English learners is to adapt instruction to meet the needs of the learner so that all students can attain academic success. This is the foundation for instruction (see Figure 2.2, p. 34). Therefore teachers are expected to learn about their learners so they can adapt lessons accordingly.

This chapter examines factors at each level (individual, cognitive psychological, social–emotional psychological, sociocultural, and societal-contextual) that affect student performance in school. Taking these factors into consideration, teachers can adapt instruction to meet the needs of individual students.

Each student has a unique *background,* including name, age, primary language, second-language learning experience, previous schooling, likes and dislikes about schooling, hobbies, and so forth. This background is an indispensable knowledge base that the teacher needs to have about each learner.

Delving deeper into the individual, a teacher discovers that the learner has unique *cognitive psychological factors*—the way he or she uses a combination of learning styles and strategies that may or may not be academically successful. Linked to these cognitive factors are *social–emotional psychological* aspects of learning such as self-esteem, emotions, and attitudes that affect the learner's school life.

The individual is situated within a *sociocultural milieu* of family and culture. Culture provides the lens through which the individual learns about reality—the beliefs, behaviors, and values that shape everyday life are the foundation of the learner's approach to schooling. Moreover, the home and community provide more than simply the learner's primary language: They are the context within which that language makes sense and furnish the goals, desires, and dreams that language makes possible. Therefore the tensions—or, more positively, linkages—between the primary language and English serve as focal points for conflict or cohesion between home and school.

Surrounding the psychological, social–affective, and sociocultural environment are *societal–contextual factors* that affect the learner's schooling—larger, less tangible forces and conditions in society that act as invisible determinants of academic possibility for each student. Society at large elevates or denigrates the status of the primary language of the student, creating a halo of prestige around some home languages (in the United States, Parisian French or any British-sounding dialect of English) and the reverse, a sense of unimportance or—worse—shame around other languages or dialects of English.

Continuing this pattern of relative privilege or disenfranchisement, schools are funded disproportionately well for those students in wealthy neighborhoods, and the types of language and discourse structures used in schools reflect the relative respect that social class buys privileged students. Teachers with integrity have clarity about the relationship between English learners and the sociocultural context in which they are acquiring or learning English. All of these factors affect teachers as they adapt lessons to meet the needs of learners.

Box 3.1 summarizes these factors in the form of a questionnaire that can help to organize the teacher's knowledge about each learner. This questionnaire can serve as an organizer for the information in this chapter. Box 3.2 provides assistance in administering the questionnaire to English learners in the form of question prompts.

Learner's Background

Name and Identity

What's in a name? A learner's name represents not only the learner's individuality and human dignity but also his or her connection to the family. If a person's name is treated with disrespect, how can the person feel validated? In the past, teachers and administrators often

English Learner Profile

Learner's Background
Learner's name _____ Age _____ Gender M/F
Grade _____ L1 proficiency _____
Type of bilingualism _____
Previous L2 experience _____
Academic success _____
Likes/dislikes _____

Cognitive Psychological Factors
Cognitive learning styles _____
Learning strategies _____

Social–Emotional Psychological Factors
Self-esteem _____
Motivation _____
Anxiety level _____
Attitudes toward L2 _____
Attitudes toward school in general _____
Level of oral interaction w/ peers in L1 _____ L2 _____

Sociocultural Factors
Family background _____
Family, community use of L1 _____ L2 _____
Degree of family assimilation _____
Institutional support for L1 _____
Support for L1 in classroom environment _____
Use of L1 during instruction _____
Assessed L2 level: Reading _____ Writing _____ Listening _____ Speaking _____

altered students' names in an attempt to encourage assimilation. The following excerpt recounts one English learner's experience:

> Before I started school in America I was Edite. María Edite dos Anjos Cunha. . . . I loved my name. It was melodious and beautiful. [In Peabody, Massachusetts, a well-meaning second-grade teacher changed her name on the first day of school.] "Your name will be Mary Edith Cunha," she declared. . . . My name was María Edite dos Anjos Cunha. . . . I wanted to scream out my name. . . . Day after day she made me practice pronouncing that name that wasn't mine. . . . Later my teachers shortened it to Mary. I never knew quite who I was. (Pedrosa, 1990, p. 36)

Despite some educators' belief that a name change promotes cultural assimilation, it can lead students to a sense of shame and a feeling that their name, hence their identity, is somehow flawed. Changing someone's identity without their consent can lead to a sense of confusion and disrespect. Skutnabb-Kangas (1981) cited an example of discrimination that took place against a minority student in a Swedish school. This example demonstrates the

English Learner Profile: Facilitating the Questionnaire

An important feature of teacher performance is the ability to articulate and address the needs of English learners. In a tutorial situation, prospective teachers can use the English Learner Profile as a means to investigate and address the needs of English learners.

While achieving an informal tone, use the questionnaire to interview the learner briefly. Try to ask questions in a way that is comprehensible to the learner, in a conversational tone.

Component	Facilitation
Learner's Background	
Learner's name	(Full name—spelled correctly; any nicknames?)
Age _____ Gender M/F	(Complete this in advance, if possible.)
Grade _____	
Observed L1 proficiency level	(Use levels of the Natural Approach: preproduction, early production, speech emergence, intermediate fluency.)
Type of bilingualism	(Additive/subtractive; concurrent): When did you start to learn English?
Previous L2 experience	(How many years has the student been educated in English?)
Academic success	(Investigate previous academic record): Do you think you are a good student?
Likes/dislikes	What are your favorite subjects in school?
	What do you do to have fun after school or on the weekends?
Cognitive Psychological Factors	
Learning styles	(Sensory modality strengths—visual/auditory/hands-on): How do you learn best? Do you like to read new things, or listen to someone explain it to you?
	(Holistic/analytic, etc.): If I taught you a card game, would you like to hear all the rules before you play, or learn the rules as you go along?
Learning strategies	(Study skills, problem solving, information processing): Do you have a special place you write down homework assignments? When you have to memorize something, how do you do it? When you have a hard math problem in your homework, how do you solve it?
Social–Emotional Psychological Factors	
Self-esteem	Do you think you are good at most things?
Motivation	How do you get yourself going if you have something hard to do?
Anxiety level	How do you feel about school? Explain.
Attitudes toward English	Who are your best friends? Do they like English?

(continued)

box 3.2

(Continued)	
Component	**Facilitation**
Attitudes toward school	Do you and your best friend like school? Why or why not?
Level of oral interaction with peers in English/L1	Do you speak English on the playground?
Sociocultural Factors	
Family background	Do you have brothers and sisters? How old are they? Do you all live together?
Family, community use of L1/L2	Who speaks English at home? Describe. Do your parents like to read? What things do they read? Do your parents read to you? What language do your neighbors speak?
Degree of assimilation	What movies/TV/music does your family watch in L1/L2?
Support for L1 in the classroom environment	(Does the room show evidence of L1?)
Use of L1 during instruction	(Does the teacher use any L1 during class?)
Institutional support for L1	(Does the school show evidence of support for L1? Is L1 used on school notices or hallway bulletin boards?)
L2 learning level (CELDT levels?)	(Use CELDT level if on file.)
Reading/writing	(Check evidence from classroom performance.)
Listening/speaking	(Check evidence from classroom performance.)

way that a name can be used to encourage students to internalize a sense of shame in being foreign.

> The headmaster said, "You have a name which is difficult for us Swedes to pronounce. Can't we change it? . . . And besides, perhaps some nasty person will make fun of your name."
> "Well, I suppose I'd better change it," I thought. (p. 316)

Cultures have distinct naming habits. The custom in mainstream U.S. culture is for an individual to have three names. The first name may represent a family name or a name that is commonly popular. Boys are much more likely to have a nickname variant of the given name ("Bob" for "Robert," but more rarely "Steph" for "Stephanie"). The second, or middle, name for a girl may be another popular girl's name or, for boys and girls alike, it may be the mother's maiden name or a family name. In any case, the middle name is rarely used together with the first name in address, except in the case of regional dialects (e.g., "Sally Sue").

The last (or family) name is usually the father's last name; much more rarely, it is a hyphenated name combining mother's and father's surnames. It is not uncommon for the mother and child to have different last names if the mother keeps her maiden name and

gives the child the father's name. On attendance lists, the first and last names are often reversed to organize or alphabetize the names.

In contrast, other cultures put the family name first not only in organized lists but also
in social address. In Vietnam, for example, names also consist of three parts, in the following
order: family name, middle name, and given name. The names are always given in this order
and cannot be reversed, because doing so would denote a different person—Nguyên Van Hai
is different from Hai Van Nguyên. Similarly, Chinese and Korean names are presented family name first, and the given name consists of the next two syllables. For example, for Huang
Mei-Ling, "Huang" is the family name and "Mei-Ling" is the given name. In U.S. schools,
in an effort to assimilate, the student may introduce herself as "Mei-Ling Huang."

Although some names are arbitrary (does *Claire* really mean "clear"?), some names
carry special meaning. A teacher can learn a lot by asking about the meaning of a child's
name. If a child was named after a family member, the connection may be especially meaningful. If a child was, for example, named after the Catholic saint sharing the same birth-
day, this may indicate a highly traditional home environment. Conversely, if a child is named
"Moon Unit," the opposite may be true!

Puerto Ricans and other Latinos generally use three names: a given name (which may
be compound, like "José Luis"), followed by the father's surname and then the mother's surname. If one last name must be used, it is generally the father's surname. Thus, Esther Reyes
Hernández can be listed as Esther Reyes. If the first name is composed of two given names
(María Elena), both are used. This person may have a sister who is named María Teresa; for
either to be called simply María would be tantamount to a loss of identity.

Name and Identity: Adapting Instruction.   A sensitive teacher strives not only to understand the use and order of names but also to pronounce them correctly. This may require a
private session with the individual student. Practicing a student's name repeatedly in public
is often embarrassing for that student and is a stigmatizing indicator of "otherness." The
teacher may also wish to check again a month later to see if the pronunciation is still accurate; too often over time the teacher's once-correct pronunciation of someone's name will re-
vert to English phonemes and therefore needs to be learned anew.

Issues of Age

A student's age is an often-overlooked factor in school success. Because school districts enforce different birth dates as a requirement to enter school, a kindergarten student born just
before the enrollment cutoff date may be the youngest student in the class, whereas a child
born just after the last permissible date may be a full year older than the first child mentioned. This year of developmental difference is huge at all levels of schooling. Given the
reality that on any skill there is a wide range of attainment, one 5-year-old may acquire new
vocabulary at the level of a 2-year-old while another is operating at the level of a 7-year-
old. A teacher who looks closely at the birth date of the student in relation to that of others
can more fully understand developmental differences due to age.

Language is one of the many skills a young child must master, and there are distinct
developmental differences between individuals in such areas as language fluency and vocabulary acquisition. Second-language acquisition skills, like other kinds of language skills,
shows variation in performance among individuals according to both age and aptitude.

Generally speaking, a child is fluent in the primary language at the age of 5. This means that the child, as a native speaker, can create well-formed sentences, pronounce the basic set of phonemes of the language, and use language to meet basic social needs. This does not mean that the child can create grammatically complex sentences perfectly, can pronounce all phonemes, or can use language to negotiate a car purchase (negotiation expertise develops during the third and fourth decade of life). However, the lament that a young child "does not have language" is rarely true.

One issue that surfaces repeatedly is the myth that the younger the child, the quicker the second-language acquisition. Second-language acquisition is a complex process that occurs over a long period of time, and the optimum age for this process has been widely debated. Research has shown that contrary to popular belief, older children acquire a second language faster than younger children, and adults master early stages of syntax and morphology faster than do children (Krashen, Long, & Scarcella, 1979; Collier, 1987). Research comparing adults to children has consistently demonstrated that adolescents and adults outperform children in controlled second-language learning studies (Marinova-Todd, Marshall, & Snow, 2000). Adults have the advantage over children in self-discipline, strategy use, and prior knowledge; and, as a rule, they are more socially comfortable and have more experience with language in general.

Lenneberg (1967) postulated that a child can learn a second language more rapidly than an adult can because the brain has a language-acquisition processor that functions best before the child becomes a teenager—the so-called *critical period*. Despite the fact that the critical period hypothesis has not been proved, people continue to believe a child learns a second language rapidly (Snow & Hoefnagel-Hoehle, 1978). The language that children tend to use is relatively simple compared to that of adults, with shorter sentences and fewer vocabulary words, making it appear more fluent.

People also once believed that children are less inhibited than adults when speaking a second language, but this is not so. Children are just as likely to be embarrassed around their peers as are adults, and they are more likely to be shy when speaking before adults (McLaughlin, 1992). Prepubescent youth may have one advantage: the acquisition of native-speaker-like pronunciation skills. Oyama (1976) found that the earlier a person begins to learn a second language, the closer the accent will become to that of a native speaker.

One last aspect of the learner's age is the difficulty experienced by preteen and teenage immigrants from Mexico and Central America in U.S. schools. Some students may not have achieved literacy in their primary language—which may not even be Spanish, but rather an indigenous language such as Mixtec, Zapotec, or Triqui (Flores & Gage-Serio, 2003). This poses an unusual challenge to second-language educators. It is often difficult to find age-appropriate materials for these students at the level of emergent literacy.

Age: Adapting Instruction.   The varying ages of students within the same grade cause developmental differences that show up in three basic ways: learning readiness, social–emotional adjustment, and behavioral maturity. The younger the child in a class in comparison to others, the more the child needs cognitive "catch-up" due to developmental factors. The older the child in relation to others, the more learning is affected by lack of success in previous schooling (usually due to retention) or, in the case of nonliterate immigrants, the lack of previous schooling. These situations require different adaptations.

Students are increasingly able to master concrete operations and begin to think abstractly as they progress through school. This is true for every K–12 grade. Older students are better able to acquire concept-related vocabulary than such age-related abilities as correct pronunciation of phonemes. Adjustments can be made for younger students by encouraging more manipulative (hands-on) tasks that strengthen concrete operations. This is also true for second-language acquisition—making sure that the second language is linked to, and advances, academic learning at every step. An example follows:

Selena and two other sixth-grade students were doing a Full Option Science System (FOSS) lesson that involved building a go-cart of dowel rods and Tinkertoy wheels that was self-propelled by means of rubber bands. (See www.lawrencehallofscience.org/foss/index.html for more information on FOSS.) The go-cart was able to spin its wheels if the rubber band was wound tightly, but that's all it did: spin its wheels. What was missing? The teacher asked Selena to make a hypothesis.

"I don't know," was the reply. Obviously some scaffolding was needed. The teacher looked for a way to teach the missing concept: traction. Without rubber bands wrapped around the Tinkertoy wheel to create traction, the wheel would not grip the ground and the power supplied to the wheel would not result in forward motion.

In this case, hands-on experience was not enough to solve the problem. Concept attainment would also be necessary.

Social–emotional adjustment is age-related and is a large part of an individual's success as a student. This is treated at greater length under the discussion of social–emotional psychological factors.

Behavioral maturity is also linked to age. Success in school learning depends on long periods of cognitive focus and mental self-control. Students who are younger or older than the norm may need more frequent breaks from this routine, possibly including teacher-led stretching sessions.

Behavioral maturity is particularly evident in the adolescent years. Middle school is a time when students are still in many ways children; classroom activities should strike a balance between a high level of cognitive challenge and a high level of sensory involvement and activity.

Grade-Level Performance

For preliterate students mentioned earlier, correct grade-level placement is often difficult. They often have difficulty competing with students whose cognitive academic language is well developed, but they cannot be placed with younger children for social reasons. This poses a particular problem for adolescent immigrants, who are vulnerable to peer pressure and might be ridiculed if forced to take classes with younger children.

Holding English learners to standards of grade-level performance for purposes of accountability is an issue being contested in every state under the No Child Left Behind federal guidelines. English learners need enough time to acquire cognitive academic language proficiency in English in order to do well in academically challenging instruction. Most school districts now understand that grade-level proficiency expectations cannot be applied in a simplistic, one-size-fits-all formula.

Grade-Level Performance: Adapting Instruction.   Grade-level-appropriate materials must be used for all students, despite the second-language acquisition stage they may have attained. Although some adolescents, for instance, may be lacking in concepts and experiences, materials to address their needs should reflect their age. If a student is at the beginning stage of English, he or she remains a part of the grade-level curriculum in all subjects, with modifications such as simplified texts and specially designed academic instruction in English (SDAIE, see Chapter 5) to increase comprehension.

First-Language (L1) Proficiency

Evidence has shown that the firmest foundation for academic success is educating a student in his or her **first language (L1)** so that access to academic content is not lost while the student acquires a **second language (L2)**. Thus it is particularly important for the teacher to have data on a student's **primary-language** proficiency.

Various instruments exist for measuring students' primary-language skills, such as the Bilingual Syntax Measure (BSM), which measures oral proficiency in English and/or Spanish grammatical structures and language dominance, and the Student Oral Language Observation Matrix (SOLOM). (Chapter 10 addresses student assessment.)

Teachers who are bilingual in the language of the student can supplement more formal test results with anecdotal evidence of the student's proficiency. Informal measures of proficiency can be obtained by asking a primary-language-speaking aide, parent, peer, or teacher to spend some time with the primary-language-speaking student. These volunteers may be able to provide additional anecdotal opinions about the student's abilities, proficiency, and interests.

First-Language Proficiency: Adapting Instruction.   Academic proficiency in L1 is a direct result of schooling. Parents need clear information about the type of primary-language instruction their children will be provided so that they can seek a program of primary-language maintenance if they so desire and the school does not offer such services. Teachers who support L1 maintenance programs have a major role in setting up such programs, including two-way bilingual schools.

Teachers who take responsibility for students' L1 maintenance can monitor L1 proficiency. If opportunities for peer interaction in L1 are available and the student does not seem to respond, a family conference may be helpful to check whether the family believes the student is, for example, excessively shy, has the attitude that the primary language is not important or not valued, or has a speech/language delay.

Types of Bilingualism

Most people have just one primary language and acquire their second language some time after the first language. These people might be called *serial bilinguals*. The rare case of an individual acquiring two primary languages is known as *concurrent bilingualism*. This is the case in a country such as Nigeria, in which English is acquired as a primary language in the context of the simultaneous acquisition of a tribal language such as Ibo.

The level of **bilingualism** that students eventually attain is an important factor in educational development (Cummins, 1979). If the first language is maintained during schooling, students gain **additive bilingualism;** if the first language is compromised, stunted, or discontinued by the acquisition of the second language, the situation is called **subtractive bilingualism.** Many adults in the United States find that they were systematically discouraged from acquiring fluency in their parents' or grandparents' language, causing intergenerational loss of the **heritage,** or ancestral, **language.** Often the children themselves make the decision to discontinue use of the heritage language, responding to social pressures to "fit in" with mainstream monolingual English-speaking society.

Type of Bilingualism: Adapting Instruction.   The single greatest factor in achieving additive bilingualism is family support for proficiency in two languages. Teachers should play a major role in encouraging families to sustain their children's heritage-language skills, as well as in encouraging the school district as a whole to invest in linguistic multicompetence by providing materials and programs in all major languages of the community. Chapter 11 suggests ways for families to promote additive bilingualism.

Previous Second-Language (L2) Experience

In parts of the United States that have implemented bilingual education, a typical third-grade classroom might contain students who have been schooled in vastly different ways. One student may have gone through kindergarten and first and second grades in a primary-language classroom and be literate in the primary language; however, this student may have had little exposure to English. Some students may be fluent in listening and speaking their primary language without having attained literacy—reading and writing in English may be their only literacy achievement. Other students may have experienced submersion in English without L1 support. Other students may have had no formal schooling at all. Yet other students may have had a high level of schooling as reflected by grade-level-appropriate mathematics skills, yet be totally new to English.

Of course, two students who have attended identical instructional programs for three years might emerge with very different skills. In addition, no two students are exposed to exactly the same input of English outside of class. Thus students' prior exposure to English and attainment of English proficiency are often uneven.

These conditions create the typical class of English learners characterized by mixed levels of L2 proficiency. Teachers will find it useful to investigate exactly what degree of L2 instruction a student previously attained, even if it means visiting the student's previous classroom to make an independent assessment of how English is used and taught.

Previous L2 Experience: Adapting Instruction.   Proficiency testing in L2 offers the instructor a direct measure of current proficiency that can be matched to instructional modification, making the history of prior services useful to have in order to design instructional adaptations.

Previous L2 experience has major ramifications for students' motivation to learn English and their attitudes toward English. If an overemphasis on accuracy in grammar and pronunciation and use of Standard English occurs too early in the acquisition process, students "shut down" and are unwilling to risk experimentation, a vital part of second-language acquisition. Teaching with integrity means accepting with delight a student's language, supplying corrections indirectly and with respect. Students may need to undergo a process of healing if they have had negative previous English-language experiences in school.

Adapting to varying degrees of English proficiency means striking a balance between homogeneous and heterogeneous grouping. Grouping students at the same English level helps them to complete similar objectives. Grouping students across proficiency levels helps to expose the students with a lower proficiency level to more fluent speech, and helps those with higher proficiency levels to relax and enjoy speaking in a low-stress environment.

Previous Academic Success

Because grade-level academic success is built on prior schooling, teachers must have access to prior school records in order to understand a learner's background. Some teachers wait until the end of the first month of school before reviewing students' cumulative files in order to evaluate the student before being influenced by evidence of a student's prior record.

However, if a student transfers from another school, the cumulative file is often not immediately available; the destination school must make a written request to the school of origin. Even more pressing if delayed in transfer is the confidential file that is kept if the student has been enrolled in special education classes. Often this must be requested by the receiving school.

Previous Academic Success: Adapting Instruction.   Teaching with integrity is a process of making scholars out of students. A gifted teacher believes in students' success to a greater degree than they believe in their past mediocrity.

A crucial instructional adaptation is a change in teachers' attitude from cynical acceptance of the image of the bell-shaped curve (only a few are gifted, most are average, and a few have to be left behind) to profound embrace of a more empowering image: the boat leaves port for the Promised Land (academic success) with every single class member on board.

The Learner's Likes and Dislikes

Every student has favorites: academic subjects, television shows, and extracurricular activities. Teachers who spend time informing themselves about the hobbies and interests of their students can help to create teacher–student rapport and enhance students' interest in instruction. Equally important is the ability of teachers to create links between academic content and the activities that students do at home. This helps to bridge the home–school gap and to motivate students to take a personal interest in school.

Likes/Dislikes: Adapting Instruction.   Students who report that they do not like school are at risk of dropping out prematurely. Every effort should be made to communicate to students that learning is enjoyable; it may not be "fun," in the sense of playing in a video arcade, but students can discover that genuine pride is possible in accomplishment and that there is beauty in numbers aligned correctly on a math page, happiness in reading a work of literature, and delight in showing one's peers how a science experiment works. The alchemy of teaching is in converting "dislike" to "like" where schooling is concerned.

Cognitive Psychological Factors

Psychological factors are those that help the individual form a relatively stable approach to learning. According to sociocultural theorists such as Vygotsky, nothing is internalized that is not first a part of the social–cultural surroundings; people learn how to learn by being part of a culture. Therefore the psychology of the individual learner cannot be separated from the surrounding culture, or, as Cole (1998, n.p.) put it, "mind is interiorized culture and culture is exteriorized mind."

Nevertheless, even though internalized from the exterior, psychological factors influence learning. These factors can be divided into two categories: *cognitive psychological* and *social–emotional psychological.* Cognitive psychological factors influence the input and processing of information, whereas social–emotional psychological factors have more to do with the disposition to learn. Teachers can help students become aware of those psychological factors that further their language learning, and they can work with students to ensure that these factors promote rather than impede their learning.

Learning Styles

Students vary considerably in their approach to learning tasks, including language-learning activities. Many researchers have documented differences in the manner in which learners approach the learning task and offer several definitions of **learning styles.** "Learning styles are the preferences students have for thinking, relating to others, and for particular types of classroom environments and experiences" (Grasha, 1990, p. 23). Much research has taken place on learning styles since the 1980s, and each researcher defines the concept in a slightly different way.

Learning styles are generally classified into three types: perceptual modality (reactions to the physical environment based on the way each individual receives information), information processing (the way information is organized and retained), and personality patterns (the way in which each individual pays attention, values, and responds emotionally while learning) (see www.learnativity.com/learningstyles.html). McGriff (2005) called these three types physiological, cognitive, and affective styles. Each of the five systems described in the following paragraphs—Hruska-Riechmann and Grasha, Sonbuchner, Keefe, Tharp, and Cohen—represents a combination of perceptual modality, information processing, and personality patterns, making these five systems difficult to categorize. Those who are interested in using one of these systems might check the Websites provided, take the learning styles quizzes that are offered on those sites, and thus discover which system is most understandable and appealing.

Hruska-Riechmann and Grasha (1982) offered six learning styles: competitive versus cooperative, dependent versus independent, and participant versus avoidant. Students may show characteristics of more than one of these styles (see also Grasha, 1996). If instructors can anticipate the different needs and perspectives of students, the information can be used to plan and modify certain aspects of assignments. To find out more about the Grasha–Riechmann Student Learning Style Scales (GRSLSS), teachers can explore www.ltseries.com/LTS/sitepgs/grslss2.htm.

Sonbuchner (1991) viewed learning styles as information-processing preferences (reading, writing, listening, speaking, visualizing, or manipulating) and work environment preferences (differences in motivation, concentration, length of study sessions, involvement with others, level of organization, prime times for study, amount of noise, amount of light, amount of heat, and need for food/drink). To read more about Sonbuchner, see http://64.233.179.104/search?q=cache:SilcXDheO00J:wilearns.state.wi.us/apps/default.asp%3Fcid%3D653+&hl=en.

The following vignette illustrates a learning style with a preference for listening.

Noorwahida likes to talk. Coming from a Malaysian family background, she has learned long passages from the Koran by heart by practicing with her mother. She talks to herself as she reads, although last year's teacher deemed this a stage she needs to "get over." But Noorwahida just smiles and says, "I like the sounds of the words."

Four categories of learning style variables—physiological, affective, incentive, and cognitive—influence the way a learner approaches a task in Keefe's (1987) system. Physiological variables include personal nutrition, health, time-of-day preferences, sleeping and waking habits, need for mobility, and response to varying levels of light, sound, and temperature. Affective variables include requirements for structure or supervision, anxiety and curiosity, and the degree of persistence used to pursue a task in the face of frustration. Students' responses to incentives vary according to personal interests; levels of achievement motivation; enjoyment of competition versus cooperation; preference for risk taking versus caution; reaction to rewards and punishment; social motivation arising from family, school, and ethnic background; and locus of control (internal, seeing oneself as responsible for one's own behavior, or external, attributing circumstances to luck, chance, or other people).

Keefe's (1987) last category—cognitive learning style variables—includes field independent versus field dependent; conceptual/analytical versus perceptual/concrete; broad versus focused attention; easily distracted versus capable of controlled concentration; leveling (tendency to lump new experiences with previous ones) versus sharpening (the ability to distinguish small differences); and high cognitive complexity (accepting of diverse, perhaps conflicting, input) versus low cognitive complexity (tendency to reduce conflicting information to a minimum).

Tharp (1989) suggested two sets of contrasting learning styles: visual/verbal and holistic/analytic. Students who have a visual orientation learn by observing rather than by reading or talking. Similarly, a student with holistic thought processes dislikes reducing phenomena to disassembled parts. This person may understand pieces of a process only when the whole pattern is visible. Traditional classrooms tend to be organized to favor verbal and analytic learning styles, so schools tend to reward students who are both verbal and analytic. Tharp's work applied to Native Americans is presented at www2.sjsu.edu/depts/it/edit226/learner/lrngstyl.pdf.

Some English learners use learning styles that are a result of previous schooling. Some students have been taught to learn by means of rote memory; others have been taught to observe closely until it is their turn to do something by themselves. In many Western cultures, learning by doing is emphasized, and trial-and-error is preferred over a more passive approach (Helmer & Eddy, 2003). Teachers may observe that some students feel more confident with direct instruction accompanied by rote memorization; others blurt out answers or compete for a chance to answer, whereas still others speak only in small-group settings.

In East Asia, for example, teaching is dominated by a book-centered, teacher-directed transmission mode. Many students dislike ambiguity and prefer closure. Many are visual learners; lectures and conversation without visual input can be confusing for them. Many students are field-independent learners, oriented toward thinking rather than feeling, and they are reflective rather than impulsive. They prefer concrete-sequential approaches such as following detailed lists and structured reviews of information (Rao, 2004).

Rather than offering a summary of these five diverse systems, Table 3.1 presents a summary of Cohen's (2004) system, which is specifically adapted for English learners. An "assess yourself" survey can be downloaded from www/carla.umn.edu/about/profiles/ Cohen. A larger questionnaire is available from Soloman and Felder (2005) at www2.ncsu. edu/unity/lockers/users/f/felder/public/ILSdir/ilsweb.html. A summary of learning styles counseling is presented by Griggs (1991) at www.ericdigests.org/1992-4/styles.htm.

Learning Styles: Adapting Instruction.   In the typical classroom, some modification can be made to take learning styles into account. If students score high on dependency and competitiveness, for example, assignments that enhance collaborative and independent learning might be developed. Teachers who incorporate variety into learning activities can accommodate distinct learning styles.

table 3.1   **Summary of Learning Style Preferences**

Learning styles are either this . . .	. . . or this
Extroverted Enjoying social, interactive tasks	Introverted Preferring to do tasks by oneself or with one other
Abstract-intuitive Enjoys speculating about future possibilities and the "big picture"	Concrete-sequential Prefers the present, one step at a time
Open Enjoys discovery learning without concern for rules or boundaries	Closure-oriented Seeks clarity, precision, planning ahead, and meeting deadlines
Global Gets the main idea without having to know all the details	Particular Focus is on details and specifics
Synthesizing Summarizing material quickly and noticing similarities	Analytic Pulling ideas apart for purposes of contrast
Field sensitive Needs to see context in order to understand	Field independent Separates and focuses on items without context
Reflective Processes material at low speed with high accuracy	Impulsive Processes material at high speed with low accuracy

Visual Relying on the sense of sight	Auditory Preferring listening and speaking tasks	Hands-on Working with objects

Source: Adapted from Cohen (2004).

Given the complex ways in which students may differ, instructional adaptations can be based on the theme of variety and choice. In delivering information, the teacher uses variety (see Table 3.2). Independent learning centers, such as self-tutoring stations, listening centers with audiotapes or CD-equipped computers, and so forth, offer a range of activities to meet varied learning styles (see Table 3.3). Assessment is varied and samples various types of attainment (see Table 3.4).

Of course, not all adaptations are used every day. In planning lessons, the teacher draws on a repertoire of ideas to add variety with respect to students' learning style preferences, making distinct modifications throughout the weekly or monthly plans. Reid's *Learning Styles in the ESL/EFL Classroom* (1995) is a comprehensive source for the incorporation of learning styles into second-language acquisition instruction.

Learning Strategies

Some students may use cognitive, metacognitive, and social–affective **learning strategies** routinely. More commonly, however, is the intermittent use of these strategies even by the

table 3.2   Variety in Teacher Presentation to Adapt to Learning Style Preferences

Learning Style	Adaptation for Learning Style Preferences
Extroverted	Let students interview one another to receive instructions from an information card.
Introverted	Let students receive instructions directly from an information card.
Abstract-intuitive	Let students brainstorm alternative ways to do a task before beginning and explore ramifications of alternative ways.
Concrete-sequential	Let students do the first three steps of a task and then return for further instructions.
Open	Let students experiment with materials before beginning formal instructional segment.
Closure-oriented	Let students take inventory of materials before beginning a task and advise them at intervals of time remaining.
Global	Describe to students the whole task before beginning.
Particular	Advise students what specific products or outcomes will be required, and show examples.
Synthesizing	Describe how each part of the task fits into the whole.
Analytic	Describe how each part of the task contributes differently to the result.
Field sensitive	Have students watch a model and discuss how it worked for the model.
Field independent	Have students try a task individually and then have them share how it worked for them.
Reflective	Let students sit and think for a moment, going through the task in their minds; then ask if anyone needs clarification.
Impulsive	Actively involve students as models; let students guess what comes next.
Visual	Show: Use posters, charts, pictures, videos.
Auditory	Let some students be "designated listeners" who in turn explain the task to others.
Hands-on	Tell-and-do: Alternate speech with students' doing subparts of task.

table 3.3 Variety in Independent Practice to Adapt to Learning Style Preferences: Diverse Roles in Cooperative Research Tasks

Learning Style	Adaptation for Learning Style Preferences
Extroverted	"Extrovert" can do interpersonal research (perform interviews, give questionnaires).
Introverted	"Introvert" can do library research.
Abstract-intuitive	"Abstract" learners can inform team of the categories of information that need to be included.
Concrete-sequential	"Concrete-sequential" learners can plan task steps.
Open	"Open"-style learners can gather diverse information in early phases of project.
Closure-oriented	"Closure-oriented" learners can be in charge of shaping information in middle and end phases of project.
Global	"Global" person visualizes final result at beginning of project.
Particular	"Particular" learners can use a checklist of task features to ensure inclusion in final product.
Synthesizing	"Synthesizers" can compare information from various sources to note similar data and address possible information gaps.
Analytic	"Analytic" learners can divide large ideas into smaller segments for further, more intensive research.
Field sensitive	"Field-sensitive" students can act as a team coordinator to see that each person is contributing.
Field independent	"Field-independent" students can work on a "one-person" feature of the task.
Reflective	"Reflective" learners can proofread written product.
Impulsive	"Impulsive" learners can scan drafts to check for missing features.
Visual	"Visual" students can draw pictures and charts.
Auditory	"Auditory" team members can describe verbally what they are doing to the coordinator, who gives further direction.
Hands-on	"Hands-on" learners can build physical products or models.

best students. Throughout the years of K–12 schooling, explicit instruction in *how* to learn should accompany instruction about *what* to learn. This is consistent with the cognitive approach to learning (see the discussion of the cognitive academic language learning approach in Chapter 5).

The use of cognitive strategies may be difficult to observe (who can readily measure the extent of a student's schemata?), but students who have careful study skills and the habit of critical or creative thinking often are the most impressive as serious scholars.

Metacognitive strategies are observable when students set goals, plan, monitor, and use self-assessment to organize themselves, self-check their understanding or progress, and redirect their activity if necessary. Monitoring and evaluation strategies are noticeable when students make on-course corrections as they learn. Together these strategies sustain the impression that a student is careful, thoughtful, and self-managed.

table 3.4   **Variety in Assessment to Adapt to Learning Style Preferences**

Learning Style	Adaptation for Learning Style Preferences
Extroverted	Can give oral quizzes to others or ask for progress reports as formative assessment.
Introverted	Can do paper-and-pencil test.
Abstract/intuitive	Can answer essay questions asking for abstract comparisons of subtle features.
Concrete-sequential	Have students display results as a step-by-step chart.
Open	Students benefit more from formative monitoring than from summative results.
Closure-oriented	Students benefit more from focus on summative results than on formative monitoring.
Global	Each phase of result is assessed.
Particular	Best, or most interesting part of, result is chosen for assessment.
Synthesizing	Synthesizers give progress reports on whole task.
Analytic	Analytic types can display results as a comparison chart.
Field sensitive	Students can work together to create assessable features.
Field independent	Would prefer to be measured against already-existing standard.
Reflective	Test features fewer questions requiring longer, thoughtful responses.
Impulsive	Test features many questions, requiring shorter answers.
Visual	Test may require interpretation of graph or picture.
Auditory	Assessment may require verbal explanation of steps or meaning.
Hands-on	Creative product or object is assessed.

Social and affective strategies are evident when learners manage their emotions and social relations well, use positive self-talk, and gain satisfaction from working with others. These strategies are used deliberately but overlap with the more basic individual differences in general attitude and emotional state described below.

Learning Strategies: Adapting Instruction.   In each lesson, in addition to the content objectives (drawn from content standards) and language objectives (drawn from ELD standards), the teacher includes learning-strategy objectives. This means that every lesson teaches *how* to learn as well as *what* to learn. The objectives might fulfill long-term strategy training, such as the fourth-grade teacher's lessons that are built on a gradual increase in students' ability to work in cooperative groups. Early in the year, a lesson might focus on students learning how to praise one another; another lesson might feature students learning peer assessment; and so on.

It might be wise for a teacher to make a chart at the beginning of the school year stipulating what learning strategies the class will acquire over the course of the year. These become "learning-strategy standards" that resemble content standards and are defined and practiced on a daily or weekly basis. These become a road map toward cognitive teaching.

Social–Emotional Psychological Factors

Social–emotional psychological factors are those having to do with the disposition to learn. The social–emotional side of human behavior helps determine how communication takes place. Some factors within this domain pertain specifically to individuals' feelings about themselves, whereas other factors pertain to their ability to interact with others. Affective factors discussed here are motivation, self-esteem, anxiety, and attitudes.

Motivation

Motivation has been defined as the impulse, emotion, or desire that causes an individual to act a certain way. Students' motivation to learn English can be influenced by the desire for academic success or peer interaction—in positive or negative ways. Most language learners experience both types of motivation.

Pierce (1995) conceptualized motivation in terms of investment, identity, and language choice. The way an English learner interacts with others influences the way identity is constructed and affirmed. Unfortunately, an English learner often has marginal status as a newcomer, which may detract from a stable sense of identity.

Motivation can be seen as an individual or personal *trait* that is relatively consistent and persistent; or as a social or environmental *state*, a more temporary condition that can be influenced by the use of interesting materials or activities, reward, or punishment. If a teacher defines motivation as an individual trait, he or she may blame the student, the parents, or the student's culture for low student interest or achievement. Conversely, if a teacher believes that motivation is a social–environmental state, he or she may make more attempts to alter classroom teaching if students appear unmotivated, in order to make lessons more interesting and involving.

English learners, like other students, respond to efforts on the part of teachers to support intrinsic motivation. Teachers can offer students learning alternatives; support their work on difficult tasks without hovering over them or micromanaging the project; ask directive questions without manipulating students through guilt or control; and encourage students to choose a topic of study, reading, or research that interests them.

Motivation: Adapting Instruction. Staying on focus as a student and scholar is not easy for students whose families do not have a history of supporting academic achievement or the means to motivate students' daily efforts. Scholastic endeavor is not easy, nor should teachers underestimate the sacrifices students must make in the service of acquiring **cognitive academic language proficiency (CALP)** in the second language. Support for difficult tasks is the responsibility of the teacher and the family, working together.

Self-Esteem

People with a positive evaluation of themselves have high **self-esteem.** This involves attitudes toward the self—what people believe about their abilities in general, as well as the ability to learn a second language. These cognitions and feelings are often hidden and may be resistant to change.

High self-esteem may *cause* success or *result from* success. Students who feel proud of their successes and abilities and who have positive images of themselves, their families, and their cultures are better language learners. Self-esteem is not made up solely of beliefs about the self but also of successful learning experiences. Some schooling practices, such as tracking and competitive grading, damage self-esteem. Authentic cooperation and a sense of accomplishment enhance the success of English learners. Self-esteem–building techniques (see Díaz-Rico, 2004) can help to foster positive attitudes.

One big setback in self-esteem takes place during **culture shock,** or transition shock, the stage in which a newcomer is uncomfortable and disoriented in an unfamiliar culture, resulting in frustration, depression, anger, or withdrawal (Bennett, 1998). The severity of this shock varies as a function of individual personality, the emotional support available, and the perceived or actual differences between the two cultures.

Adaptation to a new culture can take several months to several years. Ideally, the newcomer accepts some degree of routine in the new culture with habits and customs "borrowed" from the host culture. This results in a sense of comfort, and the newcomer feels capable of negotiating most new situations. On the other hand, individuals who do not adjust as well may feel lonely and frustrated, with a resulting loss of self-confidence. They may reject certain aspects of the new culture. Eventually, successful adaptation results in newcomers finding value in the differences and similarities between cultures and being able to actively express themselves and create a full range of meaning in the situation.

In the classroom, some students may experience mental fatigue from continually straining to comprehend the new culture. Individuals may need time to process personal and emotional as well as academic experiences. The teacher must take great care not to belittle or reject a student who is experiencing culture shock.

Related to self-esteem is the concept of *inhibition.* Students are inhibited when they defend themselves against new experiences and feelings. Emphasizing fluency over accuracy in the first stages of language learning may help students feel less inhibited. The ability to take risks may facilitate second-language acquisition. Learners who are willing to guess at unclear meanings and to risk creating errors will progress in language skills more rapidly than their more inhibited colleagues. Moderate risk takers stand the best chance at language development.

Self-Esteem: Adapting Instruction.   Self-esteem, whether affirming the uniqueness of the individual or the worth of community efforts toward social betterment, is fed by success, not by empty praise. The genius of the gifted teacher is to identify students' praiseworthy talents and provide a showcase for them.

Díaz-Rico (2004) offers a variety of ideas and resources for involving students in self-esteem-raising activities, including the Name Game ("Introduce yourself by first name, adding a word that describes how you are feeling today—using a word that begins with the same letter as the first name." Each subsequent person repeats what the others have said in sequence. The teacher provides an alphabetized list of adjectives so that students prepare in advance). Another activity is Lifeline ("Using a string and index cards, enter six to ten points that represent important events you are willing to share. Compare your life stories with a partner's."). These and other activities are designed to increase English learners' pride in their identity, personal history, and skills.

Anxiety

English learners may be tense, self-conscious, and afraid of making mistakes. Using English can threaten a learner's sense of self, because English learners may fear they cannot represent themselves fully in a new language or understand others readily (Horwitz, Horwitz, & Cope, 1991).

Students learn better in a supportive, nonthreatening environment with low tension and high student-to-student communication. Peer work, small-group work, games, simulations, permission to use L1, and an atmosphere of warmth and friendliness reduce students' feelings of apprehension. Beginning students tend to feel comfortable with activities that require hands-on involvement, such as activities that do not require complex languague production or a verbal response in English.

Learners at intermediate levels of English might work with maps or create simple puppet shows in which the puppeteer is behind a curtain or below a table. Activities requiring slightly more oral production include group singing and retelling simple stories. If students are capable of more complex activities, they can be paired to interview classmates, read aloud in small groups, or work on group projects (Koch & Terrell, 1991).

One element that **anxiety** and self-esteem have in common is their role in school bullying behavior. Research on bullying has shown that major characteristics of victims of bullying are low self-esteem and high social anxiety (Lane, 1989; Slee, 1994). Because most bullying behavior takes place at school, and urban schools in lower socioeconomic areas have a higher incidence of bullying (Whitney & Smith, 1993), teachers must be aware that English learners are at greater risk of being victimized by bullying behavior in the schools they attend. More about bullying and conflict resolution is presented in Chapter 4.

Anxiety: Adapting Instruction.   Teachers can use a variety of tactics to reduce students' anxiety during learning tasks. Activities can be carefully monitored to reduce undue pressure (such as exaggerated pressure for students to be accurate on a task, such as creative writing, that promotes fluency). Students learning a second language should not be doing so in an environment of highly competitive tasks.

Anxious students, or students in the beginning stages of language acquisition, should not have to perform in front of large groups. When students are starting a new type of task, the teacher can give examples or provide models of how the task is done, teaching skills explicitly and providing study guides. Assignments should vary over different modes of language learning. Anxious students benefit from a brief chance to be physically active, as well as from activities that provoke curiosity or surprise. Oral interaction with peers is one way for students to relax and enjoy learning.

Attitudes about Learning

Attitudes toward Learning English.   Prior experience, parents, and peers influence students' **attitudes** toward English and those who speak it. If a student has a negative attitude toward English, the cause may be the experience of discrimination or racism. Stavans (2001) quotes Amy Tan's essay "Mother Tongue" as an example of a young child's sense of shame about her mother's English:

> When I was growing up, my mother's "limited" English limited my perception of her. I was ashamed of her English. I believed that her English reflected the quality of what she had to say. That is, because she expressed them imperfectly her thoughts were imperfect. And I had plenty of empirical evidence to support me: the fact that people in department stores, at banks, and at restaurants did not take her seriously, did not give her good service, pretended not to understand her, or even acted as if they did not hear. (p. 166)

Parents may encourage or discourage their children's use of English outside of school. Peers may incite attitudes against English, or may mock those who do not speak English well. On a more positive note, if a teacher—and the school as a whole—models support and appreciation for students' developmental **interlanguage** and encourages peer-language use in school, attitudes that enhance dual-language use are much more common.

Attitudes toward the Primary Language.   Students' negative reactions toward their own primary language are often the result of internalized shame. Peñalosa (1980) pointed out that English learners may have a defensive reaction to or ambivalent feelings about their primary language if they are made to feel inferior. Students who acquire English while neglecting their primary language may be considered traitors by their peers or families. Either of these situations can create a backlash against maintenance of the primary language. Peers may incite attitudes against the L1, or may try to tease or bully those who speak the same primary language with a different dialect.

Attitudes toward the Teacher and the Classroom Environment.   A family's positive attitude toward school can influence their child's success. However, parents who have had negative experiences at school may subconsciously pass along these attitudes to their children and subtly communicate to their children ambivalence about and disillusionment with the value of academic effort (Ogbu & Matute-Bianchi, 1986).

Students often cling to the language of their subculture as a way to oppose the type of language used in school and engage in resistance in the form of misbehavior, vandalism, and poor relationships as a reflection of the destructive patterns of subordination and socioeconomic deprivation they have experienced. This element of opposition is not always overt but may instead take the form of mental withdrawal, high absenteeism, or reluctance to do classwork. On the other hand, students' prior schooling may have encouraged them to be more willing to participate in class. These variables affecting learning are understood by teachers who seek to see schooling through the eyes of the student, rather than to judge or blame the student for a poor attitude. This is a part of teaching with clarity of vision.

Attitudes toward English, the Primary Language, the Teacher, and the Classroom Environment: Adapting Instruction.   Negative attitudes are usually the result of negative experiences; these attitudes will only change over the long term, when students have been treated well enough to overcome previous poor instruction. Teachers can do much to model positive attitudes toward the students' primary language, in ways that are covered elsewhere in this book. However, a consistently negative attitude may stem from a student's home environment.

A teacher's willingness to be fully human—to admit to the student that an attitude is an interpersonal barrier to communication—is an honest response that does not blame the student, but rather invites a dialogue and shares responsibility for change.

Level of Oral Interaction with Peers

Young children extend their understanding through talk with peers. Teachers can learn a lot about a student by studying the language that is used during peer chat. Children are most likely to develop into competent talkers when they have the chance to practice with one another. A classroom in which teacher talk dominates leaves young children without adequate time and opportunities to improve their oral skills.

Teachers observing classroom interaction should note not only the amount of talk but also the quality of the conversation. Questions to ask are as follows: Who initiates and sustains conversation? Who talks to whom and in which languages? What kind of code-switching takes place between L1 and L2? What is the content of the talk? What are the topics about which students feel comfortable talking in L1 versus L2? Who takes more turns? Who talks to both boys and girls, and who does not?

Oral Interaction with Peers: Adapting Instruction.   After a brief period of teacher-in-front instruction, as much time as possible should be spent on student–student interaction. Ongoing observation is important to ensure that students are making progress in speaking English. Use of a checklist aligned with the ELD standards encourages teachers to advance English learners in a systematic way in their oral skill development.

Overall, the social–emotional adjustment of students goes a long way toward their acculturation, language acquisition, and school success. The teacher who can observe this process skillfully can help promote students' success by practicing a pedagogy that is responsive to English learners.

Sociocultural Factors

Second-language teaching and learning occur within communities that use language to carry out social and cultural activities during which people interact with one another and carry out the business of daily life. Learning English means learning how to act appropriately within a new set of cultural norms that differ from those of the home culture. Thus, sociocultural factors play a major role in second-language acquisition.

Culture includes the ideas, customs, skills, arts, and tools that characterize a given group of people in a given period of time. The primary culture forms the template of reality, operating as a lens or filter through which some information makes sense and other information does not. When two cultures come in contact, members of these cultures have different perceptions, behaviors, customs, and ideas. This can cause curiosity and attraction or misunderstanding and fear.

For some students, prolonged exposure to English does not result in proficiency. They may not feel that their primary language and culture are accepted and validated by the school. The most up-to-date pedagogy may still fail to foster achievement if students are socially and culturally uncomfortable with, resistant to, or alienated from schooling. The teaching with integrity model emphasizes that teachers seeking a wider repertoire of intercultural understanding make an effort to understand students' need to have their primary language and culture validated by the school and by teachers.

Students' success in learning a second language depends on certain factors beyond language—the pattern of acculturation for their community, the status of their primary language in relation to English, the view their own speech community holds about the English language and English speakers, the dialect of English they are hearing and learning and its relationship to Standard English, the patterns of social and cultural language usage in the community, and the compatibility between the home culture and the cultural patterns of the school. These issues are explored here with a view toward helping teachers to bridge the culture and language gap that may exist between themselves and their students.

Family Background

Knowing and understanding the family background is critical to knowing and understanding the learner. Although many teachers in mainstream U.S. schools have been taught to view students through the lens of a field-independent cognitive style that isolates the figure from the background—and mainstream culture focuses on the value of the individual self—in other cultures the individual is viewed as deeply embedded in the family context. Getting to know the family provides valuable information and should be a priority for teachers with integrity.

Home visits are one of the best ways teachers can learn about family background. Scheduling an appointment ahead of time is a courtesy that some cultures may require and provides a way to determine whether home visits are welcome. Dress should be professional. The visit should be short (20 to 30 minutes) and the conversation positive, perhaps avoiding discussion about the student's schoolwork. Viewing the child in the context of the home provides a look at where and how the child lives, the nature of the parent–child interaction, the resources of the home, and the child's role in the family.

In secondary school settings in which the number of students poses a challenge to the concept of home visits, teachers can visit neighborhoods where students live to get a sense of that aspect of students' lives. Also, phone calls are an efficient way to introduce oneself to families. It is vital that the first school–family connection be a positive one. Many parents have come to fear calls from school because teachers too often call only when there is a problem.

If a home visit is not feasible, teachers can learn about families through monthly open house events, in which the classroom is open to the whole family, perhaps featuring simple art or craft projects that the family members can do together. This lets the teacher interact with the students' families on a friendly, nonacademic basis.

Family Background: Adapting Instruction.   Families exist in a wide variety of contexts, with a diversity of means and goals. The teacher walks a fine line between high expectations and unrealistic or unfair expectations, and between encouraging family support and violating familial expectations. There are no easy answers to these dilemmas.

Culturally responsive pedagogy is a key to using information obtained about the family background to adapt instruction (see Chapter 5). Curricula can be adapted using the funds of knowledge approach outlined in Chapter 5.

L1 and L2 Use in Home and Community

Some parents may use only English in the home, hoping children will learn English more rapidly; or, conversely, they may forbid English in the home as a defense against assimilation pressures. Either of these situations can cause problems within the family. Other families code-switch, using whichever language is appropriate for the needs of the situation.

In the homes of some immigrants in the United States, the children speak English with one another, and one or more parents may not speak English at all. This may cause alienation and loss of family cohesion. Lily Wong-Fillmore (1990) recounted a sad conversation that resulted from loss of a common family language.

My younger sister became a lawyer, but lost the ability to speak Mandarin to my mother, who did not speak English. When my mother became incapacitated due to a lingering illness, it was time for the family to arrange transfer of the power of attorney. My sister tried to explain to my mother why the family needed a power of attorney—in case the need arose for someone to sign papers for her. The conversation went badly. My mother started to cry, thinking that her family was ready to sign papers to end her life. My sister meant only, "in case of terminal illness. . . ." But without a common language, key meaning was lost. (n.p.)

Teachers seeking information about the family's use of L1 and L2 might observe interaction when a family member picks up the child after school, invite family members to class as volunteers, or arrange for family members to visit the classroom for social interaction. In the process, the teacher can observe family language use. Chapter 11 suggests many ways to involve parents in schooling.

Knowing about the language used in a student's community helps teachers to know what that community's expectations are for the acquisition and use of English. Much can be learned about a community by walking or driving through it, perhaps stopping to make a purchase in local stores and markets. Through community representatives, teachers can learn about important community living and language patterns. Teachers can attend local ceremonies and activities to learn more about community dynamics. Community activities might be reported in a local newspaper or church bulletin, and much can be learned about local communities through such publications.

The Language of the Home and Community: Adapting Instruction.   Schools cannot change the language used in the home and the community, but teachers can build on this language by encouraging students to use their language abilities creatively and critically in the classroom. The following vignette illustrates one way to bring the values and the language of the home into the classroom:

Traditional proverbs, meant to convey cultural knowledge and wisdom, are often closely tied to a culture's values and everyday experience. Amy Oliva challenges her seventh-grade ELD students to ask a parent for a traditional proverb that is used at home. Students translate the proverbs into English and then update the maxims in their own words. After reading a few of Aesop's fables, they write an animal fable of their own in which the proverb is the moral. They then write an imaginary scenario in which they use the proverb in conversation with one of their friends. This brings the wisdom of the home into English in both an imaginative and a communicative way.

Degree of Family Acculturation

The process of adapting to a new culture is called **acculturation.** *Assimilation*, one extreme of acculturation, means taking on the values and behaviors of the **mainstream culture** at the expense of the native culture. How acculturation/assimilation proceeds depends on the family's long-term goals. Assimilation may not be a desirable goal for all groups. During the process of acculturation, many families choose to retain a lifestyle that differs in key ways from the mainstream U.S. culture.

The success of acculturation depends on such variables as the immigrant status of the family, the socioeconomic status, and the rural-versus-urban environment. **Racism** on the part of the **dominant culture** is also a factor. Racial prejudice in the United States has usually meant that the lighter a person's skin, the quicker they were able to acculturate into the mainstream.

One quick way to assess how much the family has assimilated is to ask the student what movies, television programs, or magazines the family consumes, and in which language. These are the primary vehicles that the mainstream culture uses to win cultural "converts."

Schumann's (1978) acculturation model predicted that the degree to which a learner acculturates to the target-language group governs the degree to which the second language is acquired. Table 3.5 describes the social variables Schumann considered important factors in acculturation. The more acculturation factors the learner embraces, the faster the acculturation to the new culture. Yet the acculturation process poses risks, the greatest being loss of the native tongue.

Research has shown that the **cultural congruence** or lack thereof between mainstream and minority cultures has lasting effects on students. Students from families whose cultural values are similar to those of the European-American culture may be relatively advantaged in schools. In contrast, students from cultures that do not have a long history of classroom learning may not demonstrate such behaviors and thus not achieve well in U.S. classrooms.

Teachers can informally assess the degree of family acculturation by encouraging a discussion or taking a poll of which television shows students watch and who in the family

table 3.5   Factors in Schumann's Acculturation Model

Acculturation Factor	Description
Comparative language status	The primary-language and English-language groups view each other as socially equal, of equal status.
Welcome	The primary-language and the English-language groups both desire that the L1 group assimilate.
Sharing	Both the primary-language and English-language groups expect the primary-language group to share social facilities with the English-language group.
Group size and cohesion	The primary-language group is small and not very cohesive.
Cultural congruence	The primary-language group's culture is congruent with that of the English-language group.
Mutual attitudes	Both groups have positive attitudes toward each other.
Residency goals	The primary-language group expects to stay in the area for an extended period.

Source: Schumann (1978).

watches television with the student. The channel(s) the family watches is a good indicator of the culture of the home.

Degree of Assimilation: Adapting Instruction. Intercultural educators are responsible for educating students from diverse cultures. Many find it relatively easy to help students whose values, beliefs, and behaviors are congruent with U.S. schooling. But teachers with integrity can find common ground with diverse students to promote their further education, help them achieve within the cultural context of the school, and not compromise their culture, identity, or primary-language use.

In the movie *Stand and Deliver,* math teacher Jaime Escalante goes to a family's restaurant and gently but firmly reminds the owner that pulling his gifted daughter out of high school to work as a waitress is wasting her talents. The father, angry at Escalante's chiding, rebukes him—but Ana returns to school. Open communication with family members is key. If a teacher does not share a common language, every effort must be made to find translators and intermediaries who can facilitate this communication for the good of the student.

Institutional Support for the Primary Language

Schools vary in the degree to which they welcome students and parents whose primary language is not English. A welcoming environment features school administrators and office staff members (secretaries and attendance clerks) who speak the primary language of the community. Posters in the hallway welcome families in the primary language. Bulletins and announcements are sent home in the primary language as well as in English. School outreach workers and translators are available for parents whose primary language is of low incidence in the community. Bilingual school counselors and school psychologists help students with emotional or learning problems.

In the same community, various schools may communicate vastly different messages to the community. At one extreme—the use of diversity as exotic flavoring—school personnel may pay lip service to diversity, allowing a token number of students to attend whose presence brings an exotic flavor chosen to enrich the intercultural experience of the mainstream population; but there is little support for the primary language. At the other extreme—school as cultural hub—the school is the vibrant center of a largely immigrant community whose rooms house a variety of social services: adult English classes for families, with a staffed babysitting center for young children whose parents attend class; after-school ethnic dance classes; and a Saturday school for classes in the heritage language of the community. What a vast difference in support for L1!

Classroom Support for Primary Language. Classroom environments can show welcome and support for the primary language of the students, whether it be one or many languages. Bulletin boards in two or more languages express a commitment to dual-language proficiency. With the help of family members, different alphabets and scripts can be displayed around the classroom. Objects used in the classroom can bear labels in different languages. A display of appropriate books in dual or original text in the primary language(s) of the students communicates interest and support. A few phrases of welcome or comfort in the children's home language make newcomers feel more at ease (Morgan, 1992).

Because it is tiring to listen to a new language for long periods, the classroom may feature a quiet area in which a student can escape to listen to audiotapes in the home language. If the student is literate in the primary language, books and magazines in that language can reduce feelings of homesickness or culture shock.

Use of Primary Language During Instruction.   In a classroom whose teacher values multicompetent language use (see Chapter 8), students are free to chat with one another in whatever language they feel most comfortable. Teachers who are themselves bilingual encourage "sharing time" in the home language with translation for others. If the teacher does not share the primary language of the student, parent or community volunteers can provide home-language models in the classroom. If a student is a newcomer to the classroom and to English, he or she can be seated next to a bilingual speaker as a way to get involved with others.

Children are most likely to develop into confident language learners in a climate in which they believe that their own language and way of speaking are respected and their opinions are taken seriously. If the physical environment and organization of learning encourage collaborative talk, students will feel free to make mistakes, to speak tentatively, and to think aloud knowing they will not be judged harshly.

Institutional and Instructional Support for the Primary Language: Adapting Instruction. Support for dual-language competence at every level—in the classroom environment (posters, bulletin boards, alphabets, signage), during instruction (producing bilingual books, plays, and presentations), and in the school itself (in the hallways, in the school office, and in publications)—helps parents to have trust and confidence in the role of their family's language in the present and future life of their child.

An important aspect of a teacher's integrity is the way in which the teacher models **multicompetent language use.** Because Spanish is by far the most frequent second language spoken in U.S. classrooms, a teacher who makes the attempt to learn Spanish goes far in creating a bridge toward rapport with Spanish-speaking students and families. Several books are available that can help teachers become more professional in two languages: *A Bilingual Dictionary of School Terminology, Reporting to Parents in English and Spanish,* and *School Office Spanish* (online at www.ammieenterprises.com).

Societal–Contextual Factors

Teachers with clarity of vision recognize that all factors that influence the education of English learners do not reside within the learner, or even within the immediate context of the learner's family and cultural community, but rather are a part of the larger society. Such factors as the prestige accorded to the learner's language, attitudes toward the language, **socioeconomic status,** the structure and culture of the schools, issues of social class, and racism and prejudice affect the social surroundings of teaching and learning.

Differential Status of Languages

In modern U.S. culture, the social value and prestige of speaking a second language varies with the second language that is spoken. Many middle-class parents believe that learning a second language benefits their children personally and socially and will later benefit them professionally. In fact, it is characteristic of the elite group in the United States who are involved in scholarly work, diplomacy, foreign trade, or travel to desire to be fully competent in two languages. However, the languages that parents wish their children to study are often not those spoken by recently arrived immigrants (Dicker, 2003). This suggests that a certain bias exists in being bilingual—that being competent in a "foreign language" is valuable, whereas knowing an immigrant language is a burden to be overcome.

In the following informal sociolinguistic ranking task, rate from 1 to 5 the following language situations according to the probable socioeconomic status of the individual in one situation relative to another (1 = highest socioeconomic status; 5 = lowest socioeconomic status).

_____ A recently immigrated child in a Miami neighborhood speaks Haitian French.

_____ A child in a Washington, D.C.–area suburban preschool learns French.

_____ A student in an El Paso middle school is placed in a Spanish-for-native-speakers class.

_____ A student in a Minneapolis high school studies Spanish as a second language.

_____ A student in northern Maine celebrates Christmas in French at the local parish church.

Did you rank the preschool child as representing the highest socioeconomic class? In the United States, members of the upper middle class in the diplomatic communities of New York and Washington place great value on the acquisition of French, to the extent of enrolling young children in preschools that feature French instruction. In contrast, a native speaker of French from Haiti receives very little social status (rank = 5) from the knowledge of French because it is not acquired in the context of possible use in the activities of the upper classes.

Middle-class students in U.S. high schools routinely enroll in French, German, or Spanish classes to meet college entrance requirements. Therefore, this middle-class language acquisition probably represents a ranking of 2 on the exercise. Spanish-speaking students in the Southwest do not need Spanish taught as a foreign language, but their social status as Spanish speakers is lower than that of mainstream U.S. students who acquire Spanish as a foreign language (rank = 4). Americans of French Canadian background tend to be lower middle class in New England (rank = 3). This task illustrates the differential social status of second languages in the United States.

Not only are second languages differentially valued, but so too are various aspects of languages. Judgments are made about regional and social varieties of languages, "good" and "bad" language, and such seemingly minor elements as voice level and speech patterns.

There are many ways in which a second-class status is communicated to speakers of other languages, and, because language attitudes usually operate at an unconscious level, school personnel and teachers are not always aware of the attitudes they hold. Teachers need to be honest with themselves about their own biases, recognizing that they communicate these biases whether or not they are aware of them. Generally, attitudes toward second languages need to be broadened. If Americans, consciously or unconsciously, are going to maintain only certain foreign languages as the prestige languages in the twenty-first century, they are cutting themselves off from the social and economic advantages available to those who value a wide range of languages and cultures.

Dialects and Standard Languages

Teachers of English learners who understand the connection between dialects and standard languages are, in the long run, much more accepting and supportive of students' second-language acquisition efforts. All speakers have three or more levels of correctness in their language usage, levels of which they may or may not be aware. These are (1) an intimate speech used in the home, (2) an informal but slightly restrained speech used in semi-public situations, and (3) the carefully prepared, deliberate formal speech of public address. Some of this speech may belong to the standard dialect, some to other regional or social dialects. The terms *standard* and *dialect* indicate that certain forms are more acceptable than others.

Standard English operates on both a formal and an informal level. The formal standard is the style used when writing, giving public speeches, or talking on television. It is the form taught in schools for expository or argumentative writing and is characterized by strict adherence to grammatical elements such as subject–verb agreement, pronoun–antecedent relationships, complex tense sequences, and use of elaborate sentence structures. The informal standard is more subjective and flexible and is sensitive to the context in which it is used. The language used in a store when asking for assistance and for chitchat at parties are examples of informal standard. Its written form is personal correspondence and business and social notes.

A **dialect** is a variety of a language, usually regional or social, that is distinguishable from other varieties by differences in pronunciation, vocabulary, and grammar. Everyone speaks a dialect and, as stated previously, no dialect is good or bad in itself. The difference in the prestige of certain dialects comes from the prestige of the speakers of that dialect. Teachers in general often feel that their role is to enforce Standard English in the classroom and not to accept or validate other dialects. Teachers may take various positions on the teaching of Standard English.

Teachers who see their role as correcting students' "errors" may see their role as *eradicating* the dialect of the students. Teachers who encourage students to use colloquialisms to lend flavor to creative writing or dialogue, while reserving Standard English for formal classroom contexts, are practitioners of *additive dialectalism* or *bidialectalism*. Teachers who do not feel the need to enforce Standard English at all times may help to promote the *dialect rights* of English learners (Wolfram, 1991).

Regardless of teachers' attitudes toward nonstandard dialects, the language spoken by a child—whether standard or nonstandard—is the best means of direct communication between teacher and child. Having an understanding of the child's language is a necessary first step toward understanding the child. If, on the other hand, teachers use dialect to evaluate students' potential or use proficiency in Standard English to predict school achievement, it is possible that the teacher's own attitude toward the students' dialect—either positive or negative—has more to do with students' cognitive and academic achievement than does the dialect. A continuing pattern of interruptions and corrections can silence a child.

Just because a teacher does not engage in overt linguistic racism—racial slurs—does not mean that linguistic discrimination is not taking place. Corrective repronunciation of accented speech, manner of address, inattention, and delegitimization of ideas that are not expressed in "acceptable" discourse are subtle ways in which teachers convey negative attitudes. "Discrimination may occur in tone of voice, choice of vocabulary, facial expression, gesture, and posture that encode attitude and engender reaction" (Attinasi, 1994, p. 329).

Linguistic racism also manifests itself in silencing students and not supporting their use of L1, or in rendering them invisible by lack of attention to their needs. Rather than the teacher's assuming the dialect of the nonstandard speaker for purposes of communication, it is usually the student who is forced to change:

> [S]peakers of "other" (other than standard American or British) varieties of English are generally in less powerful positions in society and carry a disproportionate burden in making themselves understood. [T]he dominant culture expects the nonstandard speaker to make the adjustment at all times. . . . Drawing on Delpit's (1988) notion of the *culture of power,* I argue that confronting power differentials and linguistic prejudice in the classroom could begin to open pathways for changing language attitudes. (Nero, 2005, p. 1)

If teachers devalue the accent that students use as they learn English, English learners receive the message that their dialect is not accepted. A teacher can model correct usage without overt correction, and in time the student will self-correct—*if* the student chooses Standard English as the appropriate sociolinguistic choice for that context.

Teachers' Attitudes toward Bilingualism

The linguistic ideology that monolingualism is the accepted norm in U.S. classrooms restricts the range of pedagogical options that teachers can offer students. Monolingual teachers cannot help but silence those students who speak a language the teacher cannot understand. Institutional silencing processes have a cost, both for those who are silenced and those who silence (Santa Ana, 2004). Freire (1970) wrote,

> Each time [the teachers] say their word without hearing the word of those whom they have forbidden to speak, they grow more accustomed to power and acquire a taste for guiding, ordering, and commanding. They can no longer live without having someone to give orders to. Under these circumstances, dialogue is impossible. (p. 129)

If a teacher acts threatened or displays resentment of the students' first language, or appears insensitive or uncompromising about the use of L1 in class, students may react in a variety of ways: with hostility or with covert or overt resistance. Conversely, if a teacher discusses the value of being bilingual, models bilingualism, encourages students to use L1 if it is helpful in their learning, sets boundaries when and where the L1 is appropriate, and is sensitive to the increased cognitive and affective demands of operating in a second language, students will feel a sense of acceptance (Curran, 2003).

Social Class Issues

In the United States, societal–contextual factors involving **language-minority students** are compounded by social class issues. Classism—the distaste of the middle and upper classes for the lifestyles and perceived values of the lower classes—is often directed against linguistic and cultural minorities. A typical poor person is portrayed in the American imagination as urban, black, and young, although statistics document that the vast majority of the poor are white. Depicting poverty in racial, linguistic, or cultural terms makes it easier to stigmatize the poor (Henwood, 1997).

Often, middle-class teachers view the poor as unwilling or unable to devote resources to schooling. Ogbu (1978) postulates that indigenous minorities often bear the brunt of a castelike status in the United States, which may lead to their resisting the academic identity of successful student. Needless to say, bias against English learners because of their poverty makes it harder for teachers to fully invest and believe in students' success. If students are blamed for being poor or for holding values and beliefs related to lower-class living conditions, teachers may lower expectations for their academic success.

In many parts of the United States, class differences are sharply defined by language—degree of acceptability of accent, choice of words, or even talkativeness: lower-class students may feel a lack of confidence based on real or perceived lack of academic preparation, causing them to be less visibly engaged in the classroom. A struggle for economic security may require such students to work outside of school rather than study, affecting their achievement (Warren, 1998–1999).

Cultural Patterns and Organization of Schools

Often, minorities in U.S. society experience school failure. Several conflicting hypotheses try to explain this failure. One is that students of these groups are unmotivated—the students and/or their parents are uninterested in education and unwilling to comply with teacher-assigned tasks. A second hypothesis is that students who grow up as native speakers of another language are handicapped in learning because they have not acquired sufficient English. A third hypothesis is that there are cultural differences, a **cultural mismatch,** between the ways children learn at home or among their peers and the ways they are expected to learn at school.

A fourth hypothesis, one that is examined in Chapter 2, is that teachers have lower expectations for their non–European American students and thus provide them with a less rigorous instructional program. A fifth hypothesis is that schools operate in ways that advantage certain children and disadvantage others, and that these distinct outcomes align with social and political forces in the larger cultural context. In this section, organization and patterns within the school are examined in order to explore this fifth hypothesis and extend the understanding of societal–cultural factors that influence schooling for English learners.

Some social theorists see the culture of the school as maintaining the poor in a permanent underclass and as legitimizing inequality (Giroux & McLaren, 1996). In other words, schooling is used to reaffirm class boundaries. McDermott and Gospodinoff (1981) postulate that students who come to school without an orientation toward literacy present organizational and behavioral problems to teachers who are pressured to produce readers. Teachers who lower their expectations create an educational "engine" in which English learners are pulled slowly and inexorably toward failure.

Nieto (2003) identified numerous structures within schools that affect student learning: tracking, testing, the curriculum, pedagogy, the school's physical structure and disciplinary policies, the limited roles of both students and teachers and limited parent and community involvement. Each of these is examined in turn.

Tracking. Placement of students in classrooms of matched abilities, despite its superficial advantages, in reality often labels and groups children for their entire schooling experience and allows them little or no opportunity to change groups. **Tracking** is sometimes initiated as early as kindergarten. Secondary school personnel who place ESL students in low tracks or in nonacademic ESL classes preclude those students from any opportunity for higher-track, precollege work. Furthermore, tracking systems divide a campus and can increase prejudice.

Testing. Part of the meritocracy myth (see Chapter 2) is that testing creates an equal playing field by separating the high achievers on the basis of test results. Students who respond poorly on standardized tests are often given basic skills in a remedial curriculum that is fundamentally the same as the one in which they were not experiencing success.

In the current climate of high-stakes testing, students are often seen as workers who must produce results in order for the school to merit results-based funding. This places students under the unfair pressure to score well despite their having been educated in an environment that lacked effective resources to begin with.

Curriculum Design. Standardized curriculum is often at odds with the needs of learners. The knowledge that is codified in textbooks and teacher's guides is rarely the knowledge that English learners bring from their communities. In addition, the curriculum is systematically watered down for the "benefit" of English learners due to the mistaken idea that such students cannot absorb the core curriculum. As a result, students' own experiences are excluded from the classroom, and little of the dominant-culture curriculum is provided in any depth.

Pedagogy. In lower-track classrooms, teaching methods are often remedial, tedious, and uninteresting, particularly for students who are given a basic-skills curriculum. The pressure to "cover" a curriculum excludes learning in depth and also frustrates teachers. Teachers in lower-track classes tend to lower their expectations of student performance, rely excessively on worksheets and other forms of drill-and-practice activities at the expense of student discussions and critical thinking, and spend more time on disciplinary speech.

The Physical Structure of the Schools. Many inner-city schools are built like prisons to forestall vandalism and theft. English-language development classes tend to take place in temporary classrooms away from the main campus buildings. Rich suburban school districts, by contrast, often provide more space, more supplies, and campuslike schools for their students, a hallmark of educational advantage.

This inequity exacerbates the contrast between the dialogic, critical-thinking-based curriculum afforded the academic-track students, versus the prisonlike thinking of the basic-skills, drill-and-kill curricula that discourage school achievement for those students who receive the low-end treatment.

Disciplinary Policies. Discrimination against certain types of students is rampant in some schools, particularly those who have high physical activity levels or who are resistant to schooling. By interpreting this as delinquency, teachers create more disruption and rebellion. Rather than defining students' predilections as deviant or disruptive, teachers can channel these feelings in more positive ways to allow students to express themselves and learn at the same time.

Disciplinary policies may be the unfortunate result of poor communication between home and school.

Two girls of different cultures (European-American and Hispanic) got into a pushing match during lunch, and the European-American girl's friends testified to the assistant principal that the Hispanic girl was the instigator. The Hispanic girl was suspended, and a letter was sent home requesting that her parents appear at a disciplinary hearing. The family never received the notification.

Because of the family's frequent moves, the Hispanic girl's family had changed their home address, and the district office had failed to inform the school of the change of address. When the family failed to appear at the disciplinary hearing, the girl's status was changed to "expelled." It took a local activist's appearance on her behalf before the county school board to reinstate the girl in the school.

The Limited Role of Students.   Alienation and passive frustration may result when students are not encouraged to take an active part in their own schooling. For example, in classrooms on the Warm Springs (Oregon) Reservation, the European-American teachers tried to control the social and spatial arrangements of the classroom—where desks were placed and who talked, when, and with whom. Students did not go along with this program. Schooling became more successful for these students when they were able to take a more active role. The following summarizes Philips' (1972) description of this adaptation.

The Native American students preferred to wander to various parts of the room to talk to other students while the teacher was talking, and to "bid" for each other's attention rather than that of the teacher. They frequently refused to read aloud, did not utter a word when called on, or spoke too softly to be audible.

A look at the daily life of the Warm Springs children revealed several factors that would account for their willingness to work together and their resistance to teacher-directed activity. Outside of class, they spend much time in the company of peers with little control from older relatives. No single individual directs and controls all activity, and there is no sharp distinction between audience and performer. Individuals are permitted to choose for themselves the degree of participation in an activity. When teachers stopped trying to direct the class from the front and let students control and direct interaction in small group projects, they concentrated completely on their work; very little group talk was spent disagreeing or arguing about how to go about a task. (Philips, 1972)

Cultural difference influences the way students collaborate. In the Punjabi culture, for example, teenage boys and girls avoid conversation in mixed company, and girls do not speak up in the presence of males (Gibson, 1987). Classroom structures, the importance of individual performance, the authority of the teacher, and the amount and kind of student participation varies across cultures. Students can gain psychological support from one another and the teacher as they acquire English to achieve a workable sociocultural compromise between the home culture and the culture of the school.

The Limited Role of Teachers. Just as students are disenfranchised when they are excluded from decision making, so are teachers. A scripted, mastery-learning curriculum that is touted as "teacher-proof" promotes a climate that "de-skills" teachers, treating highly educated professionals as low-skilled labor. This may lead teachers to have negative feelings toward their students, manifested in a low-status curriculum and low expectations for student success.

Limited Parent and Community Involvement. In inner-city schools with large populations of English learners, parents may find it difficult to attend meetings, are uninvolved in the governance of the school, or feel a lack of welcome from school authorities. School personnel, in consultation with community and parent representatives, can begin to change such perceptions by enhancing communication and interaction. School administrators and teachers may need to rethink traditional notions of parental involvement and reach out to the families of English learners in nontraditional ways. Home–school communication translated into the primary language is fundamental.

People from various cultures view the parental role in schooling differently than do middle-class parents from the mainstream U.S. culture. Some cultures view schools and teachers as all-powerful and do not dare to intervene if the child is treated with disrespect or is not experiencing academic success. In contrast, the U.S. middle-class parent often acts on the assumption that the child's success in schooling can be affected by parent–teacher negotiation. In contrast, parents from other cultures may be unable or unwilling to alter negative perceptions through negotiation, and become frustrated or disillusioned in response. Teachers who are aware of a family's cultural background can draw on skills in intercultural communication to avoid alienating parents.

Prejudice, Racism, and Discrimination

One factor that inhibits the schooling of English learners is **prejudice** on the part of educators and mainstream students. This can take various forms: excessive pride in one's own ethnic heritage, country, or culture, so that others are viewed negatively; ethnocentrism, in which the world revolves around oneself and one's own culture; and negative stereotypes toward members of certain racial groups. Prejudice is often based on fear—fear of the unknown, fear of engulfment by foreigners, or fear of contamination.

Racism. The view that a person's race determines psychological and cultural traits—and, moreover, that one race is superior to another and thus has more rights to a higher quality of life—is racism. *Cultural racism* is the belief that the traditions, beliefs, language, and artifacts of other cultures are inferior to one's own. *Linguistic racism* is the belief that some languages are superior to others.

On the basis of such beliefs, racists justify discriminating against other groups. Weinberg (1990) regarded racism as a system of privileges and penalties, in which people are rewarded or punished by simply belonging to a particular group regardless of their individual merits or faults. More important, racism is tangible: Social and economic goods and services as well as respect are distributed in accordance with such judgments of unequal worth.

Racism is often expressed in hate crimes, which are public expressions of hostility directed at specific groups or individuals. Perhaps due to feelings of frustration at social and economic forces they cannot control, those who are marginally employed and poorly educated often seek out scapegoats to harass. Too often the targets are immigrants, particularly those of color. Schools are often prime sites at which hate crimes are committed (Bodinger-deUriarte, 1991). This fact underscores the urgency of educators' efforts to understand and combat racism.

Racism and ethnocentrism are difficult to combat because these types of prejudice are irrational. Furthermore, many teachers feel that teaching about values and beliefs is not a part of the curriculum, and therefore they are reluctant to address topics such as racism, prejudice, and discrimination. To work effectively with diverse student populations, however, teachers can open the dialogue and help students understand the harm in racist ideas and behaviors. An ideal outcome of discussions of racial and cultural heritage would be that students feel an ethnic pride in their own background without becoming ethnocentric.

A famous author expressed the necessity even for small children to learn about cultural relativity:

> A first grader should understand that his or her culture isn't a rational invention; that there are thousands of other cultures and they all work pretty well; that all cultures function on faith rather than truth; that there are lots of alternatives to our own society. Cultural relativity is defensible and attractive. It's also a source of hope. It means we don't have to continue this way if we don't like it. (Vonnegut, 1974, p. 139)

Overcoming Racism.   School curriculum and instructional practices can be used to help students be aware of the existence and impact of racism. Positive interracial attitudes can be fostered whenever students have an opportunity to work together (Alder, 2000). Students and teachers alike must raise awareness of racism. Antiracist topics include the following: the lack of scientific basis for the concept of race; the history of racism and its impact on oppressors and victims; the reasons why people hold racial prejudices and stereotypes; ways to recognize racist images in texts and other media and racist practices in the immediate community and society as a whole; specific ways of combating racism; and self-examination of attitudes, experiences, and behaviors concerning racism (Bennett, 2003; see also the Southern Poverty Law Center's Website, www.splcenter.org).

The Southern Poverty Law Center publishes the magazine *Teaching for Tolerance*, which is rich in resources for teachers. Also, grants are available to K–12 teachers for antiracist projects in their classrooms, schools, or communities.

Institutional Discrimination.   **Discrimination** refers to social actions—often implemented through laws and policies—that limit the social, political, or economic opportunities of particular groups on the basis of race, language, culture, gender, and/or social class, and that legitimize the unequal distribution of power and resources. An institution's policies and practices may effectively discriminate against a group of people as a class. Blatant discrimination, in which differential education for minorities is legally sanctioned, may be a thing of the past, but discrimination persists.

Institutional racism consists of "those laws, customs, and practices that systematically reflect and produce racial inequalities in American society" (Jones, 1972, p. 131). Classroom teaching that aims to detect and reduce racism may be a futile exercise when the institution itself—the school—promotes racism through its policies and practices. For example, minority-group teachers are often nonexistent in classrooms where children are predominantly of minority backgrounds, because the institution of schooling itself has made it difficult for minorities to attain the education and certification needed for employment as a teacher.

Segregation in fact still exists. Most students of color are still found in substandard schools, receiving a watered-down curriculum (Harvard Civil Rights Project, 2002). Today, Latinos have the dubious distinction of being the victims of school segregation, often justified by the need to provide primary-language support services. Teachers who do not share the ethnic background of their students may not communicate well with their students or may tend to avoid interaction, including eye contact (Ortiz, 1988). Thus, school continues the discrimination experienced by minorities in other societal institutions (Grant & Sleeter, 1986).

Symbolic Violence. In the past, those in power often used physical force to exclude people and to discriminate. Those who did not go along were physically punished. With the spread of literacy, there is a trend away from the use of physical force and toward the use of silencing, shame, and guilt—what Skutnabb-Kangas (1981, 2000) calls *symbolic–structural violence*. Direct punishment is replaced by self-punishment, adding to the emotional and intellectual bonds of internalized injustice.

School programs in which children are separated from their own group are examples of this symbolic–structural violence. Students are not taught enough of their own language and culture to be able to appreciate it and are made to feel ashamed of their parents and origins. The message is that the native language is only useful as a temporary instrument in learning the dominant language. Majority students, on the other hand, are seldom taught enough about the minority culture to achieve appreciation.

Status, School Organization, and Racism: The Teacher's Role as Advocate. It is not easy for students to maintain pride in cultures that represent minority points of view if these cultures suffer low status in the majority culture. Students feel conflict in this pride if their culture is devalued. Many students face the burden of having to either deny or lose their culture if they want to succeed, or keep it and fail (Nieto, 2003).

When the languages and cultures of students are highly evident in their schools and teachers refer to them explicitly, students feel a sense of pride and enhanced status. Schools that convey the message that all cultures are of value—by displaying explicit welcome signs in many languages, by attempts to involve parents, by a deliberate curriculum of inclusion, and by using affirmative action to promote hiring of a diverse faculty—help to maintain an atmosphere that reduces interethnic conflict, models integrity, and promotes a high level of achievement for English learners. Welcoming schools set the tone for society as a whole by practicing democratic principles.

This trust and confidence helps to create a vision for the future of the United States as a country in which multicompetent language users have a leadership role. This is the best contribution that dual-language educators can make toward a healthy and vibrant nation.

This chapter offers ways for teachers to inform themselves about students' backgrounds and prior learning and language experiences, levels of proficiency in first and second languages, and psychological and sociocultural factors so that they can adapt and differentiate instruction to enhance students' academic progress.

The teaching with integrity model stipulates that teachers face with clarity the social, political, and economic realities of the learners' lives while communicating the highest possible academic expectations. Intercultural communication skills make it possible to communicate with students and parents of other cultures—not perfectly, but with willingness to acknowledge misunderstandings when they exist and work through any communication challenges that arise. The challenges of a diverse classroom bring out the best in human beings who are dedicated to teaching all students in the best way possible.

4

Theories of Learning and Second-Language Acquisition

English is best acquired when students interact in the context of meaningful instruction.

expectation

■ The prospective teacher understands how cognitive, pedagogical, and individual factors affect students' language acquisition. *(Element 7.15 of the California Teaching Performance Expectations. Reprinted by permission of the California Commission on Teacher Credentialing.)*

Theories of learning and language **acquisition** underlie the teaching of English learners. The decisions and actions that teachers make on a daily basis are based on beliefs about what is good teaching. If a teacher provides in-class time for structured review before an examination, the underlying belief may be that structured practice is a key to higher test scores. If a teacher encourages students to recount briefly what they did over the weekend before class begins on Monday morning, the underlying belief may be that not only students' intellectual lives but also their personal lives are important. These beliefs enact theories of pedagogy, ways that key assumptions and principles are connected to predictable outcomes.

As an example of a learning theory in action, suppose that a fifth-grade teacher sets an explicit goal for students—high scores on a weekly spelling test, for example. He then takes class time each day to drill and practice on the week's spelling words. Behavioral learning principles underlie this practice, including the teacher-selected objective ("scoring high on weekly spelling test") and the direct instruction (drill and practice) used as a means to achieve the goal. The decisions that teachers make, the pedagogical practices employed, and the beliefs that underlie these stem from learning theories.

A second example relates specifically to theories of second-language acquisition. A teacher who plans creative writing activities for English learners *only in English* is enacting a theory of subtractive bilingualism, with principles that result in low support for primary-language skills after the student has made a transition into schooling in English. This decision is derived from a theory about second-language acquisition.

This chapter surveys basic theories of learning and language acquisition, with the goal of aligning educational practice with key foundational principles. Theories of learning and language acquisition are one part of the foundation of instruction (see Figure 2.2, page 34).

Theories of Learning

Traditionalism and Rationalism

Traditional schooling emphasizes the authority of parents, teachers, and school administrators. Learning is based on the acquisition of authorized knowledge. English learners and their families who have emigrated from traditional societies may approach schooling in the United States with expectations framed by religious or philosophical beliefs, such as those based on the Koran or Confucianism, that have been transmitted from ancient times and are still a vital part of various cultures. Educators in countries with a western European cultural heritage have been influenced not only by traditional philosophies and religions but also by Enlightenment rationalists (those who believed in the power of reason and individual rights). Educators in the United States often experience conflicting pressure from these two sources.

Huang, Shao-Hung attended elementary school in Taiwan, where educational practices stemmed from the point of view that the teacher and the textbook are the sole sources of authorized knowledge. When Shao-Hung attended a large urban middle school in Denver, Colorado, the social studies teacher explicitly encouraged students during classroom discussion and debate to call into question information presented in the textbook. Shao-Hung found it difficult to meet the expectation that she play the role of critic. She seldom spoke up in class.

The western European rationalist framework entails the expectation that an individual can rationally debate issues, separating rationality from an emotional position. Students like Shao-Hung who were raised in a traditional culture might find it difficult to assume a point of view, solely for the sake of argument, that conflicts with deeper cultural beliefs. Western European liberal values also underlie the belief that placing individuals in competition with one another is necessary to promote achievement. Such beliefs are not as prevalent in cultures that value harmony and cooperation among community members.

Progressivism in Opposing Trends

In early twentieth-century U.S. classrooms, rote memorization was the prevailing method of instruction. At the turn of the century, John Dewey, an educational philosopher, founded a progressive laboratory school affiliated with the University of Chicago to implement learning theories based on democracy in action. Dewey's philosophy advocated educational practices consonant with American ideals of individual rights, freedom, and creativity.

According to Dewey (1916, 1963; see also Boydston, 1967–1991), teaching practices must help to develop thinking citizens in a democracy. Over the years, this philosophy has justified pedagogy based on active learning. Dewey tried to introduce into schooling more engaging, experience-based forms of teaching and learning. Aligned with this philosophy was an emphasis on problem-based learning. Dewey has often been called the single most influential American educator of the twentieth century.

Three trends have opposed progressive education since Dewey's time. First, education has become ever more hierarchic, with government- and school-district-mandated curricula and policies forcing classroom teachers to act as semiskilled workers conducting routinized pedagogy. Second, corporate values influence school policies, with textbook content increasingly dictating lesson plan content and business leaders acting as advisors about educational quality. Third, students are expected to be passive recipients of knowledge who are categorized, classified, and competitive with one another (Fuller, 2003). Nevertheless, some progressive schools flourish on the fringes of U.S. education, largely as private schools.

Behaviorism

Educational psychology, with its history of scientific experimentation, provides the main foundation for instructional practices in the United States. **Behaviorism** was the dominant paradigm of psychology in the United States from the 1920s to the 1970s. B. F. Skinner's success in using laboratory animals to discover basic principles of reward and punishment was applied to human learning.

Behavioral Management.   Basic principles of behavioral management are that teachers reinforce approved behaviors, using immediate and desirable rewards such as praise, candy, points, or privileges; and teachers punish undesirable actions with scolding or loss of points, rewards, or privileges. Providing grades, gold stars, and so on for learning or demerits for misbehavior is an attempt to motivate students by extrinsic means. Behaviorism only works if students value the rewards or fear the punishment—if school-based tokens are an incentive for students to behave. External rewards tend to decrease internal motivation, but many students respond in the short term to material rewards, and teachers persist in using them (Brophy, 1988).

Direct Teaching and Mastery Learning.   **Direct teaching**, a behaviorist approach, focuses on a controlled sequence of facts or steps, with moment-to-moment teaching carefully scripted for the teacher. Two contemporary reading programs, Open Court and Direct Instruction, use the direct teaching approach (Groves, 2001).

Mastery learning is another type of behaviorist instruction. Learning is divided into small units of basic skills, each with specific objectives. Students progress at their own rates and must master each unit before proceeding to the next. Mastery learning provides immediate feedback and reinforcement.

Advantages and Disadvantages of Behavioral Methods.   The strength of direct teaching and mastery learning is the ability to build basic skills; the weakest part of direct teaching is students' lack of ownership of the goals of learning. These teaching techniques persist because they are easily packaged into "teacher-proof" materials that permit administrators to control and monitor what is taught. Elaborate systems of external outcome measures, however, minimize the role of the teacher and undermine professional integrity. The teacher's ability to meet the needs of individual students is reduced to a one-size-fits-all approach.

Cognitivism

Cognitive psychology began to overtake behaviorism in the 1960s as a way to understand human learning. Jean Piaget's work with children emphasized the development of cognitive functions. Noam Chomsky postulated innate language-processing rules unique to human beings. Cognitive psychologists studied human thinking directly, rather than basing principles of behavior on animal studies. The emergence and availability of computers led researchers to speculate that humans think in the same way that computers process data, leading to information-processing models of human thinking.

Information-Processing Theories of Mental Functioning.   As computers became more widespread in the late twentieth century, various models of computer processing were used to represent the operation of the brain. According to information-processing theorists, the human mind is like a computer; it receives, stores, and retrieves information guided by internal and external control processes. The sensory register receives and briefly holds environmental stimuli, as either images or sounds (perception), and selects input for further processing. Next, short-term memory (also called working memory) holds an image or a sound for about 20 to 30 seconds, keeping information activated while it is processed. Information is stored in long-term memory as either visual images, verbal units, or both. A *schema* is a structure for organizing information or concepts. A *script* stores a common language/action sequence.

Mrs. Alban believes that perception is the key to success for students. Changing the arrangement of the room or moving to a different setting gets their attention. She plans lessons that require students to touch, smell, or taste to shift sensory channels. Using movements, gestures, and voice inflection (speaking softly and then more emphatically) or writing with colored pens or chalk stimulates perception.

The Focus of Cognitive Teaching   Cognitive psychology views people as active learners who seek experiences and reorganize what they already know to achieve new insights, pursue goals, solve problems, and make sense of the world (Bruner, 1986). Learning occurs at both conscious and unconscious levels of awareness through controlled and automatic processes. Students learn best when they engage their natural abilities, interests, and imagination and develop critical thinking skills, self-knowledge, and goal-setting, planning, self-monitoring, and self-evaluating skills.

Cognitive training includes the use of learning strategies; memory enhancement; text processing, study, research, and test-taking skills; and problem solving. A cognitivist view of learning means teaching students *how* to learn. A cognitive lesson needs two kinds of objectives: **content objectives** (knowledge of subject matter) and *learning strategy objectives* (building cognition) in addition to the **language objective** (see Chapter 8). This focus on learning strategies expands traditional forms of learning (for example, a focus on reading comprehension and study skills) to foreground the idea that a key outcome of learning is that the learner gains a "toolkit" of thought.

Comparing the Cognitive View with Behaviorism.   Behaviorists and cognitivists differ on many basic assumptions about the nature of learning. These contrasting positions are summarized in Table 4.1.

Alternative Theories of Mental Functioning.   The input–process–output information–processing models of human thinking that emerged in the 1960s, have been replaced by models of parallel-distributed computer processing that may serve as a better model for the

table 4.1   Comparing Behaviorist and Cognitivist Views of Learning

Component of Learning	Behaviorist	Cognitivist
Belief about the mind	The mind is a blank slate.	The mind is an active organizer.
	All minds are basically alike.	Brains vary, with multiple intelligences and learning styles.
Goal setting	The teacher plans and sets goals.	Students participate in planning and goal setting.
Motivation	Reward is a motivator.	Learning is a motivator.
Teaching styles	One "best" way to learn (usually the teacher's).	Teaching with variety; no one "best" way.
Content of curriculum	Students are taught "what."	Students are taught "what" and "how."
Assessment: Who does it	The teacher assesses.	Students are actively involved; self-assessment.
Assessment: What is evaluated	Product is important.	Product and process are important.
Role of culture	Culture is irrelevant.	Culture is the basis for social interaction patterns; learning results from social interaction.

Source: Díaz-Rico, Lynne T. *Teaching English Language Learners: Strategies and Methods.* Published by Allyn and Bacon, Boston, MA. Copyright © 2004 by Pearson Education. Reprinted by permission of the publisher.

operation of the brain. In this view, information is received in the brain, and then a simultaneous adjustment of a net of neural connections creates a pattern that adjusts over time by repeated exposure (see Clark, 1993). This provides a good explanation for unconscious learning, such as first-language acquisition. The parallel-distributed model would explain the acquisition of grammatical forms, for example, in the following way:

> Joey, a 2-year-old, is learning to use past-tense verbs forms. He uses *went* as the past tense for *go*, but he also uses the incorrect form *goed*, because he has acquired the past-tense rule: "add /—ed/ to the base form." Thus his brain has associations for both *went* and *goed*. Eventually, the form *went* will be heard more often, and Joey's association network in the brain will strengthen the connection between *go* and *went*.

Ratey (2001) uses a contrasting metaphor for brain functioning—the ecosystem. Perception, function, consciousness, and identity components alternately take precedence, depending on the thinking task of the moment. Functions such as thinking and consciousness are thus somewhat separate, involving a mix of conscious and unconscious performance.

Brain-Compatible Learning.   Brain-compatible learning helps to align teaching with the way the brain learns, using its vast potential to optimize learning (Sylwester & Cho, 1992/1993; D'Arcangelo, 1998; Jensen, 1998). Understanding how the brain learns may require the reshaping of teaching and learning in schools toward the complexity found in life (Caine & Caine, 1997). The search for meaning is innate, and the role of teachers is to channel and focus learning to offer the brain complex and meaningful challenges.

The brain automatically balances new stimuli with stored patterns while creating and expressing unique patterns of its own (Hart, 1983). Good teaching avoids focusing on isolated, unrelated bits of information, making efficient use of the brain's ability to create meaningful patterns. Teachers who use a great deal of "real life" activity (classroom demonstrations, projects, field trips, etc.) immerse the learner in a multitude of interactive experiences, thus enhancing brain function. Brain-compatible teaching incorporates stress management, nutrition, exercise, and other facets of health in the learning process.

Some learning is unconscious. Teachers send out many subtle signals that affect students' learning, such as muscular tension and posture, rate of breathing, and eye movements. A classroom emotional climate that is supportive and respectful creates a state of relaxed alertness in students. In contrast, under stress the brain "down-shifts" (Hart, 1983), and learners literally lose access to portions of the brain. Emotions and cognition cannot be separated—emotions facilitate the storage and recall of information in memory.

Whereas traditional definitions of intelligence have been limited to verbal and logical intelligence, the concept of emotional intelligence is now expanding how intelligence is viewed. Emotional intelligence (EI) is a construct proposed by Salovey and Mayer (1990) that consists of five competencies: self-awareness, self-regulation, motivation, empathy, and social skills. Recognizing the importance of EI underscores the need for humanistic education.

Each person's brain integrates mental processes differently. In a healthy person, the left and right brain hemispheres interact whether a person is dealing with words, mathematics, music, or art. Teaching should be multifaceted in order to allow students to express individual interests as well as visual, tactile, emotional, or auditory preferences.

Multiple Intelligence Theory.   A well-known form of brain-compatible teaching is Howard Gardner's theory of multiple intelligences. According to Gardner (1983), students possess a variety of abilities that naturally direct them to learn in different ways, using at least eight separate kinds of "intelligences": linguistic (verbal), musical, spatial, logical–mathematical, bodily–kinesthetic, interpersonal (understanding of others), intrapersonal (understanding of self), and natural (using cues from nature). Teachers who respect multiple intelligences offer variety in instruction, appealing to an individual's strengths and providing additional support when necessary (Gardner, 1993).

Ana Maria is one of the most avid readers in the third grade. Her favorite chapter books are those that feature girls as heroines. Mrs. Oliva, her teacher, connects Ana Maria's strong reading skills to her linguistic intelligence: She learns English words quickly, often compares words with the Spanish cognates, and has picked up some words in a third language (a classmate's Vietnamese). To strengthen Ana Maria's logical intelligence, Mrs. Oliva plans to introduce her to the Nancy Drew Girl Detective series and then later the Encyclopedia Brown series.

Learning Strategies.   A **strategy** is a mental procedure used by a learner to think, study, monitor, and evaluate while doing academic work. Learning strategies can be indirect or direct.

Indirect strategies (such as learning styles and language-use strategies) tend to originate as unconscious performance but can be brought into awareness by the use of learning style questionnaires or self-analysis, and then used or modified in a deliberate manner. Learning styles were addressed in Chapter 3 as a part of the focus on the learner. Second-language-use strategies are implemented when a second language is used for communication—when second-language speakers want to sustain conversation or transmit an idea but cannot produce the precise linguistic forms in the second language. This is discussed later in this chapter.

Direct strategies originate at the level of deliberate performance and can be taught as learning strategies, as when a teacher models the process of monitoring one's use of time when taking a timed test. Direct strategies, once acquired, can be made automatic through repeated performance.

Mr. Liu noticed that the ninth-grade algebra students were making computational errors. He introduced two direct strategies for error correction. He cautioned students first to check by estimating what range of numbers would make sense in the answer. He then modeled the strategy of substituting the answer in the equation to see if it fit, as a way of checking.

Direct learning strategies include literacy and oracy strategies, which are addressed in Chapter 8; CALLA strategies such as cognitive, metacognitive, and social–affective strategies (Chamot & O'Malley, 1987); and academic adjustment and study skills. **Cognitive learning strategies** are ways to use thinking to complete a task. **Metacognitive learning strategies** include ways to set goals, plan learning, monitor progress, and self-assess results. **Social–affective learning strategies** can be used to manage emotions and gain satisfaction from working with others. Academic adjustment and study skills are useful in preparing for tests and attaining good grades. Learning strategies are summarized in Table 4.2.

Explicit Teaching of Learning Strategies.   Learning strategy instruction can raise students' awareness of strategies and learning style preferences, introduce and reinforce systematic strategy use in daily lesson plans, and help learners expand their repertoire of possible strategies (Weaver & Cohen, 1997). Learning strategies are taught by *awareness training*—keeping notes, diaries, or journals; taking self-report surveys; or interviewing one another (Oxford, 1990). Learners can perform an activity and then match their approach to a chart of learning strategies; or they can read brief scenarios or stories about learners who use various strategies in various task situations.

Learning strategies are also taught explicitly, as an objective in a lesson plan in addition to content objectives and language objectives. As part of the cognitive approach to learning, teaching students *how to think* (learning-strategy objective) as well as *what to learn* (content objective) and *how to use language to learn* (language objective) follows the adage, "Give people fish and you feed them once; teach them to fish and you feed them for life."

Using Learning Strategies in Classes with English Learners.   Unfortunately, most instruction in classrooms with culturally and linguistically diverse learners does not include learning-strategy instruction. This may be due to the mistaken assumption that English learners do not have the academic readiness to become strategic learners. The **cognitive academic language learning approach (CALLA)** was the first learning-strategy instruction designed explicitly for English learners, and use of this method has done much to alter the assumption that English learners must be taught using solely behavioral, drill-and-practice instruction.

Applying Learning Strategies to Second-Language Acquisition.   For the most part, learning strategies are just as useful for second-language acquisition as other kinds of knowledge. When a second language is treated as a set of facts (such as vocabulary lists), learning strategies can be helpful. In contrast, when a second language is used for communication, the face-to-face nature of the interaction involves a much more subtle, indirect kind of language-use strategy.

Teaching Direct Strategies: Cognitive.   Cognitive strategies can be divided into two main areas: (1) enhancement of cognitive functions through the use of specific psychological tools, including schema building, scaffolding, and use of alternative information representations such as graphic organizers; and (2) critical/creative thinking.

A **schema** (plural: schemata) is a unit of understanding that is used to store knowledge in long-term memory. Teachers evoke students' use of existing schemata when they help them to link new learning to prior knowledge. If students have little prior knowledge about the topic at hand, teachers will need to help students to develop new schemata.

table 4.2 Learning Strategies Applied to Second-Language Learning

Learning Strategy	Definition	Example(s)
Indirect strategy	A learning practice that originates as an unconscious predilection or habit but that can be brought to awareness for purposes of augmentation or modification	Learning styles Second-language-use strategies
Learning style	"Learning styles are the preferences students have for thinking, relating to others, and for particular types of classroom environments and experiences" (Grasha, 1990, p. 23).	Physiological: personal nutrition, health, time-of-day preferences, sleeping and waking habits, need for mobility, and need for and response to varying levels of light, sound, and temperature Incentive: level of achievement motivation, enjoyment of competition versus cooperation, risk taking versus caution, reaction to rewards and punishment
Second-language-use strategy	A second-language behavior that is employed for transmitting an idea when the learner cannot produce precise linguistic forms	Cover strategy: used to communicate despite a gap in proficiency (use of gesture instead of word) Code-switching from L2 to L1
Direct strategy	A learning practice that is taught deliberately, and that can be automatized through repeated practice	Oracy Literacy Cognitive Metacognitive Social–affective Academic adjustment and study skills
Oracy	Strategy for speaking or listening	Getting a turn in an informal conversation Listening for specific facts
Literacy	Strategy for reading or writing	Getting the main idea Using a topic sentence
Cognitive	Techniques a person uses to think and to act on in order to complete a task	Using psychological tools (schemata, scaffolding, alternative ways to represent information) Using critical/creative thinking
Metacognitive	A person's cognition about cognition	Goal setting, planning, self-monitoring, self-evaluating
Social–Affective	Emotions, attitudes, motivations, and values that help create and maintain suitable internal and external climates for learning	Asking for help Using positive self-affirmations
Academic adjustment and study skills	Ways to accommodate to the culture of the classroom and to organize, store, and retrieve academic information	Text processing Time management

A **scaffold** is a temporary support for learning used to help the learner construct knowledge (Berk & Winsler, 1995). During scaffolding, the teacher might ask key questions to focus the learner's attention on relevant parts of the task, or help to divide the task into smaller, manageable subcomponents. Assistance is sensitively withdrawn when it is no longer required. Learners can also do these steps for themselves.

A variety of representational formats for knowledge (text, visual, oral, figurative, etc.) helps students use a variety of learning modes. Computers have expanded knowledge formats, including art, hypermedia, color graphics, text animation, and graphics programs, that supplement text as a source of information and experience for many young people.

Graphic organizers, visual frames that organize information, are an alternative form of text. These can also be used to help students focus their ideas and access core content even when students' reading skills are weak. Graphic organizers are used to promote language (e.g., brainstorming in a word web), explain content (e.g., the periodic chart in chemistry), or evaluate (e.g., compare-and-contrast diagrams) (Early, 1990). Graphic organizers can be classified into five types (see Table 4.3).

Critical thinking plays an important role in citizenship. An important aspect of schooling in a democracy is helping students develop the ability to analyze ideas, separate fact from opinion, support opinions from reading, and make inferences. Materials are available that incorporate the teaching of critical thinking into English-language development (ELD) instruction providing activities for English learners that combine reading, dialogue, and discussion (Little & Greenberg, 1991).

Critical thinking used to create *critical consciousness* is an extension of critical thinking that examines issues of fairness, social justice, and equity in society. Many teachers avoid controversial subjects for fear that students will become angry or hurt because of discussions that touch on the social injustice or economic inequities that are all-too-prevalent in some language-minority communities. However, the alternative—so much unsaid or omitted

table 4.3   Types of Graphic Organizers

Type	Use
Sequential	Shows events in order, such as a chain of events in a story, a cycle of repeating events, a sequence of cartoon frames, or a set of dates on a time line
Relational	Compares or contrasts items, or shows concepts nested in layers or connected as flowcharts
Classification	Shows specific structures such as a hierarchy, a matrix, or a two-dimensional plot
Concept development	Used to brainstorm: K-W-L chart (K = what we Know, W = what we Want to know, and L = what we Learned) is used to introduce a theme, a lesson, or a reading; the Mind Map (basically a circle with the topic in the center, and lines, bubbles, arrows, or other connectors) connects ideas to a topic
Evaluation	Shows degree of positivity such as grade scales (A to F), Likert scales (extreme values are 5 = strongly disagree to 1 = strongly agree), or rubric scales (needs work → satisfactory → good → excellent)

from discussion—is more damaging. The long-term harm is that students are given no specific tools of truth or justice with which to grapple with the realities of their lives.

Creative thinking can be used in reading lessons to expand the reader's point of view: What if Joan of Arc had been male rather than female? What if her story were set in the modern era? Using the imagination can stimulate readers to explore a whole range of activities to promote creativity, including creative movement and storytelling. Tools of creativity are especially necessary in the contemporary milieu of schooling, with its excessive pressure on teachers to standardize and mechanize the teaching–learning interaction.

Teaching Direct Strategies: Metacognitive. **Metacognition** means "beyond cognition" and "learning about learning"—assessing and monitoring the state of one's own mind. *Planning strategies* help students learn how to organize themselves for a learning task, sequence task features, and arrange learning activities to suit personal preferences.

> Before beginning a cooperative learning activity, Mr. Kajiwara asks the seventh-grade students as a whole group to think through the task in which they will engage. Does the task have distinct phases (information gathering, notetaking, reporting)? About how much of this work can be done in the time allotted, and what time on the clock represents halfway through as a checkpoint?

Monitoring strategies help students check their comprehension and production and pay selective attention to specific aspects of a task. In the previous example, the teacher might ring a "progress" bell at the halfway point and ask the group monitor to check the group's progress so that members can change speed if they must hurry to finish the expected work. Students might also use a model, exemplar of the task, or rubric to see if their work is developing within expectations.

Evaluation strategies teach students how to assess their own performance on a task using learning logs or other reflective tools to keep track of their progress (Wellman, 1985; Chamot, 1987; Chamot & O'Malley, 1994). When a rubric such as a checklist of required elements is available, students can use it to self-monitor their progress; this reduces the stress of wondering about the criteria on which the final evaluation will be based.

Thus, using metacognition requires a double mental process during tasks. For example, while reading a text, the reader must plan before reading, adjust effort during reading, and evaluate the success of the ongoing effort of making meaning from the text—in addition to the doing the reading itself. Additional kinds of metacognition involve self-knowledge about one's own learning style preferences, about one's own strategy repertoire, and about the state of one's own prior knowledge.

Although to some extent metacognition is innate, it must be modeled, made explicit, and integrated into learning through regular guided practice like other strategy training. A teacher can model metacognitive processes such as self-checks and self-awareness as a regular part of instruction; make time during instruction to plan, monitor, and reflect as a group; and help students match self-reflection to replan and set new goals. Metacognitive strategy training and use is an integral part of cognitively stimulating teaching and is essential in educating English learners.

Teaching Direct Strategies: Social–Affective.   Students use social–affective strategies to support or advance learning. Affective strategies are emotions, attitudes, motivations, and values that help to "create and maintain suitable internal and external climates for learning" (Weinstein, 1988, p. 291). These strategies help language learners lower their anxiety and find ways to encourage and reward themselves when they have accomplished their learning goals.

Teachers can include opportunities for students to talk cooperatively about key concepts, using their primary language for clarification. Support in the affective domain outside of the classroom for English learners may include home visits by teachers, counselors, or outreach workers and informal counseling by teachers—visits that are initiated not because of problems but because of positive interest in the lives of students.

Implementing social-affective strategies is the best way to create a low-anxiety environment for students, so that English learners do not view their second-language acquisition experience as threatening. Explicit attention to the "feeling" side of learning helps learners understand that their achievement in school is not always about how much they *know* but about how much they *desire* to learn and to grow as human beings. The ultimate purposes of social–affective strategies are for learners to take full advantage of whatever emotional support is available and to learn to sustain themselves and their peers with positive self-talk and supportive friendship.

Academic Adjustment and Study Skills.   Many English learners use the academic behaviors and competence acquired in their native culture to adjust to U.S. schools as they acquire English-language skills. Other students may have had little prior schooling and lack the skills to participate and study. Study skills become increasingly necessary at higher levels of schooling.

Students need to know how to use reference materials, take notes, make an outline, use a library, and keep track of assignments and notes; how to allocate time during test taking; when to take the relevant textbook home from school; how and when to ask for help from peers and authority figures; how to use their cultural knowledge as a topic for essays, term papers, or autobiographical writing; how to verbally interact in question-and-answer sessions; how to use clarifying strategies to make sure they understand the assignments they are expected to do; and how to solicit cooperation from English-speaking peers (Gonzales & Watson, 1986). The role of the teacher is to create the scholar from the mere student.

Text processing presents a challenge for English learners. English learners need to vary study strategies according to the type of processing required, whether broad and comprehensive recall, specific types of critical or creative thinking, or memorization of facts. Effective time management allocates text processing and assignment preparation into phases. The early phase is the time to identify requirements and assemble materials. The middle phase of an assignment may require extensive reading and note taking. The late phase is the time to prepare for deadlines or tests.

Together, these types of skills lead not only to academic survival but also success. Possible resources for help with studying are after-school programs, peer tutoring, and Dial-a-Teacher for homework help in English and in the primary language. Additionally, the classroom teacher may designate specific times for homework help during the school day, or middle and high schools may offer an elective class that offers study skill strategies.

To summarize cognitive views of learning, learning stimulates the brain to search for the best response to challenge. Learning how the brain works is a key to operating more strategically. Teaching English learners to understand and use a cognitive approach not only helps them to be better students but also to learn English more rapidly. Teachers with integrity include cognitive instruction as an integrated part of lesson planning and delivery.

Constructivism

Constructivist learning is an offshoot of cognitivism in which students are encouraged to take responsibility for constructing their own knowledge and mastering their own thinking and learning in the face of complex, challenging learning environments. Students and teachers share responsibility for the knowledge-construction process, collaborating on planning how to meet the goals of instruction (Wells & Chang-Wells, 1992).

Constructivist learning is based on student autonomy and initiative (Brooks & Brooks, 1993). Students discuss ideas, ask questions, and explain things to one another as they solve problems together. Project-based learning, for example, is a constructivist technique in which teams of students pool resources and expertise to accomplish large undertakings. Teachers are also learners, constructing knowledge and solving complex problems alongside the students.

Learner Autonomy: Self-Motivation.   *Learner autonomy* can be defined as the learners' sense that studying is taking place due to their own volition. Autonomy enables students to feel pride in their own achievement. A major aim of classroom instruction should be to equip learners with self-directed learning skills, efficient learning strategies, and the ability to set their own learning objectives and plan realistic time frames (Nunan, 1989).

Many learners are highly disciplined yet passive, willing to do everything necessary to achieve high grades but with little desire to learn anything beyond what is required. Given the choice, most teachers would prefer learners who are both self-motivated and self-managed. Three areas of learner autonomy are particularly important: students' belief in themselves as agents of their own learning, control over topics (goals), and freedom of choice in activity (means).

Freedom of choice in activities assumes that teachers provide flexibility not only in what to study (topics) but also in what kind of performance or product can be selected as the outcome of the learning experience. With help, students can construct their own rubric that reflects the criteria of the worth of such a product or performance.

Learner Autonomy: Self-Management.   Marshall (1999a, 1999b) offered classroom strategies that foster self-managed learning: assigning regular duties to *all* learners within the classroom, expecting that *all* students will answer when a question is asked, using question-and-answer techniques for making this possible, and helping *all* students set goals and plan assignments to achieve these goals.

In summary, strategic teaching addresses high-level instruction that gives English learners the tools they need to extend their academic potential. Rather than solely focusing on cognition, however, learning strategies that are emotional, social, and organizational are also important.

Humanistic Teaching

Educators have long recognized that learning improves when it is both cognitive and affective—involving the head *and* the heart. Students who accept the emotions that accompany learning (not only joy, curiosity, and excitement but also sometimes frustration and anxiety) will mature as learners. Good teachers target a level of performance that is within the learners' skills and abilities, support students' collaboration, and offer the chance for students to explore issues that interest them.

Humanistic approaches promote the idea that learning should be a positive, holistic experience in which each student's individuality is valued as he or she uses inner resources, competence, and autonomy in the pursuit of knowledge. Agne emphasized that humanistic education is not a single technique, but "a deep emotional belief that pervades every teacher's thoughts and behaviors" (1992, p. 123), placing emphasis on the worth of the individual, trusting and accepting the strengths and weaknesses of learners, and empathizing with their thoughts and feelings.

Teachers with a humanistic approach to teaching show students that they are cared for and that high standards are the highest form of caring. They demonstrate that they value creativity and individual uniqueness. They listen to students' opinions about classroom occurrences deemed unfair, teaching practices that are ineffective, or ideas that would benefit the whole group.

However, a caring teacher cannot entirely overcome the negatives of the dehumanizing "get-tough" administrative policies of inner-city schools, or the negative messages that students may receive about their home culture. Promoting humanism is not enough to achieve effective education. In fact, "having positive self-esteem is almost impossible for many young people, given the deplorable conditions under which they are forced to live by the iniquities in our society" (Beane, 1991, p. 27). Teachers with integrity are dedicated to working with school administrators and community members to expand funding and resources for schools, providing the financial hope and high-quality ambience that can lead to improved self-esteem.

Addressing Emotional Needs.   English learners may need emotional support during their adjustment to language and schooling in a new culture. Teachers who are "kind and helpful, inviting and stimulating . . . fostering tolerance, cooperation, and self-respect" (Kottler & Kottler, 1993, p. 6) can help students deal with the stress and anxiety of daily life, whether by private conversation, by group discussion, or by using a story in class that touches on a theme relevant to common problems.

A humanistic educator is willing to take time outside of class to hear about students' lives, if this is appropriate in the context of the school. Nonjudgmental listening supports students' efforts to seek their own solutions to problems. Courses in listening skills and intervention strategies may be available in programs that train school counselors. Communication training often helps teachers themselves cope with job-related stress.

Conflict Resolution.   Intercultural miscommunication and misunderstandings often occur in communities of mixed races. Language differences can cause conflict, among many other possible sources of unrest. Schools can benefit from clear antidiscrimination policies combined with structured programs of intercultural communication. Conflict resolution programs are available that train students as peer counselors to assist with structured processes when conflicts arise.

Preventing conflict is as important as intervention after the fact. West-Windsor-Plainsboro School District in New Jersey instituted a series of programs to improve the intercultural climate after an incident of racially motivated crime. The interventions included a peacemaking program at the elementary level, training for middle school students in facilitating human relations, a ninth-grade elective course in conflict resolution, an elective course for 11–12 grade students to prepare student mediators, a minority recruitment program for teachers, and elimination of watered-down, nonrigorous academic courses in lieu of challenging courses accompanied by a tutoring program for academically underprepared high school students (Bandlow, 2002).

Bullying—defined as a single or series of intentionally cruel incidents in which the intent is to put the victim in distress—may be a problem for some non-English-speaking students, as it is for many others. Students who are the victims of bullying can become suicidal or suffer lifelong emotional scars. One-third of students report bullying or having been bullied. Victims report being lonely, with problems making friends, and they are more likely to dislike and perform poorly in school (Mestel, 2001; Mestel & Groves, 2001).

Sociocultural Theory

In recent years, cultural anthropologists have contributed rich insights into the practices of schools, investigating the relative successes and failures of members of various subcultures who have attended public schools in the United States. School administration and pedagogy are dominated largely by European-American learning models, social behaviors, and customs, and learning is seen as the consequence of the behavior of individuals.

In contrast, teaching and learning can be seen as social and cultural interaction. The Russian psychologist Lev Vygotsky emphasized the role played by social interaction in the development of language and thought. According to Vygotsky (1986), cognitive ability is not a "natural" entity but a sociocultural construct that emerges from a child's interaction with the environment. Learning is a process of applying ever more complex cultural tools to one's own psychological processes (Kozulin, 1998).

Vygotsky emphasized the role of social interaction in the development of language and thought: Language joins with thought to create meaning (Wink, 2000). Vygotsky recognized that all teaching and learning takes place within the context of the memories, experiences, and cultural habits found within families. Families form the matrix that underlies the schooling in which students participate. The wise teacher draws on families' stories and social histories to enrich the classroom. Children appreciate their parents and parents' friends more as they see that their experiences are worthy of regard.

English learners take on multiple social languages as they engage in specific social interactions. They negotiate to gain these abilities as they assume various identities associated with their first and second languages. The sociocultural perspective also takes into consideration the power relationships that students experience and the limitations they experience as newcomers to schools and to English. Teachers with clarity of vision pay attention to the ways in which the **sociocultural context of schooling** provides or denies access to privileges according to perceptions of students' possibilities, language, and status (Hawkins, 2004).

Communities of Practice.   Learning is an integral part of participation in a community (Lave & Wenger, 1991). Children are not only members of the school community but also participants in dynamic and interactive communities after a day at school. Teachers must come to know and respect what the community offers students and encourage knowledge to circulate from school to home and back to school as the cultural practices of households and communities function as resources for the school curriculum. Thus learning is both an individual and a communal activity (McCaleb, 1994).

Culture and Schooling.   **Culture,** though largely invisible, influences instruction, policy, and learning in schools. Knowledge of the deeper elements of culture—beyond superficial aspects such as food, clothing, holidays, and celebrations—can give teachers a crosscultural perspective that allows them to educate students to the greatest extent possible.

Schools, as institutions of learning and socialization, are representatives of a particular society, a *macroculture*. Moreover, each classroom has a unique *microculture*. Understanding the discourse practices used in the classroom is an important step forward for students who are new to English.

Teachers of English learners have a repertoire of teaching/learning strategies available for use in a given context. Some educators believe that nonmainstream students should change their cultural patterns to match those of the society at large—an assimilationist view. Other teachers believe in accommodating instruction to facilitate learning for nonmainstream students. This view has been called **culturally responsive pedagogy**—teachers use the cultures of the students as a means to support their learning. Students' real-life experiences legitimize their contribution to the "official" curriculum.

Scholars are still engaged in intense debates about the extent to which schooling should be based on such disparate foundations as behaviorist, cognitivist, humanistic, or sociocultural theories. These provide a range of lenses through which to examine teaching and learning. An attempt to examine the principles that form the foundation for practice is an effort that ultimately benefits instruction, because what a teacher believes about learning will influence his or her teaching and ultimately affect student success or failure. A critical stance is all-important for implementing change and increasing the voices of those who advocate for high-quality education for language-minority students.

Theories of Language Acquisition

First-Language Acquisition

Before exploring various theories of second-language acquisition, a quick review of how children acquire a first language provides a useful framework for comparison. The research done by linguists has drawn from experimental paradigms in a variety of fields.

Most parents are aware that babies first coo, then babble, and then learn to say syllables, words, phrases, and finally sentences. Research on first-language acquisition (FLA) by Brown (1973) showed that there appears to be a natural order of acquisition of English morphemes for child language learners.

Here is an example of the developmental sequence for the structure of negation in a native English speaker:

1. Negative marker outside the sentence
   No Mommy go.
2. Negative marker between the subject and verb
   I no take it.
3. Negative marker in correct position
   I don't want this one.

These data are typical of the early research on L1 acquisition in that they represent the study of individual children at carefully recorded age intervals, and they came out of studies of the acquisition of forms, or discrete "pieces" of language. Chomsky's work on innate language processing and the grammatical competence of native speakers dominated FLA in the 1980s. Throughout the 1990s, the focus on grammar expanded to that of other kinds of competence, including the acquisition of strategic and sociocultural competence.

The behaviorist view of first-language development—that language is learned through constant verbal input shaped by reinforcement—was summarized by Skinner in *Verbal Behavior* (1957). Noam Chomsky (1959) refuted this position by asserting that language is not learned solely through a process of memorizing and repeating, but that the mind contains an active language processor or **language-acquisition device (LAD).** Children are not formally taught their first language but emerge from this experience as competent users of their native language by the age of 5. Chomsky concluded that language is an inborn skill that is externalized in specific ways by the various languages of the world.

Bruner's influential book *Child's Talk* (1983) and the cumulative effect of Piaget's constructivist ideas led to examination of the active and experimental role of language in the intellectual development of the young child. Together, Chomsky, Piaget, and Bruner are lumped together as cognitivists, but in fact Chomsky showed little interest in children's language in his enterprise of characterizing Universal Grammar (Gillen, 2003).

Vygotsky's explanation of language acquisition as internalization—that children gradually come to understand language as they start to use it—has been enormously influential in the study of first-language acquisition. Children first talk to themselves, what Vygotsky called "private language," as they make the transition from external to internal speech. This is the foundation for not only their language skills but also their capacity to think. Berk (1994) and other researchers have pursued this line of research in the sociocultural tradition.

Overall, the first language is intricately bound up with cognitive development and primary socialization. The relationship between L1 and L2 acquisition remains controversial, particularly the issue of the continued development of the primary language during the period of second-language acquisition. Learning that things have names, that language classifies reality, and that language is a means for sharing experiences with others—none of these insights needs to be discovered anew in the second language. Two questions are important here: What is the best way to use L1 in the service of learning, and what is the best way to use L1 to acquire L2?

The Role of the First Language in Learning in General.　Most students are fluent in their primary language before they enter kindergarten, having learned language from personal experience. *Building* on the language of the home allows students to benefit from their prior knowledge and in return bring home the knowledge they learn at school to benefit their home lives. *Replacing* the language of the home with language and experience that is disconnected from the culture of the community confuses children and leads them to undervalue and distrust the home–school connection. Both building on and replacing the home language have consequences for academic achievement, cognitive development, self-esteem, and identity.

Advantages of Bilinguality.   The Bilingual Education Act of 1968 originally authorized funds for the education of limited-English-proficient students on the grounds that they were "educationally disadvantaged because of their inability to speak English." This law was explicitly designed to remediate the "handicap" of being bilingual. But does being bilingual cause learning problems, or does it involve associated cognitive strengths?

Research performed before 1962 built a case for a "language handicap" in bilingual children, suggesting that they were hampered in school because of cognitive interference. However, these early studies were often flawed by the failure to separate the economic status of children from the measure of their academic ability (Cummins, 1976). Moreover, Díaz (1983) found that these studies systematically failed to define *bilingual* in a satisfactory manner, often confusing such factors as parents' birthplaces and family name with bilingual proficiency.

A study involving 10-year-old French-Canadian children showed a positive correlation between bilingualism and general intelligence (Peal & Lambert, 1962). In this research, however, the students chosen as subjects had equally developed French and English skills; critics have charged that these students were likely to have been gifted or from privileged families.

Proficient bilinguals with high levels of primary- and second-language ability outperform monolinguals on a variety of cognitive tasks (Duncan & De Avila, 1979). This research indicated that a strong bilingual program provides an important boost to subsequent academic success. Cummins (1976) proposed a *threshold hypothesis:* Children must attain a critical level, or threshold, of linguistic proficiency in order to avoid the negative cognitive effects of being transitioned to education in a second language. If students attain a strong foundation in the first language, learning a second language may lead to accelerated cognitive growth.

Subsequent research has shown that higher degrees of bilingualism correlate with high test scores in such areas as concept formation, creativity, knowledge of the workings of language, and cognitive flexibility (Díaz, 1983; Galambos & Goldin-Meadow, 1990). Additionally, a number of studies showed that bilingual children have been generally shown to develop more positive, open views toward members of other ethnic groups than their monolingual counterparts (Tucker, 1990). Skutnabb-Kangas (2000) has summed up other research that shows a positive effect of bilingualism on general intellectual development.

Common Underlying Proficiency.   According to some critics of bilingual education, primary-language schooling reduces minority students' opportunities to learn English. Cummins (1981b) has termed this belief the **separate underlying proficiency (SUP)** hypothesis, which asserts that proficiency in English is separate from proficiency in the primary language. In contrast, Cummins claimed that the fundamentals of cognition and language, once learned in the primary language, augment subsequent learning in any language. This position assumes a **common underlying proficiency (CUP),** the belief that a second language and the primary language have a shared foundation, and that competence in the primary language provides the basis for competence in the second language.

Metalinguistic Awareness.   One common underlying proficiency is *metalinguistic awareness,* knowledge about the structural properties of language, including sounds, words, and grammar, as well as knowledge of language and its functions, such as knowing there is more than one way to represent meaning: to "realize the arbitrary nature of language in that form of language, either written or spoken language, is something different from meaning" (Yaden & Templeton, 1986, p. 9).

Metalinguistic awareness may develop alongside first-language acquisition, or during middle childhood as the child learns to think about the linguistic system. Bilingual individuals outperform monolinguals on tasks requiring metalinguistic abilities (Hamers & Blanc, 1989). Teachers can promote metalinguistic awareness through such practices as helping students judge the adequacy of messages and their context, guiding students to find cognates between languages, and teaching students about word denotation and connotation.

Recent research on the anatomy of the brain has found that people who speak two languages develop more gray matter in the language area of their brains, particularly early bilinguals who learn a second language while they are young. The more proficiency in the second language is achieved, the larger the gray area. (See "Bilinguals Brainier . . . ," 2004.)

Transfer from the First Language to the Second Language.   How does knowledge of a first language benefit an individual's learning a second language? Individuals who have learned a second language sometimes find that the first language interferes with the second: In trying to say "language" in English, for example, Korean speakers sometimes mistakenly say "languaji" because in Korean the final sound is a syllable, not a single phoneme, as in English. This is called *cross-linguistic influence,* or *transfer.*

Language transfer occurs when the comprehension or production of a second language is influenced by the first language (Odlin, 1989). *Positive transfer* allows people to respond appropriately and meaningfully in new language situations. The use of cognates from Spanish to English is a helpful resource (cognates are words in two languages that look alike and have the same or similar meaning). For example, almost all nouns in English that end in "ion" have a Spanish cognate (e.g., *transportation/transportación, attention/atención, action/acción*).

Numerous studies have compared various features of languages in order to predict which language features will promote positive transfer. However, even though the first language is a valuable resource, it is usually not helpful for learners to compare specific forms of the first and second languages as they learn.

What kind of transfer can be expected from the first language to the second? Students can transfer sensorimotor skills (eye–hand coordination, fine muscle control, spatial and directional skills, visual perception and memory); auditory skills (auditory perception, memory, discrimination, and sequencing); common features of writing systems (alphabets, punctuation rules); comprehension strategies (finding the main idea, inferring, predicting, use of cueing systems); study skills (taking notes, using reference sources); habits and attitudes (self-esteem, task persistence, focus) (Cloud, Genesee, & Hamayan, 2000); the structure of language (speech–print relationships, concepts such as syllable, word, sentence, paragraph); and knowledge about the reading process (Thonis, 1981).

A second general cognitive strategy used by all learners is generalization: applying a rule, once learned, to a new context. In the first language, a child may learn that past-tense verbs are created by adding "-ed" and happily create *jumped* from *jump* and *popped* from *pop*. English learners whose L1 is Spanish may benefit from the understanding that like Spanish verbs, some English verbs are regular in the past tense and some are not, thus generalizing the idea of regular–irregular verbs.

Sometimes learners generalize rules from their first language that are not applicable to the second. As an illustration, Natheson-Mejia (1989) describes errors that Spanish speakers may make when writing in English. These include "es" for /s/, as in *estay,* "d" for /t/ or /th/, as in *fader;* "ch" for /sh/, as in *chirt;* "j" for /h/, as in *jelper;* and "g" for /w/, as in *sogen* (sewing).

Teachers can use positive transfer as a learning strategy by helping students draw on prior knowledge of "how language works" as they learn English. Explicit attention to transfer, both in teacher attitude (welcoming dual-language use, understanding code-switching) and in teacher assistance (providing support for literacy in multiple languages, recommending specific strategies) helps students build second-language acquisition on a firm foundation of first-language proficiency.

According to Skutnabb-Kangas (2000), many bilinguals feel that their second language is somehow poorer in emotion and less rich in communicative power than the first language. The native language dominates the heart, leaving little emotional space for the second, no matter how rich the experience of learning the second language. For others, however, the second language represents new learning opportunities and experiences that can be supported by knowledge from the first language—the second language augments, rather than interferes with, the first language.

Second-Language Acquisition

Second-language acquisition (SLA) is one of the most difficult domains of learning. Becoming proficient in another language requires precise control of meaning, careful attunement to intonation, and mastery of behavioral subtlety. Prior knowledge about language—one's first language—is only partially helpful.

Acquiring a second language—defined as any language that is learned after the first language, whether it is the second or the sixteenth—is difficult, for many reasons. First, this language learning is usually not a life-or-death situation. The first language, the so-called mother tongue, fulfills the majority of a person's social and emotional needs. Second, a second language, for most people, seems to be learned in a way different from the first, with far more frustration.

To make matters more difficult, the better a person becomes in a foreign language, the more difficult it becomes to improve. Some second-language learners attain a level of intermediate fluency and then make no further progress, satisfied at having established basic communication but not motivated to refine pronunciation or syntax toward a native-speaker's level. A second factor that makes SLA difficult is that native speakers are often

table 4.4   The Challenges of Learning a Second Language

Characteristic	First Language	Second Language
Sense of urgency	High—many social and survival functions take place in L1.	Low—can rely on L1 for many social and survival functions.
Possibility of mastery	High—almost everyone achieves native-speaker proficiency in L1.	Low—almost no one achieves native-speaker proficiency in L2.
Ease of acquisition	High—almost all humans learn L1 by the age of 5.	Low—L2 is seldom as easy as L1.
Learning process	Usually learned by informal acquisition and augmented by formal schooling.	Usually learned by formal schooling and augmented by informal acquisition.
Feedback during learning	Informal—oral utterances are seldom corrected.	Formal—errors are often corrected.
Motivation	Mostly unconscious.	Mostly conscious.

more critical of an intermediate learner than of a beginner, perhaps because expectations for proficiency are higher. In addition, the closer a speaker approaches to native-speaker fluency, the higher the degree of mastery of the target culture must be attained, which is a long, subtle process. Thus there are multiple cognitive and emotional obstacles to second-language proficiency. Table 4.4 summarizes these difficulties.

The nature of English as a target language compounds the difficulty of acquiring it as a second language. English has a huge vocabulary that is continually growing due to fast-paced cultural innovation. Spelling and pronunciation quirks are a learner's nightmare (compare *sad* and *wad*), as are irregular plurals (*memorandum/memoranda, forum/fora*). Idiomatic phrasal verbs are hard to learn (*shut up* versus *shut down*). Finally, English dialects vary widely in vocabulary and accent—to pick just two examples, the English spoken in Tennessee and in Scotland may be mutually incomprehensible, not to mention the Englishes of Jamaica and Korea. The challenges of English as a target language are summed up in Table 4.5.

How, then, does this complex process of second-language acquisition take place? What best motivates SLA? How can teaching and learning of a second language be accomplished with greater ease, especially so that students who must learn academic subjects in a second language can be more successful? These are the questions and challenges facing teachers of English learners.

Many approaches have been tried throughout the long history of language teaching, and certain techniques have been retained as a part of the complex repertoire of second-language professionals. Teachers of English learners who are cognizant of second-language acquisition theories can be assured that their pedagogy is substantiated by research rather than by common practice.

The following section explores theories of second-language acquisition and connects these theories to teaching. How a language is taught depends on how the teacher believes students learn. Beliefs about second-language teaching and learning have changed in much the same way that beliefs about learning in general have shifted over the course of centuries.

table 4.5   Some Challenges of Learning English as a Target Language

Aspect of Language	Examples
Phonology	English dialects vary widely in vocabulary and accent.
Morphology	Many verbs are irregular.
Semantics	Vocabulary is large and continually growing due to fast-paced cultural changes.
Graphemics	Spelling–pronunciation correspondence is irregular.
Syntax	Idiomatic phrasal verbs are hard to learn (*shut up* versus *shut down*).
Pragmatics	A "low-context" culture means interpersonal interactions vary greatly from person to person, rather than featuring fixed cultural rules; many aspects of culture must be negotiated using language.

Traditionalism and Grammar Translation.   The earliest type of language teaching was grammar translation pedagogy, which began in the monasteries of medieval Europe and has continued to the present day in many parts of the world. This pedagogy can be seen as a form of traditionalism. Teachers explain the meaning of vocabulary words and the structure of sentences, students learn only what is required, and rewards are explicitly connected to precisely defined actions, including a focus on memorization of vocabulary words.

This methodology is still widely employed for learning English. The curriculum is carefully structured and controlled, with students' access to L2 limited to that which the teacher or other authorities determine to be valuable. Grammar translation pedagogy is thus compatible with traditional education (see discussion of traditionalism and rationalism earlier in this chapter).

The drawbacks to grammar translation as a methodology are that learning is not self-motivated or self-managed, and this goes against the intrinsic nature of cognition as curious, playful, and explorative. When English becomes a measure of how much rote memorization learners are willing to suffer, it becomes hated and feared as a second language.

The Audiolingual Method.   Some instructors expect students to develop correct second-language habits through repetitious training, often using technology such as tape recorders in language laboratories. Correct pronunciation was considered the first step and was achieved using oral language pattern drills based on carefully ordered grammatical structures in the target language. For example, a complete lesson might be focused on tag questions (*She wants to go, doesn't she?*). Reading and writing may be delayed until the student has an adequate oral base.

Audiolingual pedagogy is behavioral because of the emphasis on drill and practice. The chief goal of instruction in the second language is to produce correct speech and syntax, modeled after a correct stimulus. However, even though audiolingual instruction results in good pronunciation of the second language, it does not seem to be a major cause of second-language proficiency beyond a basic level. Learners pressured to perform accurately under classroom or laboratory conditions often find it difficult to communicate spontaneously with native speakers.

Transformational Grammar.   Transformational grammarians (followers of Noam Chomsky) posit that the human mind has an inborn capacity to internalize and construct rules, which means that human beings, once exposed to the language(s) of their environment, use this innate ability to understand and produce sentences they have never before heard. The goal of transformational grammar (also called *generative grammar*) is to understand and describe these rules.

Despite its widespread influence on language-acquisition research, transformational grammar has not been useful in second-language teaching. Due largely to Krashen's influence (see the subsequent discussion of monitor theory), explicit grammar instruction is no longer seen as a useful way to achieve fluency at the beginning stages of second-language acquisition. At advanced stages of second-language acquisition, however, explicit instruction of grammar rules is necessary to achieve native like competence.

Interlanguage Theory.   The language produced by second-language learners is an intermediate language or continuum. Selinker (1972, 1991) calls this "interlanguage." This "language-learner language" is a different language from that of the native speaker but similar to that of other language learners. Interlanguage researchers look for ways in which the rules of the first and target language influence language learning, as well as ask what rules—and what kind of rules—are universal to the human mind.

Teachers who are knowledgeable about interlanguage see learners as intelligent, hypothesis-forming individuals. Instead of criticizing the language that learners produce as error-ridden and deficient, a teacher can recognize it as a dynamic system that is in constant progression toward increased proficiency. The teacher's role is to help students make progress by assessing learners' strengths and providing support for interlanguage production.

Monitor Theory.   An idea similar to that of Chomsky's language-acquisition device was incorporated into Krashen's (1981, 1982) theory of SLA. Krashen's theory included five hypotheses. The *acquisition-learning hypothesis* distinguished acquisition (an unconscious process that occurs when language is used for real communication) from learning (which involves "knowing about" language and its formal rules). Krashen considered acquisition more important than learning in achieving fluency and de-emphasized direct instruction of syntax rules.

Krashen asserted in the *natural-order hypothesis* that morphemic and syntactic rules of a second language are acquired in a gradual yet predictable order that is similar to that of the first language. Children acquire correct usage of grammatical structures in their L1 gradually, as do children acquiring a second language.

In the *monitor hypothesis,* Krashen postulated that the mind employs an error-detecting mechanism—the monitor—that scans utterances for accuracy in order to make corrections. When an individual initiates an utterance, that individual's monitor edits—that is, confirms or repairs—the utterance either prior to or after attempted communication. This may be useful only when there is ample time to be concerned with grammatical correctness, as in slow, relaxed speech production.

The *input hypothesis* claimed that language is acquired by understanding messages. According to Krashen, second-language learners benefit most by participating in language that is slightly more complex than they can themselves easily understand, such as conversation with peers that mixes more- and less-skilled speakers. Krashen introduced the expression $i + 1$, where i stands for the current level of the acquirer's competence and 1 is the next structure to be acquired in the natural order. Comprehensibility increases when teachers use a variety of modalities, including visual and kinesthetic, to give the learner context for language. A focus on the message and its relevance for the language learner makes language comprehensible.

In the *affective filter* construct, Krashen hypothesized that emotional variables, including anxiety, motivation, and self-confidence, influence the second-language learner. Mental and emotional blocks can prevent language comprehension, whereas a positive affective context increases the functioning of the monitor. People acquire a second language only if their affective filters are low enough to allow them to receive adequate input. Therefore the language learner needs a supportive, nonthreatening experience.

Krashen's work has led teachers to the view that acquisition helps students learn some aspects of language un-self-consciously in a nonstressful, "natural," language-rich environment.

The Natural Approach.   Teachers now understand that intensive focus on language rules does not produce perfect formation of grammatical structures. When children interact with one another in English as they learn, they are in fact improving their language ability. In this way, students learn language while actively engaged in other pursuits, and the teacher can use the students' errors as an impetus to improving their language.

Although individuals vary greatly in their acquisition of a second language, many progress through similar stages of development in what Krashen and Terrell (1983) call the Natural Approach. In *preproduction*, learners become attuned to the sounds and rhythms of the new language and begin to isolate specific words. They generally communicate nonverbally and rely on context clues for understanding. In the *early production* stage, learners can attempt single words ("yes," "no," "OK," "you,") and two- or three-word combinations ("where book?" "no go," "don't go," "teacher, help"), and can memorize simple poems and songs. In the *speech emergence* stage, learners can respond with longer and more complex utterances, although syntax errors may increase as learners attempt creative constructions. Once in *intermediate fluency*, students begin to initiate and sustain conversations and are often able to recognize and correct their own errors.

Total Physical Response.   Total Physical Response (TPR) (Asher, 1982) associated language and body movement. In TPR the teacher models actions and gives oral commands, and students follow along. The instructor repeats the commands ("Step forward, step back") followed by the appropriate action until students perform without hesitation. The instructor then begins to give commands without modeling to allow students the opportunity to demonstrate understanding. Eventually, the number of commands is increased and novel commands are given that combine previously learned commands in a new way.

Reading and writing can be introduced through TPR. The instructor might write on the board "Touch your nose" and gesture to the students to perform the action; then the teacher reverses the procedure and makes a gesture for which students write the correct phrase. TPR is associated with early stages of second-language learning and is useful in classrooms where more than one primary language is spoken. Advanced techniques such as TPR storytelling can be used at later stages. The strength of TPR is the reinforcement of memory provided by physical action.

Communicative Competence and Functional Grammar. Hymes (1972) introduced the term **communicative competence,** meaning the ability of language users to convey and interpret messages and negotiate meanings interpersonally. The competent speaker is one who knows more than grammatical forms, such as when, where, and how to use language appropriately—the use of language in the social setting. "Communicative competence comes from opportunities to use language in real ways for real reasons with real people" (Townsend & Fu, 1998, p. 194).

Halliday (1978) elaborated on this definition by stating that the social structure is an essential element in linguistic interaction. Linguists have thus gone beyond merely linguistic components of a language to analysis of language in use—including social, political, and psychological domains.

> Many children from immigrant families are called on to be the translators for their parents in social service encounters. Teachers and administrators decry this practice and criticize families for making use of their children's linguistic skills in this way. A more authentic approach to second-language acquisition would be to acknowledge these encounters and help children learn to communicate competently under these circumstances—know what phrases to use, how to ask questions, and how to ask for information to be repeated if a misunderstanding takes place.

Communicative competence is complex because real-life language is complicated. Real second-language use is more than pronouncing words accurately and understanding the grammar of sentences. Canale (1983) described communicative competence as comprising of four basic aspects: (1) *Grammatical competence* is the focus on sentence formation, vocabulary, and so forth; (2) *sociolinguistic competence* involves language used in different social contexts; (3) *discourse competence* involves the ability to create meaningful spoken conversation or written text; and (4) *strategic competence* involves the use of language to enhance the effectiveness of communication or to repair breakdowns in communication.

Second-Language-Use Strategies. Even when they use strategies for acquiring language learners sometimes have to plunge into conversations with only their proficiency to help them. In this case, they must employ language-use strategies, ways to get messages across when a speaker is challenged to maintain communication when proficiency is not adequate.

Many strategies are available for communicating ideas when the learner cannot produce the correct linguistic content. *Communication strategies* comprise gestures, nonverbal pleas for help, and prememorized phrases. *Cover strategies* are used to create the impression that the learner is in control when in fact there are gaps in proficiency (a speaker may repeat a word just heard, change the subject to one in which the vocabulary is more familiar, or avoid using certain syntax if it is difficult).

Code-switching is a language-use strategy that alternates use of the first and second language at the level of words, phrases, clauses, or sentences (see Valdés-Fallis, 1978). Code-switching may occur when a speaker (perhaps upset, tired, or distracted) is not able to express himself or herself in one language and switches to the other to compensate for the deficiency. Code-switching is also used to enhance sociolinguistic competence as speakers cross social or ethnic boundaries to express group identity and status, to be accepted by a group, to enhance rapport between speakers of the same language, to express an attitude, or to ease tension in a conversation (Crystal, 1987; Skiba, 1997).

In classrooms, students should learn in whatever manner they feel most comfortable, including code-switching, if it reduces anxiety or increases group solidarity. Research has shown that the fact that students code-switch does not indicate dysfunctional language behavior; rather, it is a feature of multicompetent language use.

Teachers can help students increase their skills in sociolinguistic, strategic, and discourse competence by involving students in designing projects, solving problems, and exploring areas of interest. But creating a supportive, student-centered environment is not enough to accomplish communicative competence. Students need content that is both compelling and comprehensible, that involves the participants because they have a stake in it, and that focuses on issues that are relevant and meaningful to students.

The first type of second language that children learn what Cummins (1981b) called **basic interpersonal conversational skills (BICS)**. Children of a young age will naturally switch from BICS in their primary language to BICS in English, depending on with whom they are speaking and their purpose for communicating. Teachers do not need to fear that this use of the primary language is regressive for the student or in any way undermines instruction; likewise, parents do not need to worry that this language use jeopardizes the "purity" of their child's first language.

Semiotics.   Semiotics is a discipline that studies the ways in which humans use signs (symbols, icons, and indexes) to make meaning. Thus the way chairs are arranged in a classroom, and the manner in which students are expected to respond to the teacher, are both signs that signal meaning. Semioticians strive to make the implicit explicit.

Semiotics is a way of looking beyond the obvious of what can be observed to discover the underlying meaning of phenomena: "Semiotics provides a potentially unifying conceptual framework and a set of methods and terms for use across the full range of signifying practices, which include gesture, posture, dress, writing, speech, photography, film, television, and radio" (Chandler, 2004b, n.p.).

Semiotics can also help us realize that whatever meaning seems to be obvious, natural, universal, given, permanent, and incontrovertible is actually generated by the ways in which sign systems operate in discourse communities. Although things can exist independently of signs, the only way they can be known is through the mediation of signs. Social semiotics alerts us to how the same text can generate different meanings for different readers. Art historian Keith Mosley comments:

Semiotics makes us aware that the cultural values with which we make sense of the world are a tissue of conventions that have been handed down from generation to generation by the members of the culture of which we are a part. It reminds us that there is nothing "natural" about our values; they are social constructs that not only vary enormously in the course of time but differ radically from culture to culture. (cited in Schroeder, 1998, p. 225)

Teachers of culturally and linguistically diverse students are aware that signs can serve as symbols. A poster of Mexico—or of any student's homeland—on the bulletin board is a welcome sign. For older students, a rainbow sticker on the door may mean that a gay or lesbian student can discuss issues in confidence with an understanding teacher.

Learning even a few words in a student's native language is a sign that the teacher is making an effort to see the world through the eyes and ears of another. Many nonverbal signs—ways of interacting that honor and show respect for students who may be marginal or shy—go a long way toward creating a semiotic message of support and willingness to accommodate instruction to meet students' needs.

If signs do not merely reflect reality but are involved in its construction, those who control the sign systems control the construction of reality. One role of ideology is to protect the interests of dominant groups. Various codes contribute to reproducing dominant ideology, making it seem natural, proper, and inevitable. Many semioticians see their primary tasks as revealing ideology at work and demonstrating that "reality" can be challenged.

In an increasingly visual age, an important contribution of semiotics has been a concern with imagistic as well as linguistic signs, particularly in the context of advertising, photography, and audiovisual media. At present, many people feel unable to draw or paint, and even those who own video cameras seldom know how to use them effectively. This is a legacy of an educational system that still focuses almost exclusively on the acquisition of verbal language at the expense of most other semiotic modes, whether auditory, visual, or tactile.

This institutional bias not only excludes many from engaging in nonlinguistic representational practices (e.g., drawing, painting, dancing, singing), but also handicaps them as critical readers of the majority of texts to which they are routinely exposed throughout their lives—texts such as television and films, especially those soaked in advertising and other types of visual propaganda.

A working understanding of key concepts in semiotics—including ways to interpret gestures, visual icons, and television and print advertising—is essential for everyone who wants to understand the complex and dynamic communication terrain of modern society: "Those who cannot understand such environments are in the greatest danger of being manipulated by those who can" (Chandler, 2004b, n.p.).

By adopting a semiotic perspective, teachers accept that students learn not just the content of a specific lesson but also the entire context in which the lesson is embedded. Through the interplay of multiple meaning systems, students study the various ways in which culturally authentic materials (phone books, voicemail messages, advertising brochures, music videos, etc.) communicate meaning.

Semiotics has become increasingly important as visual information, rather than primarily text, has become salient in the lives of students and as propaganda of all sorts becomes increasingly subtle in its influence. Clarity of vision is needed on the part of teachers and students alike to interpret signs and symbols wisely.

Discourse Theory.   Discourse theorists have looked at the ways in which language is used in the classroom. Schools, as institutions of learning and socialization, are representatives of a society's *macroculture;* but, in addition, each classroom has a unique *microculture* composed of language and the deeds used to deploy power. Understanding the discourse practices used in the classroom is an important step forward for students who are new to English.

In U.S. classrooms, teachers often use a *recitation* pattern of discourse, in which they ask "known-answer" questions—that is, the teacher knows the "correct" answer and wants to see which students are also knowledgeable. Students then volunteer to answer or are called on to answer. Teachers follow the answer with an evaluation or with added information meant to clarify the question. This three-part sequence (initiating a question, picking someone to respond, and then giving evaluative feedback) sustains a predictable, teacher-centered rhythm and enables the teacher to maintain control, monitor students' attention, and assess the general level of the class's knowledge and interest in a topic.

Discourse theorists note, however, that this sequence may not meet the needs of English learners. The questioning segment may not be comprehensible, the English learner may be slow to comprehend and thus slow to volunteer to respond, and the question may require prior knowledge unavailable to the learner. The response may be difficult for the beginning learner to produce. In the evaluation segment, the teacher may focus more on the grammar than on the intellectual content of the response, depriving the English learner of content-based feedback.

Moreover, cultural differences may preclude the English learner from understanding what turn-taking behaviors are required during this discourse, leaving the learner frustrated and unwilling to participate. Teachers with integrity are aware of the limitations of this discourse pattern and vary its frequency, alternating with discourse patterns that are more student-centered.

The Future of Second-Language Teaching.   Teachers of English learners are poised at the edge of new opportunities. Teaching no longer concerns a search for methods and techniques that are so useful that they transcend learner, culture, and context. Instead, teaching must be specific to the learners' cultures and needs. Learners who understand themselves and affirm their own culture are the most productive.

Teachers are most successful when they fully understand the foundations of learning theory and the role of first- and second-language acquisition in learning. Exploring the mind deeply, eliciting its potential for self-regulatory and accelerated learning, and honoring the interlanguage of English learners frees teachers of English learners to embrace strategic teaching and maintain integrity in their teaching.

5

Pedagogy for English Learners

Parents provide vital resources for culturally responsive teaching.

expectations

Each prospective teacher . . .

■ Knows and applies pedagogical theories, principles, and instructional practices for comprehensive instruction of English learners. *(Element 7.1 of the California Teaching Performance Expectations)*

■ Uses English that extends students' current levels of development yet is still comprehensible. *(Element 7.8 of the California Teaching Performance Expectations)*

■ Uses questioning strategies that model or represent familiar grammatical constructions. *(Element 7.13 of the California Teaching Performance Expectations)*

■ Makes learning strategies explicit. *(Element 7.14 of the California Teaching Performance Expectations. Reprinted by permission of the California Commission on Teacher Credentialing.)*

Teachers cannot teach what they do not know. To teach with integrity, teachers must be skilled in their craft by having expertise in the necessary aspects of their work. What is pedagogy for English learners—what do teachers of English learners need to *know* and *do* to teach effectively? This chapter addresses how to provide effective, comprehensive instruction for English learners.

Implementing a pedagogy grounded in democratic principles can occur only when teachers know and honor what the learner brings to teaching and learning. This issue is addressed in this chapter, as well as the view that bilingualism is an asset and that a humanistic approach to classroom management is a necessity. Second, the chapter addresses pedagogy for English learners by focusing on issues of curriculum design, culturally responsive teaching, cognitive academic language proficiency (CALP), adapted instruction, questioning techniques, and learning strategies as core elements in a comprehensive approach to teaching English-language development and content area knowledge. Last, the chapter includes a focus on two additional pedagogical features: service learning and computer-assisted learning.

Figure 2.2 (see page 34) presents a model of instruction that shows pedagogy as a critical element of the foundations of instruction.

Key Assumptions Underlying Effective Pedagogy

Clarity in How and What to Teach

Teachers make a difference. Both common sense and research support this position (Balderrama, 2001). This assumption is at the core of the pedagogy-for-English-learners model, suggesting that it is the teacher (with family support) who is in the best position to promote students' classroom success. For this reason, teachers must understand the centrality of their role in designing curriculum that not only is comprehensive, humane, and empowering but also teaches students to "read the English word" and the English-speaking world.

More Than Methods and Good Intentions

Good intentions are not sufficient. Teachers practicing pedagogy for English learners must take a critical stance, reflect critically, and, if necessary, make adaptations in their own behaviors and attitudes. Bartolomé (1994) identified this as a humanizing pedagogy that requires a shift in perspective so that teachers do not get bogged down in seeking the solution to their students' underachievement *solely* through methods, but instead realize that "by robbing students of their culture, language, history and values, schools often reduce these students to the status of subhumans who need to be rescued from their 'savage selves'" (p. 233). Bartolomé (1994) further suggested that "any discussion having to do with the improvement of subordinated students' academic standing is incomplete if it does not address those discriminatory school practices that lead to dehumanization" (p. 233).

Thus pedagogical knowledge is more than a collection of "how-to" methods to teach English and academic knowledge. A much broader definition of pedagogy for the English learner places the English learner at the center of the curriculum while also taking into consideration the macro level or larger issues that may affect teaching the English learner. In short, pedagogy does not exist in a vacuum, and teachers with integrity and clarity of vision maintain a vigilant stance about the implications of specific pedagogies, techniques, or methods they have chosen to use with English learners. Teachers with clarity of vision do not compromise humanity for the sake of methods.

The most advanced technological tools or the most innovative curriculum will fail if the teacher is unable to show and convince students that they are seen as humans first and students, or English learners, second. This statement is often contested, however, particularly in the secondary context; some secondary school teachers are unwilling to accept this position, believing that teaching the subject matter is their primary role and that they are not there to "coddle" their students. Prospective teachers often claim that they are supposed to "teach the subject, not the student."

Humanizing pedagogy does not "coddle." To the contrary, a pedagogy that sees students as full partners in the teaching and learning experience does not place students in a subordinate role, but instead accepts them in a status that is fair and equal. It also places students in a position in which their humanity is more important than the subject matter: Teachers teach the student first, *then* the subject matter. Pedagogy for the English learner is grounded in a commitment to honor and respect the integrity of individual English learners, their families, and their communities.

Democratic Practices as Pedagogy

Another principle is that pedagogy for English learners must incorporate a multicultural curriculum emphasizing social justice and critical thinking skills. Nieto's (2002) definition describes how multicultural teaching frames the pedagogy for English learners:

> Multicultural education is a process of comprehensive school reform and basic education for all students. It challenges and rejects racism and other forms of discrimination in schools and society and accepts and affirms the pluralism (ethnic, racial, linguistic, religious, economic, and gender among others) that students, their communities, and teachers reflect. Multicultural education permeates the schools' curriculum and instructional strategies as well as the interactions among teachers, students, and families, and the very way that schools conceptualize the nature of teaching and learning. Because it uses critical pedagogy as its underlying philosophy and focuses on knowledge, reflection, and action (praxis) as the basis for social change, multicultural education promotes democratic principles of social justice. (pp. 29–30)

This definition of **multicultural education,** although not explicitly naming it, has teaching with integrity at its core because it assumes that the teacher is a political actor within a social system (schooling) that is connected with a broader reality, or society. By recognizing this, the teacher with integrity accepts the role and the responsibility of teaching for social change and justice, and with that, the active pursuit of democratic principles.

Bilingualism as an Asset

The use of multiple languages in teaching and learning is another tenet of this book. Bilingualism is an asset, and all languages are created equal. Students' linguistic repertoires are varied, and their dialects should be honored, respected, and used as a linguistic bridge toward their acquisition of English. This pedagogical stance affirms that the use and maintenance of a child's primary or home language is essential to maintaining the child's and family's integrity.

Because classrooms are complex social systems that include many individuals, learning is a social enterprise. Teachers tap into the resources of this social system, providing and orchestrating ample opportunities for students to talk, work, and learn together around academic tasks. The pedagogy for English learners acknowledges that two languages can be used and practiced in numerous contexts.

Comprehensive instruction for English learners requires that teachers use strategies that develop English-language skills (listening, speaking, reading, and writing) and content area knowledge. Chapter 7 addresses numerous strategies for teaching academic and content area knowledge in elementary and secondary settings, and Chapter 8 focuses on English-language development strategies.

Pedagogical Theories, Principles, and Practices for Comprehensive Instruction of English Learners

The following sections address specific pedagogical strategies effective in working with English learners, including curriculum that builds on knowledge available in the learner's home and community, adaptation to the learner's family and cultural background, and culturally modified techniques of discipline and management.

Community-Sensitive Curriculum: Funds of Knowledge

Last year I was teaching a methods class to secondary school teachers, and the discussion centered on what resources students bring with them to school. A science teacher in the group raised his hand and stated that he did not believe English learners, or other students for that matter, came to school with much prior knowledge. "I don't expect my students to know much when they come to my classroom," he stated, "and English learners know even less since they do not speak English." Many in the class were speechless, finding it hard to believe that someone within the teaching profession could hold the archaic belief that students are "blank slates" when they enter the classroom, and that students are deficient if they do not speak English. (MVB)

Contrary to the beliefs evident in this anecdote, a major assumption underlying the contents of this book, including the theoretical framework of teaching with integrity, is that all students, including English learners, bring extensive prior knowledge to the classroom. This assumption aligns with a pedagogical stance grounded in Freire's (1970) work whereby teaching and learning are viewed and practiced as reciprocal processes. Teaching and learning are two-way activities: Students (or learners) bring much to the table, and they too are teachers.

Local Community Knowledge as a Resource.   Inspired by Lev Vygotsky's work, and intentionally moving away from the cultural deficit model, Moll and González (1997) tapped into the cultural resources of local communities, primarily working-class households, to develop pedagogies that view this knowledge as a resource, or **funds of knowledge.** He suggested that teachers can intentionally plan and create "activity settings" that combine cultural practices and resources, thus providing opportunities for students to contribute and integrate their knowledge into schooling and classroom tasks.

The focus in this curricular approach is on what students know and bring to school, regardless of their English-language proficiency levels. Teachers visit their students' homes and communities as learners, seeking to understand the households, and particularly the practices of life, as a way to gain a "deep appreciation of how people use resources of all kinds, most prominently their funds of knowledge to engage life" (Moll, 2001, p. 17). Questions are addressed, such as, "What do the activities of a household reveal about a family's knowledge base? What are the family networks, labor history, educational history, language use, and child-rearing practices? How do households function within the broader socioeconomic context, and how do individual members obtain and distribute their material and intellectual resources?"

The Responsive Curriculum. The intent of the funds of knowledge approach is to render the cultural resources of households visible and explicit so that teachers can use these as starting points for their curricular planning and for creating strategic connections with classroom instruction. Moll (2001) describes how one teacher built a curriculum unit based on the information she obtained from visiting many of her students' households:

> One teacher built a curriculum unit based on the information that many of her students' households had extensive knowledge of the medicinal value of plants and herbs. She was able to draw on this ethnobotanical knowledge in formulating a theme unit that reflected local knowledge of the curative properties of plants. Other teachers have created similar units with a variety of content. In some instances, individuals met during the household visits became participants, visiting the classrooms to contribute in English or Spanish their knowledge or experiences. (p. 19)

Linking Knowledge and Biliteracy. The funds of knowledge approach to the curriculum can also be instrumental in the development of **biliteracy** competencies. Moll (2001) suggested that knowing what funds of local knowledge exist in a household or community can provide teachers with opportunities to create meaningful connections between classroom learning, literacy, and modes of engagement. That is, if teachers are cognizant of the breadth and depth of local knowledge a child brings to the classroom, literacy experiences can address and tap into this knowledge to make literacy a meaningful and useful activity. In this way, the funds of knowledge approach can extend student experiences and enrich awareness while also building on what students already have in their cultural repertoire.

Teaching Responsively to Learners' Family and Cultural Backgrounds

A prevalent mythology in schools is that one can teach the individual child without needing to know about a child's cultural background. This is a position taken frequently by those who oppose multicultural education. In taking this position, teachers may think they can avoid facing cultural issues. What one finds, particularly in secondary school settings, is that teachers' knowledge about their learners' backgrounds is limited. Thus, ignorance about other cultures is compounded by linguistic miscommunication between teachers and English learners. The resulting cultural and linguistic chasms undermine the academic success of English learners.

Knowledge about Students' Cultures.　Teachers with integrity must be informed about their students. Knowing students' familial, cultural, and linguistic backgrounds is essential to effective planning within a humanizing and academically challenging pedagogy. Furthermore, the role of the teacher as intercultural educator is central to teaching with integrity because learning builds on previous learning. If teachers do not know what their students already know, it is difficult to teach by building on these funds of knowledge.

Although an individual's identity comprises many factors, perhaps the most important influence is that of the family. Basic patterns of living and existence are learned in the context of the household. For example, verbal, nonverbal, and age- and gender-appropriate behaviors are learned from observing models within the immediate household or family. Interpersonal relationships, expression of emotions, use of personal space, cooperation, competitiveness, and even conceptions of time are all cultural patterns learned within the family.

These values are learned in many ways: through the patterns of daily life, through creative expression (art, music, and dance), through contact with nature, through care for living things (children, relatives, pets, gardens). Language is also acquired within this context. The home and community are places that have taught students how to use language with all of its multiple functions (Halliday, 1978). When is it appropriate to speak, and when to listen? When is it appropriate to talk about oneself and others and to share feelings, beliefs, and values? All of these issues are learned within the context of the family and must be acknowledged because they affect teaching and learning.

Culture provides a road map of life for human beings and is an essential tool for giving meaning to the world. The household or home is the cultural system with which an individual first comes in contact, and thus it is the foundation for learning in and of the world. No child is culturally deficient or deprived, because all cultures provide an adequate pattern of living and survival for their children. Although some students may come from homes where there is economic deprivation, or speak a dialect or language different from that of Standard American English, this does not mean that these students lack culture. What these students lack are middle-class resources, which if provided can bridge gaps in knowledge or experience. And because culture affects learning, teachers must go beyond merely recognizing cultural differences (Chapter 3).

Intercultural educators have cultural knowledge about themselves and others and use this knowledge to organize their classrooms and teaching to incorporate students' cultural backgrounds. Table 5.1 outlines some fundamentals that teachers need to know about their students in order to begin to plan and deliver effective pedagogy for English learners.

Finding Out about Students' Cultures.　Effective teachers are skillful observers of their classrooms and their students. They learn to look beyond the surface of what they see, suspend judgment, and instead use a unique lens—the ethnographic lens—that allows them to perceive and understand a particular situation, gain insight into student behavior, and even enhance their own understanding of why they view or react to a specific situation as they do. George and Louise Spindler (Spindler, 1982; Spindler & Spindler, 1963), cultural anthropologists, were some of the first to begin to use **ethnographic study** to understand the cultural processes underlying schools, school customs, and student behavior. The Spindlers suggested that teachers use a cultural lens—a different way of seeing—to understand and identify patterns and practices of life within classrooms.

table 5.1   Fundamentals That Teachers Should Know about Their Students

Category	Sample Questions
Basic and daily living patterns	Where does the student live? Who is present in the home? What are the routines in the home (waking/sleeping hours, for example)? What are the values about the extended family (the role of grandparents, other relatives living in the home, for example)?
Attitudes toward language usage	What language(s) are spoken in the home; who speaks which language(s) and to whom? How does the family/student see the role of primary language? How does the family value learning to speak English?
Literacy	Does the student read/write in native/primary language? What are the levels of literacy of household members? Are books or other printed materials present in the home? In which languages? Does the student have a library card?
Family occupation	What is the socioeconomic status or occupation of household members? Do both parents/guardians work?
Values	What role does "education" (various levels, elementary, secondary, higher) play in the household? How is success defined? How is ability or intelligence defined?
Social customs	What are the views of "time and space"? How are punctuality and speed in completing assignments viewed? Which activities do students complete quickly? How is personal space used in relation to self and others?
Symbolic systems	How does the student dress, comb hair, use accessories? Does student appearance reflect differences for male/female? What is culturally appropriate dress?
Rituals, ceremonies	Which celebrations (religious and otherwise) are celebrated, and how? What are the rituals important to students and families?
View of nature	How do students see themselves in relationship to nature? What is their behavior during natural phenomena such as lightning, earthquakes, and thunder?
Leisure	How do the individual and family members use their spare time?
Health and medicine	How is health viewed? How is disease treated? Does the family have non-Western approaches to healing and medication?
Interaction with institutions	Are the student and family familiar with how social institutions (educational, judicial, health) operate? Does student/family see social institutions as supportive and accessible to their needs? How is "authority" viewed?

Using an "ethnographic lens" also allows the teacher to shift perspective and begin to see and understand behavior from an insider's point of view. Henry Trueba (1989) was one of the first ethnographers to use this lens to examine specific student populations such as Mexican and Asian students. Delgado-Gaítan and Trueba (1991) also used ethnographies in their work with immigrant students and their families. This perspective is a powerful way for teachers to view the classroom, the lesson, or life in general from the perspective of a child who is learning to speak English.

A useful, clear source for conducting ethnographies is *Ethnographic Eyes: A Teacher's Guide to Classroom Observation* (Frank, 1999). Frank defined the ethnographic perspective as the study of culture based on multiple perspectives. Ethnographies are written descriptions of culture that allow teachers to open their eyes to other meanings of culture. The insights thus provided help teachers develop awareness and consciousness of a new way of thinking, leading to a change in their thinking about themselves and their own cultures. Ethnographic research and observation allow for an understanding that reality is not fixed, given, and objective, but rather is socially constructed, learned, and heavily dependent on perspective. It helps make explicit the role of language in shaping reality. This observational skill is an important tool in the pedagogical repertoire of the teacher of English learners.

For example, the questions in Table 5.1 can be useful in beginning to generate ethnographic data about a particular student. These questions can guide the teacher interested in finding out specific information about a child, which can later be used to inform his or her teaching.

Cultural Accommodation.   Culturally relevant teaching acknowledges the role that culture plays in teaching and learning, and is a way to bridge what students bring to school and the teaching practices found in schools. To make instruction culturally relevant, teachers use teaching strategies and methods that recognize and build on the way students have been taught to learn, behave, and use language. This model of responsive teaching also suggests that teachers examine the shortcomings of the Eurocentric cultural perspective—the learning styles, values, and academic content—that may create a cultural incongruence between teachers and English learners. Instructional accommodation allows students and teachers to meet halfway. This examination includes attaining clarity about the use of American Standard English.

Classroom Management Aligned with Humanistic Education

Pedagogy grounded in humanity and rooted in democratic principles is provided optimal conditions in a classroom that is also managed humanistically. Larrivee's work *Authentic Classroom Management* (1999) is an exemplar of a humanistic model of management that dramatically shifts the paradigm away from the view that student behavior is problematic or in need of reform. Larrivee's approach to management rests on the assumption that "effective classroom management begins with teacher self-awareness, self-control and self-reflection, not with the students" (p. viii).

Larrivee supported this position by suggesting that teacher responses to student behaviors reveal how secure and competent teachers feel as teachers. If teachers feel confident in their potential to be effective, they tend to solve problems and use management strategies that humanize, rather than dehumanize, students. Larrivee (1999) advocated that classroom management be humanizing and reinforced the idea that, like effective pedagogy, effective classroom management is more than a collection of skills and strategies, but instead a deliberate philosophical and ethical code of conduct:

> If teachers latch onto techniques for handling student behavior without examination of what kinds of responses to students would be congruent with their beliefs, aligned with their designated teaching structures and harmonious with their personal styles, they will just have a bag of tricks. (p. ix)

Although recognizing the challenge of managing today's classroom, Larrivee further explained, "The path cannot be preplanned—it must be lived. Meeting the challenge calls for teachers to resist establishing a culture of control in order to create an authentic community of learners" (p. ix).

Management That Creates a Community of Learners.   The classroom is a community; in a classroom that encourages humanistic behavior, students and teacher build relationships based on mutual respect and integrity. Student–teacher classroom interaction patterns are collaborative and equitable, with minimal favoritism. Daily routines and tasks are proactively planned so that classroom practices and teaching–learning structures promote acceptance of students from all cultural, social, and linguistic backgrounds.

Classrooms with low-achieving students (and English learners are often erroneously perceived as such because of their level of English proficiency) may have a restricted focus on interactions related to classroom behavior and may feature teacher–student interactions that reduce genuinely intellectual activities. Unfortunately, English learners are often perceived as "low status" and less able or competent to participate in class discussions or group projects. Teachers with integrity must be vigilant about the interactions in their classrooms and constantly reflect on how opportunities to talk and participate are structured.

Classrooms dominated by a few privileged students obstruct the possibilities for creating a community of learners. The community must involve all students authentically. Creating a community of learners involves the following factors:

- Becoming a reflective practitioner
- Planning that is preventive, not reactive
- Building democratic learning communities
- Communicating by keeping channels open
- Managing collaborative decision making
- Promoting student self-management and responsibility

Building Relationships.   Effective classroom management that is authentic and inclusive of all students requires more than discipline, rules, and routines. It includes building relationships between students and students, and between students and teacher, and is characterized by a safe and caring environment. A community of learners is grounded in integrity and collaboration, and students' emotional and personal needs are concurrently addressed along with their academic and social needs.

Such a classroom tends to focus on shared views of power and is less hierarchical and teacher-centered. Power is used collaboratively instead of coercively (Cummins, 1996). The role of the teacher is redefined as the teacher moves from manager to facilitator. Larrivee (1999) suggested that the shift in teacher role has tremendous implications and possibilities for transforming student–teacher interaction patterns.

An Adaptive Model of Classroom Management.   Hoover and Collier's (1986) model of classroom management, which is based on interactions and adaptations of classroom elements also provides a useful tool for creating communities of learners. Their model has been used primarily in classrooms comprising minority students and minority students with learning disabilities, but it is also applicable to classrooms in general. It integrates classroom management and curricular adaptations of four basic elements: content, instructional strategies, instructional settings, and student behaviors.

t a b l e 5 . 2   Adapting Instruction to Facilitate Classroom Management

Adaptation	Implementation
Response alternatives	Provide alternate modes of response, such as oral, rather than written, visual, or graphic.
Segmentation of assignments	Shorten assignments by dividing complex tasks into segments.
Student input, ownership	Incorporate students into the curricular planning process and decision making.
Student choice	Provide options for students—alternative assignments and activities.
Primary-language options	Provide opportunities for students to use primary language as they work.
Explicit communication	Communicate academic and behavioral expectations explicitly and repeatedly; restating in different ways if necessary.

Source: Hoover and Collier (1986).

Hoover and Collier (1986) proposed that curricular elements (choices made by the teacher) have important consequences for management. Thus, content, classroom setting, strategies, and student behavior are interdependent, and change in one will affect the others. Although Hoover and Collier did not focus on the teacher's role explicitly, their model posited implicitly the centrality of the teacher in planning and organizing a curriculum that is student-centered. Table 5.2 presents some of the techniques they suggest for adapting instruction.

Both Larrivee (1999) and Hoover and Collier's (1986) models of management support the idea that effective classroom managers are teachers with integrity. Classrooms characterized by respect and learning are student-centered, without the assumption that students must be controlled and managed by a set of rules that rest on coercive and dehumanizing power. Instead, teachers are facilitators and experts in human relationships—in being fully human—as well as in academic content, and they are able to create learning environments that honor and maintain their integrity as well as that of the students.

Conversational versus Academic Language

One of the most important theoretical concepts for teachers of English learners is that language plays a variety of roles in instruction. Language varies in difficulty depending on the functions for which it is used and the skill needed to use language in these various ways.

Language Functions

Halliday (1978) distinguished seven functions for language: instrumental, regulatory, representational, interactional, personal, heuristic, and imaginative (see also Chapter 8). More recently, Christie, Enz, and Vukelich (1997) proposed three broad domains of language use, each with specific functions (see Table 5.3.) Teachers of English learners recognize the wide range of language functions and use this knowledge to provide students with multiple opportunities for self-expression and social interaction.

table 5.3   Domains and Purposes of Language

Domain	Purpose
Self	Reveal, assert needs; fulfill personal needs; reach goals; direct and control self/others
Self and others	Interdependence; social interaction; share about self; express feelings
Self, others, world	Create, comprehend, find out, and communicate; expand knowledge, information; pretend, fantasize

Source: Adapted from Christie, Enz, and Vukelich (1997).

The language used in the classroom is a mix of Halliday's seven functions. Language is heuristic when it is used for problem solving, imaginative when art and poetry are evoked, personal and interpersonal when used for informal expression of feelings or relationships, instrumental when teachers use language to organize classroom activities, and regulatory when discipline is necessary. However, the key function of academic language is representational. Knowledge of all sorts is represented, often in abstract ways; students are expected to use language to re-represent knowledge by comparing, inferring, synthesizing, and so forth, developing and using higher-order thinking processes. Language used in these abstract, cognitively demanding ways is called cognitive academic language.

Cognitive Academic Language Proficiency

Cummins (1979, 1980) proposed two different, yet related, language skills: basic interpersonal conversational skills (BICS) and cognitive academic language proficiency (CALP). BICS is the language that allows students to communicate in daily social contexts in school; it is social, everyday, playground or hallway language. The mass media, particularly television viewed by English learners, is filled with BICS-type language; and the language required for classroom chores and social interaction with peers and adults also utilizes BICS.

The BICS–CALP distinction is one of the most useful concepts for teachers of English learners, and it greatly helps to explain student academic performance. The following anecdote by a seventh-grade science teacher, Mr. Sutton, aptly captures the usefulness of this distinction and its application to teaching.

Before I learned about the different types of language, I remember blaming my students because of what I thought was their refusal to speak English in my science classroom. Because I had no explanation for their not speaking in my classroom, I resorted to blaming them.

I recall two students, Tomas and Huey, speaking English in the hallways with their English-speaking peers. They were both sociable students and quite competent. I remember their speaking to me before class; they were polite. Yet once we began to "do science," it was as if they knew nothing, or didn't even know how to speak English. I remember talking about this in the faculty lounge. Mrs. Pointe (a seventh-grade social studies teacher) commented that she thought Tomas knew English, yet when he came into her social studies classroom he would say little and even refused to participate in most classroom activities.

We attended a seminar for teachers that dealt with the differences between the different types of language we can see in the school setting. The language that students like Tomas needed in English for my classroom was academic, technical, formal language—the language of science. This was very different from the conversational language he was using with his friends. We also learned that this conversational language is acquired and develops much quicker, and that the academic language takes much longer and requires more complex skills because it is used for literacy in the content area. The lights went on for me!

I realized that Tomas and Huey needed my support in acquiring this academic language so that they could function in my science classroom. Everything fell into place for me—or rather for them—after I learned this important distinction. I quickly began to look for ways to teach them this academic language. And more important, I didn't view their not doing science as lack of motivation or unwillingness. I realized they just did not know the language of science and part of my job was to teach them that language.

More about BICS.   According to Cummins (1981a) and others (Collier, 1987; Hakuta, Butler, & Witt, 2000), BICS can reach nativelike levels within two years of exposure to English. This finding rests on the assumption that the social environment of students is BICS-rich. It follows, then, that this is the linguistic repertoire students acquire first.

Another important aspect of BICS is that it is context embedded, meaning that students can communicate without relying exclusively on the linguistic code. BICS operates and is acquired in socially meaningful settings in which the situation can provide information to enhance or complete the meaning of what is said. For example, communication that takes place between two or more people in their everyday activities may not rely on or require words exclusively.

Thus an English learner can begin to understand that "hi" is an informal greeting because it is also accompanied by a smile or a wave of the hand. The oral expression of "hi," then, is quickly assimilated and understood because the context has provided much rich information to give it meaning and usefulness. CALP, on the other hand, is more challenging to acquire because it involves context-reduced communication. English learners tend to acquire BICS successfully without any intentional strategies, whereas CALP is taught almost exclusively and explicitly in schools.

Academic Language for School Tasks.   Performing school tasks successfully requires abstract and decontextualized language. CALP requires language background and knowledge to attain meaning. This linguistic cycle suggests that words cannot be separated from knowledge or learning. It is not possible to understand a topic without first understanding specific terminology relevant to that topic. And in order to learn specific terminology, a person must have some understanding of language. CALP also provides language for fundamental cognitive processes necessary for systematic thought such as categorizing, comparing, analyzing, and accommodating new experiences and knowledge. Content area academic knowledge and CALP tend to coexist—one cannot succeed without the other. Academic literacy requires in-depth knowledge necessary for college entrance and success; it also characterizes the language of a well-educated citizen in a democracy.

Transfer of Proficiency. One of the reasons English learners have difficulty acquiring CALP is that the linguistic resources these students bring through their primary language are not tapped or used. That is, most bilingual education programs transition students into English as quickly as possible based on the erroneous assumption that proficiency in English is separate from proficiency in a primary language, and that content and skills learned through the primary language do not transfer to English. Cummins's (1981b) common underlying proficiency (CUP) assumption is that primary and secondary languages have a shared foundation; this shared foundation provides the basis for transfer of cognitive language from L1 to L2.

An individual has to learn a new concept, and learn to read and write, only once. For example, he or she needs to learn the concept "book" only once; if learned in German (*buch*), for example, the concept does not have to be relearned or taught again—only how to say "book" in other languages. The same holds for literacy in general; acquiring deeper understanding of the functions of reading and writing and their relationship to thought and learning needs to occur only once. Therefore, once a student has a strong linguistic and literacy foundation in the primary language, learning a second language—and learning in general—builds on this foundation, and elements once learned do not need to be relearned. This accelerates acquisition of academic language in English.

Specially Designed Academic Instruction in English

Specially designed academic instruction in English (SDAIE) (also known as "sheltered instruction") was a response to the growing need for monolingual-English-speaking teachers to adapt and modify instruction for their English learners. As the population of English learners grew yet the number of bilingual teachers did not grow proportionately, teachers and schools had to do something about the "getting behind in content areas" phenomenon. SDAIE emerged in the 1980s to fill this gap under the assumption that if teachers adapted their traditional ways of teaching, English learners would be given access to content area curriculum, and ultimately could be participants in the academic discourse without falling behind in subject matter knowledge.

Students at the intermediate level of fluency or above can benefit if subject area teachers incorporate specific teaching modifications to make a lesson understandable. This provides additional instructional support to English learners rather than allowing them to "sink or swim" in a content class designed for native English speakers (Echevarria, Vogt, & Short, 2000).

What is SDAIE? What does it look like in classrooms? This section attempts to answer these questions and provide examples of adaptations embedded in the SDAIE approach.

What Is SDAIE?

Adapted instruction is intended to meet the needs of English learners in the following ways. According to Echevarria, Vogt, and Short (2000), students

1. Learn grade-appropriate content
2. Master English vocabulary and grammar

3. Learn "academic" English (this includes CALP, as well as ways in which English is used in content subjects)
4. Understand and use appropriate classroom behavior, such as turn taking, participation rules, and established routines

Teachers implementing SDAIE focus on their communication strategies to ensure that the messages used to present content area instruction are comprehensible to English learners. What this implies is that teachers address their students' language needs and present material by creating opportunities for students to be active learners and by designing curriculum that integrates student interaction, hands-on learning, use of visuals, and other pedagogical practices of good teaching.

Effective SDAIE teachers organize instruction by modifying complex information to demystify and simplify it so that students understand. SDAIE does not mean changing the curriculum; SDAIE means changing how teachers present the curriculum.

Challenging Students to Perform to their Maximum Potential.   In SDAIE instruction, teachers hold students to high expectations by using academic standards that are not watered down for English learners and that push students into higher zones of proximal development. Regardless of students' level of English proficiency, SDAIE teachers hold students to the same academic standards and push students to excel. Having limited literacy skills in English does not let students off the hook; instead, SDAIE teachers provide opportunities for students to perform to the limit of their potential on a daily basis.

Content Plus Language Objectives.   SDAIE also implies that teaching English learners is not an either/or proposition, which is how it has been posed in many secondary schools (that is, they either receive English-language development or they receive content area instruction). Effective sheltered instruction is proof that students can receive *both*, because content area knowledge is provided alongside English-language development.

The only thing that changes is that SDAIE teachers also address language objectives and implement these language goals by adapting the instructional delivery or activities of the lesson.

Reducing SDAIE to "Just Good Teaching."   Many student teachers, when presented with SDAIE, regard it as "just good teaching." This is a myth. Díaz-Rico and Weed (2002) and Echevarria, Vogt, and Short (2001) made the important distinction between SDAIE and good teaching: SDAIE teachers know their students' English-proficiency levels, acknowledge how these levels affect comprehension of content, and accordingly incorporate techniques that will provide comprehensible input by teaching language as well as content.

Many teachers fail to understand that, for English learners, achievement requires more than "trying hard." English learners can try their hardest and still encounter academic failure if the teacher does not modify lessons so they can understand what is expected of them in that particular class. SDAIE teachers teach with integrity and understand that it is their duty to adapt and modify their lessons so that all students have access to their rich curriculum. Table 5.4 compares "good teaching," which tends to exclude English learners, with SDAIE practices, or "good teaching that includes English learners."

table 5.4   The Myth of "Only Good Teaching" Compared to SDAIE

"Only Good Teaching"	SDAIE
Excludes English learners.	Includes English learners.
Includes academic goals.	Includes academic goals, language goals, and learning goals.
Uses teacher centered teaching.	Uses student-centered teaching and learning.
Talk is teacher dominated.	Opportunities for students to use language are designed and planned.
Learners tend to be passive.	Learners tend to be active.
Students are expected to adapt to the curriculum.	The curriculum is adapted by the teacher.
Modifications are random.	Modifications are planned and guided by students' language needs.
Curriculum is changed, or watered down, to make it accessible to English learners.	Curriculum remains the same but is modified to make it accessible to English learners.
English-language development issues are not incorporated or made visible in planning.	English-language development issues are incorporated in planning and/or teaching.
Comprehension errors are seen as due solely to content misunderstandings.	Comprehension errors may be due to language misunderstandings.

SDAIE: Overview of Core Elements

The goal of SDAIE is to provide access to content area knowledge through instructional modification and language development. In doing this, teachers know their students' academic and language needs, respect their humanity by believing that their students can and want to learn, and then begin to plan accordingly. Thus the disposition and attitude of the teacher is critical in setting the stage for a lesson that is successful and supportive of its students.

Teaching must take place in an environment that is rich in mutual respect and based on the belief that English learners have linguistic resources that teachers can tap to teach content and English-language development—these assumptions are the backbone of a successful SDAIE lesson. SDAIE includes the following pedagogical core elements: (1) content, (2) creating meaning through connections, (3) comprehensibility, (4) language interactions, (5) use of L1, (6) assessment, and (7) reflection/critical stance. Table 5.5 presents these core elements.

Access to Content

Content is the heart of a lesson that focuses the teaching and learning goals. Thoughtful planning is guided by content objectives, which ultimately help inform pedagogy and facilitate necessary modifications in the presentation of the curriculum. Language and learning-strategy objectives should reflect content selection and be closely aligned with content goals.

table 5.5   Core Elements of SDAIE

Content

Academic

Language

Learning

Materials and resources

Creating Meaning through Connections

Prior knowledge (personal background, content-related)

Connecting to students' lives

Connecting to other lessons, other subjects, schooling, previous learning

Linking previous to new knowledge
  Schema building
  Scaffolding
  Learning strategies

Comprehensibility

Messages with meaning (visuals, gestures, intonations, dramatization)

Use of multiple intelligences and learning styles

Modeling

Speech adjustment

Language Interactions

Opportunities to use language informally and formally

Questioning strategies

High expectations for language development by challenging students to perform beyond their potential

Language Interactions *(continued)*

Opportunities to use social and academic language
  Teacher to teacher (team teaching)
  Teacher to whole class
  Teacher to student
  Student to teacher
  Student to group
  Student to whole class
  Student to content or specific discipline
  Student to self
  Student to parents

Use of L1

Preview content

Clarification

Primary-language materials

Student interaction

Collaborative work

Assessment

Informal and formal

Ongoing comprehension checks

Multiple opportunities to show understanding

Alternative assessment

Self-assessment

Reflection/Critical Stance

Strengths

Areas for improvement

Academic Content Objectives.   How do teachers know what to teach? Content is guided by content standards in each of the discipline areas according to grade level. The content standards delineate what students are expected to know for each grade level. State committees develop these content standards and publish curricular goals for teachers to adopt. In lesson planning, teachers divide these curricular goals into units of study and then into daily lessons. Objectives are then developed for each lesson.

Language Objectives. Traditional lesson planning did not include language objectives. Language arts lessons may have included some aspects of language objectives, but these were not targeted at promoting English-language development for English learners. SDAIE lesson planning takes into account specific language demands in the content areas as well as student language needs and, in recognizing these, incorporates these in the planning. In California the English Language Development Standards provide the specific language standards that should be addressed as teachers plan. These standards are represented by proficiency levels and by grade level. Teachers identify the specific standards and then translate these into language objectives related to the academic goals of the lesson. These language objectives then help the teacher design the language demands of the academic lesson.

Learning-Strategy Objectives. Learning strategies are being recognized more and more as an integral part of teaching, an idea made explicit in Chamot and O'Malley's work in CALLA (see the discussion of CALLA later in this chapter). Learning strategies are the "how" of learning that should be made explicit to English learners. How does each student learn, and how do these strategies relate to academic work? By making learning strategies explicit and by developing them into specific objectives, SDAIE teachers can plan to target them in their instruction. This chapter suggests numerous ways in which teachers can select these learning strategies, incorporate them in their teaching, and make them visible to students. Learning strategies are addressed more fully later in this chapter.

Materials and Resources. The materials a teacher chooses in order to teach a lesson play a central role in the success of a lesson. Therefore, material selection is an important task when planning an SDAIE lesson and in modifying curriculum for English learners. This is particularly important given the central role that textbooks play in schools. The SDAIE teacher should be familiar with the textbooks used in the content areas, including the reading level required to access the content.

With this knowledge, the teacher can make appropriate modifications or adaptations when using the text and incorporate other resources that can supplement and enhance instruction. Teachers should also check the comprehensibility of the text and identify discourse patterns or jargon that may pose reading or comprehension challenges for English learners. Also, how are graphs, tables, or charts labeled? Is the text user-friendly? Does the text have a glossary? Does it invite the student to open the book and use it?

Many teachers have resource libraries in their classrooms stocked with primary-language materials such as dictionaries (some that are visual), encyclopedias, maps, charts, books, and computers bookmarked to specific sites related to the academic content. Para-educators or tutors often use these resource centers to provide further support to English learners.

Creating Meaning through Connections

Brain-based theory postulates that learners are engaged when the brain is able to create meaning by blending knowledge from previous experiences with that of present experiences. Effective SDAIE teachers thus orchestrate meaning by making connections explicitly instead of leaving this to chance. These connections can be made by tapping into students' prior knowledge, connecting to students' lives, connecting to their previous academic knowledge, and, finally, by linking or anchoring new knowledge to previous knowledge.

Prior Knowledge.   *Prior* means "occurring before." In the teaching context, prior knowledge refers to knowledge that students bring with them that can be tapped and built on during the lesson. In the following section we suggest that prior knowledge exists in two forms: (1) that gained from personal or life experiences and (2) academic knowledge that has been learned at school. SDAIE teachers pause in their lessons to create opportunities for students to display prior knowledge in whatever form it occurs, because both can be ultimately linked to academic content.

Personal Prior Knowledge.   Many English learners have rich backgrounds that have given them extensive funds of prior knowledge they can access and share given the opportunity.

A seventh-grade student from the state of Michoacán in Mexico worked with his father raising horses. Manuel began to talk about this one day when the teacher was talking about domestication of animals. After Mr. Thompson explained the concept of animal domestication, he asked the class if anyone knew examples of domestication and/or had experiences. Manual raised his hand and began to speak about how his father worked with horses. He began to explain at length about raising horses and how his father had told him about how horses, like dogs, had been "tamed" by people, and that this process had taken a long, long time.

Mr. Thompson was surprised to learn about Manuel's previous life experiences, which provided a natural link or bridge to the academic content of the lesson. He acknowledged the valuable knowledge and insights Manuel had as a result of his experiences with his father, and then selected key points Manuel had made (such as taming horses and history) to expand on the lesson on domestication. (MVB)

This example illustrates how teachers can provide opportunities for open discussion that allow students like Manuel to share experiences with others that not only enrich the academic content but also allow other students to see that English learners are not underachievers and unidimensional, but instead complex human beings with a wide range of experiences.

Academic-Related Knowledge.   Teachers tend to see prior knowledge primarily as those previous academic experiences students bring to the lesson. And as suggested earlier, some teachers view a lack of English proficiency as synonymous with lack of academic or intellectual knowledge. Many English learners who have had previous schooling possess rich academic knowledge in many content areas. Teachers who know their students' backgrounds can actively plan to tap into what students already know about the subject and extend this knowledge into the lesson.

Connecting to Students' Lives.   Manuel's experience served as an example of how personal prior knowledge can enhance a lesson by allowing students to share their experiences when discussing the content of a lesson. For example, Mr. Thompson can connect the academic and abstract concept of animal domestication with Manuel by talking about horses as one example of animal domestication. Mr. Thompson also knows that many of his students have dogs, so he continues connecting this concept to his students' lives. Learners tend to remember what has meaning. By thinking about the numerous ways in which an academic concept can be linked to students' lives, teachers can hook their students into the lesson, as well as involve them in retaining the information.

Connecting to Other Lessons.   Part of the cycle of teaching and planning is that teachers connect what is to be learned, or today's academic goals, with what has been studied earlier. In this way, students find coherency in their learning and see that concepts and learning are interrelated and interconnected. Again, using Mr. Thompson as an example, we can hear him connect previous lessons to today's lesson on domestication: "Remember last week when we studied about wild animals? Well, today we will study about another type of animal that was once wild but today is tamed or domesticated."

Linking Previous Knowledge to New Knowledge.   Examples from Mr. Thompson's class suggest that students may have previously acquired knowledge, or schemata, that he can tap in order to teach the lesson on domestication. However, in many instances students lack prior knowledge about the topic and will not succeed without the teacher's intervention and support. Schemata must be created, and this can be done successfully by scaffolding or using instructional techniques on a temporary basis to get the learner to master the content. Scaffolding provides the cognitive links that build new concepts and connect these newly learned concepts with previous knowledge. Scaffolding techniques include semantic mapping, graphic organizers, and discussions that tap into prior knowledge.

Comprehensibility

Krashen (1981, 1982) suggested that people acquire language by getting comprehensible input—messages that have meaning or that the listener understands. Those messages that we hear and do not understand sound like a "blob"—it is hard to hear where words begin and where they end. Knowing this, teachers make efforts to present messages or concepts in more than one way. Variety in the presentation of messages tends to increase comprehensibility; if students fail to get the message through Method A, the teacher can switch to Method B. The message remains the same—all that changes is the delivery.

Messages with Meaning.   Some messages with meaning provide visuals, holding true to the expression that "a picture is worth a thousand words." Pictures tend to provide a setting or context, which gives the listener cues that increase the meaning of the concept. The concept is introduced alongside the picture, providing a backdrop the listener can use to find meaning in the spoken-language message. Gestures, intonation, and role-playing or dramatization emphasize language by increasing its context and providing additional clues the listener can use for interpretation. Speech adjustment is also important, because many speakers of a foreign language state that they could understand if only the native speaker did not speak so fast. SDAIE teachers adjust their speech by slowing down (which is not the same as using baby talk) and enunciating clearly.

Table 5.6 presents a brief summary of the ways in which teachers modify speech to make themselves more understandable to English learners.

table 5.6   Teachers' Language Modifications in SDAIE

Type of Modification	Definition	Example
Precise articulation	Increased attention to enunciation so that consonants and vowels in words are understandable	"Trade your *homework* with the person *beside* you."
Use of gestures	Showing with hands what is to be done	[Make a swapping gesture with papers to act out "trading homework."]
Intonation	Increased stress on important concepts	"The number of *correct* answers goes at the top of the page."
Simplified syntax	Shorter sentences, with subject-verb-object word order	"Mark the papers. Give them back."
Semantic clarity	More concrete, basic vocabulary; fewer use of idioms	"Turn in your work. I mean, give me your homework."
Pragmatic distinctness	Frequent and longer pauses; slightly slower delivery	"Check the chemicals. . . . Check the list. . . . Be sure your team has all the chemicals for your experiment."
Use of discourse markers	Careful use of transition words, emphasis, and sequence markers	"Note this" to denote importance, or "now," "first," "second," and "last" to mark a sequence.
Use of organizational markers	Clearly indicating change of activity	"It's time for recess; . . . put away your books."
More structured discourse	Main idea easily recognized and supporting information following immediately	"Today we are learning about mole weight. . . . I will show you how to calculate mole weight to make the correct solution."
Use of clarification checks	Stopping instruction to ask students if they understand; monitoring students' comprehension	"Hold your thumb up in front of your chest if you understand how to use the formula for acceleration."
Soliciting written input	Having students write questions on index cards	"I have a card here asking for another explanation of longitude degrees and minutes. OK. . . ."
Repetition	Revisiting key vocabulary terms	"*Precipitation* means overall rain or snowfall; we are going to study the precipitation cycle."
Use of mini-TPR lessons to preteach key terms	Acting out terms to increase understandability	"'On the other hand': Carlos, stand over here, and Elena, stand here—you are 'on one hand,' he is 'on the other hand.'"
Use of primary language	Saying simple directions in the students' language(s)	"Tsai jher, over here, tsai nar, over there." (Mandarin)

Use of Multiple Intelligences.   The concept of multiple intelligences opens up additional opportunities for students to participate in a learning task. For example, traditional classrooms tend to be characterized by tasks that require verbal (Standard English) and logical or mathematical abilities. Many English learners are automatically excluded from these learning tasks and consequently denied access to the content area curriculum. Planning for a curriculum that incorporates multiple intelligences (Gardner, 1983, 1993) increases the possibilities of students gaining access to the content area.

In other words, teachers who plan learning tasks that incorporate abilities along the numerous intelligences open the door for many of our students to enter. Finding Out/ Descubrimiento (De Avila & Duncan, 1980) is an example of an elementary math and science curriculum that incorporates multiple intelligences in its work.

A relevant question teachers can ask as they plan is the following: How many kinds of intelligences are required to complete this task? The answer provides an accounting of how many opportunities are provided for students to succeed. Use of one intelligence will mean only one way to show success in a learning task, whereas the use of four intelligences will provide at least four opportunities for students to perform well. Teachers can do simple surveys of their students to establish which intelligences may be preferred by a class. In this way, the SDAIE lesson is sure to include all learners in the process.

Use of L1.   A theme running throughout this book is the importance of coming to know the students, which includes knowledge about their primary-language usage and skills. Teachers use students' primary-language experiences as prior knowledge and linguistic resources that students can tap to learn content area knowledge and improve English-language development. The use of the primary language can be a type of scaffolding that teachers use to introduce new knowledge; unfortunately, this strategy is frequently underutilized.

> When a language arts teacher in an eighth-grade classroom introduced the new theme for literature circles, she told the class, "This quarter we will be reading different novels with a central theme on speaking out, and today I will introduce all the books you can choose from." She wrote this theme on the board and asked several ELLs how to say "speaking out" in their language. Some ELLs used their bilingual dictionaries to translate the phrase. This was done in Korean, French, and Spanish. The teacher created a web and wrote students' translations phonetically around the English word, asking the class to repeat after each student. She made references to these words throughout the lesson (Sumaryono & Ortiz, 2004).

Preview of Content.   The primary language can be useful in previewing content and giving students an academic heads up on what to expect in a future lesson. This alleviates much anxiety because students know what to expect, and they can focus on the content and not on understanding what is being said. SDAIE teachers can plan this by having a para-educator preview material using the students' primary language, or teachers themselves can bring English learners together to preview content the day before the lesson.

Clarification.   Comprehension implies understanding, and the primary-language materials can be useful in clarifying concepts that may be difficult for students to grasp in English. Visual, multilingual dictionaries are useful in this clarifying process, because it is not unusual for a single word or concept to be a stumbling block in a learning task that may require more time. Student-centered classrooms abound with student-friendly materials that supplement texts and include primary-language materials for English learners.

Interaction

Planning how students will interact and use language in the classroom is important when the goal is both content mastery and language development. Teachers should plan for ongoing student interaction centered on academic tasks. Rather than same-ability grouping, collaborative work in mixed ability or heterogeneous groupings provides ample opportunities for English learners to interact, use language, hear native speakers, and share and learn from their peers in a low-anxiety setting. From these interactions, the SDAIE instructor can glean important information about student progress in both content learning and academic language development.

Group work, for example, allows students to collaborate on learning tasks and use language freely without having to worry about the presence of the teacher. SDAIE teachers recognize that student-centered classrooms provide multiple and ongoing opportunities to use language. One way to plan for language use is to consider the language interaction scenarios in Table 5.5.

Teachers can also have students conduct surveys of language use to identify the opportunities students have to use language in a day or even in a week. This activity can shed light on how students (and teachers) are using language.

Plans for Language Use.   Teachers might ask, "How am I planning for students to listen, speak, read, and write language on a daily basis?" Allowing students to speak and hear themselves and others is an important step in helping them develop language and acquire content knowledge. Most of us have experienced times when we have read a particular word again and again yet have not had the opportunity to speak it. Once we say the word (even if we pronounce it incorrectly), it takes on a life all its own and ceases to mystify or intimidate us. An analogy can be drawn with English learners when they are given the chance to use language in a low-anxiety environment.

Using Language Informally and Formally.   Language and the ability to use it remind us that there is a time and a place for certain kinds of language. Social contexts often determine the appropriateness of language, and English learners should be taught how language requirements can vary. Speaking English informally (using BICS), students communicate with their friends. For many classroom functions, however, the setting and content require formality and specific language. Therefore, part of SDAIE planning should include communicating to and modeling for students those certain disciplines that require different types of language. The formal language used in science, for example, is quite different from that used in the social sciences or to talk about historical events. Making these distinctions allows students to understand the complexity of human communication and to not feel intimidated by formal or academic language.

Assessment: Formal and Informal

Teachers implementing SDAIE strategies are also aware of the importance of assessing their English learners. Chapter 10 examines assessment of English learners in more depth, whereas the following discussion briefly touches on key considerations teachers need to make in evaluating their students.

Experiences with prospective teachers have shown that informal methods of assessment such as observation often go unrecognized by many SDAIE teachers. Interestingly, many teachers tend to identify assessment only with more formal measures such as quizzes, portfolios, or standardized tests. However, informal methods can be just as informative about students' work and progress if teachers include them in their repertoire and acknowledge them as integral parts of their lessons. Indeed, informal assessments can be useful and practical, particularly in secondary school settings, where a teacher may work with more than 125 students each day, and correcting that many papers on a frequent basis becomes unrealistic.

Ongoing Comprehension Checks.   Monitoring the progress of English learners involves checking for understanding of the concepts covered. Teachers can conduct ongoing comprehension checks to ensure that students are "with the lesson" and following along. Examples of ongoing comprehension checks include asking students to paraphrase to another student or to a group what is expected or learned in the lesson. Some teachers use hand signals to get a reading of how students are following along. The most important point is that teachers do not wait until the end of the lesson or unit, or until the day of the test, to find out if students are comprehending the lesson, but instead establish a conscious routine that checks for student comprehension. Also, asking students if they understand is not an effective way to check for understanding because most students will respond "yes" even when they do not understand.

Multiple Opportunities to Show Understanding.   Teachers of English learners should not rely on just one way for students to show that they are learning, but instead use multiple ways to determine whether students show understanding. Beginning students might show understanding by responding to questions with "yes" or "no," and intermediate students might report on their laboratory findings in a brief oral presentation or in a written report. More advanced English learners can participate in dramatizing or role-playing. Students of all levels can show understanding through drawings.

Alternative Assessment.   Teachers who provide multiple modes of assessing student knowledge are engaging in alternative modes of assessment. Thus teachers do not rely on one measure to determine whether a student has understood and can apply concepts. Alternative assessment includes methods such as **authentic assessments** that tend to capture what students have been taught and what they have learned in a genuine way.

Self- and Peer-Assessment.   An integral part of English learners' education is to help them take responsibility for their own learning. In modeling **self-assessment** and teaching students to self-assess, teachers provide students with an important skill. In this way, teachers can develop activities that help students pause to evaluate themselves to see how they are doing. Monitoring their own progress and learning allows students to become independent learners and to establish teaching and learning relationships with their teacher that prevent them from being embarrassed to ask for support or clarification.

English learners are quickly socialized to hide their gaps in knowledge and to avoid errors in their English-language development. Encouraging students to practice self-assessment creates learning environments in which not knowing everything is simply part of being a student; this is critical because errors or lack of comprehension can be common occurrences in the life of an English learner.

Peer assessment is also useful. To be useful, however, peer response must be modeled and taught as part of the learning process from the beginning, so that students are aware of ways they can prepare to become more deeply involved in the discussion of ideas and substantive issues. This helps students focus on the communicative content of the project and draws them together in a more respectful sharing of the messages they send.

Reflection/Critical Stance

As suggested in Figure 2.1 (see page 21), teachers with integrity look back and reflect on their teaching, their practices, and their own learning. Successful completion of the cycle of teaching involves taking a critical stance when looking back on the lesson for its strengths—those parts of the lesson that went well—and also those areas that need improvement. Future planning can be modified or enhanced by consciously knowing what needs to be maintained or improved, thus starting the cycle of teaching once again.

Questioning Strategies for English Learners

Effective questioning skills are closely linked to effective pedagogy. Skill in knowing what questions to ask and how to evaluate the responses is among the most important skills a teacher can have because of the link to cognitive and academic learning gains. Teachers' questions not only develop a framework for the subject matter involved (Woolfolk, 2004) but also set the tone for student engagement and participation (some questions engage students, whereas others disengage) and establish behavioral and cognitive expectations.

Teachers use questions frequently and for several purposes in their teaching. At times it is to check for comprehension, and other times it may be to probe for prior knowledge. The following section focuses exclusively on questioning and provides numerous ideas for teachers as they prepare their questions. What is important to remember is that good questions must be planned and thought out in lessons designed for English learners.

Students become aware of what is expected of them by the kinds of questions that teachers ask. Teachers who have high expectations for their students tend to spend less time on managerial or procedural questions, which focus on whether students know what to do, and dedicate more time to challenging students with more cognitively demanding or higher-order questions.

Core Elements and Goals of Good Questions

Groisser (1964) suggested that all good questions have the following core elements: They are purposeful, clear, brief, natural, thought provoking, limited in scope, and adapted to the level of the class. Furthermore, questions should be guided by specific aims, and teachers should ask themselves what they hope to gain from their questioning. Are questions intended to arouse student interest in the lesson or topic? Do the questions develop insights or provide the teacher with new knowledge? Is the purpose to support and strengthen students' learning, to encourage their thinking to go beyond the lesson or classroom, or to stimulate critical thinking? Is the purpose to test students' preparation, or to see if objectives have been met?

Classroom Discourse Patterns

The traditional **discourse** pattern for teachers when questioning students consists of a three-part pattern: *initiation* (teacher asks questions), *response* (students answer questions), and *reaction* (the teacher reacts by giving feedback that is praising, corrective, or expands or builds on the student response) (Burbules & Bruce, 2001). Although this tends to be the general pattern that is repeated again and again, what is important on a daily basis is how the teacher "spins" each of these elements of the pattern. In other words, the kinds of questions the teacher asks (not all questions are the same), how the students respond, and how the teacher reacts to the responses (not all responses are the same) will influence, to a high degree, the cognitive gains students make.

Sociocognitive Aspects of Questioning

According to Woolfolk (2004), questioning strategies play several roles in cognition; they do the following:

- Help students rehearse information for effective recall
- Work to identify gaps in students' knowledge base
- Provoke curiosity and long-term interest
- Initiate cognitive conflict by introducing new knowledge that may contradict previous knowledge
- Serve as cues, tips, or reminders that provide cognitive guidance and facilitation

The English learner benefits from questioning because the context automatically engages the learner in using language in various ways. Listening and speaking skills are immediately activated, shifting the learner into an active role. As they ask English learners questions, teachers challenge them cognitively and linguistically, integrating language skills with academic knowledge. Students are included in the curriculum because they are not allowed to be silent; instead, they are participants in the discussion.

Involvement is particularly important because English learners are frequently relegated to the role of mere observer or voyeur of classroom interaction. If they are questioned, however, their status is sustained with their peers, because students tend to believe that those who are asked and who answer questions are high-status students. Thus, when teachers ask English learners questions, they elevate these students' status within the social system of the classroom.

Questions at Various Levels

Bloom's taxonomy (1956) is a frequently used method for organizing thinking skills in the cognitive domain using a hierarchical system that ranges from lower-level to higher-level thinking skills. Table 5.7 lists the levels of the taxonomy, with a brief explanation and examples of questions within each of the levels.

table 5.7   Bloom's Taxonomy: Explanation and Questions at Each Level

Category	Explanation	Examples
Knowledge	Remembering	"What does *perspective* mean?" "Define *mitosis*."
Comprehension	Understanding and demonstrating understanding by using one's own words	"What does the chart on page 10 suggest?" "Explain the process of mutation in cells."
Application	Applying and using information to solve a problem; usually with a single answer	"Calculate the size of this room." "What would you include in the summary of this story?"
Analysis	Critical thinking; breaking or dividing material into parts and explaining relationships; making inferences	"Who influenced Mark Twain's writing style?" "Why was George Washington chosen to be the first president of the United States?"
Synthesis	Creating a new pattern or structure using original, divergent thinking	"What would you have done if you had been Abraham Lincoln during the Civil War?" "What title would you give this book?"
Evaluation	Using criteria to making judgments; assessing the merits of an idea	"Which story do you believe to be scarier? Why?" "Why do you choose this ending?"

Lower-level questions are referred to as those that include knowledge, comprehension, and application, whereas higher-level questions require analysis, synthesis, and evaluation. The Center for Teaching Excellence–Searle (2005) suggested that lower-level questions are generally appropriate for:

■ Evaluating students' preparation and comprehension
■ Diagnosing students' strengths and weaknesses
■ Reviewing and/or summarizing content

Higher-order questions are usually used for the following:

■ Encouraging students to think more deeply and critically
■ Problem solving
■ Encouraging discussions
■ Stimulating students to seek information on their own

Questions can also be categorized as convergent or divergent. Convergent questions tend to be lower-level questions that have only one right answer and usually deal with facts, such as

"When was the first steam engine built?" Divergent questions are viewed as being higher level and have many possible answers, such as "Which president is your favorite, and why?"

Questions That Match Student Needs

How does a teacher decide whether to use high- or low-level questions? In general, this depends on which thinking skills the teacher is trying to develop. With regard to English learners, the kinds of questions asked in English should also be informed by the learner's level of English proficiency. For example, beginning-level students should be encouraged to practice their English skills and be given opportunities for success by having low-level questions posed that require simple answers and focus on comprehension. This does not mean that students are let off the cognitive questioning hook, because teachers can ask high-level questions in the students' primary language and challenge English learners to analyze, synthesize, and provide evaluations.

Although questions are categorized as low level or high level, this does not necessarily mean that one type of question is better than the other, particularly when the skilled teacher can use questions intentionally for English-language development. Knowing one's students is critical, because only the teacher will know what is appropriate questioning in English for each child.

California's English Language Development Standards and the California English Language Development Test provide useful references about appropriate linguistic expectations for English learners that can inform and guide teacher questioning while encouraging the success of their English learners.

Increasing Wait Time

Wait time is another important aspect of the questioning pattern. Rowe (1974) found in her classic study that teachers wait an average of only one second for students to answer! She also found that by prolonging wait time to five seconds or longer, the length of student responses increased (short wait time, short answers). With more wait time, students used whole sentences with increased confidence, evidenced by their higher tones and increased speculative thinking. If there is a shift from student–teacher to student–student interaction, students' questions increase; and as teachers benefit by having more time to hear responses and to think, they revise their expectations of students and begin to increase the variety in the kinds of questions they ask.

Extending Rowe's important findings to English-learner populations, an important adaptation teachers can make in questioning English learners is to allow additional wait time for students to respond. If monolingual English speakers can make such tremendous gains by being given only four additional seconds to respond, we can only imagine how this can benefit English learners, as well as their teachers. Again, teachers need to consider students' levels of English proficiency because beginning students may need more time to respond to a question than those more advanced in their English skills.

Teachers' Reactions to Student Responses.   The way a teacher reacts to students' answers is also important, because reactions bring closure to the question-and-answer cycle and also give students feedback on the quality or accuracy of their answers. Sadker and Sadker (2003) report that nearly half of teachers' responses or reactions to student answers are simple affirmatives, such as "OK," with little specific feedback provided. To this point, Woolfolk (2004) suggested the following:

> If the answer is quick, firm and correct, simply accept the answer or ask another question. If the answer is correct, but hesitant, give the student feedback about why the answer is correct. . . . This allows you to explain the material again. . . . If the answer is partially or completely wrong, but the student has made an honest attempt, you should probe for more information, give clues, simplify the question, review the previous steps or reteach the material. If the student's answer is silly or careless, it is better simply to correct the answer and go on. (p. 451)

These tips can be useful to teachers of English learners as they encourage their students to practice their language skills, because the teacher's response focuses on what is said, not how it is said. Furthermore, English learners, like all students, need feedback that is explicit so that they can know about their progress.

Questioning Our Questioning

Research reveals that teachers ask from 30 to 120 questions an hour, or 210 to 840 questions in a seven-hour school day (Sadker & Sadker, 2003). This seems reason enough for teachers to be thoughtful in and mindful about their questioning. Teachers can reflect on and examine their questioning, activities that allow them to know what kinds of questions they are asking.

The Center for Teaching Development suggests four methods for collecting feedback: self-reviewing by video- or audiotaping a lesson, inviting a colleague to observe a mini-lesson, inviting a colleague to a videotape review of a lesson, and asking students about questions asked in class. The center's Website, www.oir.uiuc.edu/did/docs/QUESTION/quest4.htm, provides observation and feedback instruments teachers can use, including a sample of a student survey used with university-level students that can be adapted for elementary and secondary levels.

Challenging Students to Perform to Their Potential

Having high expectations is an important aspect of challenging students to perform to their potential, but this may not be sufficient if teachers fail to purposefully engineer and create opportunities that extend students' current levels of development. Faltis's "meaning-making invite" (2001) is a useful model of how teachers can coerce learners into a new knowledge system that challenges and pushes them into a new cognitive and intellectual space: "Meaning-making invite includes (a) language *beyond* what students currently understand and use for communication about academic content and (b) language that invites students to actively participate in the construction of meaning about academic content" (p. 116). Faltis (2001) purposely used the word *coerce* because it is the teacher's responsibility to make the learning in school enjoyable and challenging rather than boring or frustrating.

Meaning-making utilizes some of Vygotsky's theories as well as situated learning theories. According to Faltis (2001), Vygotsky found that students could understand more and communicate better about academic content in interaction with adults than they could on their own. Learning theory from a socially situated perspective suggests that using language and trying new things is socially motivated.

As suggested earlier, English learners must be provided ongoing daily opportunities to participate in second-language activities so that they begin to understand that language has different communicative purposes and can begin to apply this knowledge. As English learners are invited or coerced to participate in the discourse of the academic classroom,

> [T]hey have to work to come up with meaning that is precise, coherent, and appropriate to the particular community. In other words they have to negotiate meaning with the teacher or peers as they grapple with new academic content. (Faltis, 2001, p. 116)

As English learners are trying to figure out what is expected of them, they are negotiating meaning, and this automatically encourages them to acquire and try out the new language they need to make themselves understood. As the negotiation of meaning continues, discourse is again sustained, challenging students to extend their current levels of development. Faltis (2001) provided the following example to illustrate meaning-making invitation:

English learner: Uh how—how you feel 'bout elephants in movie Tarzan?

Teacher: How did I like the elephants in the Tarzan movie?

English learner: Yeah, how you feel about elephants?

Teacher: How did I feel about them? Did I like them?

English learner: Yeah, how did you feel about them. Were they good or bad? (p. 118)

By interacting with native speakers, English learners are challenged to produce language that approximates English, even if they have not been previously exposed to it. The teacher as native speaker can engage students in an academic discourse that asks for clarification, checks for understanding, and paraphrases learners' language to ensure comprehension.

Interestingly, Faltis (2001) suggested that being pushed into developing new language does not promote language acquisition, but it does confirm to the learner how new language can be used to discuss topics that matter and that have meaning for them, thus challenging students to work up to their potential.

Learning Strategies

Learning-strategy objectives were discussed earlier in the context of SDAIE. As suggested then, teachers must explicitly teach strategies that help students to think about how they learn and what steps are involved in all learning tasks.

Different learning strategies are appropriate for different content areas, just as different disciplines have different cognitive demands. Teachers should become familiar with these differences and ask, for example, "What are the strategies necessary for my students to learn to succeed in mathematics?" Teachers can then break down some of the learning demands of mathematics, recognizing, for example, that math requires adequate note taking and use of deductive reasoning. SDAIE teachers can then target these learning strategies by making them visible to their students and engaging students in opportunities to practice them during their learning tasks.

The CALLA Model as Strategic Teaching

Chamot and O'Malley's (1994) **cognitive academic language learning approach (CALLA)** model is useful in teaching mathematics, science, social sciences, and language arts to English learners. The strategic processes emphasized in teaching content area literacy to English learners involves explicit teaching of academic knowledge, language skills, and learning strategies.

Academic knowledge is guided primarily by content standards mandated by states and districts. Language skills are those that teachers need to target with regard to the needs of their English learners. In California and a few other states such as Texas, English-language development standards have been developed that identify the specific language skills teachers should target in listening, speaking, writing, and reading activities. As teachers prepare lessons and language objectives, they need to be aware of their students' English-proficiency levels and select language skills corresponding to those levels. Finally, learning strategies involve those skills that help students learn. Chamot and O'Malley (1994) suggested that academic learning is more effective combined with learning strategies (cognitive, metacognitive, and social–affective).

Strategic Instructional Practices for English Learners

Proficient, competent readers use a wide range of strategies to read; these strategies must be taught so that English learners can become strategic readers in English. Researchers such as Chamot and O'Malley (1994), in their work with English learners, suggest that language, content area knowledge, and literacy are not mutually exclusive and should be taught in an integrated, holistic manner. In teaching these strategies, teachers should explain and model and allow students to practice and accept responsibility for their learning.

This approach is collaborative and supports the teaching with integrity model proposed in this book because it is based on the assumption that students are equal partners in the teaching and learning process.

Service Learning

Service learning is a curricular option that teachers of English learners can use with their students because it lends itself to a community-relevant view of learning. That is, English learners who come from communities that have been historically subordinated may view schooling and learning as an opportunity to "give back" to their families and communities. Therefore, service learning is culturally congruent with many English learners, their families, and their communities. César Chávez's work is a model for leaders serving their communities, not as an obligation but as a way of life. Chávez believed that service strengthened not only the community but also those who served.

Service learning also provides opportunities for multiple experiences that benefit academic development. It helps students improve their language skills and social skills as well as their understanding of the target culture, the English-speaking community. Service-learning pedagogy connects decontextualized classroom experiences with the real world or outside experiences. Thus, as O'Grady and Chappell (2000) suggested, "service learning is an activity in which the academic and the experiential converge" (p. 209).

Service learning is not new to the U.S. educational landscape. The YMCA, for example, stands out as one example of an organization founded on the principles of community service.

More recently, AmeriCorps, the national service program founded during President Clinton's administration, created service-learning programs in K–12 and higher education settings through the program Learn and Serve America. Many high schools and under-graduate programs have established service-learning activities as a graduation requirement. Thus, service learning has become an integral part of the school curriculum.

What is service learning and, more specifically, what are its benefits? According to the National Society of Experiential Education (n.d.), service learning is any service expe-rience that is monitored, involves intentional learning goals, and incorporates active reflec-tion on the part of the learner. Another definition, by Jacoby and Associates (1996), suggests that service learning is experiential education in which students engage in activities that address human and community needs. Learning and development must involve structured opportunities with reflection and reciprocity as key concepts.

Service learning differs from field education and volunteerism in that the focus is on the persons being served as the main beneficiaries. Service learning that is shorter term is fre-quently referred to as project-based learning. An example of service learning is tutoring, in which a person may become involved in performing a service in a program already established.

> The best service learning projects provide students with an opportunity to develop skills and knowledge in real-life situations and meet a real community need. They reinforce the connections between school and community and teach students how to work collabora-tively with others to create change. (Díaz-Rico, 2004, p. 403)

For English learners, service learning provides numerous opportunities that benefit their learning of the English language by placing them in meaningful activities that lead to productive social and educative engagement.

Computer-Based Education

Computers have altered life in the United States in many ways and have had a significant impact on pedagogy. Their appearance in schools dates back to the early 1970s (Cotton, 1991), and today it is nearly impossible to find a school that is not equipped with comput-ers. Computers and textbooks sit side by side in many U.S. classrooms.

Cotton (1991) claims that the use of microcomputers expanded during the 1980s, and by the 1990s, U.S. schools had acquired over two million microcomputers, the number of schools owning computers increased from approximately 25 percent to virtually 100 percent, and more than half the states began requiring—or at least recommending—preservice tech-nology programs for all prospective teachers.

The information age has arrived, and the role computers play in disseminating, process-ing, and accumulating knowledge will undoubtedly continue to grow. The educational micro-computer and computer-assisted instruction are here to stay. What is computer-assisted instruction, and what kinds of learning activities are associated with this method of instruction?

Definitions Pertaining to Computers in the Classroom

Educators who use computers in the classroom use a diverse list of terms to describe learning activities. These include *computer-assisted instruction, computer-based instruction, computer-based education, computer-enriched instruction,* and *computer-managed instruction.* Several researchers (Bangert-Drowns, Kulik, & Kulik, 1985; Batey, 1986; Grimes, 1977) have attempted to synthesize some of the definitions. For example, *computer-based education (CBE)* and *computer-based instruction (CBI)* are the broadest terms and can refer to virtually any kind of computer used in educational settings. Table 5.8 lists computer terms used in education.

Benefits of Computer-Assisted Instruction

Extensive research summarized in Cotton (1991) supports the finding that the use of computer-assisted instruction (CAI) as a supplement to traditional, teacher-directed instruction produces achievement effects superior to those obtained with traditional instruction alone. Generally, these findings hold true for students of different ages and abilities, as well as for learning in diverse curriculum areas.

The positive effects of CAI on writing have also been documented (Batey, 1986; Bialo & Sivin, 1990; Collins & Sommers, 1984; Dickinson, 1986; Kinnaman, 1990; Rodríguez and Rodríguez, 1986). The evidence seems to be favorable, particularly when teachers emphasize the teaching of writing as a process. The writing-as-process approach encourages students to engage in prewriting activities, followed by drafting, revising, editing, and final publication, with each phase receiving frequent feedback from teachers or peer editors. Thus, writing is not viewed as a mere product, or finished text, but as a process.

English learners engaged in the writing process with computer-assisted instruction can undoubtedly reap these benefits. However, using computers for drill and practice on isolated subskills such as grammar and mechanics is not associated with improved writing skills. Again, researchers suggest that desirable outcomes are obtained when computers are used as part of a holistic writing-as-process approach. Collins and Sommers (1984) suggested that "microcomputers are counterproductive when used in a theoretical vacuum" (p. 7).

CAI also positively affects reading. Soe (2000) examined the effects of CAI on reading achievement. Soe conducted a meta-analysis of 17 research studies based on K–12 students and found that CAI does have a positive effect on reading achievement.

table 5.8   Computer Terms in Education

Term	Connotation
Computer-based education	Broadest term; can refer to any kind of educational use
Computer-based instruction (CBI)	Any educational use (drill and practice, instructional management)
Computer-assisted instruction (CAI)	More frequent term used in educational settings; activities usually supplement teacher-directed activities, but can stand alone (drill and practice, tutorials, simulations)
Computer-managed instruction (CMI)	Use of computer by school staff to organize student data, make decisions about students' test performance, keep records of student progress
Computer-enriched instruction (CEI)	Learning activities in which computers generate data or execute programs developed by students to provide enrichment; more unstructured
Computer-assisted language learning (CALL)	Use of computer to teach language and to drill specific language skills

Computer-assisted instruction yields other beneficial effects. Research studies have found that learning rates increase and content retention improves (Capper & Copple, 1985). Attitudes are also affected by use of microcomputers in that students' attitudes improve toward the use of computers in education, course content, school in general, and self as learner; attendance, time on task, and interstudent cooperation also improve (Cotton, 1991).

Several researchers have examined the effectiveness of CAI in different curricular areas. Although their findings are not conclusive, they indicate that CAI activities are most effective in the areas of science and foreign languages, followed by mathematics, reading, language arts, and English as a Second Language.

The Center for Applied Research in Educational Technology (CARET) (http://caret. iste.org/index.cfm) reports that technology in general can be used effectively to increase the learning of lower-performing, at-risk, and learning-disabled students. Technology is most effective when students use programs that are appropriate to their own language experience; when students use technology applications selected to address their unique needs, strengths, and weaknesses; and when students use instructional programs that continuously assess individual performance by adjusting the task difficulty to the ability and experience of the student.

The Best Use of Computers

How can teachers infuse technology into curriculum and instruction effectively? Table 5.9 presents recommendations provided by CARET indicating the conditions by which educators and education decision makers can most effectively integrate technology into instruction.

Computer-Assisted Language Learning (CALL).   English learners have unique needs for computer assistance in learning English. Computer-assisted language learning (CALL) uses microcomputers to support the language- and content area learning needs of English learners. Classrooms can be transformed through the use of computer multimedia, the Internet, and the World Wide Web. CALL has infinite potential, extending instructional experiences beyond the four walls of the classroom, the local school site, or the community. CALL supports the trends recommended earlier in the discussion of language teaching, such as writing as a process.

Classrooms integrating CALL use both software programs and online resources to help students achieve their individual language goals. The Internet connects students with

table 5.9   Effective Integration of Instruction with Technology

Type	Explanation
Align curriculum	Review and analyze the content of technology applications to determine whether new skills align with content standards.
Maximize use of technology	Enable students to acquire proficiency with the technology application prior to the onset of the content standards–based lesson.
Extend core curriculum	Support the development of instructional lessons and units that use technology to reinforce core curricula.
Integrate technology	Develop detailed plans to integrate technology as a tool to increase learning opportunities.

Source: http://caret.iste.org, retrieved June 30, 2004.

other parts of the world in real or delayed time (synchronous or asynchronous communication). Chat groups and listservs (electronic discussion groups on specific topics and/or resources) can connect students with their classmates, schoolmates, or students in other parts of the world. The Internet provides opportunities for students to talk to native speakers through e-mail and collaborate with other students as they develop their English skills.

Teachers can provide opportunities for students to have their own e-mail addresses or accounts (much like their own library cards in previous years). Many teachers now have students develop personal web pages, or collaborate in constructing a classroom web page. Search engines such as Google or Yahoo! help students find materials for individual research topics (Díaz-Rico & Weed, 2002).

Brave New Schools.   Cummins and Sayers (1997) described electronic communities of learning as essential elements in creating intercultural learning networks. Their book *Brave New Schools* presents portraits of teachers who are creating learning environments that showcase the use of microcomputers to prepare their students with the intellectual and cultural resources essential for success in multicultural global communities. Equity, literacy, and praxis are themes running throughout this book.

Cummins and Sayers (1997) suggested that inequity of access to technology resources, including computer networks, mirrors the unequal distribution of other human resources in public education. Therefore, schools and communities must be vigilant about providing equal access to computers for historically subordinated student populations such as English learners, students from lower socioeconomic backgrounds, females, and Latino, Native-, and African-American student populations. If unaddressed, the "cultural digital divide" will grow.

Computers should be part of the process of developing critical literacy and of involving students in understanding and resolving social issues (Cummins & Sayers, 1997). Computer literacy should not be an end in itself, but rather part of a process of awareness, understanding, and agency, or what Freire (1970) called *conscientizao*. In "brave new schools," computers are useful tools for engaging the individual in improving both local and global communities.

Conclusion: Pedagogy for English Learners

In summary, pedagogy for English learners requires more than providing stimulating, high-level academic content, more than curriculum design that is relevant to the community, and more than adapted instruction that includes cognitive academic language proficiency, appropriate questioning techniques, and explicit teaching of learning strategies, although these elements are essential. English learners also need culturally responsive teaching that connects their daily lives to the lives of their future, a future that undoubtedly will involve computer technology—but a future that we hope will foster communities awash in the beauty and originality of local cultures, full of neighbors that care for and serve one another, and rich with multiple languages. This is the United States we await, and English learners will play a key role.

6

Integrity in Designing and Planning Instruction for English Learners

Teachers plan instruction guided by standards while addressing students' needs.

e x p e c t a t i o n

■ Prospective teachers take cognitive, pedagogical, and individual factors into account in planning lessons for English-language development and for academic content. *(Element 7.16 of the California Teaching Performance Expectations. Reprinted by permission of the California Commission on Teacher Credentialing.)*

Teaching with Integrity and Standards

Standards-based instruction. Outcomes-based education. Performance-based teaching. High-stakes testing. National standards. State standards. Standards for teachers. Standards for content. Standards-based instruction for English-language learners. These are some of the concepts that are part of the most recent educational reform in the United States, the "standards movement." Teachers who understand the meaning of these concepts and their relationship to teaching and learning can plan lessons that facilitate access to high-status academic knowledge, as well as promote development of English-language skills.

This chapter is intended to place standards-driven instruction for English learners in a sociohistorical context, allowing the reader to gain a broader picture of the connection between designing lessons for English learners and broader schooling issues.

This discussion also addresses one of the key elements in the teaching with integrity model—clarity of vision. It focuses on planning standards-based instruction for English-language learners and includes examples of practical ways to plan for English learners using the backward design approach. Next, the importance of taking a critical stance to reflect on planning is addressed. This chapter closes with a discussion of how standards-based instruction for English learners can avoid compromising the integrity of the teacher and the learner.

Standards: A Brief History

Diane Ravitch, historian and former assistant secretary of education under President Ronald Reagan, is frequently cited as one of the architects of the modern standards movement. Her book *National Standards in American Education: A Citizen's Guide* (1995) suggested that just as standards have improved the daily lives of Americans, so will standards in education improve the effectiveness of education in the United States:

> Americans . . . expect strict standards to govern construction buildings, highways and tunnels; shoddy work would put lives at risk. They expect stringent standards to protect their drinking water, the food they want, and the air they breathe. . . . Standards are created because they improve the activity of life. (pp. 8–9)

> Standards can improve achievement by clearly defining what is to be taught and what kind of performance is expected. (p. 25)

Earlier, however, the national publication of *A Nation at Risk* (National Commission on Excellence in Education, 1983) initiated the modern standards movement by tracing the interconnectedness between the nation's financial security, economic competitiveness, and educational system. The educational preparation of the nation's youth (and ultimately teachers) prompted an educational summit led by President George H.W. Bush, which led to the publication of *The National Educational Goals Report: Building a Nation of Learners* (National Education Goals Panel [NEGP], 1991).

Shortly thereafter, the National Education Goals Panel (NEGP) and the National Council on Education Standards and Testing (NCEST) were established to implement these educational goals, and were charged with "addressing unprecedented questions regarding American education such as, what is the subject matter to be addressed? What types of assessment should be used? What standards of performance should be set?" (Marzano & Kendall, 1996, p. 3).

More recently, mandates resulting from the reauthorization of the Elementary and Secondary Education Act, December 2001, were manifested in the national legislation No Child Left Behind (2001), which instituted the role of the federal government within the standards movement in several ways. First, while the act sought to address the importance of maintaining high standards in education, it also "threatened" local districts by eliminating grants and other federal support if students did not meet specific testing expectations and if teachers were not fully certified or credentialed. The No Child Left Behind Act also set a precedent by addressing the importance of the language needs of English learners and by imposing pedagogical remedies as to how best to teach English.

Following the lead of the federal mandates, national subject matter organizations moved quickly to establish standards in their respective jurisdictions and content areas. Thus began the standards movement in teaching academic content, educating teachers, and teaching English to English-language learners.

What Is Standards-Based Instruction?

Standards-based instruction is intended to expose all students to high levels of academic learning and prepare them to attain high levels of performance. There are three dimensions to standards-based instruction: content standards, benchmarks, and performance standards.

Standards-based instruction tends to focus on **content standards** (language arts, science, social studies, and mathematics) that define what students should know and be able to do. Content standards are determined by external standard-setting bodies and are uniform across teaching contexts. As suggested earlier, there are different sets of standards at the national, state, and local levels. National subject matter organizations such as the National Council of Teachers of Mathematics and the National Science Teachers Association are also major players in underwriting national and state standards in their respective content areas.

The second dimension of standards-based instruction, *benchmarks,* identifies the expected understandings and skills for a content standard. Benchmarks are different for each grade level. Finally, *performance standards* describe how students are expected to perform or achieve so as to meet the desired content standards.

What Is Performance-Based Instruction?

An integral part of standards-based education involves performance-based standards, as these not only describe what students are expected to accomplish or perform, but also measure their academic progress. **Performance-based instruction** depends on teacher planning, because it is the teacher's responsibility to ensure that students meet the standards. Teachers must first design learning activities that will produce the desired evidence of learning and then detail what kind of evidence will substantiate this performance.

Performance-based assessment is the systematic observation of a pupil's actual performance and includes rating that performance according to preestablished criteria. This type of assessment involves both process and product in the performance of a task and frequently measures what students can do with what they know rather than how much they know. The term *authentic* is often used with performance assessment, connoting that the performance uses information, concepts, and skills in the ways people use them in the real world. Problem solving, thinking skills, cooperative learning, and the use of diverse learning styles are elements of performance-based tasks.

Standards-Based Instruction and Curriculum Objectives

State agencies publish standards documents that spell out what students should know and be able to do. Districts and schools then follow with curricular guides consistent with the state-initiated documents. Some districts provide their teachers with "pacing sheets." These allow the school to set a pace or a timeline that dictates the day(s) of the academic year on which teachers should be teaching specific standards or objectives.

For example, a pacing sheet might suggest that on or by October 22, Mrs. Johnson, the ninth-grade mathematics teacher, should be covering specific standards and addressing the specific objectives to meet those standards. In another school site, a classroom teacher plans instruction using curriculum guides at the specific grade level. Units might be organized based on a theme or, if the course is text driven, based on chapters in the text (instructional planning is discussed in greater detail later in this chapter).

Units or chapters are further divided into specific lessons. Each lesson contains the essential content area objectives. The classroom teacher is responsible for presenting the material in a comprehensible and meaningful way, arranging for students to participate in learning activities, and then evaluating the extent of the student's mastery of the material. Thus instruction and assessment are linked.

Standards-Based Instruction for English Learners

Additionally, in states such as California with an increasing number of English learners, there is a third type of standard, one that focuses on English-language skills in speaking, listening, reading, and writing. These **English Language Development (ELD) Standards** (CDE, 1999a) are population specific and identify five incremental levels of language proficiency: beginning, early intermediate, intermediate, early advanced, and advanced. Traditionally, most standards have been subject area specific, yet the fact that states such as California as well as the federal government, through No Child Left Behind, are instituting standards for the teaching of English learners points to the growing needs of this student population in U.S. schools.

The group Teachers of English to Speakers of Other Languages (TESOL) has also proposed English-language development standards, which address the following goals: (1) to use English to communicate in social settings, (2) to use English to achieve academically in all content areas, and (3) to use English in socially and culturally appropriate ways.

The National Board for Professional Teaching Standards (NBPTS) also includes the English as a New Language Standards as part of their English as a New Language Certificates:

> Accomplished teachers of linguistically and culturally diverse learners may be bilingual education teachers or English as a second language (ESL) teachers. Regardless of assignment or approach, such teachers work toward the same goals for their students: to develop students' proficiency in English; to provide students with access to important subject matter; and to assist students in becoming part of the fabric of the school and responsible members of democracy. (National Board for Professional Teaching Standards, 2005, p. 1)

Teachers in California and those certified by NBPTS, for example, must integrate English-language development standards within traditional content area instruction along with other standards. Table 6.1 provides an example of California's ELD standards for beginning and advanced levels of proficiency in reading and writing.

table 6.1   California English Language Development Proficiency Standards for Beginning
and Intermediate Learners in Grades 3–5 and 9–12

English Language Acquisition Category	Grades		
Listening and Speaking Strategies and Applications			
Beginning	3–5	Comprehension	Begin to speak with a few words or sentences, using some English phonemes and rudimentary English grammatical forms (e.g., single words or phrases).
			Answer simple questions with one- to two-word responses.
			Retell familiar stories and participate in short conversations by using appropriate gestures, expressions, and illustrative objects.
		Comprehension, organization and delivery of oral communication	Independently use common social greetings and simple repetitive phrases (e.g., "May I go and play?").
Beginning	9–12	Comprehension	Begin to speak with a few words or sentences, using some English phonemes and rudimentary English grammatical forms (e.g., single words or phrases).
			Ask and answer questions using simple sentences or phrases. Demonstrate comprehension of oral presentations and instructions through nonverbal responses.
		Analysis and evaluation of oral and media communications, comprehension	Respond with simple words or phrases to questions about simple written texts.
			Orally identify types of media by name (e.g., magazine, documentary film, news report).
Reading and Comprehension Strategies and Applications			
Advanced	3–5	Comprehension and analysis of grade-level appropriate text	Use resources in the text (such as ideas, illustrations, titles, etc., to draw inferences, conclusions, and make generalizations).
		Comprehension and analysis of grade-level appropriate text and expository critique	Describe main ideas and supporting details, including supporting evidence.
			Use text features such as format, diagrams, charts, glossaries, indexes, etc., to locate and draw information from text.

(continued)

table 6.1   California English Language Development Proficiency Standards for Beginning and Intermediate Learners in Grades 3–5 and 9–12 (Continued)

English Language Acquisition Category	Grades		
Reading and Comprehension Strategies and Applications			
	3–5 *(cont.)*	Structural features of informational materials	Identify significant structural (organization) patterns in text such as compare/contrast, sequence/chronological order, and cause/effect.
		Comprehension and analysis of grade-level appropriate text and expository critique, structural features of informational materials	Distinguish between fact/opinion, inference, and cause/effect in text.
Advanced	9–12	Comprehension and analysis of informational grade-level appropriate text	Apply knowledge of language to achieve meaning/comprehension from materials, literary text, and text in content areas.
		Comprehension and analysis of grade-level appropriate text and expository critique	Analyze the features and rhetorical styles of different types of public documents and how the authors use these features and devices.
		Structural features of informational materials	Identify how clarity is affected by patterns of organization, hierarchical structures, repetition of key ideas, syntax, and word choice in texts across content areas.
		Comprehension and analysis of grade-level appropriate text and expository critique, structural features of informational materials	Prepare an oral and written report that evaluates the credibility of an author's argument or defense of a claim by critiquing the relationship between generalizations and evidence. Prepare a bibliography for the report.
			Prepare a brief research or synthesizing paper in which content areas and ideas are analyzed from several sources to present a coherent argument or conclusion, including proper format and bibliography.

Source: Adapted from California Department of Education (1999), *English Language Development Standards for California Public Schools, Kindergarten through Grade Twelve.*

Standards for Teachers

Teacher education is also being driven by standards-based and performance-based reform. Therefore the course work in teacher education programs is organized to teach and evaluate what teachers should know and be able to do; this is also known as performance-based teacher education. For example, the National Commission for the Accreditation of Teacher Education (NCATE) developed, with the consensus of 33 constituent organizations, a set of standards that focuses on performance-based learning outcomes.

These new standards, known as the NCATE 2000 standards, require colleges and schools of education to use performance-based evidence to demonstrate that teacher candidates in all programs are gaining the knowledge, skills, and dispositions necessary to have a positive impact on K–12 schooling. These standards also emphasize the significance of discipline-specific pedagogical and content knowledge, increase accountability in teacher education and elevate the role of assessment.

Standards for Teachers of English Learners

State teaching commissions such as the **California Commission on Teacher Credentialing (CCTC)** are increasingly specific in their expectations for teachers' performance. The California Standards for the Teaching Profession (CSTP) is an example of a set of expectations for teacher performance adopted for statewide use as a standardized description of the expertise required of beginning teachers (see Chapter 1, Box 1.1, page 15).

More recently, California's Senate Bill 2042 (2002) furthered the implementation of performance-based teacher education by legislating teacher performance expectations for prospective teachers. Teachers credentialed under this new legislation are expected to complete a series of performance tasks to demonstrate their knowledge of pedagogy, discipline-specific knowledge, and planning for teaching specific populations such as students with special needs and English learners.

The need to educate English learners adequately is so critical that California designed a performance expectation specifically for English learners. "Teaching English Learners" is California's Teacher Performance Expectation Number 7, which explicitly defines the standards and expectations for teachers in planning and teaching English learners. Box 6.1 describes Teaching Performance Expectation Number 7, Teaching English Learners.

Standards and Testing: The Stakes Are High

The major element that differentiates the current reform in education from previous educational reforms is the testing element embedded in the standards movement. Curriculum standards must be implemented within a context of standardized teaching that measures how well standards are being met. Although this accountability appears innocuous and necessary to motivate student achievement, Wirt and Kirst (1997) suggested that this accountability is at the expense of equity. As equity is undermined, it becomes glaringly apparent that these "reforms" tend to be problematic and unfair, particularly with student populations such as the English learner.

> I believe that today's high-stakes tests, as they are used in most settings, are doing serious educational harm to children. Because of unsound high-stakes testing programs, many students are receiving educational experiences that are far less effective than they would have been if such programs had never been born. (Popham, 2001, p. 1)

For example, a high school exit exam might determine whether a student receives a high school diploma, regardless of passing grades in required schoolwork. Grade retention,

box 6.1

Teaching Performance Expectation 7 (Teaching English Learners)

Candidates for a Teaching Credential:

- Know and can apply pedagogical theories, principles, and instructional practices for comprehensive instruction of English learners
- Know and can apply theories, principles, and instructional practices for English Language Development leading to comprehensive literacy in English
- Are familiar with the philosophy, design, goals, and characteristics of programs for English-language development, including structured English immersion
- Implement an instructional program that facilitates English-language development, including reading, writing, listening and speaking skills, that logically progresses to the grade level read/language arts program for English speakers
- Draw upon information about students' backgrounds and prior learning, including students' assessed levels of literacy in English and their first languages, as well as their proficiency in English, to provide instruction differentiated in students' language abilities
- Understand how and when to collaborate with specialists and para-educators to support English language development
- Based on appropriate assessment information, select instructional materials and strategies, including activities in the area of visual and performing arts, to develop students' abilities to comprehend and produce English
- Use English that extends students' current level of development yet is still comprehensible
- Know how to analyze student errors in oral and written language in order to understand how to plan differentiated instruction
- Know and apply pedagogical theories, principles and practices for the development of academic language, comprehension, and knowledge in the subjects of the core curriculum
- Use systematic instructional strategies, including contextualizing key concepts, to make grade-appropriate or advanced curriculum content comprehensible to English learners
- Allow students to express meaning in a variety of ways, including their first language, and if available, manage first language support such as para-educators, peers, and books
- Use questioning strategies that model or represent familiar English grammatical constructions
- Make learning strategies explicit
- Understand how cognitive pedagogical and individual factors affect students' language acquisition
- Take these factors into account in planning for English language development for academic content

Source: California Teaching Performance Expectations. Reprinted by permission of the California Commission on Teacher Credentialing.

promotion, and school funding might depend on test scores, and in some situations depend on raising test scores. Auerbach (2002) noted that teachers and principals can be held accountable for raising test scores, and staff can be reassigned if test scores do not improve.

Testing: The Pressure Is On

The No Child Left Behind Act of 2001 put teeth in the standards movement by requiring all states to institute systems of accountability covering all public schools and students. All students in grades 3 through 8 are to be tested against rigorous standards in reading and math. Schools meeting or exceeding their progress will receive achievement awards, whereas those who fail to improve are subject to "corrective action." The stakes are high for those schools whose student populations tend to score lower on standardized tests because of socioeconomic status and/or English-language proficiency.

Assumptions Underlying Reform

Valdez Pierce (2003) questioned three assumptions underlying the "test as reform" movement and their implications for English learners. The first assumption is that standardized test scores are objective indicators of student learning. In reality, these tests reflect students' access to content area knowledge and their native-speaker levels of English-language proficiency. English learners may have neither the content area knowledge to perform well on these tests nor the native-speaker fluency these tests require.

Second, it is unreasonable to assume, as the standards movement does, that standardized tests will force the education system to be accountable based on the simple equation that increases in test scores imply increases in student learning. Because standardized tests scores are not normed on English learners' performance, it is incorrect to make inferences about performance based on these test scores.

The third assumption is that externally imposed, nationally developed tests will guide and improve classroom instruction. Teachers may be pressured by administrators to teach to the test in order to increase and maintain test scores, bringing into question the validity of the test scores into question. Furthermore, English learners' language development and progress are not fully captured by standardized testing, which fails to show improvement in their language learning.

Research has demonstrated that socioeconomic status is a strong predictor of standardized test performance. A significant majority of English learners in the United States live in poverty and occupy the lower socioeconomic stratum, placing them in double jeopardy. Also, English proficiency affects student performance, making tests and test results inaccurate at best and invalid at worst. Low testing performance by English learners may be difficult to explain and address, as it may not be clear whether the cause for low performance is limited English knowledge, insufficient knowledge in the content area tested, or a combination of both.

Standards versus Learners' Needs

Standards-based instruction, along with performance-based teaching and learning, tends to leave behind English learners and/or students who do not have middle-class family backgrounds. For example, a major assumption underlying standards-based instruction is that school funding and resources are equitably distributed and that teaching conditions are adequate across districts and schools. Research into access to challenging curricula provides evidence that Latino and African-American youth are less likely than whites to be placed in educational tracks with a curriculum that will adequately prepare them to meet content standards that will help them to attend college (González, 2002).

Proponents of standards-based reform argue that rigor in examination will motivate schools to improve service to economically disadvantaged students, many of whom are English learners. However, standardized testing does not accurately assess student achievement, and yet many educational interventions are made based on these testing results. Low scores for English learners, for example, may not be an accurate measure of a student's achievement or ability, but may be directly tied to ineffective instruction or lack of proficiency in English. Also, data reveal that Latinos and children from working-class backgrounds tend to attend schools with inexperienced, unprepared, and ineffective teachers.

How can these built-in contradictions be reconciled with the stated goals of the 2001 No Child Left Behind federal education act, which are that each student master a set of designated and standardized content? Although some may applaud the idea that educators are to be held accountable for maintaining high standards, the problem remains: how to implement these standards in a manner that does not further discourage already struggling students such as English learners. In California alone, English learners make up 40 percent of the student population and are growing up in poverty-level families in which English is not the home language. High performance expectations for teachers can prove effective only if classroom professionals are able to adapt instruction to meet the needs of English learners.

Identification, Assessment, Placement, and Reclassification of English Learners

It is critical to planning and teaching with integrity that teachers know about their English learners. Knowledge about the learner is an integral part of the process of instruction for English learners because this knowledge has direct implications for teacher planning. The individual backgrounds and academic knowledge that students bring to the classroom vary tremendously. The more teachers know their students as both individuals and members of linguistic, ethnic, racial, or religious groups, the more likely it is they can design meaningful learning opportunities. Knowledge about the learner also includes knowing a student's English-language levels (listening, speaking, reading, writing) and their literacy levels in their primary language, as well as their academic abilities. When teachers know what their students know and bring to the instructional circle, they can increase their English learners' opportunities to engage in lessons.

Many states recognize the importance of knowing the English learner's academic history and have mandated school districts to develop "master plans" describing how they will assess their students' English-language proficiency and primary-language skills. In some instances, students are interviewed about their background and previous schooling experiences. Many schools also interview the English learner's family and use this as an opportunity to establish positive communication between school and family. These school-level processes support effective instruction because, by systematically assessing their students' language abilities, teachers have access to information and can plan appropriately.

The following section describes the four dimensions central to a master plan for educating English learners: identification, assessment, placement, and reclassification.

Identification

In California, as in other states, districts and schools are required to deploy a systematic, standard way of identifying potential English learners. In California, for example, students are flagged as English learners when they first enroll in school and fill out the home language survey (HLS). A mandatory part of the enrollment process for all students in public schools, the HLS asks approximately four questions about the use of language(s) in the home, including the child's primary language. The HLS merely flags the child as having a language other than English in the home, without further assessment.

Assessment

After the student's home language is determined, assessment procedures enter the picture. The child is referred to a specialist who can properly assess the child's English skills, including literacy level. Some districts have established an assessment system whereby a battery of tests is administered to the student to obtain listening, speaking, reading, and writing levels in English and in the primary language. In California the **California English Language Development Test (CELDT)** (CDE, 2004a) is used to determine the level of English proficiency of new English learners, and it annually assesses their progress toward becoming fluent-English proficient. The CELDT is required by law and is aligned with the state English Language Development Standards adopted in 1999. Teachers are provided results of the assessments and given opportunities to understand how to read these results and apply them to their planning. By law the school must inform parents of test results within 30 calendar days of receiving data from the test publisher.

Many districts also give placement tests in mathematics to establish the child's performance level in mathematics. Other districts also interview the child and his or her parents to obtain background information and to establish whether any special concerns or circumstances exist. The fundamentals of identification, assessment, placement, and monitoring include the following:

1. A uniform way to identify students, preferably built into the enrollment/intake process of all new students
2. A uniform way to flag potential English learners, including assessment, placement, and reclassification information that is clearly outlined, documented, and given to teachers and staff
3. A team of credentialed individuals assigned to oversee this process
4. Determination of which standardized test(s) will be used to assess listening, speaking, reading, and writing skills in English
5. Additional tests selected, if necessary, to be a part of this assessment (including local, school, or teacher-developed tests)
6. A procedure established for assessment and disseminating assessment results to teachers, parents, and students, with appropriate accommodations for student with disabilities
7. Guidelines and timelines established for periodic assessment and reclassification of students
8. Close collaboration between counselors and other school staff responsible for placement of students in classes (particularly important in middle and high schools)
9. Meetings of teams of teachers and staff working with English learners at least once a year to review student progress
10. Close collaboration with the school study team to identify and observe English learners who may demonstrate the need for special education services, including gifted and talented placement

Placement

Placement refers to the instructional program assigned to an English learner that includes ESL and core classes. In secondary schools, this includes elective classes. The language program available at the site is the primary determiner of placement. English learners enrolling in a two-way immersion school may be fortunate to receive quality bilingual education; other students, enrolled in a school with a structured English immersion program, will receive all of their classroom instruction in English, with limited oral assistance in their primary language. Unfortunately, placement is not generally driven by student needs but by local language policies and preestablished language programs that increasingly do not use students' primary language for instruction.

In some cases, students simply are placed where there is room, because many schools and classrooms are filled to capacity. In these situations, teachers will want to flag these students in some way to remind themselves that these students have been inappropriately placed and require careful monitoring of their performance. Those students who are identified as "bilingual special education," or English learners with learning disabilities, also require careful placement so as not to deny these students English-language development opportunities.

Reclassification/Redesignation

One of the major goals of the programs for English learners is to help these students develop academic proficiency in English. **Reclassification** (also referred to as **redesignation**) of English learners involves the use of a set of criteria that students must meet in order to be reclassified as fluent-English proficient. Once a student meets the district's redesignation criteria, the student's linguistic status changes, and he or she ceases to be formally identified as "limited-English proficient."

Local districts, guided by policies consistent with state education codes, generally define redesignation. One local district in southern California defines redesignation as the stage attained by an English learner who has demonstrated that she or he is ready to participate fully in all-English instruction without special support services while meeting the district's multiple criteria. English learners must show English proficiency in reading, writing, listening, and speaking standards comparable to the proficiency of average students in the district of the same age and grade level. These multiple criteria include standardized tests, student performance (recent grades), teacher recommendation or input, and, in California, scores of intermediate or higher in listening/speaking, reading, and writing on the CELDT examination. In many secondary schools, a minimum of a C grade in all core subject areas must be earned. Many districts redesignate students throughout the year, and many states are now requiring that parents be notified (verbally and in writing) about the redesignation process.

Lesson Planning

Effective planning is essential for effective teaching. And effective teaching reflects careful and mindful planning. Although there are numerous definitions of **instructional planning,** the following general description is appropriate for our purposes: a design guiding student-learning activities toward specific intended outcomes. Instructional models also vary widely

box 6.2

Planning Pays: Research on Lesson Planning

- Students who tend to achieve more have teachers who planned and organized instruction prior to their teaching on a daily basis. (Brophy & Good, 1986)
- Teachers tend to consider content and instructional strategies before objectives as they plan. Less time is spent on objectives and assessment. (Morine, 1976)
- Students tend to achieve more if the teacher informs them of the lesson's objectives and if the teacher is specific about these objectives. Objectives tend to provide students with a sense of direction and security. (Levine & Long, 1981)
- Classroom management and subject matter tend to drive a lot of planning, with classroom management often taking priority in the planning. (Thornton, 1991)
- Teachers utilize mental imagery, indicating that more planning goes on in the mind than on paper. (Earle, 1992)
- Development of routines in planning increases efficiency. Developing schedules, groupings of students, time management, for example, develop practice and familiarity that makes planning easier for teachers. (Evertson & Emmer, 1982)

(from direct instruction to the inquiry method, for example), yet traditional activity-based lesson plans tend to have three fundamental components: what is to be taught (content objective), how students will be taught (instructional approach), and what students have learned (assessment).

The Research on Lesson Planning

Although planning is central to effective teaching, little research has been conducted in this area, with most of it being descriptive, occurring within the past 20 years, and conducted at the elementary school level (Wilen, Ishler, Hutchison, & Kindsvatter, 2000).

Some generalizations can be made from the research on instructional planning that help to address relevant issues as teachers prepare to teach English learners. Box 6.2 highlights some of the research findings on planning.

In short, research findings support the importance of teachers' making careful instructional decisions, and standards-based instruction is intended to focus the content, activities, and assessment in planning so that lessons are more than fun and engaging and loosely guided by arbitrarily selected content.

Planning to Teach English Learners

Standards-based instruction for English learners has introduced two new dimensions to traditional lesson planning. The need to address language development issues in a classroom comprising English learners has prompted teachers to address language objectives. Including learning-strategy objectives in lesson plans is the second adaptation, which addresses the importance of explicitly teaching students how to be successful learners. The following summarizes the three dimensions of beginning to plan to teach English learners:

1. *Content objective:* address grade-level content standards
2. *Learning-strategy objective:* how to learn; strategies

3. *English-language objective:* language standards
   Speaking
   Listening
   Reading
   Writing

These planning modifications are discussed below in detail.

Choosing Content Objectives.   The question of what to teach is primarily driven by content standards at a particular grade level. This procedure is straightforward and rather systematic. After selecting a content objective in line with district and state mandates for the specific grade level and the unit of instruction, teachers examine the curriculum from the perspective of their English learners, or from a language perspective (Short, Echevarria, & Vogt, 2003; Short & Echevarria, 2004/2005). For example, what are the specific linguistic demands of the content? This can help teachers begin to break down and deconstruct how specific language abilities are embedded (and assumed) in the content standard and, ultimately, what is required of students to meet this objective.

Looking at content standards with "language eyes" can also help teachers identify what aspects of English (listening, speaking, reading, and writing) students need to apply in order to succeed in the class, or to attain the content standards. Furthermore, examining the curriculum from a language perspective begins to set the stage for teachers to see curriculum planning as an integrated whole instead of as isolated parts. Content, language, and learning objectives are thus seen as interdependent and not as separate pieces in planning.

Choosing Learning-Strategy Objectives.   As suggested in Chapter 2, learning strategies are not a traditional element of lesson plans. As teachers recognize the importance of explicitly teaching students how to learn, learning-strategy objectives increasingly are included in their planning. Chamot and O'Malley (1994) suggested the following about the importance of teaching learning strategies:

> The basic premise is that students will learn academic language and content more effectively by using learning strategies. That is, students who use strategic approaches to learning will comprehend spoken and written language more effectively, learn new information with greater facility, and be able to retain and use their second language better than students who do not use learning strategies. (p. 58)

Learning strategies are framed in a cognitive model of learning representing the dynamic process underlying learning. These strategies can be taught explicitly so that these strategies transfer to new tasks.

The learning-strategy objective is chosen from a repertoire that is appropriate for the cognitive development level of the students. Learning strategies are chosen from five areas: Piagetian developmental stages (concrete or formal operations); cognitive (graphic organizers, critical or creative thinking techniques); metacognitive (student goal setting, planning, self-monitoring, or self-assessing); social–affective (cooperative learning, emotional self-control, self-esteem building); or study skills (text processing, time management, etc.) (see Chapter 5). Chamot and O'Malley (1994) suggested the following in choosing learning strategies:

- The curriculum (content) determines the strategy selected: Which strategies are needed for this discipline or course?
- Start with a small number of strategies.
- Use tasks of moderate difficulty.
- Use strategies grounded in research or shown to work.
- Use strategies that apply to different content domains such as social studies, science, physical education, as students are more likely to adopt the strategy as part of their repertoire (p. 66).

The teacher who keeps a list of these strategies can draw on a repertoire of skills that students revisit in subsequent lessons throughout the year. For example, a fourth-grade science lesson might have as its objective a Piagetian concrete operations task: classifying plants according to biological characteristics. A high school history lesson might include a critical thinking objective, separating fact from opinion. A middle school mathematics learning-strategy objective might be to learn how to work in groups to generate algebra-themed story problems. All these learning-strategy objectives have in common is that they teach a skill that students can use to enhance their cognitive, metacognitive, social–affective, or study skills repertoire—skills not specific to one content but generalizable over a variety of contents and contexts.

Choosing English-Language Development Objectives.   In many schools, placement data may be available for each English learner as a result of assessment tests that were given upon classification (in the case of California, the results of the CELDT). In Alhambra Unified School District, for example, a file for each English learner, the English Language Development Progress Profile, comprises a folder that has the five levels of the ELD framework (beginning, early intermediate, intermediate, early advanced, advanced) printed on the front and back cover; as a student completes each item on a particular level, a check is entered in that box and evidence is stored in the folder, if required. Yearly CELDT scores are registered as benchmarks. The folder travels with the student until he or she is reclassified (redesignated).

For example, under listening and speaking (beginning), the following four items are available:

1. Responds to simple directions and questions using physical actions
2. Answers simple questions with one- or two-word responses
3. Demonstrates understanding of social interaction/conversation in small-group and face-to-face contexts
4. Demonstrates comprehension of stories through active listening/participation.

When planning a lesson for a class in which a beginning-level English learner is present, the language objective of the lesson for this student (or usually a group of such students) might be chosen from one of these four items. If the lesson involves reading, an item might be chosen from the reading comprehension items at the beginning level (example: "Identifies the basic sequence of events in stories read aloud using key words, pictures, or student-generated drawings"). See Table 6.1 for examples of strategies and applications using English-Language Development Standards. When the lesson is completed successfully, the particular item on the student's profile can be checked.

Two ideas are important here. First, the lesson contains specific language objectives adapted to the student's needs. Second, when the lesson is successful, the assessment documents not only the success of the lesson but also the advancement of the student's ELD progress. In some cases, such as the writing strategies and applications section of the ELD framework, actual student work samples are put in the folder as documentation. Thus the language objective of a particular lesson might be to produce and evaluate such a work sample.

For those schools in which the language objectives are not delineated as they are in California's English Language Development Standards, there are several steps teachers can take to develop language objectives. Using language eyes, the teacher examines the curriculum and content standards that must be addressed from a language perspective and identifies the language demands posed by the content standard. What is the language (listening, speaking, reading, or writing) that students need to know? Which areas of language may be a challenge to English learners, given their abilities? What is realistic to expect given the students' language skills and English-proficiency levels in listening, speaking, reading, and writing? Which aspects of the language need to be targeted to facilitate success for English-language learners? Answering these questions helps teachers plan language objectives and helps them identify necessary adaptations of the lessons in order to provide English learners with access to academic knowledge.

Assessment.   Assessment is an integral part of planning and instruction and should not be an afterthought or add-on to the instructional process. There is tendency for teachers to leave assessment out of the planning cycle when addressing the need to meet the content objectives. And because planning for English learners includes both the learning-strategy and the language objectives, this poses another challenge to ensuring that assessment is considered appropriately. Teachers must be vigilant in their planning of how they will assess what students learned (in all three dimensions—content, learning, and language); otherwise it is difficult to complete the process of instruction if assessment is lacking, as suggested earlier in Figure 2.2 (see page 34).

Beyond Design for Assessment.   In their discussion of backward design (a useful planning method), Wiggins and McTighe (1998) claim that teachers think as "assessors" when they are guided by the primary question, "What counts as evidence of understanding?" and not, "What would count as evidence of successful teaching?" They suggest:

> Urge teachers to think of students as juries think of the accused: innocent (of understanding) until proven guilty by a preponderance of evidence that is more than circumstantial. That is why it is vital for teachers to think like assessors and not just activity designers. (p. 65)

Wiggins and McTighe reiterate the importance of using multiple and varying methods to assess, and the importance of assessing in-depth understanding (quality of understanding, or, do students really get it?) rather than superficial knowledge.

Also, teachers of English learners must determine whether the assessment(s) will capture the academic gains (in language and learning) made by English learners. Determining whether the culminating activities are inclusive in such a way that English learners will have an opportunity to demonstrate what they have learned with regard to content, language, and learning strategies is also important.

Evaluation provides feedback to the teacher and students about what was learned (academic, learning, and language goals attained) and provides evidence of meeting the desired standards. Reflecting on the effectiveness of the lesson is essential in making necessary adjustments for future lesson plans.

Student Self-Assessment.   Teachers do not always have to be involved in designing and implementing assessment activities. Teachers can teach students to be active players in monitoring their own progress and work. Helping students acquire academic habits and facilitating student empowerment involves providing students with opportunities to take responsibility for their learning, which includes monitoring their growth and progress.

As teachers plan assessment, activities should be included that put students in the "assessor's seat," or allow them to evaluate and, when appropriate, grade their own work. These self-assessment activities can be done individually; the teacher routinely meets with individual students and engages them in self-monitoring, assessment discussions, or progress reports.

Authentic Assessment.   The discussion in this chapter focuses primarily on assessment as part of lesson plans and used primarily to monitor student academic and language progress in the classroom. This assessment is often referred to as *alternative* or *authentic assessment,* which includes teacher-made tests and multiple forms of evaluation. Teachers who teach for student understanding (as opposed to regurgitation of knowledge) have no choice but to assess students' understanding in multiple ways.

Planning performance-based instruction begins with assessment, in asking the preliminary question, "What student competence will be documented, and how will the evidence look?" The instruction, then, becomes a process of preparing this evidence, although in some learning contexts, authentic assessment is naturally integrated with the learning activity. Take physical education classes, for example, in which the specific outcomes are based on performances that capture the level of learning that has been achieved. In this setting, the assessment occurs as a natural extension of the content objective (as well as learning and ELD objectives) and can be observed and documented readily.

Portfolios are one of the most popular forms of authentic assessment and are particularly useful in assessing content, learning, and language objectives. A **portfolio** is a collection of student work that represents student progress. Teachers of English learners view portfolios as excellent methods of assessment because they provide clear evidence of student progress while also providing teachers with information to help make and modify instructional decisions. Box 6.3 lists numerous examples of authentic or performance-based assessment, along with the four elements of lesson planning for English learners (objectives, instruction, assessment, and critical stance).

In performance-based assessment, the emphasis is on students' ability to demonstrate specific skills and competencies and their ability to apply these skills and competencies. It is not uncommon for teachers to create activities that assess reading and writing, for example, when the intent is to assess content knowledge of specific skills. As assessment is planned, it may be useful to consistently check, asking the following questions: What

box 6.3

Examples of Authentic Assessment Guided by Content, Learning, and Language Objectives

1. *Producing a product:* Early intermediate English learners in Ms. Nakao's sixth-grade science class are asked to work as a group (learning-strategy objective); to develop a graph showing data they have collected of a plant experiment (content objective); and then prepare and deliver a short oral presentation (language objective) of the findings of their experiment.

2. *Realistic word problems:* Mr. Santini's third-grade early advanced English learners in mathematics are challenged to make notes (learning-strategy objective) and write a word problem (language objective: writing) that is relevant to their class by applying multiplication concepts (content objective) recently learned.

3. *Text retelling:* Intermediate English learners in Mrs. Taylor's ninth-grade language arts class are encouraged to read a passage from *To Kill A Mockingbird* (content objective) in a small cooperative group (learning-strategy objective) and then retell the section read by identifying the main idea and using detailed sentences (language objective).

4. *Drawing to demonstrate comprehension:* Mr. Arciniega's beginning English learners in his senior art class are asked to visualize and design (learning-strategy objective) an advertising campaign (content objective) for a forthcoming theater production as a way to demonstrate comprehension (language objective) and application of concepts learned.

content, learning, and language skills are assessed? Is this what standards-based instruction intends? Performance-based assessment *can* be used to evaluate reading and writing if that is what is intended. What is important is that teachers be clear and focused about what skill they are measuring.

Rubrics for Assessment.   Rubrics translate the evidence obtained in authentic assessment into letter grades. **Rubrics** are general descriptions of predetermined outcomes, behaviors, or criteria that can be correlated with a grade, if necessary. Rubrics make the standards for performance explicit and can be used in all content areas.

In some ways, the ELD framework is performance based. Language objectives in the lesson plans are designed so that in completing the lesson, the English learner also advances systematically in English skills as documented by the ELD profile—and, ultimately, by yearly CELDT scores (in California).

The Lesson Adapted to the English Learner

Each lesson, then, accomplishes three goals. First, content is taught in alignment with content standards. Second, learning strategies are taught that systematically build a student's learning capacities. Third, the lesson is specifically adapted for English learners by including a language objective that advances their English skills in a systematic, documented way.

These three objectives are not isolated from one another but are integrated. For example, a lesson about right triangles has a content objective drawn, perhaps, from the third-grade mathematics framework. The learning-strategy objective may be to practice the cooperative learning strategy of reciprocal teaching, in which students create questions to quiz one another on the elements of "right-triangle-ness." The language objective for beginning English learners might be, "Answers simple questions with one- or two-word responses," and for intermediate English learners, "Ask/answer instructional questions using simple sentences." (Note that different language objectives are built into the lesson to meet the needs of English learners at two different ELD levels.)

The Primary Language: A Useful Adaptation.   Another planning adaptation for English-language development is the inclusion of the primary language, including primary-language materials. For example, those teachers who speak their students' primary language(s) can target specific concepts or terms central to the lesson and present these in the students' primary language(s). These can be planned in advance and integrated with the content objectives.

It is not uncommon in secondary classrooms to see teachers with a list of technical or discipline-specific terms that they want students to learn as part of the content. Why not translate and present these terms to students in English and their primary language(s) as another way to provide access to a lesson? Monolingual English-speaking students also benefit from being exposed to academic concepts in different languages. Teachers can plan to incorporate materials in their students' primary language(s) by having available dictionaries, encyclopedias, and, when possible, bilingual textbooks. Technology can also be useful when computer stations are "bookmarked" to specific sites that provide English-language support to students in specific content areas and with specific topics.

What Teachers Need to Know to Adapt Lessons

Chapter 7 contains extensive suggestions on ways to adapt instructional delivery to the assessed needs of learners across various content domains. Following is an outline describing general knowledge that teachers of English learners must possess to plan and implement adaptations:

Adapting lessons requires teachers to do the following:

- Know their students' backgrounds and academic, language, and learning needs
- Possess subject matter knowledge
- Possess pedagogical knowledge in teaching content areas
- Possess knowledge of the role of language in teaching
- Understand how language is used in the classroom
- Understand academic language
- Possess knowledge about language development
- Possess knowledge about language teaching
- Understand relevant issues related to English learners' learning
- Understand the purpose of assessment in learning
- Understand the role of assessment in standards-based instruction for English learners
- Possess knowledge of multiple ways to assess

Conclusion: What Makes an Effective Instructional Plan?

Lesson planning, then, is drawn from district, state, and national content standards. It is augmented by professional training of teachers in preservice programs, in-service institutes, and

professional conferences. In planning to teach English learners, teachers make three considerations: addressing the standards through content objectives, including learning strategies that
help students to learn, and adapting lessons by including English-language objectives to address
English-language development. Teachers must also plan assessment activities that capture all
three aspects of lesson planning in order to complete the cycle of teaching for English learners.

Planning for English learners must be grounded in high-quality instruction in the
content areas and in language development. It must also incorporate learning strategies to
help students learn, and must include modifications appropriate to the language levels of
English learners, including the use of the primary language.

Critical Stance

Taking a critical stance is the final step in lesson planning; it allows the process of instruction for English learners to end and, in turn, renews the cycle of teaching and planning. As
teachers contemplate and reflect on their work with a critical eye, they are reflecting on their
planning, on their implementation, and on student learning. Some questions teachers can
use to frame critical contemplation of their teaching are listed in Box 6.4.

When planning, teachers draw from the foundation and application domains as seen
in Figure 2.2 (page 34). Effective planning must be informed by knowledge about the
learner, by theories of learning and language acquisition, and by pedagogical knowledge. Applying or implementing successful lessons requires planning that is framed in the learner's
academic, English-language, and primary-language development. These areas of application are then contemplated critically or assessed, and new information is added to update
learning theories, learner characteristics, and pedagogical foundations—all providing feedback to the cycle of application, foundations, planning, and assessment. This results in new
planning, and the process of instruction for English learners continues.

Critical Contemplation in Lesson Planning

- Identify strengths in the lesson.
- Were content, learning, and language objectives clearly stated to students?
- Were students, including English learners, engaged in the lesson?
- How many opportunities were provided for English-language development?
- What evidence do I have to demonstrate that lesson adaptations for English learners were adequate?
- Which evidence demonstrated learning by English learners?
- Which opportunities allowed for students to self-assess and be responsible for their own learning?
- Identify areas that may require changes for improvement in the lesson:
     ____Planning
     ____Objectives
          ____content
          ____learning-strategy
          ____language
     ____Instruction
     ____Assessment

Teaching to the Humanity of Students

The most important aspect of planning and, ultimately, teaching using the English-language development standards is to know students. The teaching with integrity model suggests that because teaching is a humanistic enterprise, grounded in art and science, teachers must use pedagogy that is humanizing, and that acknowledges the learner as a person first, and as an English learner second.

Students vary in motivation, self-esteem, primary-language skill, and academic background knowledge. All of these factors (and other environmental factors) affect their progress and speed in English-language acquisition. This knowledge becomes extremely useful and practical when planning adaptations.

It is not uncommon to hear students in teacher preparation classes claim that they do not know who their English learners are, or whether they have any in their classes. This invisibility is particularly evident in middle and high schools, where teachers work in busy, crowded classrooms and the schools often lack adequate communication channels.

Elementary or secondary school teachers may want to implement beginning-of-the-year activities and include student questionnaires or surveys to get to know about the academic and English-language backgrounds of their students, as well as their interests. In secondary schools, activities to identify English learners in the classroom should be included as part of these icebreakers. Many websites offer ideas about activities for getting acquainted and ways to get to know one's students (www.daveseslcafe.com, for example).

Establishing a relationship with students is central to a teacher's ability to reach and teach them. Not speaking the students' primary language should not discourage teachers from making and maintaining contact with students and their families. Teachers can be creative in seeking linguistic resources and ways to reach their English learners. They will learn much about their students (and themselves) that will be invaluable in creating a positive learning environment in their classroom.

The Art and Science of Teaching

Teaching is both a humanistic enterprise and a science. It is a science because extensive research on teaching and learning has taken place over the past 100 years, research that has been used to establish relationships between specific pedagogy and desired outcomes. It is a humanistic enterprise because many psychological and sociocultural factors must be considered in the challenge to elicit the highest quality learning from each student.

As teachers begin to plan to teach English learners, they must remember that if they do not maintain a critical stance or perspective, curriculum development can become a technical activity rather than a creative decision-making and empowering endeavor. Poplin and Weeres (1992) found that students become more disengaged as the curriculum, texts, and assignments become more standardized. The multiple demands placed on teachers by the different standards of accountability can keep a teacher so preoccupied that focus is lost on what students most need.

Teachers must be vigilant about the implications of teaching to the test. Teachers with integrity understand their role in designing curriculum that is rigorous, engaging, and accessible to all students and take a critical stance toward the testing frenzy that is part of their context. Teaching with integrity means preserving the humanity inherent in the teaching act in the face of the inhumanity imposed by external, never-ending demands such as standards.

7 Promoting Academic Achievement of English Learners

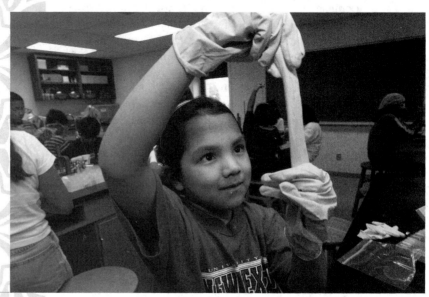

Hands–on projects involve students actively with science content.

expectation

Prospective teachers . . .

■ Select instructional materials and strategies, including activities in the area of visual and performing arts, to develop students' abilities to comprehend and produce English based on appropriate assessment information. *(Element 7.7 of the California Teaching Performance Expectations)*

■ Know and apply pedagogical theories, principles and practices for the development of academic language, comprehension and knowledge in the subjects of the core curriculum. *(Element 7.10 of the California Teaching Performance Expectations)*

■ Use systematic instructional strategies, including contextualizing key concepts, to make grade-appropriate or advanced curriculum content comprehensible to English learners. *(Element 7.11 of the California Teaching Performance Expectations. Reprinted by permission of the California Commission on Teacher Credentialing.)*

Many teachers of English learners are first and foremost responsible for content area instruction at specific grade levels rather than specifically ELD. Most teachers of English learners see content instruction as a priority; hence, it is the primary area of instructional application (see Figure 2.2, page 34). This chapter addresses pedagogical adaptations for standards-based instruction in the content areas for English learners at the elementary and secondary levels.

Content Standards for English Learners

Each **content area** has a specialized knowledge base, specific outcomes, content standards, content vocabulary, and particular means for organizing information. Applying content standards for English learners has been a contentious issue. Are they expected to achieve the same **standards** as their native-English-speaking peers? How are they given access to the same challenging content as their peers? How can teachers address the dual tasks of teaching content *and* language (McKeon, 1994)?

Incorporating both content and language objectives has been problematic for content teachers. This chapter specifically addresses language difficulties for English learners in mathematics, science, social studies, physical education, music, and visual arts. Literature as a content area is addressed in Chapter 8. *The CALLA Handbook* (Chamot & O'Malley, 1994) helps teachers understand the language demands of various disciplines. SDAIE instruction is addressed in Chapter 5 of this text.

Academic Content in Multiple Subjects

No matter what the subject, good teaching for English learners requires attention to five aspects (see Box 7.1). In the following sections, and again when single-subject instruction is discussed, each of these aspects is addressed.

Elementary School Mathematics

Common wisdom holds that mathematics, characterized by symbols, is "language-free" but mathematics is not a subject that students with little proficiency in English can easily master. Specially designed activities and teaching strategies must be incorporated into the mathematics program so that these students have the opportunity to develop their mathematics potential.

---

box 7.1

Five Keys to Content Adaptation for English Learners

- How do the content standards address English learners?
- What are the academic language requirements of the content?
- What activity system is used to teach the content (including teacher and student activity)?
- How is mastery of the standards assessed?
- What resources are available to teach the content?

Content Standards for Mathematics.   The document *Principles and Standards for Mathematics* from the National Council of Teachers of Mathematics (NCTM, 2000), features three principles specifically relevant for English learners: equity (high expectations and strong support for all students); teaching (challenging and supporting students to learn mathematics well); and learning (actively building new knowledge from experience and prior knowledge to learn mathematics with understanding).

NCTM has proclaimed equity as the first principle in *Principles and Standards for Mathematics* (2000):

> All students, regardless of their personal characteristics, backgrounds, or physical challenges, must have opportunities to study—and support to learn—mathematics. Equity does not mean that every student should receive identical instruction; instead, it demands that reasonable and appropriate accommodations be made as needed to promote access and attainment for all students. (p. 12)

The document suggests best practices that are applicable and relevant for teaching English learners, such as depth over breadth ("Curricula can be offered so that students can explore mathematics more deeply rather than more rapidly" [p. 368]) and use of grouping ("Students can effectively learn mathematics in heterogeneous groups if structures are developed to provide appropriate, differentiated support for a range of students" [p. 368]). Exploring mathematics in depth allows English learners to move beyond superficial, rote understanding (Sheffield & Cruikshank, 2005).

The Language of Mathematics.   Language difficulties for English learners lie in vocabulary, syntax, semantics, and discourse. Vocabulary in mathematics includes technical words such as *numerator, divisor,* and *exponent.* Words such as *regroup, factor,* and *table* have a meaning different from everyday usage. Two or more mathematical concepts may combine to form a different concept: *line segment, cross multiply.* A variety of terms can signal the same mathematical operation: *add, and, plus, sum, combine,* and *increased by* all represent addition (Dale & Cuevas, 1992).

Problems with meaning (semantics) occur when natural language becomes the language of mathematics. For example, in the problem "Five times a number is two more than ten times the number," students must recognize that "a number" and "the number" refer to the same quantity. Technical language has precise, codified meaning and must be learned in context. Discourse features that are unlike those of everyday English characterize the text used in mathematics. Also, charts and graphs are an integral part of mathematics text, not a supplement, and must be read up and down as well as left to right.

The teacher's use of language in mathematics can be tailored to elicit different responses from students in various stages of language acquisition. For example, when teaching triangle shapes, the teacher may ask a beginning English learner the question, "Show me the right triangle"; to intermediate students, "What do we call this shape?"; and for advanced students, "What makes a right triangle?"

The Activity System: Using Students' Interests and Experiences.   Teachers can incorporate students' interests into mathematics instruction. For example, sports fans can learn to calculate batting average or points per game. Students who shop can help to keep purchases within budget, determine the best-priced item, and estimate the added tax.

Student interaction and group work can encourage students to try out ideas and learn mathematical strategies from their peers. Using inquiry-based approaches that emphasize open-ended problems with multiple solutions allows students to solve problems in their own ways. Heterogeneous group work provides opportunities for students to use and practice mathematical language in English as well as in the primary language.

Many activities in mathematics lend themselves to multicultural reference. Systems of numeration and measurements that originated in ancient civilizations (Egypt, Inca, Aztec, Maya) can be explored and contrasted (Hatfield, Edwards, Bitter, & Morrow, 2004). Such basic operations as regrouping to subtract, finding the greatest common factor, and performing long division are done differently around the world, and students may have insights to share.

Assessment in Mathematics. Although traditional assessment in mathematics focuses on the mastery of algorithms, many alternative forms of assessment can be used to measure mathematical thinking and problem solving. Authentic assessment allows the teacher to assess mathematics understanding while students are actively engaged in such learning as running a school store or simulating trade on the stock market. Flexible expectations allow different pacing for students in basic versus advanced math skills.

Resources for English Learners. An organized support system for teaching math includes resource books, technology, and human resources. To supplement classroom instruction, the World Wide Web features a vast source of problems, contests, enrichment, and teacher resources that are not addressed in textbooks. Mentors who represent diverse linguistic and cultural groups within the school system, volunteers from the community, and experts who agree to respond to questions by e-mail can help students understand how math opens doors to professions and careers.

Family Math is a program that focuses on families learning mathematics together in support of the elementary math curriculum. Adults and children come to Family Math classes together once a week for several weeks, doing activities in small groups of two or three families working together. As a follow-up, family members use inexpensive materials found in the home (e.g., bottle caps, toothpicks, coins) to practice ideas that were presented in class. Materials are presented in English and Spanish (University of California at Berkeley, 2005).

Adapting math instruction for English learners takes many forms. Table 7.1 provides ideas for several types of adaptations in a math center set up to teach multiplication.

Elementary School Social Studies

Social studies helps young people develop the ability to make informed and reasoned decisions as citizens of a culturally diverse, democratic society in an interdependent world, and to gain a historical perspective as a lens through which to understand current events.

Standards and Goals for Social Studies. By implementing certain strategies on a regular basis, teachers have found that their English learners are able to achieve the broad goals of social studies: global education, multicultural education, environmental education, law-related education, gender-equity education, character/values education, current events, and personal identity and critical thinking in the modern world (National Council for the Social

table 7.1   Adapting Math Centers for English Learners: Multiplication Station Activities

Unadapted Center	Suggested Adaptations
1. Shopping Spree: Students look at a menu of items to buy. Their task is to spend exactly $25.	Directions can be in pictorial form.
2. Circles and Stars: Students play a multiplication game with a partner by rolling 1 die to determine how many circles to draw and then rolling a different colored die to draw the number of stars in each circle. They express the problem in a mathematical sentence and find the product.	A peer or older tutor can be stationed at the center to explain directions in L1.
3. Patterns of Multiples: Students place number tiles on a 0–99 chart to explore patterns of multiples.	Students of various English levels can work together.
4. Comparison Game: Students draw two cards from a standard deck of cards in which the face cards have been removed and ace is equal to one. They express the problem in a mathematical sentence and find the product. Their partner repeats the process above. Finally, they spin a "more or less" spinner to determine the winner for that round.	A pair of students can observe while another pair plays until they get the idea.
5. 4 in a Row: Students spin spinners to determine the product of two numbers and then cover the product on a hundreds board. The winner is the first person to cover 4 squares in a row. If the number is already covered, the student doesn't play that turn.	Instructions can be written in the primary language(s).

Source: http://mathforum.org/t2t/message.taco?thread=5024&message=4.

Studies, 1994). These goals represent major opportunities for English learners to acquire intellectual tools and communicative skills.

The National Council for the Social Studies (1994) emphasizes that learning social studies is a constructive process in which students experience social studies topics and then define, refine, and integrate their knowledge. In this process, higher-level thinking skills are identified as goals: understanding concepts (e.g., change and continuity), understanding generalizations, decision making and problem solving, and developing attitudes and dispositions about the social world (such as willingness to suspend judgment about a situation until sufficient evidence is available).

Language: Using Family Histories.   Because history has taken place in many languages, a strong social studies curriculum builds on dual-language skills. Students can use communication skills in two languages to gather oral histories from their families and communities. For more information about oral history projects, read "Junior Historians: Doing Oral History with ESL and Bilingual Students" (Olmedo, 1993).

As a discipline, social studies is concept-rich in ideas that may be difficult to depict in visuals. Student interaction is necessary if students are to acquire concepts and then be able to apply them in situations different from the one in which they acquired them. Inquiry skills that are used first in the classroom and then in the community help students to practice what they are learning in authentic situations (Sunal & Haas, 2005).

The Activity System: Using Thematic Curricular Units.   Thematic units combine language skills with concepts in the social studies curriculum. For example, students studying a fifth-grade unit on "Settlement of the West" can examine the legal issues involved in the Chinese Exclusion Act, compare the various cultures that came into contact in the Southwest, and delve into the history of local communities. Films, videos, computer simulations, literature, nonfiction texts, and oral discussions help students develop conceptual knowledge. Research skills, group work, and even classroom dramatics are involved as students act out the signing of treaties and other cultural events.

Assessment.   Assessment of all students must be equitable in a social studies program. English learners can show proficiency in multiple ways: portfolios, performance assessments, written reports, role-plays, and research projects. When high-stakes educational decisions for individual students are made, the decisions should be based on a variety of assessments rather than on a single test score. Assessments of students in social studies should be designed and used to further the goal of educating students to be active citizens in a democratic society (see Chapter 10 for more on assessment).

Resources for English Learners: The Internet.   Classroom teachers can combine the enormous range of resources from the Internet with other instructional resources and methods. For instance, imagine reading Tacitus's eyewitness account of the burning of Rome, including the descriptions of "helpless old and young" fleeing the fire; or Corporal E. C. Nightingale's frightening memories from the deck of the battleship *Arizona* in 1941. Both of these are available to teachers and students at www.ibiscom.com. Field trips via the Internet include visiting the White House (www.whitehouse.gov), exhibitions of African and pre-Columbian Native American art (www.artic.edu), or a tour of the Egyptian pyramids (www.pbs.org/wgbh/nova/pyramid). Many of the virtual field trip sites are designed specifically for education, featuring lesson plans and interactive student activities (see www.internet4classrooms.com/social.html).

Students can create their own virtual field trips of local historical sites, or even of their school. Ms. Rosie Beccera Davies's third-grade class at Washington Elementary School in Montebello, California, made a historical Website for their community, beginning with the Gabrielino Indians and including many local historical sites.

Elementary School Science

Science teaching is a complex activity. To teach science well, teachers must adapt instruction to make the content accessible to English learners and firmly believe that all students can learn science.

Science Content Standards.   The National Science Education Standards as well as specific standards set by the states have themes in common: a focus on the process of scientific inquiry and development of interests and abilities across a wide spectrum of science domains, including life science, earth science, and physical science. Most science instruction uses a variety of means by which students have the opportunity to learn by receiving direct instruction, reading textbooks and supplemental materials, solving problems, and doing investigations and experiments both in the classroom and in the outside world.

The Language of Science: Building on Cultural Backgrounds.   Across the domains of life, earth, and physical science, the vocabulary load can be extreme. All the basic principles of SDAIE instruction are needed: the use of charts, real objects, pictures, audiovisual enrichment, and so forth. Students should be encouraged to draw examples from their lives in order to share information with students from different backgrounds, validating their own experiences and learning to communicate in English.

Science instruction organized around common science themes (e.g., the nature of matter, magnetic energy) or societal issues (e.g., water pollution, drug addiction) makes scientific knowledge relevant to students' lives. This makes science more approachable, allowing for more understanding and reflection, and permits key vocabulary to be used again and again.

English-language development must be an objective in all science instruction. Teachers should preview vocabulary terms to be used in a lesson before beginning, including the names of equipment and activities that will be used. Students need to be taught text-processing techniques (how to take notes, how to reread text for answers to study questions, how to read charts and picture captions) and then held to a high level of recall about the information they read (Anderson & Gunderson, 2004). To assist their scientific-language learning, students can receive special training in following written instructions for procedures or experiments and in using glossaries.

The Activity System: Inquiry/Discovery.   Misunderstandings can arise from attempts to comprehend oral lectures (Kessler, Quinn, & Fathman, 1992). In contrast, when science is taught through discovery methods, English learners construct science knowledge, allowing them to see and feel the meaning of words instead of just hearing the definitions.

Carrying out investigations within a group of students with heterogeneous levels of English skills stimulates English learners' proficiency. Writing summaries of procedures and results, preparing verbal presentations, and verbally explaining picture and diagrams extend language. To ensure maximum involvement within each group, each student should be assigned a specific task (e.g., experimenter, observer, recorder, mathematician), and tasks should rotate among the students from lesson to lesson.

Assessment in Science Education.   The hands-on nature of problem solving in science can naturally align with performance-based assessment. By performing actual science activities, students are actively demonstrating the skills for which assessment holds them responsible. The use of formative assessment involves teachers in offering guidance and feedback so the given skills can be accomplished.

Use of Science Resources Outside of School.   The school science program often extends beyond the walls of the school to the resources of the community. Teachers can work with local personnel, such as those at science-rich centers (museums, industries, universities, etc.), to plan for the use of exhibits and educational programs that enhance the study of a particular topic. In addition, the physical environment in and around the school can be used as a living laboratory for the study of natural phenomena.

A wide diversity of scientists has made significant contributions to scientific knowledge in the United States. Studying these role models promotes respect by all students for the accomplishments of people of many different backgrounds and helps students who share the culture of the scientists to imagine a successful career in science.

Physical Education in the Elementary School

Physical education in the elementary schools suffers from its marginalization as a discipline (fewer and fewer schools employ specialized physical education teachers). Increasingly, physical fitness is a part of the classroom teacher's multiple subjects. The lack of elementary-level physical education programs is often mentioned in connection with the increased incidence of childhood obesity, bringing a sense of public health urgency to its implementation.

Standards for Physical Education.   Physical education—and its associated discipline, health—has many aspects: lifetime fitness and fitness testing; developmentally appropriate activities; sports; dance, gymnastics, and games; accountability to, and relations with, the public; physical safety; self-esteem and responsibility; and inclusion of all students, including special-needs students. Each of these issues has ramifications for English learners.

Standard 6 of the National Association for Sport and Physical Education (NASPE) addresses diversity: "The teacher understands how individuals differ in their approaches to learning and creates appropriate instruction adapted to diverse learners" (National Association for Sport and Physical Education, 2005, n.p.). Box 7.2 displays sample knowledge, skills, and dispositions relating to teaching physical education to diverse students.

The Language of Sports.   Sports language is fun for students to learn and can become a rainy-day activity when outdoor recess is called off. Beginning English learners can play sports charades, acting out one-word sports motions after drawing an index card. Advanced English learners can play "sports IQ ," a question-and-answer game in which students read sports questions to one another about rules, strategies, and so forth, or Sports Pictionary in which students try to draw a concept and others try to guess the word depicted.

The Activity System: Practicing Lifetime Fitness, Health, and Safety.   Living a healthy, active lifestyle has both linguistic and cultural components. Students need to become aware in school of the values of eating well and exercising regularly. Teachers who incorporate developmentally appropriate activities into the curriculum in a healthy atmosphere of cooperative games help students learn to balance, run, jump, throw, catch, and even juggle.

Assessment: Lifetime Fitness and Fitness Testing.   The physical nature of sports leads naturally to tests of physical strength and ability. However, beyond the skills approach is the knowledge base of sports, vast in its own right and approachable in many languages. Beyond skills and knowledge lies the aspect of dispositions, the desire to excel in fitness, health, and safety. This opens the door to self-assessment, an ongoing process in which the individual uses introspection and insight to evaluate life choices and goals in these areas.

Resources for Physical Education: Public Relations and Physical Safety.   Whole-school fire safety and self-protection events can feature bilingual demonstrations and pamphlets, assisted by school-age "experts" who can showcase their bilingual skills. Programs of self-esteem and personal responsibility can involve group discussions on health and emotional

Knowledge, Skills, and Dispositions Relating to Standard 6 of the National Association for Sport and Physical Education

Knowledge

The teacher has knowledge of:

- Differences in approaches to learning and physical performance
- Areas of special need including physical and emotional challenges, learning disabilities, sensory difficulties, and language barriers
- How learning is influenced by individual experiences, talents, and prior learning, as well as cultural, family, and community values

Performances (Skills)

The teacher:

- Selects and implements developmentally appropriate instruction that is sensitive to the multiple needs, learning styles, and experiences of learners
- Uses appropriate strategies, services, and resources to meet special and diverse learning needs
- Creates a learning environment that respects and incorporates learners' personal, family, cultural, and community experiences.

Dispositions

The teacher:

- Appreciates and values human diversity and shows respect for varied talents and perspectives
- Seeks to understand and is sensitive to learners' families, communities, cultural values, and experiences as they relate to physical activity

adjustment. A bilingual school counselor or nurse can share responsibility for such a program, in which the whole family can participate.

Music in the Elementary School

The Website www.lessonplanspage.com/MusicK1.htm offers a wide variety of lesson plans, most of which can be adapted for English learners. This site helps classroom teachers

> maintain a strong tradition in teaching singing, performing on instruments, reading and notating music, and listening, while building a foundation for teaching composing, improvising, evaluating music and performances, as well as understanding music in relation to history and culture, and understanding relationships between music, the arts and other disciplines.

Standards for Music Education.   The National Association for Music Education has recognized nine standards for music education, as follows (National Association for Music Education, 2005):

1. Singing, alone and with others, a varied repertoire of music

2. Performing on instruments, alone and with others, a varied repertoire of music
3. Improvising melodies, variations, and accompaniments
4. Composing and arranging music within specified guidelines
5. Reading and notating music
6. Listening to, analyzing, and describing music
7. Evaluating music and music performances
8. Understanding relationships between music, the other arts, and disciplines outside the arts
9. Understanding music in relation to history and culture

Cultures around the world have rich histories and repertoires of music. No other content area has potential as rich as music to unite disparate individuals in enjoyment and celebration of diversity.

Language: Teaching Concepts through Song. A first-grade lesson teaches opposites through songs. Students listen to a story about opposites, discuss opposites, and find opposites in songs, using the books *Elmo's Big Lift and Look Book* and *Pooh Popping Opposites* and the musical tapes *Down on Grandpa's Farm* and *Lullaby and Goodnight.* After a warm-up in which the teacher asks students, "What are opposites?" and "How do we find them?," the teacher reads books that illustrate opposites, asks students for more examples of opposites, and states some things that are not opposites. Then tapes of songs are played that show opposites: fast/slow, number of instruments or people singing, and so forth. For assessment, students listen to two more tape selections and write the opposites found (Graves, 1996).

The Activity System: Teaching Content and Culture through Song. Songs can be connected thematically to American history, to literature, and to a multitude of other aspects of the multiple-subject curriculum. Music itself—without words—has a place in education because it stimulates or relaxes the mind and body. As lyrics are used to teach vocabulary and intonation, songs can teach history, culture, and celebration of diversity.

Assessment: Musical Performance. Showcasing musical talent by means of group and individual performance is a time-honored assessment of musical involvement. The excitement of performance and the responsibility of individuals toward their peers and their audience teach maturity and poise. Bridging cultural gaps by offering songs in many languages helps to involve the families and community in preparing for, attending, and enjoying concerts.

Resources for Music Lessons. When adapting music lessons for English learners, songs from students' primary language can be used. Audiotapes are available through Shen's Books at www.shens.com, including tapes in Spanish, Hmong, Vietnamese, Cambodian, Korean, Japanese, and Mandarin. Tapes from cultures other than the native cultures of the students can also be used.

Visual and Performing Arts in the Elementary School

In the Reggio Emilia preschools in northern Italy, schools have a live-in artist who works and teaches in the school. In U.S. schools, the multiple-subject classroom teacher delivers the art curriculum and develops individual talent for, and appreciation of, visual and performing arts. All students deserve access to the rich educational experiences that the arts provide, regardless of their cultural and linguistic background or perceived talents.

Standards for Art Education.   As an example of state standards for the arts, the following are the Montana [State] Standards for Arts (Montana Office of Public Instruction, 2000). These are matched to assessment standards (see the Assessment for Art Education section below).

> Standard 1. Students create, perform/exhibit, and respond in the Arts.
>
> Standard 2. Students apply and describe the concepts, structures, and processes in the Arts.
>
> Standard 3. Students develop and refine arts skills and techniques to express ideas, pose and solve problems, and discover meaning.
>
> Standard 4. Students analyze characteristics and merits of their work and the work of others.
>
> Standard 5. Students understand the role of the Arts in society, diverse cultures, and historical periods.
>
> Standard 6. Students make connections among the Arts, other subject areas, life, and work.

For another state's standards, Delaware's are available at www.doe.state.de.us/Standards/VisualArts/Introduction.html.

The Language of Art.   Because the standards for art are not excessively dependent on verbal language, and because art lends itself to visual cultural expression, a high-quality art program has the potential to be a rich and satisfying part of the academic content curriculum for English learners.

However, the vocabulary of visual design can provide useful practice for English learners. Following Montana's Standard Five at the fourth-grade level, students will "Recognize ways in which the Arts have both a historical and distinctive relationship to various cultures [e.g., American Indian] and media of expression." Students can use stencil designs from Native American art that are represented as stylized nature elements (for example, thunder as a zigzag design in Navajo art) and compare these same elements with the visual designs of other Native American cultures. Discussing these elements uses simple vocabulary that is nonetheless rich in crosscultural comparison, and allows English learners to practice their oral language skills.

The Activity System: Appreciating and Creating Art.   Human feelings and ideas can be conveyed through visual images. Looking at artwork requires a dialogue between the viewer and the object created by the artist as students learn about genres, symbolic meaning, and technique.

This is especially important when artist and viewer do not share similar values or life experiences. Art can be a multicultural experience, opening portals to other eras, other social classes, other nations.

Art gives second-language learners a way to voice perceptions they may not be able to express through the written or spoken word. The creative arts are also a source of career opportunities in commercial, entertainment, and other sectors. Research studies in diverse contexts across the United States show that art study in the schools improves academic test scores, school attendance, graduation rates, and discipline—for all students, not just the elite or the "talented"—as well as school climate and teacher renewal.

Art can also be integrated with other subjects, and various forms of artistic expression can be used in assessment.

Assessment for Art Education.   The Montana Standards for Arts features benchmark performance standards for grade levels 4, 8, and 12. For example, the following are the benchmarks for grade 4 (Montana Office of Public Instruction, 2000):

1. Recognize ways in which the Arts have both a historical and a distinctive relationship to various cultures (e.g., American Indian) and media of expression.
2. Identify and describe specific works of art belonging to particular cultures, times, and places.
3. Recognize various reasons for creating works of art.
4. Recognize common emotions, experiences, and expressions in art.
5. Demonstrate appropriate audience behavior for the context and style of art presented.
6. Explore [students'] their own culture as reflected through the Arts.

The Montana framework of standards and benchmarks is further enhanced by the incorporation of a rubric that features descriptions of student achievement at the four performance levels: advanced, proficient, nearing proficiency, and novice. Table 7.2 gives an example of the descriptors for each level of fourth-grade performance on Standard 3.

The standards for art—including the performing arts—include the possibility for multicultural education and crosscultural content. Performance-based assessment can provide a satisfying showcase for the talent and cultural knowledge of English learners.

table 7.2   **Four-Level Rubric for Performance in Visual Arts**

Standard 3 (grade 4): Students develop and refine arts skills and techniques to express ideas, pose and solve problems, and discover meaning.

Level	Description of Performance
Advanced	Independently creates, performs/exhibits in, and responds through a minimum of one art form
Proficient	Demonstrates the ability to create, perform/exhibit, and respond through a minimum of one art form
Nearing proficiency	Creates, performs/exhibits in, and responds with specific directions and assistance through a minimum of one art form in a limited way
Novice	Has difficulty creating, performing/exhibiting in, and responding through a minimum of one art form

Source: Montana Office of Public Instruction (2000).

Resources for Art Education.   A multitude of lesson plans can be found at www. nps.k12.nj.us/VisualandPerformingArts.htm that involve students in visual and performing arts, including arts associations that provide schoolchildren with stimuli and instruction.

Middle and High School Academic Content Instruction

The presence of English learners is pervasive at all levels of education. Statistics reveal that the population of English learners in middle and high schools is robust and growing in the United States; middle and high schools serve as ports of entry for many recent immigrant students.

Many textbooks, materials, teaching strategies, and instructional adaptations necessary for teaching English learners have focused on elementary levels. Only recently have publishing companies, for example, begun to develop materials that acknowledge the developmental needs of the adolescent English learner. This section focuses on standards-based teaching in content area for secondary settings (middle and high school).

Secondary School Mathematics

A well-planned mathematics curriculum is essential for all students and opens the doors to a wide range of future career paths. Mathematical knowledge is a must in today's world economy, and teachers of English learners recognize the importance of planning instruction that is responsive to a wide range of needs. It is important to avoid correlating English proficiency with mathematical skills. Many adolescent English learners who have had previous schooling in mathematics may have skills that are at, or above, grade level. These students have content area knowledge; they need support in language to demonstrate what they know and to continue to increase their mathematical knowledge. As suggested by the California Mathematics Framework (CDE, 1999b),

> Good teachers look for a fit between the material to be taught and strategies to teach it. They ask, "What am I trying to teach? What purposes are served by different strategies and techniques? Who are my students? What do they already know? Which instructional techniques will work to move them on to the next level of understanding?" (p. 178)

Content Standards in Mathematics: A Balanced Approach.   Teaching mathematics involves designing an instructional balance of computational and procedural skills, conceptual understanding, and problem solving. Although there tends to be an emphasis on computational and procedural skills, it is important to emphasize problem solving and address why mathematical ideas are true and important in the world. Students gain a greater appreciation for the essence of mathematics when they apply skills learned in the classroom to their daily lives.

The Language of Mathematics for Secondary Students.   Many prospective secondary school teachers believe that mathematics is easy to teach to English learners compared to other academic subjects because mathematics is a universal language. However, mathematics has a unique language all its own, and English-speaking mathematics students, to be successful, must learn this language. What is universal are the concepts embedded in mathematics; how these concepts are represented is culturally based. This poses a unique challenge for adolescent English learners because they must learn, for example, that in the United States, inches, yards, and miles are units of measurement; many learned the language of meters, centimeters, and kilometers in previous mathematics instruction.

Teachers must be aware of these differences and mediate the transition into learning a new language to express mathematical concepts. This is particularly important with word problems that assess reading skills and not necessarily mathematical or computation knowledge. Chamot and O'Malley (1994) suggested that reading skills in mathematics are those emphasized the most for grades 7–12, followed by speaking, writing, and listening skills.

The Activity System: The Three-Phase Pattern.　　Extensive research in teaching mathematics (CDE, 1999b) shows that effective instruction incorporates a variety of strategies yet follows a three-phase pattern, as opposed to the more traditional two-phase pattern of instruction (the teacher demonstrates and students practice). The first phase involves the introduction, demonstration, and explanation of the concept or strategy by the teacher. This is followed by questions and active engagement, in which the teacher involves all students and establishes how well students are grasping the concept.

The second phase involves an intermediate step designed to result in independent application of the new concept. Belmont (1989) described this phase as one in which students make the transition from "teacher regulation" to student "self-regulation." Supporting techniques can include coaching, prompting, cueing, and interaction that is informal, personal, and monitors student performance while giving specific feedback as students progress.

The third phase allows students to work independently and is relatively brief. This phase also serves as assessment of the extent to which students understand what they are learning and how they will use their knowledge. This model is flexible—if students do not do well during the guided phase, teachers can go back and provide additional instruction. If students are having difficulty during independent practice, they can receive more guidance and opportunities for practice. Table 7.3 shows the three-phase instructional model for mathematics.

Further research into high school students and mathematics suggests the importance of teachers' making the short- and long-term goals clear, as well as telling students the utility of the mathematical concept they are using. For example, using geometry to design a car stereo installation makes it clear to adolescents the relevancy of mathematical concepts in everyday life. Projects are very effective, although long projects need to be used with discretion. Table 7.4 shows additional strategic approaches to teaching mathematics to English learners.

Mathematics Homework.　　For homework to be productive, it should be an extension of class work. Too frequently students are given homework regarding concepts they failed to grasp in class, yet they are expected to go home and solve the problems without teacher support.

table 7.3   Three-Phase Instructional Model for Mathematics

Phase	Characteristics	Adaptations
One	Teacher demonstrates, explains, questions; students are actively involved in discussions	Teacher provides comprehensible input using SDAIE, uses BICS to explain concepts while introducing mathematical CALP, poses questions appropriate to students' ELD levels, connects concepts to real-life applications using students' experiences.
Two	Transition from teacher-centered to independent practice, with teacher and peer feedback; may require additional explanations of concepts; teacher provides informal and frequent monitoring on individual and group activity.	Teacher monitors individual students and gives positive and specific feedback; uses a peer tutor or paraprofessional to translate; encourages problem solving; repeats instructional goals using short sentences; reviews any goals that may be particular to the individual.
Three	Assessment	Use of assessments that test content knowledge, not language proficiency; provides multiple modes of assessment and offers choices; explicitly states what was accomplished or learned and what still needs to be done; or asks students to explain what they learned or still need to work on.

Source: Adapted from California Department of Education, Three-Phase Instructional Model (1999).

Homework should not rely on a parent's or sibling's ability to act as a mathematics teacher. Holz (1996) identified five types of productive homework:

1. *Exercises*: practice on skills is the goal
2. *Lesson development*: emphasis on concepts covered in class is emphasized or integrated
3. *Problem solving experiences*: students work individually or use others as resources
4. *Projects*: long-term investigations such as research application of mathematics to real world
5. *Studying*: for understanding, review and/or preparation for exams

Teachers of English learners sending notes or progress reports to parents with mathematics homework must make every effort to translate any forms that parents are expected to sign.

Assessment in Mathematics.   Assessment should emphasize the balanced approach whereby computation, procedural skills, and problem solving are assessed. Teachers must ask, "What is being evaluated?" Is assessment being used to determine a student's placement in a mathematics program? Is assessment being used to monitor progress, or is the intent summative evaluation, to find out which standards have or have not been met? Again, because mathematics requires subject-specific English-language skills, thereby requiring specific cultural knowledge, teachers of English learners should be mindful of the assessments they are using.

table 7.4 Mathematics Strategies for English Learners

Mathematical Teaching Strategies	Description
Encourage exploration.	Plan activities that facilitate, explore, and investigate mathematical concepts, that promote the construction of mathematical knowledge, and that nurture students' curiosity and stimulate creativity.
Use manipulatives.	Manipulatives help make abstract concepts concrete and hands-on; this tends to be particularly useful as students are building their mathematical CALP, because manipulatives provide a context that makes conceptual understanding easier.
	Manipulatives help students "see" and "touch" connections between different representations (concrete, graphic, symbolic, linguistic) of mathematical ideas.
Use real-world problem-solving activities.	Using mathematics as it applies to daily life and to solve real-life problems makes it interesting and meaningful, helping students to internalize and retain mathematical concepts.
Encourage oral and written expression.	Mathematics requires specific language and CALP, and students should be provided opportunities to practice and express their mathematical knowledge orally and in writing.
Offer an enriched curriculum and challenging activities.	Mathematics is a discipline with its own CALP characterized by specific experiences and abilities involving inquiry, problem solving, and higher thinking.
	Teachers can design a curriculum that sets high expectations for students, who learn to think like mathematicians and move away from repetition, drill, and memorization of formulas without a context.
Use a variety of problem-solving experiences.	The drill-and-practice approach to mathematics should not be the staple of a mathematics curriculum. Teachers should plan challenges that stimulate higher-order thinking and problem solving and that are nonroutine and open-ended. For example, provide math problems that may have various correct solutions and answers, problems with multiple interpretations, and problems that are not exclusively reading or writing based, with answers that can be represented in multiple ways.

Resources in the Mathematics Classroom. The resources for teaching and learning mathematics are numerous and should focus on grade-level standards. Students and their experiences can be taken into consideration when teachers design mathematical questions that are meaningful to students. As suggested earlier, Family Math is one example of a curriculum that is not only meaningful for students but also extends mathematical activities into the home, involving parents. Teachers need to be creative in finding resources in the school and the community, as plenty of resources are available.

Table 7.5 features several websites recommended by some of the mathematics teachers with whom we work, including their description of how these sites help them in working with English learners.

table 7.5   Websites for Teaching Secondary Mathematics to English Learners

Website	Description
http://matti.usu.edu/nlvm/nav/vlibrary.html	Provides manipulatives as a visual demonstration of concepts taking place in the class. The graph is an excellent tool; one can graph several lines on the same Cartesian plane and see the variations made by changing a coefficient.
www.purplemath.com/modules/translat.htm	The site translates word problems into algebraic expressions. When English learners are faced with word problems, it is rarely one word that gives them problems, but more often a phrase. That phrase is usually the key to setting up the problem. The Website provides a step-by-step account of how to set up these problems.
www.enc.org/topics/equity/articles	This site addresses the cultural aspects of teaching mathematics. It identifies characteristics of learners from different cultures, and addresses the common misconception that mathematics can be taught without taking culture into account.

Social Sciences and the Adolescent English Learner

"What does history have to do with me? Why do I have to learn about things that happened long ago?" These questions are not uncommon; many mature adults might remember asking these questions of their middle and high school social studies teachers who failed to create meaning for them.

Students should be able to see the connections between today and yesterday, and how ideas and behavior have consequences for a society. Equally important is that students know about cultures, societies, and economic systems around the world. Television and other mass media do not help students see or understand the origin, or history, of ideas; instead, they suggest that most events are a product of the "now." By understanding history, students understand human beings, their social creations, and the implications these have for their own participation in working toward a just society.

Content Standards in Teaching History.   The content standards for California suggest that core skills are important for students to acquire in social studies/history, but what is more important is that students develop critical thinking skills and learn to think like historians and social scientists. Adopting the habits and the behaviors of historians is a goal of these standards. History is more than regurgitation of facts but instead is about understanding how all of us live within a sociohistorical context that greatly affects who we are and what we can accomplish. Teachers who make history come alive connect the present with the past, including the lives of their students. They answer the question "What does this have to do with me?" through an interactive curriculum that involves and engages students. Teachers of English learners are also aware that concepts addressed in history and the social sciences increase in complexity as students move upward in grade level.

The Language of History.   Social studies is a rich area of study; many of its concepts are rooted in philosophy, economics, anthropology, and political science. The social studies curriculum thus requires a high level of literacy and depends heavily on language. Language in many textbooks is decontextualized, and the way in which topics are presented at the secondary level usually does not reflect the student's personal experiences (Chamot & O'Malley, 1994). History poses particular challenges to the English learner and requires teachers to adapt and make visible the information that English-speaking students know from their everyday experiences of living in the United States.

A second difficulty is that history is "vocabulary heavy," replete with specialized language, including historical terms and government processes. Social studies text tends to contain complex sentences, passive voice, and extensive use of pronouns. Reading history is problematic even for those English learners who are skilled because there are long sentences with multiple embedded clauses. Many sentences have a cause–effect style:

> Because there will be more people in the world in the future, we will need more land on which to build towns and cities.

> Because wheat is so often used to make bread, Kansas is called the breadbasket of the world. (Chamot & O'Malley, 1994, p. 260)

Third, many English learners students may have difficulty understanding what the teacher is saying and are unable to take notes. The discipline has technical jargon and a teacher's language may reflect this discourse. Box 7.3 shows some additional difficulties English learners may face in a social studies classroom.

box 7.3

Difficulties Faced by English Learners in Secondary Social Studies Classrooms

- Curriculum assumes prior cultural knowledge.
- Vocabulary is highly specialized, while borrowing from different disciplines.
- Vocabulary frequently refers to abstract concepts.
- Discourse in texts has complex sentences, passive voice, and extensive use of pronouns.
- Many concepts that may not exist in some cultures are difficult, such as privacy, free will, individualism.
- The concepts used to teach history such as "timeline" are culturally based; students may have no concept of "historical period" or "dynasty."
- Many students do not know how to use maps, graphs, and charts.
- There is so much material to cover; students may not know what is important and what is not important.
- Many English learners may be unaccustomed to expressing their individual political or personal opinions in public.
- The perspective that many English learners bring is seldom discussed as an alternative view when studying other countries and their relationships with the United States.

The Activity System: Teaching in Secondary Social Studies Classrooms.   The social studies curriculum is culturally based, assuming that the learner has been acculturated and has prior knowledge of U.S. civic, historical, and geographical knowledge. Many students have studied neither world history nor U.S. history and may have little knowledge about the history, institutions, culture, or geography of the United States. Success in history is more dependent on knowledge of American culture than any other content area.

What strategies can assist teachers in making history come alive and be meaningful to all of their students, including their English learners? What can social studies teachers do to encourage their students to "think and act like historians"? Table 7.6 shows some effective strategies in adapting instruction for English learners

Assessment in History.   The types of assessment used in history can be as extensive as the topic itself and can address the key issues of students' awareness of their role as citizens in a global society. Primary documents, mock interviews with historical characters, role-playing controversial historical figures, and debates are useful ways of assessing knowledge as well as critical skills. Group work projects can be useful by having students create historical artifacts and research the implications of these artifacts in society. Chapter 10 provides further ideas on assessment that is effective with English learners.

Historical Resources.   There are numerous resources for teachers who are developing history or social studies lessons that address the needs of their English learners and incorporate the numerous strategies useful in teaching English learners. One example is the History Alive social studies curriculum developed by Teachers' Curriculum Institute in northern California (www.historyalive.com). This curriculum is aligned or correlated with more than ten of the states' social studies frameworks, including California, Pennsylvania, and North Carolina (see the Website for a listing of states).

History Alive is theory based, incorporating multiple intelligences (Gardner, 1983), the complex instruction model for group work (Cohen, 1994), and a spiral curriculum (Bruner, 1986). It is interactive and innovative, with higher-order thinking skill tasks embedded throughout its activities. This curriculum is an exemplar for teachers looking for history materials to teach their English learners. Other resources cited by secondary-level social studies teachers include the Websites listed in Table 7.7.

Teachers of English learners have many resources with which to adapt lessons so that the multifaceted challenges presented by this discipline are addressed. Adaptations pave the road to making history come alive for English learners.

Secondary School Science

Content Standards.   Scientific literacy is an instructional priority throughout the United States. Science classrooms pose unique challenges to English learners and their teachers, but also provide numerous and varied opportunities for language development. In this section, what science means to English learners and teachers is discussed, followed by recommendations for instructional adaptations to make the science curriculum accessible to all students. Finally, resources and samples of inclusive science lessons are provided.

Science and Language: Breaking the Code.   Shifting perspective and viewing a situation from an insider's point of view is extremely useful when trying to design instruction for a

table 7.6 Strategies for Adapting Curricula in Secondary Social Studies

Strategy	How It Helps
Identifying similarities and differences	Helps students compare, create metaphors, and use analogies (example: comparing the U.S. Congress to a school can clarify this concept); builds vocabulary; enhances comprehension.
Historical investigation	Gives students an active role in understanding history and allows them to pursue a question using strategies that work for them; focuses on students' interests; allows students flexibility; encourages self-monitoring of progress.
Inventions	Inventions are/have been an important part of U.S. history; students are able to demonstrate comprehension, knowledge, and creativity within a historical framework while reliving history.
Role-playing	Adolescents are quite dramatic and like to be in "someone else's shoes"; students can learn about others' perspectives while using language, gestures, and body language to show their understanding.
Group work	Collaborative projects or assignments help students solve problems together as they hear and use history-related CALP in a low-anxiety environment; structured group work addresses status issues so that "everyone participates, no one dominates" and English learners have chances to talk.
Decision making	This provides for contemplation and discussion of concepts central to many historical issues; provides students a chance to hear and use language to make decisions.
"What if" stories	Help students use language to create hypothetical predictions about history: for example, what if Columbus had not sailed to America?
Puzzles, riddles	Students see representation of historical concepts in different formats that engage and incorporate multiple intelligences.
Explanations with concrete referents	Help students understand abstract concepts.
Alternative representation formats	Different ways of presenting facts; for example, graphic organizers, maps, tables, charts, and graphs can reduce verbiage and identify key concepts in a lesson; this also models the different means historians use to gather evidence.
Summarizing and note taking	An important skill of historians; allows students to make sense of extensive text and lecture by listening for key words and identifying relevant information.
Preteaching assignments	Helps students anticipate key concepts before reading an assignment.
Preparing for exams	Teacher can model how to use textbook features such as chapter goals and overviews, summaries, and glossaries; this also helps students self-monitor comprehension and progress.
Providing learning, reading, and study support	Helps students process text and use language to voice their ideas; puts them in role of experts. Teachers arrange jigsaw groups to read text, assigning students to groups and making groups of students experts on specific portions of reading; students read and discuss together; teacher reviews and addresses specific issues with the entire class.
Word association	Vocabulary enrichment; teaching students to hear a word and associate it with an image helps comprehension and retention.
Listening for specific information	Teaches students explicitly what is important in a lecture, text, or historical document; students use teacher-created graphic organizers or use fill-in-the-blank lecture notes.

table 7.7   Websites for Teaching Secondary Social Studies to English Learners

Website	Description
www.DiscoverySchool.com	An excellent supplement to world history videos. The site offers vocabulary words and terms used in the video, rubrics, and a list of additional resources. The vocabulary terms are integral for providing scaffolding for English learners. (Recommended by J. Kabel, high school social sciences teacher, Palm Desert, California.)
http://atozteacherstuff.com	This site contains many ELD lessons specifically designed for all content areas. I found several excellent lessons I can use for my English learners who are studying U.S. history and government.
www.tolerance.org/teach/about/index.jsp	A user-friendly site for teachers founded by the Southern Poverty Law Center provides extensive free educational materials that promote equity and social justice. While not exclusively a site dedicated to teaching English learners, it is an excellent resource for social studies teachers, and explores relevant issues such as immigration and appreciation of diversity that extends beyond the classroom.

specific group of learners. Ethnographies (see Chapter 5) are a useful tool in helping the teacher/observer understand and gain clarity about particular students or specific instructional concerns. Looking at a ninth-grade science classroom from an English learner's perspective, for example, can help teachers identify some of the issues that an intermediate English learner faces. Mario, a 15-year-old student from El Salvador, says the following about his science classroom:

No me siento agusto en esta clase porque siento que no sé nada. Yo creía que sabía hablar y leer inglés hasta que vine a esta clase de ciencia, donde no entiendo lo que dice la maestra y ni entiendo lo que esta en el libro que nos dio. El libro tiene muchas palabras que nunca he oido y pues, no las puedo leer; las oraciones y parrafos están super largos. No sé ni donde empezar para entenderlos. Luego salen palabras como "if . . . then" y muchas oraciones empiezan con "because." Mi maestro de English IIA me dijo que no empezara oraciones con "because." "Because" me tiene todo confundido. Y luego yo sé lo que quieren decir palabras como "energy," "work," y "mass." Pero aqui no quieren decir lo mismo.

Me gustan los "science labs" porque puedo trabajar con otros que me ayudan, pero en veces se me hacen duros porque no sé yo como escribir mis reportes y ni sé como explicar lo que veo o apriendo. Yo nunca he investigado cosas y ni sé que escribir como quiere la maestra. Ésta clase pide que uno escriba mucho usando palabras que ni sé lo que son. Me siento como que los de la clase creen que no sé nada, porque no hablo y nunca hago bien mis reportes o tareas. Ojala, mi maestra usara el español para enseñarme y que no hablara tan recio y tuviera otro libro.

[I don't feel comfortable in this class because I feel like I don't know anything. I thought I knew how to speak and write English until I came to this science class, where I don't understand what the teacher says and I don't understand what is in the book she gave us. The book has a lot of words that I have never heard, and well, I can't read them. The sentences and paragraphs are really long. I don't even know where to begin so that I can understand them. Then these words come up like "if . . . then" and a lot of sentences with the word "because." My teacher in English IIA told me not to begin sentences with "because." "Because" has me really confused. And then I know what words like "energy," "work," and "mass" mean, but here they do not mean the same thing.

I like to do the "science labs" because I can work with others who can help me, but at times these are hard to complete also because I don't know how to write reports, or how to explain what I saw or learned. I have never investigated things and I don't know how to write like the teacher wants me to write. This class wants me to write using words I don't know. I feel like the others in the class think that I don't know anything because I don't speak a lot in class and I don't do well on my reports and homework. I wish my teacher used Spanish to teach me and that she didn't speak so fast, and used another book.]

Mario's perspective points to much of what is difficult for English learners in science classrooms. First, science knowledge is cumulative and increases in complexity as students progress through the grade levels. Thus, prior knowledge in science is critical; students like Mario may not have the prior knowledge that would allow him to understand the new concepts being introduced.

Second, Mario accurately identifies that he can read and speak in English, except when he comes to this science class; he has BICS yet lacks CALP in science. Although he is likely to be making progress in his English-language skills development, this tenth-grade class presents major cognitive demands. Mario is expressing frustration, knowing that his peers, in this context, believe he knows little because he is unable to contribute to science activities or complete his lab reports and homework.

Mario also identifies key science issues that are related to the language skills required in this discipline. For example, Chamot and O'Malley (1994) suggested that all language skills are essential for academic success in a science classroom, and they ranked writing and reading as the two most frequently used, followed by speaking and listening in grades 7 through 12. Also, the difficulty for Mario is more than just listening, because students are expected not only to listen (or have comprehension) but also to follow directions and to perform complex procedures such as hypothesizing and predicting. The level of teacher talk also seems to be above Mario's ability to comprehend; it is not uncommon for a teacher's language in the science classroom to be incomprehensible to many English learners, as well as to many native English speakers.

The vocabulary in science is another challenge because the discipline uses many technical terms, as well as terms that indicate causalities *if/then* and *because*). Discourse in science features complex grammatical structures, with long sentences and paragraphs. Science also uses expository styles of writing, and students accustomed to narrative styles have difficulty comprehending.

Scientific writing goes hand in hand with oral descriptions of experiments, with language organized into a specific sequence to be followed. Describing observations, explaining a process, making predictions, developing a hypothesis, and writing the results of an experiment are dependent on highly complex language abilities, which poses major challenges for an intermediate-level English learner. The secondary science classroom demands greater literacy skills because students need to be able to read for information, write, analyze, and express in a specific format what they have learned.

Structuring Classroom Talk.   Research conducted by Gibbons (2003) in content and language scaffolding shows how to move students from BICS to CALP, or from "everyday comments on scientific phenomena to academic discourse" (p. 18). Gibbons observed two elementary school classrooms working on magnetism and described how teachers' responses to dialogue engaged students, keeping them moving to higher-level scientific understanding and science-appropriate language use. These instructional conversations show that teachers did the following:

- Engaged with their students
- Made linguistic and discourse choices to narrow the conceptual distance in the discourse between the science teacher and the students
- Modeled appropriate discourse and used academic terms and signals for clarification as clues for English learners to modify their language
- Provided comprehensible input so that students then produced comprehensible output in academic science
- Gave students the responsibility for making themselves understood in describing, explaining, questioning, hypothesizing, persuading, and analyzing
- Used instructional conversations as oral rehearsal for scientific lab writing, science journals, or other reports

This model thus uses classroom talk to move students from the personal to the academic experience, from the superficial to the more in-depth knowledge and discussion of science, from detailed oral expression to factual writing, and from knowledge of science to a deeper understanding of science as a discipline.

A science teacher aware of the demands of the language of science can address the needs of English learners by adapting lessons to accommodate some of the typical concerns expressed by Mario. Table 7.8 describes some of the adaptations that can provide English learners with comprehensible input, or access to the content material, in a science classroom.

The Activity System.   In addition to the previous suggestions for addressing the difficulties that English learners frequently experience in the science classroom, there are numerous instructional practices that science teachers working with English learners can incorporate in their planning.

Chamot and O'Malley (1994) suggested that those using the CALLA model include at least one science-process activity on a daily basis to get students to internalize the behaviors and skills related to "acting and thinking like a scientist." When the skills of the process of science are practiced as daily habits of the science classroom, students will begin to feel more comfortable and more successful in this setting. Creating a low-anxiety environment encourages students to use language freely and to be unafraid to make errors and mistakes in their work as scientists. After all, errors in scientific work have led to major discoveries. Students need to know that in science, as in language, mistakes are part of the learning process.

table 7.8   Adaptations in Science Lessons

Difficulty for English Learners	Adaptations
Teacher speaks too quickly	Slow down speech, repeat concepts, and explain in a different way; use visuals; use BICS to introduce CALP; use primary language whenever possible or select key terms in primary language; use overhead or board to present some of the concepts.
Textbook reading	What is the grade level of text(s) used in class? What is the reading level of student(s)? Use supplementary texts, visual dictionaries, materials, Internet resources, and primary-language books in science to teach.
Scientific vocabulary	Identify difficult words in lessons, involving students in this process; explicitly teach scientific vocabulary and make connections; clarify how words have different meanings in different contexts; practice vocabulary building in context; allow students to use visual and primary-language dictionaries; however, do not assume that just because students translate words they have attained conceptual meaning.
Scientific reading	Explicitly teach how to use the science textbook and how science reading is different from literature, for example; model how to read and follow directions; make lab reports and other science writing available; allow students to find information in encyclopedias and library books.
Writing in science	Explicitly model how scientific writing is different; teach the scientific method; have a chart for students to use to refer to steps that need to be followed in reports; allow students to submit drafts; begin by having students write about science concepts that are familiar to them, and then transition them into writing about more abstract concepts; have students practice answering "why" and "what if" questions, including answers to questions presented by the teacher.
Speaking	Practice and model how to describe observations orally; have students observe steps in a procedure and draw them; have students practice the scientific process and introduce it in the language scientists use to describe what they see; have them role-play and discuss what the scientific process is and why it is used; have students work cooperatively and practice using language to talk about what they see and what they learned, and have them report orally; have students draw charts or other visuals about steps they can follow in describing, using the scientific process.
Listening	Have students take notes, particularly when the teacher is demonstrating or students are watching videos or the Discovery Channel; these notes can include visuals or other drawings, or use of the primary language.

Thematic teaching is another pedagogical strategy teachers can use to plan meaningful and engaging science activities. Themes tend to focus on principles and processes, allowing for the examination of content knowledge in depth as well as numerous opportunities for connecting activities to students' daily lives.

Tapping into students' **prior knowledge** sets the stage for understanding, allowing teachers to refine and reformulate misconceptions students may have about specific concepts. By accessing this prior knowledge, students can get hooked into a lesson and, simultaneously, teachers can measure students' conceptual understanding when covering specific topics. Brainstorming, K-W-L charts, semantic maps (see Heimlich & Pittelman, 1986), and visual representations of what students know are ways to tap into what students bring into the science classroom and lesson.

Although visuals are an important element of an SDAIE lesson, in the science classroom these can take on a different spin, as in complex charts such as the periodic table. Student-developed visuals documenting processes or development, both important concepts in science, can be posted for later reference. For example, visuals that document the process of growth in plants or cells, or developmental stages in seeds, emphasize the role of observation.

Keeping logs of data is another critical skill in science. Teachers can demystify this process by initiating students into writing observations about what is familiar to them, or providing options about what they can write about in the world around them, such as growth in plants or changes in animals such as pets. Teachers can explicitly teach and model how scientists record data and draw conclusions. Computers are useful allies, and teachers can integrate technology into some of these activities.

Resources: Supplementing the Text.   The tools that teachers in science classrooms (and all other classrooms, for that matter) decide to use have a major impact on how much and what their students will learn. Relying exclusively on the textbook is problematic for teachers of English learners because the textbook and the teacher become the only two means of accessing content knowledge. Therefore, using a variety of materials is important. Building a classroom science library is one way to provide reading materials in science that supplement the text. Different genres of scientific writing can be included, such as science fiction or comic books.

Kress's book *The ESL Teacher's Book of Lists* (1993) is a useful resource that includes a list of basic and intermediate/advanced science words that can be used to develop vocabulary that is specific to the field. Teachers can mediate activities to help students develop a science glossary.

A useful website is http://csmp.ucop.edu/csp/initiative.html, the California Science Project Learner Initiative. The site includes many resources for teaching science to English learners. Materials are grounded in research and filled with practical tips for teachers.

Language Arts in the Secondary School

Literature at the Core of Content Standards.   Reading, writing, speaking, and listening can all be successfully taught through literature. This integrated approach (see Fogarty, 1991) to teaching the English language arts tends to be more successful with English learners because it is meaningful, and the skills necessary for language proficiency are integrated and embedded in a context that facilitates this challenging process.

A good English-language development program features a well-planned literature-based curriculum that hooks students into practicing and honing their skills. An effective language arts program also develops "reading the word and reading the world" (Freire & Macedo, 1987) by developing students' critical literacy and allowing them to engage with the text beyond the words. Finally, students develop academic consciousness (Houtchens, 2001) because literacy requires discipline, hard work, patience, and analysis. A commercial for the use of literature to teach language arts could honestly claim, "It teaches literacy, and much more!"

Reading Begins with the Reader.   Teachers who are successful in teaching English start with the "potential reader" by knowing, respecting, and safeguarding the integrity of these readers in this process. They maintain the expectation that these readers, given the opportunity, will find pleasure in reading. Teachers of English learners in secondary schools must first believe that these students, despite their age and advanced grade levels, can acquire English literacy skills.

Houtchens (2001) noticed that many students who are recent immigrants or English learners "hate reading, have never owned a book of their own, and have no books other than the Bible at home" (p. 201). The work of the English teacher, then, is to instill both the ability to read and a love of reading. Books and reading are modeled as an integrated part of the learning process, and this activity is interconnected with everything else that goes on in a language classroom.

Selecting a Book.   For success in reading, book selection is a critical element. Many English learners do not know how to select a book. Brainstorming about how one selects a book and understanding the importance of text selection are lessons in themselves that are replete with teaching moments that integrate language development. Reading the title (including the language of the title—*La vida loca,* for example), the back cover, the inside book flaps, the first three pages, and the last three pages are all ways to help students pick a book. These activities are critical to demystifying print, because many students have learned to see books as intimidating artifacts.

Classroom Libraries.   Another strategy in demystifying reading is building a classroom library. Books are part of the cultural milieu in a classroom that has a library, and students have access to books throughout the day that they do not need permission to use. Teacher-constructed libraries include a wide selection of print and are frequently dominated by books and dictionaries in the students' primary languages, dictionaries at various reading levels, big print, small print, picture books, and literature that is relevant to their students' lives. Many teachers bring comfortable reading chairs such as bean bags.

Reading as a Habit.   Facilitating reading habits is also important. Many teachers of English learners use a reading log, assigning and monitoring specific amounts of time daily that students must spend reading. These logs generally include specific reading tasks the teacher assigns and possibly adaptations for individual students.

It is critical to provide literature that appeals to the English learner, who may be a reluctant reader. Thus teachers who actively pursue literature that names and validates some of the experiences of adolescent English learners find few difficulties in engaging their students in reading. For example, *Lupita mañana* (Beatty, 2000), a book about an immigrant girl in southern California, is a story that engages many English learners in reading. Once reading becomes a fulfilling experience, students are more likely to expand their selections into other areas as their confidence in their reading ability, as well as their comprehension, improves.

Reading for Meaning.   The five strategies of active reading—predicting, connecting, questioning, clarifying, and evaluating—can be a focus for creating meaning. In addition, the teacher can facilitate learning strategies (see earlier discussion) to help students develop their academic skills.

Scaffolding strategies may be necessary for some students, such as sentence starters like "After reading this story, I think that _____ is going to happen because _____." These prompts can be used as a springboard to reading discussions.

The Activity System: Community-Based Reading and Writing.   Everyone wants to tell his or her story, or wants the story told. In this storytelling activity, students write a book for future students to read. This book may be placed in the classroom, school, and/or community library. The stories grow from the students' lives and can be told in the students' primary language exclusively or can incorporate English. This activity can be introduced by discussing the various genres of storytelling such as folktales, myths, legends, and autobiographies. Students collect, tell, tape-record, and eventually write their book. Teachers can create a handout or a rubric about what should be included, as well as a guide to reviewing a book.

This activity can be used for all levels of readers, and the content or format can be adapted to the abilities of the particular reader or class. Students can illustrate these stories, and all elements of a published book can be incorporated in the final product. Literacy activities involve speaking, writing, reading, and comprehension, including bringing in the students' primary language. Students are actively involved in all aspects of the writing process. This activity can be a focal point of parent conferences, parent group meetings, assemblies, multicultural events, or library events because reading and writing are connected with authentic, real-world contexts.

Contextual Redefinition.   Learning to use context to increase comprehension while reading is an important skill that proficient readers use and therefore an important reading strategy for English learners. Contextual redefinition shows students the importance of context in ascertaining meaning. This is a useful learning strategy for beginning, below, and above grade-level readers because the context can be used to define terms readers may not know and help them believe in their ability to find meaning even when there are no dictionaries readily available.

In contextual redefinition, the teacher selects a few words students will encounter in the text that are essential to understanding the reading, presents these words in isolation, and then has students offer suggestions about what they mean. The teacher then provides a context for each of the words using a definition or description clue. Students offer suggestions about the meanings and work in groups to consult a dictionary to verify the choices offered by class members. This activity builds reading, writing, comprehension, listening, and speaking skills; encourages a natural and holistic view of language learning; and provides multiple opportunities for English learners to use and hear language in a variety of settings.

The publication *Strategic Teaching and Learning: Standards-Based Instruction to Promote Literacy in Grades Four through Twelve* by the California Department of Education (2000b) is replete with reading strategies appropriate to use with English learners. Box 7.4 summarizes some fundamental reading adaptations that teachers of English learners can make in their planning and instruction.

Writing Adaptations.   Reading and writing go hand in hand, and teachers of English learners integrate these processes instead of teaching them separately. Writing, coupled with speaking, is a mental process that makes reading visible in "the mind's eye."

box 7.4

Adaptations That Enhance the Classroom Reading Environment

Provide the following:

■ Picture dictionaries that match concepts in the content area with illustrations.
■ Dictionaries in the primary language(s) of students.
■ A resource table related to the content area that has supplemental books on the topics covered in the specific area. For example, many science books talk about scientific concepts in various formats, including autobiographies, science fiction, or comic book.
■ A resource library, including access to microcomputers, where students can self-select topics related to the content.
■ Opportunities for students to talk about what they have read in the specific subject area in many contexts, including social and informal.
■ Guest speakers the students know from the community or mass media who can talk about reading in the specific area and why it is important to achievement.
■ Posters or other visuals that connect reading of the specific content area to the context of students' lives; for example, reading about the lives of mathematicians and what led to some of their discoveries.

For beginning writers, the emphasis should be on expression and comprehension, with grammar and spelling concerns being secondary. An emphasis on expression also builds the writer's confidence to "speak to the paper." For intermediate and advanced writers, strategies differ—including an increased emphasis on grammatical precision. Teachers should prioritize the specific goals of a writing assignment based on their students' abilities.

It is important that teachers keep the different aspects of writing in perspective and understand what is reasonable to expect from English learners. Table 7.9 shows a list adapted from the Association for Supervision and Curriculum Development (1995) that identifies and describes writing strategies useful for English learners.

Thus the use of an integrated approach to literature—one that involves reading and writing about great literature and learning to enjoy discussing the ideas contained in these works—is key to creating lifelong readers, writers, and conversants.

Content Area Materials Reflect Expository Writing. Content area materials are primarily informational or expository in nature. Informational text has specific patterns of organization that set it apart from other types of reading such as literary works. Students who have learned to read literary materials (primarily stories) may not have been exposed to organizational patterns of expository texts, and may have difficulty finding order or meaning to the new patterns they encounter. Science, mathematics, history, and health-science teachers should be aware of the ramifications of this factor as they teach content area literacy. Box 7.5 presents several questions teachers might ask as they begin to analyze their text and its accessibility to their English learners.

Another way to analyze the text is to involve the students themselves in a critical literacy activity by having them examine the textbook they are using. Many teachers develop lessons to demystify the textbook by having students answer specific questions about the

table 7.9   Adaptations in Writing Strategies for English Learners

Writing Strategies	Description
Write. Write. Write.	Provide a wide variety of opportunities for students to write and share their writing.
	Have students write in all subject areas.
	Encourage students to use and practice writing across the curriculum.
Use authentic writing	Assign tasks that have real purpose and real audiences.
Use examples of good writing	Provide access to a variety of written materials and examples of good writing.
	Make the expression of thoughts and ideas the primary goal, with correctness of form secondary.
Model writing as a process	Writing is developmental and takes time; steps in writing are made visible and practiced.
Use writing conferences	Confer individually with students on a regular basis to enhance students' self-assessment of their own writing skills and their understanding of the processes.
Teach students "how to write"	Provide explicit instruction, often in the form of mini-lessons, demonstrating what students are expected to do in their writing.
Allow time to learn supportive skills	Reinforce writing skills such as prewriting, planning, drafting, revising, and editing on a daily basis; establish a routine for this behavior and encourage students to use their own strategies, move naturally between stages, and work at their own pace.
Provide clear criteria for evaluation	Foster independence and responsibility by providing criteria (rubrics, exemplars, for example) students can use to evaluate their own writing.
Include contextual instruction in grammar	Grammar is taught within the context of writing, not in isolation, and also emphasizes strategies consistent with individual learner needs.
Use the inquiry method	Use structured assignments based on inquiry to help students produce writing that expands strategy use, accommodates a variety of purposes and audiences, and addresses increasingly complex topics.
Use writing portfolios	Use portfolios to monitor and evaluate students' writing abilities in different genres, and to provide students with greater responsibility for their progress as writers through the self-assessment of their own work.
Involve students in the evaluation process	Students are held accountable for their own growth and employ multiple measures to assess literacy skills.

book's usefulness and appeal, including how to use glossaries, visuals, and other supportive aids to gaining access to contents.

The Context.   Reading is a meaning-making process that takes place within specific contexts or settings. Examples of contexts for reading include physical setting, classroom environment, instructional task, and expected outcomes (CDE, 2000). The CDE's document *Strategic Teaching and Learning* (2000, p. 7) cites research on the importance of context in

Questions for Analysis of Expository Text

1. What is the content and structure of the text(s) used in my specific content area(s)?
2. Are my students familiar with expository text common to my discipline? Are students familiar with scientific reading and writing, for example?
3. Which are the patterns of organization my students use and feel more comfortable using? What are students' experiences in scientific reading and writing? What type of text do they prefer to read?
4. What are features in the presentation of the text that may appeal to my students or make text user-friendly? For example, density of print, colors used, size of print, amount of white space, learning aides.
5. Match or mismatch: What is the reading level of the text(s) I use and the reading levels of my students, including English learners?
6. How is text presented? Are sentences long and wordy? Are sentences short and facilitate comprehension?
7. How are key concepts presented? Is common language—BICS—used to provide a bridge to technical language—CALP? Are there supporting aids to present concepts?
8. What are strengths in the text(s) I am using? How do these strengths support English learners and access to content literacy?
9. What are weaknesses in the text(s) I am using? How do these weaknesses interfere with students' gaining access to content literacy?
10. What are ways I can modify these weaknesses by making adaptations to the text I am using?

reading and suggest that classroom environments conducive to reading have the following characteristics:

- Large amounts of time to read
- Varied and interesting materials with appropriate levels of difficulty
- Time to write about what was read
- Time for students to talk about what was read
- Time for students to talk about their responses to reading
- Opportunities for collaborative learning
- Instructional strategies that connect text with background knowledge
- Instruction that explicitly models comprehension strategies
- Instruction strategies that explicitly address how to access the text

Teachers of English learners in secondary schools can further enhance the classroom environment by including the adaptations featured in Box 7.6.

Making adaptations to text processing in order to increase reading success is a key to content area literacy. Text adaptation is also a key part of specially designed academic instruction in English.

Strategic Instructional Practices for English Learners. Proficient, competent readers use a wide range of strategies to read; these strategies must be taught so that English learners can become strategic readers in English. Researchers such as Chamot and O'Malley (1994), in their work with English learners, suggested that language, content area

box 7.6

Generic Reading Adaptations for English Learners at the Secondary Level

- Use read-alouds.
- Create a print-rich environment.
- Accommodate students' interests and backgrounds.
- Read, read, read.
- Use systematic, varied strategies for recognizing words.
- Use a variety of reading methods to raise interest.
- Integrate language activities.
- Activate students' prior knowledge.
- Provide authentic purpose, materials, and audiences in the development of oracy and literacy.
- Construct, examine, and extend meaning.
- Provide explicit instruction of what, when, and why.
- Provide opportunities for students to take control of the reading process.

knowledge, and literacy are not mutually exclusive and should be taught in an integrated, holistic manner.

Moreover, the instructional process should evolve from being teacher-directed to being student-centered. In teaching these strategies, teachers should explain, model, and allow students to practice and accept responsibility for their learning. As students acquire these strategies, they gain confidence in their reading and ability to access the text, and begin to extend and apply this confidence and ability to new situations.

This approach is collaborative and supports the teaching with integrity model proposed in this book because it is based on the assumption that students are equal partners in the teaching and learning process. The teacher's responsibility is to activate prior knowledge, explain and model strategies, provide extensive feedback, encourage students to apply this knowledge to new situations, and coordinate assessment. A student's responsibility is to participate and be attentive, practice the strategies with guidance, evaluate the usefulness of these strategies, and use strategies independently.

Physical Education, Adolescents, and Lifelong Fitness

The view of physical fitness and education has changed drastically during the past 10 years, moving away from always emphasizing competitive sports toward greater emphasis on lifelong fitness. Physical education classes play an important role in the schooling of English learners because these are the classes that tend to be the most integrated linguistically. Class size is usually large, and students are usually mixed with many different students who may not be in their core classes. This provides an important opportunity for teachers to mix and blend talents as students engage in the task of lifelong fitness.

Content Standards.   The relationship between health and overall well-being (social, emotional, mental, spiritual) is little recognized, yet it underlies most content standards in physical education. Given the sedentary lifestyle of many youths and the increasing social concern about overweight youngsters, the teaching of physical education becomes a lifelong process important in today's fast-paced society. Thus physical education is not solely about teaching discrete athletic skills and competitiveness and favoring only those who have obvious athletic abilities and skills. It is about taking students where they are and teaching to the uniqueness of each individual.

Treating each student as an individual is important with adolescents because the range of physical development is so broad, and early bloomers tend to be favored not only in their physical education courses but also in the social aspect of their lives. English learners are not different from their peers in this way. Teachers who teach with integrity teach to the whole child because they recognize this important aspect of a shared humanity.

The Language of Physical Education: Sports Jargon. Physical education teachers frequently comment that their subject lends itself to working with English learners because it does not rely on reading and writing; and when it comes to speaking, students can engage informally in an environment that is nonthreatening. Although this perception may be true, no one can deny that physical education, like other disciplines, has its own jargon and set of technical terms.

Any sport, for example, has a set of rules that govern participants' behavior as well as terms for specific equipment. Here begin some of the specific language demands placed on English learners. Also, students must listen to instructions, share strategies, and receive feedback on their performance. All of these activities are language dependent and therefore rely on teachers to modify and adapt their language to provide access to English learners.

The Activity System: It's All about Activity. At the core of a physical education curriculum is activity. Although many physical education departments do have their students engage in writing and reading activities, the majority of the work in physical education involves movement and activity.

As suggested earlier, activity in physical education classes does not have to be dominated by competitiveness that favors the school jocks or jockettes. Teachers can involve students in sports by tapping into the interests and prior knowledge students bring to the activity. For example, many teachers introduce cultural games that can broaden students' experiences and awareness of how physical education is a human enterprise, with people throughout the world engaging in it in different ways. Many English learners are quite skillful in popular sports such as soccer or baseball, and observant teachers can facilitate learning some of the jargon in English while also having the English learners work as peer coaches with other students.

Assessment. Because physical education has shifted to an emphasis on lifelong learning, as opposed to winning and competitiveness, teachers can use multiple alternative assessments with students that provide individual feedback on their progress and gains. For example, teachers can develop individual growth charts that students themselves maintain and that also help encourage self-monitoring. These growth charts can be a type of portfolio that shows the before, during, and after progress of a student's work in physical education.

Teachers can also ask students to perform a movement and quickly give informal and immediate feedback. Teachers can model for students those areas that may need strengthening, and the students can practice as the teacher observes. In this way, English learners receive feedback on their work in a contextualized setting filled with comprehensible input.

The physical education class also leads itself to peer assessment, as students can help and assist one another in giving feedback and correcting inappropriate movements.

Resources.   The resources selected by the physical education teacher should reflect the overall goal of lifelong learning, as well as inclusiveness of all students (English learners and special education students, for example).

Scarcity in resources often denies low-status students (such as less athletic, special education, and/or females) access to materials and thus limits their experiences in physical education. Teachers with integrity are vigilant and aware of these dynamics and ensure that resources are inclusive and accessible to all students. Technology can be a useful tool in physical education. It is not uncommon to see teachers using videos, interviews with sports personalities, and music to encourage their students in their path toward lifelong fitness. Providing all students the opportunity to experience success in physical education can go far toward creating a healthy social and emotional school climate at the secondary level.

Music in the Secondary School

As mentioned in the discussion of music in elementary schools, music is a powerful manifestation of cultural heritage. And while music can promote and encourage multicultural understanding, it also has academic benefits. Studies abound that describe the positive correlations between music and grades, and other findings suggest that concepts learned in music are transferred and applicable to core areas such as mathematics and history.

Unfortunately, music education is not made available to many students in public schools, and it is not uncommon to hear that students from urban areas have not had any music classes. English learners also tend to be excluded from music classes because administrative priority is on learning English. The contributions they can bring to a music program are systematically interrupted by discriminatory practices that do not allow these students to choose their elective courses.

Content Standards in Music.   Music instruction generally incorporates four arts components: artistic perception, creative expression, historical and cultural context, and aesthetic valuing. Listening and perceiving patterns are critical skills in music, and effective music teachers emphasize and teach these skills explicitly and routinely.

The elementary-level music curriculum should lay the foundation for the middle and high school music program that is centered on putting into practice what was learned earlier. Music, as other subjects, gradually increases in complexity, and students cannot perform musical pieces without having mastered basic skills in singing, for example. Also, music programs work closely with the performing arts, providing students with opportunities to see interdisciplinary connections and to examine topics in more depth.

Music as Language.   Music is a universal language. All cultures make music and express their cultural heritage in the sounds they select to make their music. However, music has its own language that students must learn in order to become proficient performers. Take, for example, words such as *jazz, pitch, atonality,* and *folk music.* These are important technical concepts specific to music that may pose a challenge for many English learners if not taught within the proper context.

The Activity System: Let's Sing and Play.   In the secondary school setting, music is about singing and playing—and this usually means public performance. Students participate in valuable experiences that help them display their hard work and talents when they perform. These student performances allow young musicians to demonstrate musical growth and the results of hard work to gain personal satisfaction from their achievement and to experience the joy of making music.

Active music programs promote music festivals, noontime concerts, school assemblies featuring student musicians and groups, community presentations, and participation in community events such as parades and local celebrations. Diversity is an important consideration in these performances; they provide opportunities for the audience, as well as the musicians, to broaden their musical experiences by hearing and playing more than classical music.

Assessment.   Assessment in music is ongoing, formal and informal, and closely intertwined with instruction. At times it is hard to establish where one ends and the other begins. Assessment becomes instruction when students and teachers reflect together on content standards and discuss ways of achieving those standards.

Wolf and Pinstone (1991) suggested there are five components of assessment in the arts: excellence of learning and performance; judgment and decisions based on insight, reason, and craft; self-assessment; varied forms of assessment, including group and individual performances; and reflection. Assessment viewed in this way is a snapshot of learning.

Musical Resources.   Technology is increasingly an important resource in music education. The most powerful application in music education may be the use of computers, allowing students to improvise, make arrangements, and access vast libraries of recorded music. When instruments are connected to electronic instruments and computers, these can be used to record, transcribe, and even permit practice performances.

Musical and cultural resources abound in all communities, and skillful music educators tap into these resources by working with parents, churches, and other civic organizations. Local musicians, professionals, music faculty at local universities, and students at colleges and universities can conduct sessions and workshops as supplements to the regular instructional program. Many parents also have musical backgrounds and knowledge, and they can enrich a program by attending school events.

Many students from low-income homes, including English learners, cannot afford instruments and therefore are not able to participate in the music program. Teachers should work together with parents and community groups to have a set of instruments that students can borrow while they purchase an instrument.

This was my experience. My parents were unable to purchase a flute for my band class, yet the school provided a loaner. Then when I got to high school, my parents bought one for me and by this time, I was an integral part of both marching and concert bands. Had the school not supported my musical interests in this way, it is likely that I would not have continued my musical education until graduating from high school. (MVB)

Visual Arts in the Secondary School

The visual arts express a common humanity, because all humans attempt visual expression. Visual arts have been used in all cultures to express ideas, emotions, traditions, and beliefs. Arts in the secondary school setting include creative expressions such as painting, drawing, photography, and sculpture, as well as those that combine media, such as environmental art and multimedia.

Visual arts classes in secondary schools should involve everyone regardless of their future aspirations in this field. Creative expression should be encouraged, with emphasis on the creative process and not on the product.

Content Standards: Curriculum in Visual Arts Education.   As previously suggested, effective art instruction calls for regular, planned, cumulative instruction beginning in preschool and continuing through high school. In this way, by the time students take visual arts classes in middle and secondary school, they have mastered some of the basic techniques and can specialize in specific areas.

Art programs tend to emphasize four aspects: artistic perception (an understanding of the visual characteristics of artworks and the influences of people who created them), creative expression (interpretations of thoughts, perceptions, and ideas in creating artworks), historical and cultural contexts (understanding the creative expression of human beings across time and cultures), and aesthetic valuing (analyzing and responding to their own works and the works of others).

Language in the Visual Arts.   The primary medium of visual arts is visual and therefore language often takes a secondary role. Nonetheless, artists have a way of doing art and there is a language to express those ways. Part of an effective visual arts education is learning an appropriate language that describes artistic expression and creates a common language in the community of artists. Explicit teaching of words such as *movement, medium,* and *organic* that have unique meanings in art is part of effective teaching, particularly with English learners, who may have learned these words in another context. Art lends itself to contextualization of terms but still requires careful and skillful teaching to connect language and art.

The Art Activity System: Student-Centered.   Art is individual, or student-centered. The nature of the enterprise demands engagement by the individual student and provides a unique opportunity for students to become involved. Some students may exhibit fear or be self-conscious, and it is the responsibility of the teacher to create an environment that is safe (much like a language classroom) and supports effort. Students who do not feel threatened may be more willing to risk new forms of expression.

Assessment: Evaluating Creativity?   As suggested earlier in the discussion of assessment in music, instruction and assessment go hand in hand; they occur almost simultaneously in the visual arts. The teacher and the artist interact and collaborate, creating a cycle of ongoing feedback, with self-monitoring and self-assessment as a part of the daily experience.

Portfolios are common assessment tools used by artists in the performing arts because they track individual growth. They can help high school students, for example, apply for college entrance to an art institute or apply for employment in the visual arts.

Student exhibitions are also ways in which teachers can create safe opportunities for assessment, whereby peers and other adults can give feedback on completed works or works-in-progress. These exhibitions can take place in the classroom, and rubrics can be developed by the class to look for basic elements in a work.

Our World: Resources in Art.   The world in which we live is the major resource available to artists, and students should begin to recognize this as quickly as possible. A school event can be the inspiration for a picture painted by a student, and an important person in a student's life (including himself or herself) can result in interesting portraits and self-portraits that integrate artistic skills.

Conclusion: Promoting Achievement through Academic Curricula

Teachers of English learners select and use teaching strategies with an analytical and critical eye. Research frequently suggests what works, but is equally important to ask what works for whom, when, and under what specific conditions. This is particularly important with diverse students such as English learners. The levels of English-language development are an important consideration in selecting specific strategies, as well as the student's culture, ability, age, or learning style. For example, the inquiry method, though widely used, is based on assumptions about questioning and problem solving that are not universally shared (Payne, 1977). Thus the inquiry method may be quite effective in certain cultural settings and with certain groups of students, but ineffective in others.

Joyce, Weil, and Calhoun (2003) suggest that effective teaching strategies help students learn academic skills, ideas, and information; develop values and social skills; and understand themselves and their environment; they also provide students with repertoires of powerful tools for acquiring education. Teachers with integrity accept the professional responsibility and arduous tasks involved in making decisions that make effective content area teaching a reality.

8 English-Language Development

English learners survey children's books to prepare for cross-age tutoring.

expectations

Prospective teachers . . .

■ Can know and apply pedagogical theories, principles, and instructional practices for English-language development leading to comprehensive literacy in English. *(Element 7.2 of the California Teaching Performance Expectations)*

■ Are familiar with the philosophy, design, goals, and characteristics of programs for English-language development, including structured-English immersion *(Element 7.3 of the California Teaching Performance Expectations)*

■ Can implement an instructional program that facilitates English-language development, including reading, writing, listening, and speaking skills, that logically progresses to the grade-level reading/language-arts program for English speakers. *(Element 7.4 of the California Teaching Performance Expectations. Reprinted by permission of the California Commission on Teacher Credentialing.)*

English-language development (ELD) is a specialty that is central to the role of teachers of English learners. ELD includes reading (both content area reading and literature), writing, speaking/oral language development, and listening as key skills. (ELD is represented as a key instructional application in Figure 2.2, page 34.) Teachers need an array of strategies and techniques to draw on as they teach English. The general expectations for knowledge and skills in this area are outlined above. ELD in the specific elementary- and secondary-level academic content areas was addressed in Chapter 7.

Teachers of English learners bear the responsibility for teaching English as a regular part of the school day. This is a radical departure from the days when English learners were submerged in regular instruction, expected to "swim" easily into the curriculum—when in reality many learners had that sinking feeling that they were swimming after a ship that was leaving them behind. Alternatively, teachers could place English learners in "pull-out" ESL classes, on the assumption that a half hour of focus on English would provide adequate skills to perform academic work.

However, neither the sink-or-swim nor pull-out ESL approaches were specifically designed to move English learners from the beginning levels of English through basic communication skills into a mastery of academic English, the key to success in school. Teachers of social studies, science, math, and the arts are now expected to contribute to literacy in English as a part of their classroom instruction, using ELD standards, if available, as a guide.

This chapter addresses the pedagogical theories, principles, and practices for ELD leading to comprehensive literacy. Seven major facets of English-language instruction provide the key components that lead to success or failure for English learners. These are (1) the connection between ELD standards and instruction, (2) ELD curriculum issues and design, (3) characteristics of English learners, (4) commitment to dual-language proficiency, (5) program models of ELD, (6) the political context of ELD pedagogy, and (7) teaching methods in oracy (speaking and listening) and literacy (reading and writing). Because of the importance of linking dual-language instruction with ELD, program models are discussed in this chapter.

The Connection between English-Language Development Standards and Instruction

English-language development (ELD) standards connect English learner's current level of proficiency to the language characteristic of the next desired level in a systematic way. California's ELD standards are matched to the English language arts (ELA) (K–12) standards so that the movement from ELD to ELA is clearly articulated (see Table 8.1).

Once the California English Language Development Test (CELDT) or some other placement test has determined the student's proficiency level, the classroom teacher plans ELD objectives and activities that are not only designed for the student to learn English skills appropriate to the day's objectives, but also designed so that the student can be "checked off" as having attained a proficiency characteristic at the next level in the categories stipulated in the ELD standards. An additional challenge is for the same lesson plan to contain ELD activities at two or more levels if students in the same classroom are at different levels of English acquisition. (See Table 8.2.)

table 8.1   Alignment of ELD and ELA Standards

ELD Standard	ELA Standard
Word analysis Fluency and systematic vocabulary development	Word analysis, fluency, and systematic vocabulary development
Reading comprehension	Reading comprehension Expository critique (grades 5 and up)
Literary response & analysis	Literary response & analysis
Writing	
Strategies and applications	Strategies Applications
Conventions	Written (and oral) English-language conventions
Listening and Speaking	
Strategies and applications	Written (and oral) English-language conventions

Thus, no matter what the current level of English proficiency, it is crucial to move the student systematically upward from beginner to advanced, until the learner's abilities are ready to be described and developed by the English language arts standards used to guide mainstream instruction.

English-Language Development Curriculum Issues

ELD is a complex endeavor, both as pedagogy and as a discipline. The instruction of English learners in K–12 classrooms, when well designed and implemented, adheres to the best practices recommended by researchers in the field of second-language acquisition. These principles, which were addressed in Chapter 4, are reviewed here. Second-language instruction

■ Is consonant with second-language acquisition theory, particularly interlanguage theory

■ Respects and builds on the language produced by the learner, including the dialect and accent used

■ Fully engages and develops the constructive, communicative, critical, and creative aspects of mind

■ Meshes behavioral, cognitive, and humanistic educational psychologies in addressing the needs of the learner

■ Offers language functions that augment and complement those available in the first language

■ Accompanies, and is integrated with, academic instruction in all content areas

table 8.2 ELD Activities in the Same Lesson That Provide Evidence for Different Levels of ELD Standards (Grades K–5)

ELD Standard	ELD Level	Activity
Reading Comprehension (comprehension and analysis of grade-appropriate text): E. Trivizas. (1993). *The Three Little Wolves and the Big Bad Pig.* New York: Simon & Schuster.		
Identifies the basic sequence of events in stories read aloud using key words, pictures, or student-generated drawings.	Beginning	Students draw cartoon strip of story events, using a given set of vocabulary words and "speech bubbles."
Uses simple sentences to respond to stories by answering factual comprehension questions during guided reading.	Intermediate	Students make up questions about story to ask each other in pairs.
Locates and uses text features such as title, table of contents, chapter headings, diagrams, and index.	Advanced	Students use story and an edition of *The Three Little Pigs* to make a chart comparing the two books on features such as title, author, illustrator, plot, number of characters, number of illustrations, and cover design.
Listening and Speaking		
Demonstrates comprehension of stories through active listening/participation.	Beginning	As teacher reads book aloud, students take turns acting out plot events.
Retells stories and participates in instructional and social conversations using expanded vocabulary.	Intermediate	Students make a list of key nouns in story; make a list of synonyms for key nouns; retell story with synonyms.
Identifies orally and in writing key details and concepts from information/stories on unfamiliar topics.	Advanced	Using plot device from similar version of the story (such as *The Trial of the Big Bad Wolf*), students will "put the wolf on trial" by role-playing three teams (prosecutor, judge, and defendants), using key details from the book to make or defend a case when the wolf goes on trial for what he does to the pigs.
Writing Strategies and Applications		
Produces patterned and modeled writing.	Beginning	The teacher creates a set of patterned sentences for the students to finish about what happens to the pig scene by scene.
Writes short narratives to include setting and character.	Intermediate	Students and teacher together create a new scene as a group using the Language Experience Approach showing what else the wolves might do to the pig.
Writes short narratives that describe the setting, character, objects, and events.	Advanced	Students rewrite the book in pairs, featuring new scenes showing what else the wolves might do to the pig.

With these principles in mind, teachers must also realize that there is no one best ELD method or set of methods. The skilled instructor chooses from a wide range of research-based practices, using formative and summative assessment to validate the success of a given practice. The following sections elaborate on ELD teaching that matches several of the listed principles.

Interlanguage Theory and ELD Teaching

Learners of a second language have only one starting point: their primary language. Therefore every understanding they have of the second language is filtered through their existing knowledge. As they become more familiar with the second language (in this case, English), they move toward learning that builds on their new knowledge base. Until they have that new knowledge, however, the language they produce is a hybrid form, an interlanguage.

How does a teacher explore what the learner knows? Examining what the learner produces, the teacher designs lessons that advance English proficiency by identifying a skill the learner needs (using the categories provided by a framework such as the ELD standards).

This process is built on two central ideas: First, the language a learner produces is not a flawed misrepresentation of English, but a creative expression of the learner's innate language "genius," an ability that only flourishes in humans. Second, the errors the learner makes (systematic errors that show a pattern of thinking, not random mistakes) are a necessary part of the learning process, as well as a source of information for the teacher. Thus the learner's interlanguage (and no two learners' interlanguages are identical) is the foundation for ELD teaching that respects and delights in individual creativity, channeled through the ELD standards.

ELD Respects and Builds on the Language Produced by the Learner

Because learners rely on the English they hear in their families, community, and peer conversations, many English learners learn to speak English with an accent; with code-switching; and with colloquial expressions, slang, and local vocabulary. This is a natural part of the flavor of English. At the beginning levels of ELD, the teacher encourages fluency in English. At the advanced levels and in academic contexts, the focus may shift toward accuracy of Standard English use. However, many of the most gifted writers in English have drawn on the creativity and color of dialects, so the variants of English used around the world and in U.S. classrooms are welcome as features of the learner's interlanguage.

ELD Fully Engages and Develops the Mind

Ideally, ELD activities would be the most mentally stimulating, creative, and communicative aspect of the school day. The imagination is a key element of language learning that must be engaged in order for the curiosity that impelled first-language acquisition to be deployed again for a second language. Creative dramatics, creative writing, critical thinking, and other forms of inspiring and thought-provoking endeavors are central to good teaching. Using imaginative language advances L2 proficiency because by definition the imagination goes where the mind has not previously gone.

Overreliance on Direct Instruction.   Teachers without specific training in English-language development too often rely on literacy instruction that uses direct instruction to teach basic skills. These skills-based lessons employ a heavy-handed, didactic approach that drills students with decoding skills, accompanied by comprehension exercises in which the only questions permitted are those asked of students by the teacher, and the only correct answers are those listed in the teacher's guide. Learning English is redefined as reading English, whereas in the life of a native speaker, reading is subordinated to oral language—the ability to communicate and negotiate to achieve life goals.

This overuse of basic-skills instruction undermines the integrity a teacher brings to the vocation, because it assumes that the teacher lacks the adequate professional preparation necessary to create lessons that meet the needs of the students without following a script.

The message underlying this approach is "the purpose of reading is to decode text and to read exactly what is put in front of you; and if you do it well, you can go on to read more of the same, until you grow up reading exactly what is put in front of you." Under the regime of direct instruction, reading texts are preselected, instruction is scripted for word-for-word delivery, and the short-term decoding success that may result is no guarantee that anyone has learned either to love to read or to love English.

Few middle-class native-English-speaking students are taught by means of highly scripted, routinized programs such as Open Court; instead their instruction is dialogic and teaching is considered a conversation (Page, 1991). Why, then, should direct teaching be considered exemplary practice for English learners? Literacy education that emphasizes narrow, bottom-up skills without the top-down pleasures of literature and great ideas makes schooling boring, leading to student disinterest and alienation. The message is that society is set up to push English learners away from literacy, resulting in disempowerment.

The pedagogical assumptions of the direct method of reading for English learners fit suspiciously well with the commercial and political interests of publishers who can significantly reduce their costs by producing textbooks that can be used anywhere, irrespective of the students' language and culture (Cook, 2001).

Yet it is the very specificity of language and culture that delights readers, who recognize themselves in the stories of authors and the illustrations of artists. In fact, often it is the passion, interests, and worldview of the teacher's literacy experience that reproduces that passion in students as readers. Under the stifling control of mandated direct teaching, passion has no place.

A Balanced Skills Approach.   Gifted teachers know they cannot simply teach English learners to read, write, speak, listen, or think; literacy is more than reading and writing with the purpose of finding one's place in the existing social order. If that were true, English learners would too often find themselves marginalized, floating at the edge of mainstream society, which does not extend itself to welcome or support other languages and cultures. English-language development must instead transform lives.

To make the best use of students' English language arts time, teachers implement a balanced approach that combines skills-based reading, literary reading, and independent reading with vocabulary acquisition, grammar, and spelling. These activities are carried out in combination with writing, listening, and speaking in an integrated approach to the language arts (Pappas, Kiefer, & Levstik, 2006).

As they teach reading, educators who have the learners' best interests at heart watch closely to make note of the kinds of oracy and literacy that inspire and delight learners.

Learning activities that respect the students' primary language and culture, interests, and imagination are the heart of English-language development.

ELD Combines with Educational Psychology to Address the Needs of the Learner

Learning a second language requires a combination of cognitive, humanistic, and behavioral psychology. It is a cognitive process because it challenges the brain to recode reality with new labels and new methods of social interaction. It is humanistic because teachers must carefully support the learner's ego and self-esteem through the culture shock of operating in a new language system. Teaching ELD is behavioral because learning such features of a language as vocabulary and idioms, sentence structures, and spelling requires repetition, drill, and precision, all of which can be supported by behaviorist pedagogy (use of distributed practice, rewards, etc.)

First- and second-language acquisition draw on different kinds of brain operation in ways that are only now being researched. One clue may be that in first-language acquisition, the brain cells governing language seem to soak up input until they are fully developed. In second-language acquisition, a set of brain cells may have to divert themselves from other functions to create a new network of connections that are somehow optional. In other words, ELD learning is an add-on, an option to a learner's life, so it requires every nuance of psychology on the part of the teacher to make it vital and relevant.

ELD Builds Language Acquisition through Social Functions

To fully challenge the learner, the second language should build on and advance the first language, rather than replace it. In other words, the functions of the second language should be even more advanced than the first language. How is this possible, when the learner is fluent in the first language and at the beginning stages of the second?

One answer to this challenge lies in the social-function approach to second-language acquisition. Halliday (1978) distinguished seven different **social functions of language:** *instrumental* (getting needs met); *regulatory* (controlling others' behavior); *informative* (communicating information); *interactional* (establishing social relationships); *personal* (expressing individuality); *heuristic* (investigating and acquiring knowledge); and *imaginative* (expressing fantasy). Later researchers have emphasized the importance of academic functions of language (cognitive academic language proficiency, or CALP). Providing English learners with opportunities to engage in the various functions of language is critical if they are to develop a full range of proficiency in English.

ELD Is Integrated with Academic Instruction

Learning academic functions in English advances the learner toward CALP in English. Learning sophisticated interpersonal language (for example, the language of peer editing, or how to be a peer tutor) advances overall language functioning. This approach to English instruction ensures that the second language does not become a poor shadow of the first, with dumbed-down instruction that assumes the learner is a "blank slate" that must be filled with language, starting with basic skills.

The Four-Part Literacy Curriculum

The following four-part schema guides the teaching of ELD reading and language arts in grades K–12. (See Table 8.3.) This schema would be similar in the language arts program

table 8.3   Schema to Guide the Teaching of Reading and Language Arts

	Literature	Language Arts	Grammar	Usage
Goals	Reading for enjoyment and love of language; study human nature	Use ELD materials that are aligned with content area subjects (thematic integration) to supplement content area instruction by emphasizing critical and creative thinking and cognitive academic language proficiency	Learn how language works: parts of speech and correct sentence structure	Learn spelling, capitalization, punctuation, and penmanship
Basic Skills Taught	Decoding, comprehension, and instructional conversation	Vocabulary acquisition, learning strategies	Subject–verb agreement, sentence types, verb tenses	Identifying comma faults, rules for capitalization
Texts Used	Basal readers, chapter books, books for independent reading, nonfiction texts	Content-based ESL series	Grammar textbook	Spelling workbook that groups words together according to similar rules; usage rules are usually in grammar textbooks as appendices

in the primary language. Each of the four literacy areas is based on a different set of goals, connected with the core curriculum and curricular materials.

Literature as an Art Form.   Great literature has a unique curricular contribution as an art form, featuring insights into human nature and beauty of language, and it should not be made to serve functional purposes, such as learning spelling or other subjects. The selection of stories that students read should be supplemented by, not dictated by, thematic integration with other content domains.

Vocabulary Acquisition.   The vocabulary that is acquired for understanding text—*recognition vocabulary*—is usually larger than a learner's *production vocabulary,* words that students use when they write about ideas stimulated by literature. Recognition vocabulary should be disassociated with work on spelling. It is not important to spell acquisition vocabulary correctly, but rather to understand the meaning of these words in context and be able to use them orally in discussion. This is what makes literature an exciting expansion of an individual's worldview.

Teaching Grammar.   The language arts are taught using an ELD series, coordinated with standards in the content areas taught in the core curriculum (in either primary language or

SDAIE-modified instruction). Grammar is taught explicitly using a grammar book that presents systematic references and explains grammar points with a suitable degree of accuracy; an example is Byrd and Benson's *Problem-Solution: A Reference for ESL Writers* (1994), an excellent resource that covers grammar points with clear explanation and examples.

Awareness of sentence structure can be enhanced by having students work creatively with sentences. They can *expand* sentences by adding details to a simple sentence ("I went home for lunch" becomes "I skipped home with my mama's tortilla at the tip of my tongue"). They can *link* sentences by taking an element from a simple sentence and using it to create an image-rich subsequent sentence ("My cat brought me a lizard in her mouth" [The idea = something about the lizard] links to "I couldn't tell if that lizard was dead or just pretending"). They can *rearrange* sentences by moving internal phrases to the opening slot ("Lisa drives her tricycle out front to meet Papa when he comes home from work"/"When Papa comes home from work . . . ").

A focus on correct usage and sentence structure—including spelling, capitalization, and punctuation—is important for English learners, although this should not be taken to an extreme. Often mainstream teachers base their estimation of students' academic potential on a few key features of written production—namely, the look of writing, such as legible handwriting; correct spelling of basic words; and well-formed sentences. Therefore, as students write—for purposes of critical thinking, reaction to literature, or project-based learning—some products of their writing should be taken to the final, corrected draft stage.

Writing for Grammar.   Fun and engaging writing tasks can incorporate correct usage. One example is a tongue-in-cheek book a group of students produced about points of interest in the surrounding neighborhoods: *The Homegirls' Guide to South Seventh Street*. Key stores, names of streets, and even car brands were correctly capitalized. Another group collected recipes from home for a class meal that featured the imperative form of the verb ("Slice cucumbers thinly") (Shoemaker & Polycarpou, 1993). Thus correct usage and grammar can be an integral part of learning activities.

Spelling is taught using a workbook that organizes the words that are most often misspelled according to similar spelling. Spelling can also be augmented by words frequently misspelled in students' writing. A fun spelling activity is to collect words that "should be spelled" differently based on rules of "foniks." Last, correct usage of punctuation, capitalization, and paragraph structure are emphasized in the context of composition but not treated as the sole goal of writing.

Integrating Critical and Creative Writing.   In an integrated-skills classroom, the skills that constitute language arts are not separated. In the reading class, students might also be writing, speaking, listening, or thinking. "As students use language to learn, teachers collaborate, respond, facilitate, and support their efforts" (Pappas, et al., 2006, p. 1). As a part of integrated instruction, teachers provide a broad spectrum of activities that stimulate inquiry and advance language skills.

Thematic units provide a natural environment for the practice of language skills as students learn concepts in other areas of the curriculum. Many kinds of media—films, videos, computer simulations, literature, nonfiction texts, and oral discussions—help students to develop conceptual knowledge.

Student Characteristics in ELD Classrooms

One constant characteristic of ELD instruction is the fact that students are always at diverse English-proficiency levels. This is true for both elementary and secondary students, even though there is a tendency to think that secondary students have more advanced language skills overall. In fact, students at the beginning levels of second-language acquisition are found at the secondary level also.

Students also bring diverse histories of previous schooling. Some students' families and communities offer exposure to English, whereas others live in primary-language enclaves with little daily use of English. Therefore the extent of students' prior knowledge and English proficiency varies widely. Providing differentiated instruction to groups of students with varied proficiency levels is a constant challenge.

This does not differ greatly from content area instruction, in which students are also at various levels; it is simply more noticeable. Content learning is also a creative synthesis of previous and new learning; this is the basis of constructivist teaching. The challenge in both English-language development and content instruction is to move away from didactic teaching methods toward methods that encourage students to build new knowledge on their prior knowledge and make more effective use of cognitive, metacognitive, and social–affective learning strategies.

Specific techniques of differentiated instruction take into consideration students' varying second-language proficiency. Along with this variation, the other individual difference factors detailed in Chapter 3 play a large role (a student's age, different degrees of past school success, L1 proficiency, learning styles and strategies, social–emotional adjustment, and sociocultural background). A student's degree of success in attaining English-language proficiency predicts how well the student is able to use English to obtain more English, whether from negotiation with the teacher, from reading, or by means of peer interaction.

Commitment to Dual-Language Proficiency

Teachers of English learners carry out their teaching informed by the realization that teaching is a political act. If ELD is taught in a school setting that neither involves nor supports the primary language of the student, what results lends support to subtractive bilingualism—learners are unable to benefit from dual-language proficiency. In developmental bilingual or two-way immersion programs, the primary language is a full partner in instruction. ELD teachers in transitional bilingual education or submersion programs have the professional responsibility to advocate for programs that instead support the students' primary-language development.

English-language development in the K–12 classroom, then, is most beneficial to the student if additive bilingualism is the goal. The most desirable goal is to produce students who use both languages as highly educated, sophisticated, polished tools of communication. If this is not the case, graduates of schools in the United States will be disadvantaged in comparison with those of other countries around the world whose educational systems have better prepared them to be multicompetent language users.

Both the primary language and the native culture play key roles in instruction. Academic content, English-language development, and primary-language development are the three cornerstones of instruction, but these three are inextricably bound up with culture. It is cultural knowledge about how to "do" schooling that creates and sustains the role of scholar, the cultural knowledge in English that permits a healthy participation in mainstream culture, and the love of the native culture that develops and maintains connections to family and the life of the mind in another language.

One caution here: The first language is not to be used solely as a means for learning English or disciplining students. In a program that genuinely develops first language, the primary language functions also as an advance toward sophisticated language use. The well-educated, multicompetent language user needs to master skills in multiple languages. The second language needs to pace the first language in these areas.

The Political Context of ELD Pedagogy

Clarity of vision is necessary for teachers to understand the contemporary context of ELD instruction. It is a field often rife with politicized rhetoric, ethnic politics, and politically influenced educational decision making. Discrimination sometimes creates distrust, such as preferential hiring of native speakers of English as ELD instructors or ELD administrators or, conversely, preferential hiring of native primary-language speakers as teachers or administrators of two-way immersion programs. Educators who work hard to advocate programs that support dual-language competency will dedicate themselves to achieving solidarity in the face of these politics.

Discussion of the political issues surrounding the education of English learners takes place throughout this book. The complexity of the social and political issues in which education is situated requires a high degree of clarity of vision on the part of teachers with integrity, as well as an ethical dedication to working toward the best service for students.

Oracy in English-Language Development

L2 **oracy**—learning to speak and listen in a second language—makes it possible for students to succeed in school. English learners already know a great deal about using oral language in their primary language. They know how to share their thoughts and opinions with others, to use language strategically to get what they want, to get attention, to take turns, and so forth. This is oral metalinguistic awareness—how language works.

Bourdieu (1977) called this knowledge "linguistic capital," a part of the resources that English learners bring to schooling. Of course, if native English speakers have a dialect characteristic of the middle class and are backed by a houseful of cultural capital such as atlases, encyclopedias, magazines, and other reference materials, the oral language they use is even more valuable as linguistic capital. The knowledge about life coded in the L1 is still worth quite a lot, however, if the teacher views this knowledge as a resource that can be tapped to promote academic success.

To be able to listen and speak is to communicate meaning and intent. However, these skills are grounded in knowledge and power practices that have social and political dimensions. Oracy is inextricably joined with cultural identity and social differences, and opportunities to listen and speak are differentiated according to the individual's relationship to institutions and sociocultural contexts. Direct connections to the community and to the circulation of power (Foucault, 1980) strengthen the chance that an individual's investment in learning to speak and listen will actually enhance his or her cultural capital.

Each student in Nora Bryce's ELD class created a short presentation about some aspect of the native culture. They practiced giving the presentations to one another during class. As members of the Cultural Ambassadors Club, various students went with Nora in pairs to the breakfast Kiwanis meeting twice a month. The Kiwanis members became so interested in the students' presentations that they devoted their fundraising activity to awarding the Club members college scholarships. In this way, community connections enhanced the students' cultural capital and vice versa.

Children's intellectual development is built on verbal interaction in the first language; according to Vygotsky (1981), children learn to engage in higher-level thinking by first listening and speaking. Thus the more students use language within the social context of the classroom, the better they will learn how to think. Teaching strategies provide imaginative ways to use oral language to further develop students' intellects. The following sections discuss ways to teach English oracy using processes that build on students' primary language.

Goals of Oral Language Development

At the beginning and intermediate stages of second-language acquisition, the goal is for students to become *fluent* rather than *accurate* speakers. The goal is not to reduce the number of errors made, but to have students produce more errors—the more language they produce, the more they learn, and hence the more errors made. (*Errors* in this sense means those that are systematic, rather than random, mistakes). Errors are windows into the learner's interlanguage competence and learning strategies—they show the ways that learners are thinking about English.

Language, like many other mental processes, is learned through "best-guessing"—the mind is satisfied with "almost right" and uses approximation when practicing. An atmosphere of acceptance helps the learner risk speaking. Complexification, not simplification, is the key to language growth. When output is encouraged, the learner moves toward a more complex, rather than error-free, language environment. If the teacher engenders in the learner sophisticated communication needs that require production of more advanced language, language acquisition keeps moving forward.

Listening Processes

According to a key principle of the Natural Approach (Krashen & Terrell, 1983), second-language learners go through a silent period in which they listen, without venturing to speak. They try to separate sounds into words, absorbing intonation patterns and "soaking" themselves in the foreign phonemes, learning to become comfortable in the second-language environment. Therefore, although listening may seem to be a receptive skill, it is by no means a passive act—it is a key way to construct meaning.

Listeners draw on two sources to try to understand spoken language: their store of background knowledge and their expectation of the message conveyed. The teacher's role is to set up situations in which students can develop their own purposes and goals for listening, acquire the English that is most useful in their daily lives, and feel a sense of purpose as they engage in real communication.

Listening is made up of two types: conversational listening (listening for communication) and academic listening (Long, 1987). When students listen for communication, the emphasis is on developing the abilities to communicate fluently and accurately by integrating listening and speaking. At the very beginning stages, when students need to hear sound patterns and sentence structures, they can sit at a tape recorder or computer and listen to such input as rhyming poems, songs, couplets, tongue twisters, jingles, alliterative poems and books, and dialogues. As they acquire basic interpersonal communication skills, they can receive comprehensible input from their peers.

In casual conversation, a key difficulty for learners is the use of colloquial language and reduced forms such as contractions and words that are slurred or run together. Yesenia was chatting with Alicia before class, talking about the upcoming senior prom. What Alicia actually said was "I wish I could go." Yesenia was momentarily puzzled, thinking, "I thought she was talking about herself. Who is *Awushacud?*" (I-wish-I-could!)

Academic listening is more challenging for students because this is a key factor in gaining access to the core curriculum. The following activities are divided into the three main stages of the listening process. These suggestions can be adapted for use at both elementary and secondary levels of instruction.

Prelistening tasks can include a preview of vocabulary, a cue to the type of rhetoric expected (such as chronological order), or attention to a map that cues a spatial setting for the listening task or pictures that cue visual meaning. At this time, students can become aware of the objectives for the listening task, such as listening for the main idea, for transition words, or to identify the speaker's point of view.

While listening, students can follow an outline, take notes cued by a set of questions, or take notes in a variety of ways such as idea maps, outlines, paragraphs, or lists. If possible, students can listen several times to a recorded lecture or conversation, perhaps a videotaped version so that students can first concentrate on understanding and later review the videotape while taking notes (Adamson, 1993).

In a multilevel dictation activity, students are given a passage to read. Then they write the passage while the teacher dictates. The teacher makes four versions of the dictation task available. Level 4 is a blank page; level 3 has chunks of text omitted that students must hear and transcribe; level 2 has phrases omitted; and level 1 has single words omitted. Students can choose their level of participation (Hess, 2001).

After listening, many kinds of activities can take place. Students can write, discuss, read, draw, or act out their interpretation of the content; compare formal versus informal English; focus on words that compare/contrast; or make a list of transition words by type (e.g., sequence or contrast).

A "listening area" can be set up in which the English learners can listen to books on CDs; texts should include picture books or models set up to support understanding. It may be comforting to a child if the narrators of these books speak an accented English that is similar to the English spoken by people from the child's primary-language community. Some teachers ask older brothers and sisters to tape stories.

Students benefit from exposure to a variety of speakers, for a variety of tasks, on a variety of topics, for a variety of purposes. The ideal tasks are those that resemble the real world so that students can handle authentic interactions. Listeners must use a relatively sophisticated set of understandings: what to expect from the speaker, the setting in time and place, the topic, the genre of the text, and the accompanying clues to meaning. In face-to-face conversation, the listener draws on nonverbal cues to help sustain coherence and clarity (Brown & Yule, 1983). This depends more on exposure to comprehensible input than to direct instruction, but there is a role for both.

Despite the complexity of listening tasks and the emphasis on communicative approaches, however, listening is only half of the work in oral language development. Listeners must also learn to speak.

Speaking Processes

Speaking involves a number of complex skills. In spoken discourse, words must not only be strung together in proper grammatical sequence, but must also make sense. Some student speech is informal, such as conversations between friends; other speech is more formal, such as responding in class or making oral presentations. Informal conversations are interactive; speaker and listener share common knowledge and support each other with nonverbal cues. Formal presentations involve special preparation and training. Research shows that language learners develop best when they have opportunities to interact (see Wells, 1981). The role of the teacher is to help students assimilate and produce discourse not only for the purpose of basic interpersonal communication but also for the comprehension and production of cognitive academic language.

Basic Interpersonal Communication Skills.   Learning *basic interpersonal language skills* (BICS) helps a newcomer adjust to the routines of schooling, perform classroom chores, chat with peers, or consume instructional media. After acquiring BICS, students can begin to understand and communicate with their teacher, make friends, and adjust to a new culture. BICS is clearly more than words; some exchanges with people involve no words at all. BICS is *context embedded* because factors apart from the linguistic code can furnish meaning (Cummins, 1984). Table 8.4 provides examples of BICS that demonstrate how nonverbal cues such as tone of voice, actions, and gestures add meaning to situations.

If BICS is successful, payoffs follow quickly. Studies have shown that communication skills can approach nativelike levels within two years of exposure to English (Collier, 1987; Cummins, 1981a). When parents see their child using BICS, they may assume that the child has mastered English. However, students who may appear to be fluent enough in English to survive in an all-English classroom may in fact lack sufficient development of academic aspects of English.

The Teacher's Role.   Teachers can encourage newcomers' acquisition of basic social language in several ways: by pairing a new student with a bilingual buddy who speaks the same primary language (some BICS will nonetheless be learned), and by seating newcomers with other pupils to encourage interactive learning. A Newcomer's Handbook is helpful, with sections on simple school rules and procedures, a simple map of the school with bilingual labels, English phrases to use to ask for help and volunteer, and guides for homework help.

table 8.4   Context, Language, Action, and Nonverbal Cues in Basic Interpersonal Communication Skills

Context	Language	Action	Nonverbal Cues
Trinh begs for a turn on the tetherball:	"Hey! Mines! Mines!"	He grabs for the ball.	Demanding tone of voice.
Students are playing a math facts card game:	Lisa: "You cheated! Don't look hers!"	Lisa throws down her cards.	Lisa puts her hand on her hip, elbow out. Tone of voice is angry.
A girl is braiding another's hair:	The other girl says, "OK! Now take it out!"	She tries to take out the new braid.	Impatient tone of voice.
Students are chatting:	"I did the waterslide— it was cool."	The speaker makes a twisting motion with his body.	His face is lit up, and his tone of voice is excited.
Students are looking into the fish tank:	"Oh no—the little frogs are dead."	Student reaches for the fishnet.	Facial expression looks disgusted.
Teacher-fronted discussion:	"Who wrote the story? Who can tell me?"	Teacher looks for a volunteer to answer.	She is trying to make eye contact.

Amery's (1979) *The First Thousand Words: A Picture Word Book* and its companions, such as Amery and Milá's (1979) *The First Thousand Words in Spanish,* help students match vocabulary words with pictures for common classroom objects as well as objects in other contexts. *The Firefly Five Language Visual Dictionary: English, Spanish, French, German, Italian* (Corbeil & Archambault, 2004) is an excellent resource for secondary school students; it matches pictures with colloquial and academic terms.

Students in their silent period need not be isolated from high-achieving peers— cooperative tasks of all kinds provide opportunities for speaking that do not require a high level of verbal ability in English. Student participation in cooperative groups needs to be carefully structured in order to eliminate notions of high and low status within the group, such as rotating the roles of speaker and recorder.

An encouraging classroom climate helps students feel confident that they can speak freely and make mistakes, and that their way of speaking and their opinions are respected. Teachers who listen to students with enthusiasm and interest make it clear that they value students' thoughts. A noncompetitive atmosphere encourages sharing ideas through interaction, and a "productively talkative" work environment is busy but not overwhelmingly noisy.

The Classroom Environment.   A "home corner" set aside so that students can listen to CDs in the primary language or engage in English-optional activities gives students a break from the stress of second-language acquisition (Morgan, 1992). In kindergarten, this may involve nonverbal play; at the high school level, a book on CD in the native language can be stimulating. In addition, students need frequent opportunities to talk with a variety of classmates, cross-age tutors, aides, parent volunteers, and volunteer "grandparents" (Dudley-Marling & Searle, 1991).

Integrated Activities.   Speaking can be integrated with other literacy and oracy activities as students retell the stories they read and finish them in new ways. Inviting storytellers and community elders to class to tell stories provides rich stimuli and entertainment, as well as models of speaking behaviors that students can emulate. Cooperative speaking activities are an important part of SDAIE lessons. Some instructors stop for a "pair-share" break every few minutes so each student can ask a partner one question.

Students who have attained intermediate or early-advanced levels of English can give structured presentations. The teacher might invite students to give a private trial run before the presentation. Other students can help by participating in a peer-scoring rubric in which content is emphasized over understandability. However, it is wise not to surprise students with requests for extemporaneous speaking.

Table 8.5 organizes representative oral activities into the three categories suggested by Allen and Vallette (1977). These categories range from tightly structured on the left to freely constructed on the right.

Pronunciation.   English learners need a comprehensible control of the English sound system—the correct *articulation* of the individual sounds of English as well as the proper *stress* and *pitch* within syllables, words, and phrases, and sentence *intonation*. However,

table 8.5   Formats for Oral Practice in the ELD Classroom

Level	Guided Practice	Communicative Practice	Free Conversation
Beginning	Formulaic exchanges Greetings Congratulations Apologies Saying goodbye Dialogues	Simple opinion polls Guessing games	Mini-conversations Socializing
Intermediate	Role-plays	Group puzzles Survey taking Simulations	Group picture story Story retelling Discussion groups
Advanced	Skits Oral descriptions Strip stories Oral games	Rank-order problems Values continuum Interviews Brainstorming News reports Research reports Storytelling	Debates Panel discussions Discussions Films Shared experiences Literature

Source: Adapted from Díaz-Rico and Weed (2002). Based on categories in Allen and Vallette (1977).

English learners need not necessarily try to sound like native speakers of English—if they retain an accent that indicates their first-language roots, they can identify with their ethnic community. An accent is inevitable in the early stages of second-language acquisition. The teacher's role, in this case, is to create a nonthreatening environment that stimulates and interests students enough to participate actively in producing speech.

Correction while a person is speaking is seldom appropriate. If the teacher makes such correction, the speaker may become tense and unable to be fluent or creative. If the speaker is genuinely unintelligible, the teacher might pretend to misunderstand so that the student can rephrase—or might genuinely not understand and be honest about it. However, it impedes communication if the teacher expects an imperfect sentence to be repeated correctly. *Recasting* is the best alternative; if the teacher hears an incorrect utterance, a similar sentence said correctly can be repeated to the student naturally and in the context of the conversation without embarrassing the student (Bartram & Walton, 1994).

Communicative games are useful for practicing various aspects of intonation, syllabification, or stress. A game to practice intonation is "stress clapping." A student comes to the front of the room, pulls a sentence written on a folded overhead transparency strip out of a box, and displays the sentence on the overhead projector (sentences are taken from song lyrics, poems, or limericks). The student must read the sentence aloud and clap each time there is a stressed word. The student's team receives a point for each stressed word correctly identified (Mahoney, 1999).

Using a computer program for practice is a self-tutoring way in which students can improve their pronunciation. Such programs as Pronunciation Plus are fun and easy to use.

The Speaking Process.   Prespeaking activities warm the students to the topic and activate or provide some prior knowledge. Students can prepare for an impromptu speech on a news topic by watching the evening news on television, listening to a news radio station, reading the editorial page of a local newspaper, reading a newsmagazine such as *Time* or *Newsweek,* and/or talking to people outside of class about selected issues. Students who must prepare an oral presentation can use an advance outline that includes an attention-getting opener, a preview of what will be said, enough substance to complete the main body of the speech, a summary of the main points, and a memorable conclusion (Dale & Wolf, 1988).

Teachers can plan activities that vary by speaking level. At the beginning stage, when the goal is fluency, students can work in heterogeneous groups. At later stages, when the goal is accuracy, students can work in homogeneous groups. For example, first-grade beginning students listen to a fairy tale, retell the story using pictures, and then talk about the pictures. Intermediate students can retell the story to the teacher or a cross-age tutor who can write their story for them, and then students can reread, illustrate, and rearrange the story from sentence strips. A group of more proficient students can create a new group story.

Informal class discussions are a low-key way to practice speaking. Turns are usually shared in small groups, and one person does not monopolize discussion. For the most part, oral discussion is a vital part of any other task and should be developed as a way to engage students in critical thinking and intellectually productive social interaction.

Instructional Conversation. The instructional conversation (IC) is a small-group semi-structured discourse format in which the instructor functions as "thinker leader" while encouraging voluntary oral participation. The IC model (Goldenberg & Gallimore, 1991) has both instructional and conversational elements. The most important of the instructional elements is the establishment of a thematic focus. The text that participants read in common before beginning the conversation provides the basis for the theme. Because the goal of the IC is to develop a more complex understanding of the prompt, a good theme is one that is flexible enough to grow out of the ideas of the participants, rather than being superimposed on the group by the teacher. This flexibility causes participants to share responsibility for the discussion. At the same time, however, the teacher's responsibility is to see that the theme has a genuine connection to the prompt.

The conversational elements include those aspects that defuse anxiety and promote verbal interaction. One conversational element is the establishment of a challenging, non-threatening atmosphere for the participants. It is helpful, for example, to talk while seated in a circle of chairs versus sitting around a conference table. The circle gives individuals equal access to turns and facilitates eye contact. Disagreement and difference of opinion are protected, although part of the challenging atmosphere is for students to find a way to evaluate one another's viewpoints.

By means of the instructional conversation, the teacher and student can get to know each other better. Elsa Tran, a sixth-grade teacher, found it difficult to supervise 25 students while 8 students were conversing with her. As a way of finding additional time, she scheduled two lunch periods a week for 20-minute instructional conversations, so that over a period of two weeks each student could participate. As an unexpected result, she found that discipline problems were reduced for two to three days for those students who had participated. She speculated that giving students personal attention as intellectuals in a thoughtful setting changed their attitude toward school, however briefly.

In addition to crosscultural comparisons, students benefit from learning how the other gender reacts to the various issues. When the classroom features dialogue, the students feel that they have friends, the beginning of feeling a part of a learning community.

Overall, oracy in a second language should be not only an integral part of an integrated-skills approach, but also developed as an end in itself. Use of the English-language development standards ensures that speaking and listening skills are advanced in a deliberate, rather than haphazard, way.

Reading Processes in English-Language Development

Reading is an essential skill. Children who do not learn to read in elementary school enter secondary education as severe underachievers and are at risk for dropping out. Research has shown that English learners often learn to read by becoming efficient decoders, but they may fail to attain comprehension or higher-order thinking skills. How can teachers encourage English learners to acquire skills that will result in academic achievement and an enjoyment of reading?

The term *balanced approach* signifies that reading instruction should combine the best literature-based, whole-language approaches as well as bottom-up methods such as phonics and word analysis. There is no one "best" method (see Prabhu, 1990). For example, older learners need different reading instruction than do children. For more comprehensive instruction in reading pedagogy for English learners, teachers might draw on Peregoy and Boyle's *Reading, Writing, and Learning in ESL* (2004) and Hadaway, Vardell, and Young's *Literature-Based Instruction with English Language Learners, K–12* (2002).

SDAIE techniques are just as appropriate in literature as they are in any other content area. Adapting instruction for English learners makes the content of literature accessible.

Standards-Based Reading Instruction

New basal reading texts on the market reflect the current emphasis on standards-based instruction. For example, *Launch into Reading, Level I* (Heinle & Heinle, 2002), an ESL reading series, specifically references the specific California English-language development standard to which each lesson is connected. Lesson 13, " 'Flowers' (A Poem by E. Greenfield)" addresses Reading Standard 6, 3.4: "Define how tone or meaning is conveyed in poetry." Follow-up exercises ask students to use a continuum scale to rank five "ways you can learn about people's feelings and ideas" (short story, poem, magazine or newspaper article, movie or TV program, and conversation), an activity that addresses Reading Standard 2, 2.7: "Interpret information from diagrams and charts."

Later in the lesson, students are asked to find the rhyming words in the poem "Flowers" (Reading Standard 1, 1.6: "Create and state a series of rhyming words") and then work with a partner to interpret a poem (Writing Standard 6, 2.4: "Write responses to literature: Organize the interpretation around several clear ideas, premises or images"). All teaching materials—the teacher's resource book, the student workbook, and the student reading book—contain explicit references to standards on each page.

High Point from Hampton-Brown (Schifini, Short, & Tinajero, 2002) is an ESL series that comes complete with teaching tips designed to facilitate comprehensible input; learning strategies for enhancing cognitive academic language; strategies to increase reading fluency; writing support for students whose primary language uses a non-Roman alphabet; cultural tips; and small books for phonics instruction. The texts themselves do not contain ESL standards, however, leaving the integration of standards and instruction to a separate supplemental document and/or to the teacher.

Emergent Literacy

Those students who are first learning to read are in the stage of **emergent literacy**, "the reading and writing behaviors that precede and develop into conventional literacy" (Sulzby, 1986, p. 84). Most "nonreaders" actually have had much exposure to print in the culture at large, and may have engaged in various informal kinds of reading that a teacher can build on so students can "grow" into reading.

Emergent readers draw on their prior knowledge of the world to connect the printed word with its semiotic meaning. For example, most preschool children understand that a red octagonal sign at a street corner means "stop." They also come to understand that sounds correspond to symbols, thus enhancing their phonemic awareness. They acquire reading behaviors, such as handling books, borrowing and returning books to the class library, and reading for enjoyment; and they learn to share their pleasure in reading with others and work with others to acquire meaning from books.

Learners read and write because they see others doing it. However, many English learners do not see their families reading or writing, so it takes a leap of imagination for them to see themselves as readers. It is important that they see the classroom as a place in which reading is an everyday, enjoyable activity. This socializes students into a culture of literacy.

Until recently, ESL teaching for students at the stage of emergent literacy involved direct teaching of English vocabulary and sentence syntax; however, recent instructional approaches integrate language, reading, and writing skills (Abramson, Seda, & Johnson, 1990). Oral and written language are now seen as interactional, and writing is seen as an important means of mediating meaning (Sulzby, 1986).

Language Experience Approach.   Students connect to their own experiences and activities when they use the Language Experience Approach (LEA). Students describe events in their own words, and the teacher writes these down and reads them back. Students can eventually read the text for themselves. Because their own phrases and sentences are written, students find the text relevant and interesting, and generally have little trouble reading it. Once students recognize that their oral language can be written and read, their confidence grows in composing extended oral stories.

Young children find written stories enjoyable as they learn to read. Primary-age students enjoy making and reading their own Big Books. After reading the story in the original book aloud, the teacher recopies the same story as sentences in a Big Book (basically, large manila sheets held together with a steel ring). Each page of the Big Book is given to a child to illustrate, and the book is made available in the classroom for students to read and reread. This gives students a sense of ownership.

Writing books is an LEA activity that adolescents find rewarding because it engages their imaginations. Students can write about boarding the school bus and being whisked away to a different destination, or create a *Carrie*-style horror story about the senior prom; in a biographic mode, they can write about a family member; in an autobiographic mode, about a family trip or other memory. The books can circulate within the classroom so that students can enjoy one another's work, or be displayed in the school library.

Ways to Foster Emergent Literacy.   Gunning (1996) suggested several ways to foster emergent literacy in children. First, an accessible, appealing literacy environment is stocked with attractive reading and writing materials, including commercial books, student-written books, comic or cartoon books (with words), magazines, encyclopedias, and bilingual, age-appropriate dictionaries. Group reading time is balanced with independent reading, small-group review of a Big Book, or work with language skills such as phonics. Children are encouraged to role-play or playact reading and writing activities, chant or sing based on reading the lyrics together, and share book experiences.

Despite the success of approaches based on the social construction of knowledge, a generation of students is being taught how to read through a series of controlled, behaviorally based lessons using such programs as Reading Mastery, Open Court, and Direct Instruction (Groves, 2001). Only time will tell if the students taught in this manner learn to read for enjoyment.

Preliterate Students.   Students who first enter literacy instruction when they are past their primary years present a great challenge. They may have internalized a sense of shame from having had little schooling or from failing to learn to read. These students need to experience immediate success. Collecting words from environmental print and helping students decode them sometimes reassures the nonreaders that they can read. Intensive one-on-one instruction in a reading resource room is recommended in these cases rather than in-class instruction. Various methods are recommended for teaching preliterate students. (See Table 8.6.)

The Basics of Learning to Read

Skill with print, prior knowledge, comprehension, and establishing the symbol–meaning connection are essential to the early reading process (Barr & Johnson, 1997). When these four elements are present, it is more likely that reading will take place. The following sections are designed, for the most part, for primary-level students just beginning to read. There have been instances, however, of adolescent nonreaders in ELD who needed to learn to read at a basic level.

table 8.6   Methods for Teaching Preliterate Students

Method	Description
Shared literacy	Peer reading (as the reader for younger children or "readee" for older children); cooperative reading.
High-interest literature	Can be stories written by other students.
Language Experience Approach	Teachers write down student-dictated story, then students read it.
Reading–oral language relation	Language as read sounds like language as spoken.
Age-level-appropriate reading	Older students should not read books that are meant for preschool children (unless they are peer reading to younger children).
Predictable books	Rhyme; repetition; simple expansions.
Focus on messages	Reading and writing simple notes and e-mail messages.
Writing in short phrases	Answering simple questions.
Culturally relevant literacy	Familiar songs; experiences in the community.
Process writing approach	Draft, then get peer feedback.
Environmental print	"Reading the world"—collecting and reading phrases from television, movies, or billboards.
Audio-recorded stories	"Read-alongs" in a listening center.
High-utility language	Writing one's name; reading simple directions.
Drawing-augmented text	Drawing to illustrate stories; Pictionary.
High-communicative events	Messages that exchange meaning.
Games	Memory games (matching cards), syntax games (matching halves of sentences).
Teacher read-aloud	Teacher uses highly exaggerated characterization and storytelling skills.

Source: Adapted from Cloud, Genesee, and Hamayan (2000).

Skill with Print. That the printed text contains words that carry meaning, and that printed words correspond to spoken language, are key ideas that underlie learning to read. Nine concepts constitute skill with print:

■ Language is divided into words.
■ Words can be written down.
■ Space separates written words.
■ Letters make words and words make sentences.
■ Sentences begin with capital letters.
■ Sentences end with punctuation.
■ A book is read from front to back and goes left to right and top to bottom.
■ Words, not pictures, are read.
■ A book has a title, an author, and sometimes an illustrator. (Gunning, 1996)

In a print-rich environment, students see print wherever they turn. Table 8.7 provides ideas for creating a print-rich environment.

Prior Knowledge. Knowing is the foundation for reading. Knowing comprises both word knowledge (vocabulary) and knowledge about the world. The chief hurdle faced by English learners in learning to read in English is that reading a word successfully depends on knowing the word in the first place (Tikunoff, 1988). Beyond vocabulary, students need experience and understanding of the situational contexts that help make sense of reading. Once students start to read, vocabulary acquisition accelerates because readers who have the gist of the text can predict and infer the meaning of unknown words they encounter. The teacher's job is to help students develop vocabulary breadth and background knowledge so

table 8.7 **Ideas for a Print-Rich Environment**

Type of Item	Example
Labels on objects	• Aquariums and terrariums labeled with the names of their inhabitants
	• Labels on objects in several languages
Displays in the classroom	• Bulletin boards with words and pictures
	• Calendar with students' birthdays and other important events
	• Students' stories and booklets
	• Hanging mobiles with weekly vocabulary or CALP concepts
	• "Living" bulletin board that accumulates evidence of the week's learning
	• Different scripts, languages, and number systems, with pictures of a country in which that language is spoken
Activity centers/areas	• Student-run post office
	• Advertising flyers to cut and paste
	• Magnetic letters, printing sets, typewriter, computers available
Classroom library	• Books, comic books, magazines, dictionaries in dual or primary language
Objects	• Menus available from restaurants
	• College brochures
	• Order blanks, notepads, shopping lists at play centers

Sources: Morgan (1992); Gunning (1996); Lipton and Hubble (1997).

they can connect prior knowledge and new learning. *Schema building* involves the use of other books, oral discussion, exposure to media, or pictures, combined with text.

Comprehension.   Understanding what is read is the key to meaning. Before students read, teachers ask them to predict the content or main idea of a book or a reading passage based on their expectations, the title, the first sentence, or other clues. Reading further, the reader modifies the initial prediction (Gunning, 1996). Getting the main idea of a reading passage is vital because this creates the central understanding that makes further reading more purposeful and memorable, and helps to make sense of the supporting details.

Sight Words.   Symbols are connected with meaning through sight words and phonics. When recognizing *sight words* (those that do not conform to phonetic rules—about 10 percent of English written words), the learner uses visual memory to match sound with writing. Sight words include frequently used words with nonpredictable spelling such as *the* and *could.*

Phonemic Awareness.   The insight that every spoken word is made up of a sequence of phonemes has been found to be an important precursor to learning to read. Once students grasp the principle that words are made up of phonemes represented by letters—called **phonemic awareness**—they can benefit from **phonics** instruction (Tompkins, 2002). Phonics can be taught using a bottom-up method, with students learning phonemes (individual sounds) in isolation, then learning to blend them, and finally seeing them in the context of words. Or students can begin by analyzing contrasting words that contain the target phonemes and then generating similar words. The analytic method of phonics is illustrated in Box 8.1.

Reading Readiness.   Several reading readiness activities help students develop visual discrimination. These include such tasks as matching pictures and patterns, sequencing story cards in a meaningful order, and matching uppercase letters to lowercase letters. Sound–symbol correspondence is taught phonetically in the following sequence. First, alphabet cards introduce the name of each consonant letter and the sound it makes. Then objects and pictures with the consonant as an initial letter are used so that learners can identify initial

---

box 8.1

The Analytic Method of Phonics

Steps for teaching by means of the analytic method of phonics:

1. *Planning:* Make a list of one-syllable words that include the target phonic element; for example, the consonant *d: dip, dog, dig, dot,* and so forth. Write simple, meaningful sentences for each one. Find pages in a common reading book that have these or other *d-* words, including *-d* as a final sound.
2. *Teaching:* Read the sentences aloud to the students in a smooth and informal fashion. Have the students "echo" (read the sentences after you); they then repeat each underlined target word after you, looking to see what sound the words have in common.
3. *Guided practice:* Students each make the target sound and look again at the letters that make the sound. Have students think of other words with the same sound. Students choral-read the sentences (read aloud together) and then take turns reading them aloud.

Source: Adapted from May and Rizzardi (2002).

sounds. (Ending sounds can be treated later in a similar way.) Then short vowels are introduced, followed by the short vowels blended with consonants. As a side process, sight words are memorized. Reading simple stories featuring short vowels helps students experience early success. Long vowels and vowel blends are taught next, followed by digraphs (consonants that together form a single sound, such as "ch").

However, reading based on phonetic awareness may not be the best approach for English learners. Hamayan (1994) offered key reasons why phonics-based and grammar-based approaches fail to meet the needs of English learners in the early stages of learning to read. First, learners need to acquire an understanding of the functional aspects of literacy, rather than just the form of words. Second, learners suffer when reading is taught in an unnatural way and in an artificial form. Third, focusing on form without a functional context makes learning abstract, meaningless, and difficult, and literacy becomes a boring chore.

The Alphabetic Principle.   Written English is based on the alphabetic principle, and children do need to understand that sounds correspond to letters. Teachers of English learners are encouraged to provide students with rich language experiences so that students practice sound–symbol correspondences. Awareness of sound–symbol correspondence emerges best as students use invented or temporary spelling when they write, "an important step on the way to conventional spelling . . . providing individualized phonics practice that will assist both reading and writing development" (Peregoy & Boyle, 2001, p. 153).

In alphabetic systems there is a direct correspondence between graphemes (symbols) and phonemes (sounds), even though in English there are exceptions to this correspondence (*chasm* has no "ch" sound). Learning to function in the Roman alphabet adds complexity to English acquisition if the student has achieved literacy in a non-Roman alphabetic language (Russian), a syllabic language (Korean), or an ideographic language (Chinese).

Having a totally different writing system from that of English is more cognitively demanding for learners than it would be if the two languages shared a common alphabet as well as the alphabetic principle itself (Brisk, Burgos, & Hamerla, 2004). Chinese students, for example, will need explicit instruction in the use of phonics to decode words rather than relying on memory—in contrast to learning the sound–symbol correspondences through alphabetic letters, Chinese students are taught Chinese characters through memorization more than through phonetics.

Even when two languages are both written in the Roman alphabet, as are English and Spanish, the phonemes represented by the alphabet may differ. For example, the /t/ in Spanish is palatalized (the tongue touches the roof of the mouth in a flat way), whereas in English the /t/ is not palatalized; rather, when the tongue touches the roof of the mouth, it is pointed so that a smaller area is in contact. Therefore a "taco" in Spanish is a little more like "thaco," using the /th/ in the English word *thigh*. Given this, the /th/ in the English word *thy* (unvoiced /th/, or /ð/) is a difficult phoneme for Spanish speakers.

Reading Strategies

When attempting a sentence with an unknown word, readers use several distinct strategies. One type of reader uses *semantic knowledge*. If the sentence reads, "Marco was not allowed to drive his dad's . . ." a reader might guess that the next word is *truck*, not *trunk*, because *trunk* would not make sense. Another type of reader might use *syntactic knowledge* on the sentence, "Joe found a small . . . " to reject the word *dig* as the wrong choice (a noun is needed, not a verb). A third type of reader might use *orthographic shape* to read the sentence "Elena worked alone, without a helper," knowing that saying the word *helper* as *help* would be to miss something. A single reader might use these three strategies equally often, or might use only one type of decoding; knowing the reader's preference helps a teacher use that strategy when assisting the reader or to teach the reader supplemental strategies (Newman, 1985).

Meaning is not "in" the text but is constructed by the reader, so there will always be an imperfect match between the meaning as taught and the meaning as attained by each reader. Rich, meaningful text evokes the most passionate and idiosyncratic response. This is the reason why we read literature. Reading anything less than rich text is reductionistic, especially when readers are required to accept the understandings of others rather than to glory in their own, however fraught with potential for misunderstanding.

The Three-Stage Reading Process and the Reader's Schemata

A common approach used in working with literature is called *into-through-beyond*. In this approach, activities prior to reading prepare students, text-processing strategies help students do the actual reading, and follow-up activities help students extend or retain their understanding. This sequential approach, although a popular organizing device, does not represent well the way literacy is socially constructed.

In reality, students pick books up, half-read them, and discard them. They use the table of contents, the pictures, or friends' recommendations to choose what to read. They surf the Internet, downloading information and wandering off-topic or stumbling onto topics much more interesting than their original intent. Therefore it is more useful to think of into-through-beyond as an organizer for the way reading is done in class, rather than the way readers actually read.

A useful overall means for teaching reading to English learners is to think of three types of schemata, or mental categories: cultural or content schemata, text-processing schemata, and linguistic/grammatical schemata. Each of these types of schemata can be applied at every stage of the reading process by using specific strategies.

Cultural/Content Schemata.   The categories humans deploy to make sense of new knowledge are based on content and cultural knowledge. The following example illustrates the importance of prior cultural knowledge as students try to make sense of instruction:

> A student teacher was working with a third-grade class in Jurupa, California, a community with a large number of English learners. She introduced them to the Mission Inn, a landmark hotel in nearby Riverside, by showing them pictures and reading with them a short history of the site. More than halfway through the lesson, she realized from listening to students that they did not realize the landmark was in the next town. Few of them had the prior experience of going to Riverside. The students needed a relevant cultural/content schema to make the lesson more memorable to them.

This is an example of the importance of teachers learning about the learner's culture. As a cultural broker, the teacher stands between the curricular content and the learner, ready to help the learner construct a bridge that makes the curriculum understandable. Even with secondary school students, teachers cannot assume that students are familiar with a given topic; many adolescents have not had opportunities to explore the world outside their immediate neighborhoods.

Many topics in reading shut out English learners because of their lack of knowledge about the culture or the content. One teacher was successful in using Gary Soto's *Pacific Crossing* with a class of middle school Latino youths. The book is successful in teaching about the cultural context of Japan because the point of view is a teenage Latino interested in the martial arts. Establishing a historical context is a particular challenge, requiring imaginative ways of recreating bygone conditions of life.

A variety of strategies can be used into-through-beyond to build students' cultural/content schemata (see Tables 8.8, 8.9, and 8.10). Although these are designed for reading and language arts, they may be useful in other content areas.

table 8.8   **Building Schemata *before* the Reading Process**

Type of Schema	Strategy	Activities
Cultural/content	Setting goals for reading	Students fill out a "Why?" sheet to clarify goals.
	Gaining background knowledge	Use background notes or a cultural/content briefing to understand aspects relevant to reading.
	Recognizing discipline-specific terms	Define particular technical terms.
	Brainstorming	Students pool their existing knowledge in a mind map.
	Identifying literary terms	Previewing a glossary: If book has no glossary, students can keep a private dictionary.
	Identifying genre	Define characteristics of genre.
Text processing	Previewing text	• Skimming • Scanning • Previewing • Formulating questions • Semantic mapping
	Metacognition	Planning for time management: How much time should be allocated for mastery?
Linguistic/grammatical	Sociolinguistic competence: Dialect, idiosyncratic speech, social class distinctions	"Lingo" sheet prepares students for dialect differences. How does dialogue reflect differences between characters? How does dialogue reflect the social class of the speakers or characters?
	Discourse competence: Point of view	Discussion: Whose point of view is represented?

table 8.9   Building Schemata *during* the Reading Process

Type of Schema	Strategy	Activities
Cultural/content	Understanding cultural terms and practices	Terms, beliefs, and behaviors are explained as they occur in the reading.
	Crosscultural comparison	Compare/contrast matrix or Venn diagram is used to make cultural differences explicit and similarities or to explicate content.
Text processing	Metacognition	Self-monitoring and adjusting.
	Text comprehension • Identifying the main idea and supporting details	Use group discussion to identify possible main ideas, evaluate, and vote.
	Critical thinking about text • Making inferences • Problem solving	Discuss: What is implied but not stated outright? What problems does the character create for others?
	Making a visual image	With eyes closed, each person imagines the setting, character, or detail.
	Obtaining information from pictures, charts, and graphs	Information gap: In pairs, a student describes a picture to another student who does not see it, using words.
Linguistic/grammatical	Vocabulary acquisition • Guessing meaning using context	Students keep their own glossary.

Text-Processing Schemata.   As students read, they draw on text-processing schemata, knowledge of how text works and how to make reading faster and more comprehensible. Activities building these schemata can take place as students prepare to read, perform silent or oral reading, or evaluate what has been read. Text-processing schemata permit readers to read faster and with greater understanding.

Silvia Girard holds an "encyclopedia race" every Friday after lunch for her fourth-grade students. In groups of four, students receive four encyclopedia volumes per group. She gives each group a question that can be answered using one of the four encyclopedias. In this way, students practice their text-processing reference skills.

Linguistic/Grammatical Schemata.   When an instructor devotes explicit attention to the analysis of a structure, a usage, or even a dialect feature of a text, linguistic/grammatical schemata are the focus. For English learners, to understand a writer's intent, an occasional focus on form is helpful.

table 8.10   **Building Schemata *after* the Reading Process**

Type of Schema	Strategy	Activities
Cultural/content	Cultural understanding • Cultural perspectives • Cultural immersions • Intercultural communication	Rewrite the story with the setting in another culture.
		Students put themselves in the shoes of characters of other cultures.
		Students talk with guests from another culture or content expert about issues raised in reading.
	Content application	• Project-based learning. • Make posters, do experiments.
Text processing	Review • Taking notes • Study buddies	Making flash cards, underlining, making annotations, posing questions.
	Text comprehension • Summarizing • Storytelling	Retelling the text from an outline.
		Recalling key ideas.
		"What if?" discussion: generating alternative possibilities.
	Application • Telegraph plot	If you had only 40 words to tell the plot, what would you say?
Linguistic/grammatical	Paragraph analysis • Identifying the topic sentence • Identifying logical argument	What role does every part of the reading play in creating and sustaining meaning?
		Do the paragraphs have clear, coherent content?
		Does the order of paragraphs create an accurate flow of ideas?
		Are the beginning, middle, and end apparent to the reader? Does the plot hold the reader's attention?

Jerry Holden challenges his SDAIE-college-prep literature class to Dialect Day. In advance, he provides selections from writers famous for their use of dialect, such as Twain's *Huckleberry Finn*, Faulkner's *Light in August*, or Rodríguez's *La vida loca*. One by one the members of the class speak the segment in an appropriate accent for that dialect. The class votes on the Big Dialect Dawg, who receives a Beanie Baby dog as a prize.

Into Reading.   "Into" activities activate students' prior knowledge by drawing from their past experiences or helping to develop background knowledge through new experiences.

Films, field trips, visual aids, and graphic organizers can help students anticipate the work. Brainstorming ideas is helpful because students' ideas stimulate one another. Students predict the content of a story and put the predictions into time capsules to analyze later. Then they evaluate what happened in the book and confirm or disprove their original predictions.

Using the K-W-L organizing chart (What do I Know? What do I Want to learn? What have I Learned?) allows students to place new knowledge in the context of their own memories and concepts, even if they have misconceptions that have to be unlearned. Should ill-conceived or wrong prior knowledge be corrected? The teacher may want to add a question mark with a circle around it beside ideas that are in the "maybe—well, I never heard that" category. These may be ones that can be specially investigated as part of the topic.

After the idea-generation phase, the students and teacher together can organize and group ideas to create a working model to guide learning. After the students list everything they know about a topic, they then tell the teacher what they would like to learn.

The chart is kept up throughout the duration of the unit so students can use it for reference, making additions and information updates. By starting each topic with an activity that draws forth students' prior experiences relevant to the topic, the teacher gains valuable insights.

While Reading.   "Through" activities help students as they work with the text. Some teachers read aloud, giving students an opportunity to hear a proficient reader and get a sense of the style and story line. Teachers can model thinking ("think aloud") to show how they follow a sequence of events, identify foreshadowing and flashbacks, visualize a setting, analyze character, comprehend mood and theme, and recognize irony and symbols. Commercial tape recordings of literature can be obtained for listening and review to help students develop a sense of inflection, pronunciation, rhythm, and stress.

Teachers using literature in their classrooms may find that selecting materials carefully, slowing the pace slightly, portioning work into manageable chunks, and increasing the depth of each lesson they teach can ensure that English learners have a fulfilling experience with literature. Myths and folktales from many cultures, commonly available in high-quality editions with vibrant illustrations, can be used as bridges to more complex works of literature. Students can move from these folktales and myths to short stories by authors from diverse cultural backgrounds, then to portions of a longer work, and then to an entire work (Sasser, 1992).

Students can perform the actual reading in a variety of ways. Table 8.11 offers a variety of reading methods for in-class use.

To sustain student interest in a longer work of literature, class time might be used to review the assigned reading and discuss students' understanding. A preview of the next assignment can feature interesting aspects of the new passage. A teacher can structure literature homework in a variety of ways. In the activity Character Diary, students write an ongoing record of what each character is feeling so they can step inside the character's life. In the activity Gap Summary, the teacher provides an incomplete description of the main points of the section assigned for home reading, with gaps comprised of key expressions that only a reading of the passage can reveal (Collie & Slater, 1987).

Story mapping is a graphic organizer used to summarize the plot. Younger students working with four boxes (labeled Who? Wants? But? So?) can fill in their knowledge of the

table 8.11   In-Class Reading Methods for English Learners

Method	Description
Page and paragraph	Teacher or fluent reader reads a page, then English learner reads a paragraph, then group discusses what has been read.
Equal portions	Students work in pairs, and each reads aloud the same amount of text.
Silent with support	Students read silently in pairs and can ask each other for help with a difficult word or phrase.
Choral reading	Passage is divided into sections, and various parts of the audience read various sections.
Radio reading	One student reads while others close their books and listen. After reading, the reader can question each student about what was read.
Repeated reading	Students read silently a book that has been read aloud, or independently reread books of their choice.
Interactive read-aloud	Students can join in on repetitious parts or take parts of a dialogue.
Echo reading	For rhythmic text, students echo or repeat lines.
Cloze reading	When reading Big Books, the teacher covers certain words and students try to guess words in context.
Nonprint media support	Students can follow along with a taped version of the book.

Source: Adapted from Hadaway, Vardell, and Young (2002).

progression of events in the plot (Peregoy & Boyle, 2004). Older students can use the labels "Characters," "Intent," "Conflict" (difficulty), and "Resolution" (outcome).

After Reading.   "Beyond" activities are designed to extend the students' appreciation of literature. Poems or reviews of works of literature can be written for the school or classroom newspaper. Students can express their reactions to certain pieces of literature by writing letters to authors or to pen pals. Favorite parts of a selection can be rewritten as a play and enacted for other classes. Students can plan a mock television show—for example, a game show—in which a host asks contestants to answer questions or to act as characters in the story.

"Beyond" activities in the communicative classroom, however, prepare students to use English outside the classroom. Although grammatical and linguistic training may continue to be a part of the into, through, and beyond phases of instruction, cultural/content and text-processing strategies are a priority so that the ideas obtained through reading can enrich students' lives.

Focus on Vocabulary.   New words can be introduced before a reading lesson, or drawn from context during reading. Explicit work with new vocabulary words, though, is usually reserved for the after-reading phase. Students may acquire technical words by accessing a text's glossary, sidebars, charts, or graphs. However, moving a new word from students' acquisition vocabulary (used in reading or listening) to their production vocabulary (used in writing or speaking) requires far more guided practice (Rosenthal & Rowland, 1986). Other learning strategies are useful for acquiring and retaining new words.

Transition Reading.   As students prepare to make the change from reading in their primary language to reading in English, "transition" reading instruction helps to make this process smoother. Students must translate many words they already know into English, as well as acquire many new words and concepts directly in English from their reading.

Sometimes reading instruction in English resembles reading instruction in the L1, and sometimes it does not. For example, Spanish reading instruction has traditionally relied on phonics and syllabic decoding because the sound–symbol correspondence has few exceptions. In contrast, Chinese is traditionally taught using kinesthetic memorization, with emphasis on drawing ideographs. Thus the L1-to-L2 transition period is a mixture of transfer of learning and acquisition of new knowledge.

Comprehension Strategies.   Reading comprehension can be advanced using a variety of reading strategies. When introducing a new comprehension strategy, the teacher explains when the strategy is useful, models the process, and then gives the students guided practice. Each strategy is named and explained as follows.

Finding a "text-based" answer means the reader can skim the text to find the answer to a question. Finding a "reader-based" answer means the reader must infer the answer using clues from the text (Barr & Johnson, 1997). Finding an "author and you" answer means the solution lies in a combination of what is in the story plus the reader's experience. Finding an "on my own" answer means the answer comes from the reader's own experience. Finding a "right there" answer means the answer is easily found in the book, whereas finding a "think and search" answer means the reader needs to put together different parts of the reading to obtain a solution (Raphael, 1986).

In the activity Mine, Yours, and Ours, students make individual summaries and compare with a partner, and then write a joint paragraph outlining their similarities and differences. In the activity Summary Pairs, students read aloud to one another and summarize what they have read (Lipton & Hubble, 1997). Using the activity Shrinking Stories, students write their own versions of a passage in 25 words or less. In the activity Simply Put, students rewrite a selection so that students two or three years younger might understand it (Suid & Lincoln, 1992).

A directed reading–thinking activity (DR–TA) helps boost reading comprehension by helping students understand how proficient readers make predictions as they read (Stauffer, 1970). Teachers guide students through the prediction process until they are able to do it on their own, by asking students to make predictions and then reading to confirm their ideas. Using reciprocal teaching, students predict, summarize, ask questions, and suspend judgment, using these techniques with one another (Palinscar & Brown, 1984).

Teaching Literature

Students of all ages derive pleasure from learning experiences involving high-quality literature. Literature fosters insight into behaviors, events, and narrative that stimulate the imagination by exposing a range of fictional beliefs, lifestyles, ideas, and information. Not only is literature an end in itself, but literature is also used as the core support for students' introduction to and development of literacy (Scharer, 1992).

Literature plays a varied role in literacy instruction. High-quality narrative and informational literature provide the basis for a consistent read-aloud program in which students are read to daily—even in middle and high school. Students need to read books of their own choosing and be provided with sustained time for both independent and collaborative book sharing, including discussions between students and the teacher. For an overview of the use of literature in a children's reading program, see Cullinan (1987), and Tunnell and Jacobs (2000) (see also Chapter 7 in this text).

Types of Literature.   Teachers featuring literature as the core of their reading program use *controlled readers, book sets, text sets, core books,* and *thematic units* to provide reading experiences that are rich in meaning and interest for students. Controlled readers are literature-based basal readers with specially adapted vocabulary and length. Book sets (Story Box and Sunshine Series from the Wright Group, Literacy 2000 from Rigby) feature Big Books and matching reader sets. Text sets are books that are related thematically (such as books on sports, or sets of multicultural readers on the Cinderella theme), or they may feature the same characters in a series of adventures, such as *The Babysitter's Club.* Core books are those specifically featured in a statewide adoption list for all classrooms to use. Thematic units use literature as integrated content with science, social studies, and art/music/performing arts. The unit may be on the rain forest, the settling of the West, or other integrative topics.

Selecting Good Literature.   The lives of second-language learners are often filled with books that feature language especially adapted with simple sentence structures, verb present tense, and controlled vocabulary. They are not usually as stupifying as the phonics readers ("Bob and Dot went to the prom in the smog." Get it? Short /o/!), but they may be just as boring in the long run. English learners may find little meaning in these phonics readers.

Suppose, then, that a teacher uses literature to supplement phonics readers, basal anthologies, and Open Court. Teachers can read to the whole class after lunch and on rainy days for recess, set up listening centers as choice activities, and hold contests to see who can read a quota of free-reading selections. Teachers read multicultural literature, their own favorite stories from childhood, and children's books that have won the Caldecott and Newbery Medal book awards. The key is to select works that have stood the test of time and are beloved by classes year after year.

Stories about families always fascinate children. *The Boxcar Children* is back in print, that tantalizing set of stories about children living on the edge of town without parents. Family stories can help the teacher learn more about the students if the read-aloud time is followed by sharing time. The teacher can invite an open-ended response to events in the story, or use prompts connected to the story. For example, after reading *The Velveteen Rabbit,* the teacher might say, "Tell me about your favorite toy when you were younger."

Self-selected books for independent reading require familiar techniques for comprehension, with students monitoring their own reading to make sure they understand. Students keep a simple reading log of the books they finish. Students who have difficulty finding books to read might benefit from a peer "book hunt" in which students interview one another and then go off to the library to find books that fulfill the partner's interests.

As mentioned in Chapter 7, students may need guidance in selecting books. Some adolescents, for example, have had limited experience with literacy and may not be familiar with book selection. Teachers can mediate this process by demystifying reading—modeling how to select a book by looking at the table of contents, the book cover or flaps, the illustrations, and so forth.

Age-level-appropriate reading material can be found by asking public librarians for recommendations. Schools can send out a list of recommended books, and students can make and share their own lists. Generally speaking, children respect the teacher's recommendations and enjoy what the teacher enjoys. Book conferences with the teacher allow students to benefit from the teacher's direct guidance. Students can use this time to share what they liked about the book, what they did not understand or what puzzled them about the book, and other elements of personal response (Reynolds, 1988).

Using Multicultural Literature.   Students enjoy multicultural literature because they can see life from a variety of points of view, compare cultures, and see their own culture represented in the curriculum (see Harris, 1997; Monroe, 1999). Appropriate selection of literature that reflects the cultural contributions, lifestyles, and values of various ethnic groups helps students develop a better understanding of themselves and their potential. Multicultural literature can help minority or immigrant students find their own identities as they undergo the complex process of acculturation into a new society: "As cross-cultural children hear stories of other searchers and experience the act of telling itself, they are more able to create their own stories and their own identities" (Shannon, 1988, p. 14).

Because culture plays such an important role in the formation of a child's identity, incorporating multicultural books into the classroom is essential if educators are to minimize the differences between the home life of students and the schools they attend, a major step in helping students experience success in school. Teachers who familiarize themselves with the values, traditions, and customs of various cultures are better able to teach without stereotyping cultures or lumping together distinct cultures by overgeneralizing (Reimer, 1992; Manning & Baruth, 2003).

A search on the Web for multicultural books for children and adolescents yields numerous titles for consideration. California State University, San Marcos, has a library dedicated to multicultural titles, especially those in Spanish.

Literature without Bias.   Receiving unbiased education about cultures is important for all students, because it reduces ethnic prejudice and builds an inclusive classroom spirit:

> Children's attitudes toward their race and ethnic group and other cultural groups begin to form early in the preschool years. Infants can recognize differences in those around them, and young children can easily absorb negative stereotypes. Children are easily influenced by the culture, opinions, and attitudes of their caregivers. Caregivers' perceptions of ethnic and racial groups can affect the child's attitudes toward those minority groups. (Gómez, 1991, n.p.)

Just because literature has an ethnic theme does not mean it is free from bias. In 1976 a committee of Asian-American book reviewers met to evaluate books available at that time for use in educational programs and concluded that most of the existing literature was "racist, sexist, and elitist and that the image of Asian Americans they present is grossly misleading" (Aoki, 1992, p. 113). To counteract offensive stereotypes for Asian Americans, the committee recommended that teachers avoid depictions of Asian Americans such as the following:

> Always smiling, serene, shy, reserved; short, buck-toothed, myopic, delicate; excessively obedient, passive, docile; menial, subservient, submissive; mystical, inscrutable, sagacious; dexterous, expert in martial arts; exotic, foreigner; sinister, sly, cunning, crafty, cruel. (Asian Americans in Children's Books, 1976, p. 4)

The Council on Interracial Books for Children (www.birchlane.davis.ca.us/library/10quick.htm) features "10 Quick Ways to Analyze Children's Books" (see Table 8.12). This serves as a fast rule of thumb for detecting bias.

Availability. A rich selection of multicultural materials is available. However, not all are culturally authentic. Purists might cringe at the version of *The Night before Christmas* with a south-of-the border theme, but some Hispanic readers like it. *Multicultural Voices in Contemporary Literature* (Day, 1994) presents 39 authors and illustrators from 20 different cultures; *Latina and Latino Voices in Literature for Children and Teenagers* (Day, 1997; see also Day, 2003) contains biographies of authors with synopses of their work, as well as an extensive list of resources for books in English on Latino themes. Shen's Books (online at www.shens.com) is a source for books on world cultures (not only Asian but also Islamic and Arab cultures, as well as Latino), plus a wide range of topics such as immigration, adoption, interracial families, Japanese internment, foods, music, and proverbs around the world, foreign languages and alphabets, folktales, and more.

Responding to Literature. *Reader response theory* holds that to make sense of a text, readers must first make connections with it (see Rosenblatt, 1978). In an atmosphere of trust, students are free to reveal their perceptions, personal feelings, and thoughts in relation to a text. The emphasis is on personal intellectual and emotional reactions, yet reader response must be guided by faithfulness to the text. The texts must be of high quality yet close to the readers' interests (Probst, 1988).

Literature response groups can develop a community of readers. After reading a piece of literature, a group of students and the teacher meet for discussion. Each student expresses ideas about the story. The teacher guides the students to deeper understandings by asking them to support their points with words from the text, or asking what words or devices the author used to evoke a mood, establish a setting, describe a character, move the plot along, and so forth. This helps students to appreciate the finer points of literature.

Storytelling-Reading. Perhaps the most important SDAIE technique is *storytelling-reading,* the ability to make literature come alive when read aloud. This, more than any other technique, can enrapture students and nourish the love of language. Storytelling-reading is a technique that includes characterization, vocal exaggeration for effect, strong facial expressions, and dramatic use of emotion and suspense. Literature can be read with a dramatic flair sitting in front of the class, using props or costumes, or in a tight circle with the class

table 8.12   Ten Quick Ways to Analyze Children's Books for Racism

Category of Analysis	Type of Racism	Example
Illustrations	Stereotypes	Chicanos as gang members or fiesta-loving
	Tokenism	Do minorities look like whites with a tan, or as genuine individuals with distinctive features?
	Typical activity	Subservient and passive roles, or in leadership and action roles?
Story line	Standards for success	Does it take "white" behavior standards for a minority person to "get ahead"? Do persons of color have to exhibit extraordinary qualities (excel in sports, get As)? In friendships between white and nonwhite children, is it the child of color who does most of the understanding and forgiving?
	Resolution of problems	Are the oppressions faced by minorities represented as related to social injustice? Are the reasons for poverty and oppression explained, or are they accepted as inevitable? Does the story line encourage passive acceptance or active resistance? Is a particular problem faced by a racial minority person resolved through the benevolent intervention of a white person?
Lifestyles	Place of activity	Minorities depicted exclusively in ghettos, barrios, or migrant camps
	Appearance	"Quaint-natives-in-costume" syndrome
Relationships between people	Issues of power	Do the whites in the story possess the power, take the leadership, and make the important decisions? Is the function of racial minorities essentially a support role?
	Families	In black families, is the mother always dominant? In Hispanic families, are there always lots of children? If the family is separated, are societal conditions (unemployment, poverty) cited among the reasons for the separation?
Heroes	White-acceptable only?	Are there only "safe" minority heroes—those who avoided serious conflict with the white establishment of their time? Minority groups today are insisting on the right to define their own heroes based on their own concepts and struggles for justice.
	Who benefited?	Are minority heroes admired for the same qualities that have made white heroes famous or because what they have done has benefited white people? Whose interest is a particular hero serving?

table 8.12 **Ten Quick Ways to Analyze Children's Books for Racism (Continued)**

Category of Analysis	Type of Racism	Example
Effect on a child's self-image	Color associations	Does the book counteract or reinforce this positive association with the color white and negative association with black?
	Identifications	In a particular story, is there one or more persons with whom a minority child can readily identify to a positive and constructive end?
Author's or illustrator's background	Qualifications	What qualifies the author or illustrator to deal with the subject? If the author and illustrator are not members of the minority being written about, is there anything in their backgrounds that would specifically recommend them as the creators of this book?
Author's perspective	The perspective substantially weakens or strengthens the value of the written work	Colonial, patriarchal, Eurocentric?
Loaded words	Coded language of stereotypes	Watch for *savage, primitive, lazy, superstitious, treacherous, wily, crafty, inscrutable, docile,* and *backward.*
Copyright date	Mid-1960s	A slew of "minority experience" books were published to meet the new market demand, but most of these were still written by white authors, edited by white editors, and published by white publishers.
	Early 1970s	The children's book world began to reflect the realities of a multiracial society.
	Later date, 1980s–present (does not guarantee quality)	A multilingual theme does not ensure authentic voices and experiences.

Source: Adapted from The Council on Interracial Books for Children, online at www.birchlane.davis.ca.us/library/10quick.htm.

drawn closely together. The best training for storytelling-reading is to observe experts and learn from them, and to collect literature that is interesting and entertaining for the listener.

Children invest their attention and interest in the plot and characters of a story as the reader makes use of inflection, intonation, emphasis, change of pitch, and body language, including facial expressions, eye contact, and gestures. Whether reading heroic tales, fantasy, or historical fiction, the storyteller-reader has a unique opportunity to transport the listener by means of the imagination to remote climes and times.

Picture-Enhanced Listening.   Literature can engage young English learners if they feel a connection to the characters. This can be accomplished by having each child hold a picture of one of the characters in the story glued to a wooden stick. As all children listen, an individual child waves the picture of the character who is featured in that part of the story. After the story is over, the children work with a small group to retell the story using the character pictures. A sequential story such as "The Golden Goose" (in which characters get stuck to one another because they grabbed the golden goose) works best (Malkina, 1998).

A classroom bright with posters, unusual visual images, and colorful cultural materials sparks the emotions and invigorates the spirit. When the work of literature that is read aloud has pictures, the book can become a literacy center where students can look at the picture closely throughout the day and then copy them onto drawing paper or create their own. If the story does not have pictures, so much the better—students can use their imaginations to talk about or to draw the protagonist, the action, or the settings.

Acting Out Literature.   Classroom dramatics offer a range of performance opportunities as a follow-up to the use of literature, some as simple as role-playing from a prepared script. Creative dramatics includes pantomimes, improvised stories and skits, movement activities, and dramatic songs and games. Dramatics provide students with a format for stimulating creative imagination, developing an understanding of human behavior, and participating in group work (Fox, 1987; Heinig & Stillwell, 1974).

One way to involve students in groups is through *story theater* (Gunning, 1996). As the teacher reads a story aloud, students perform actions of characters. *Aesop's Fables* may work well in this format. Total Physical Response (TPR) can be used to help students learn vocabulary as they act out parts of the reading (see Ray & Seely, 1997).

Students can develop and write plays using literary sources such as myths, fairy tales, and scenes from novels or stories. For example, students can act out fables such as "Pandora's Box." The teacher evokes the mood by asking students, "What bad things about this world would you put back in the box if you could?" Students close their eyes to picture the character in a pose from the play: Pandora being curious about the box or hiding from the evils that emerged. Students then develop the play after hearing the fable read (McIntyre, 1974).

Seeing plays performed is a first-time experience for many English learners. Major theater companies sometimes send artists to schools. Local high school or amateur productions may admit students free to a dress rehearsal. Local amateur actors provide models for students of talent and enthusiasm, and might spur the class to their own group performance. Students may also enjoy studying a play before attending a performance.

Readers' Theater.   Probably the most approachable way for students to read dramatic literature (scripts and plays) is through readers' theater, a reading activity in which readers read stories or plays with expressive voices and use gestures to help the audience visualize the action (Sloyer, 1982). Because the players are reading aloud, they expend no energy on memorization, props, costumes, scenery, music, or lighting (Wold, 1993). This stimulates students' enjoyment of literature through creative activity and promotes reading fluency.

Texts for readers' theater are matched to the age of the students, the length of the text, interesting characters, and the suitability of the language and plot to oral adaptation. To adapt a text to readers' theater, the teacher finds a selection that appeals to the students as a script and then highlights the characters' names on the left margin along with their lines (Young & Vardell, 1993). Dialogue sections are short and characters use direct speech. Parts are distributed so that characters have a proportionate number of lines. A narrator introduces the play and provides background not told in dialogue. McCaslin (2000) offers a sample readers' theater script, an adaptation of the folk tale "The Musicians of Bremen."

Before the first group reading, the teacher reads the selection to the class, clarifying the meaning of unfamiliar vocabulary. Then students repeat each line in a choral response after the teacher or alternate lines with the teacher. Students continue practicing in small groups. Parts may then be assigned for the reading.

During the performance, readers are arranged in a semicircle, wearing similar clothes or simple costumes. As a performer is reading, he or she looks up from the script as often as possible to establish eye contact with the audience (Shepard, 1994). Following the performance, students can talk about their experience either as a performer or as a listener, or write a review for a local newspaper. Readers' theater contributes to students' growth in reading skill, social awareness, and interpersonal cooperation.

Poetry.   Love of poetry is an important part of teaching literature, and special techniques can make poetry more accessible to English learners. Poetry is a universal language. All cultures deal with love, nature, religion, joy, and despair, and all languages employ devices of rhythm, rhyme, and figurative language to express deep emotions. Poetry is made up of language that makes life more beautiful, meaningful, and personal. Reading—and writing—poetry stimulates the imagination and can lead to increased appreciation for the beauty of English as a language.

Traditionally, poetry is organized by sound: end rhyme, internal rhyme, stanza, and verse. Having students tap or clap along with the meter helps to convey the rhythmic basis of poetry. Specific poems can be used to teach pronunciation patterns (Solé, 1998). Websites dedicated to musicians such as Bob Marley can show students the rhythm of sentences and rhymes made of longer, multisyllabic words.

Choral speaking has been used successfully with poetry to provide students the opportunity for speech improvement, working on pitch, volume, rate, and tone quality of spoken English. Individual voices can alternate with the group as a whole for dramatic effect, or two groups can alternate lines in a call-and-response format. Students can hold "poetry slams" to give the poetic voice a special cachet.

McCaslin (2000) suggested many poems that can be used with choral speaking, including the majestic "The Creation" by James Weldon Johnson and Walt Whitman's "I Hear America Singing," which can be dramatized with pantomime. Choral reading can be used effectively to build a sense of classroom community, perhaps in a morning routine that brings students into oral group unison (Lipton & Hubble, 1997).

Poems are rich sources of vocabulary. Students can volunteer to illustrate or define the words from poems. *Found poems* are made from vocabulary words that students discover while reading. Translating poetry into a student's native language to match the English version can result in a dramatic dual-language choral reading.

Exposure to a rich poetic environment helps students create poems in the classroom. Students who mingle with one another to share and borrow words and ideas can write collaboratively. Idea prompts that open up the world of "pretend" encourage students to fully exercise their imaginations. Chapter 7 of *Teaching English Learners* (Díaz-Rico, 2004) provides a rich tapestry of poetry types and suggestions for poetry creation.

When students do not like to read, schooling becomes a cycle of failure—poor reading habits lead to poor academic work, which in turn causes distaste for reading. If students feel they have low status in high school, are alienated from the teacher and from other students, and sense disrespect for their home language and cultures, literacy is adversely affected (Zanger, 1994). Inclusionary, multicultural learning environments help English learners feel accepted and productive, allowing them to become literate and successful in school.

Something about Literature.   Part of the genius of a work of art in literature is its plot—the story line that transfixes, the thrilling, page-turning quality that seizes the reader and does not let go until the end, and even then leaves the reader hungry for a sequel. Equally important are the characters: the main actor (protagonist) who, while not necessarily heroic, can be counted on to do the right thing (or, if a comedy, to do the wrong thing!). The setting is also a main quality: Who can forget the famous opening line that fixes the setting in time of Dickens's *A Tale of Two Cities:* "It was the best of times, it was the worst of times . . ."?

Last but not least is the language—to the good reader this is invisible, but to the second-language learner this can be a challenge. Although the good reader is carried along from page to page by language, its unique quality is not usually obvious unless literature teachers stop to point it out.

Other features of literature can be the entrance into other kinds of analysis. Who can forget the insistence of Humpty Dumpty in *Through the Looking Glass* that he could use words in any way he wanted—that "glory" could mean "a nice knockdown argument" if he so chose? That little piece of metalinguistic troublemaking is a fine opening for discussion of the arbitrary nature of language!

Literature opens the door to many adventures in language and the imagination for English learners. Many techniques, including SDAIE-modified read-aloud delivery, student enactment, TPR, classroom dramatics, readers' theater, and choral reading, can alter and illuminate the atmosphere of the English-language development classroom.

Something about fictional literature—the narrative, with its structured beginnings and endings, ritual performance, and patterned sequence of events—is deeply satisfying to the emotions, powerfully stimulating to language acquisition, memorable to the mind, and conducive to crosscultural comparison and cultural enrichment. This is exactly the kind of technique sought to educate English learners.

Writing Processes in English-Language Development

Writing and reading go hand in hand. Writing in English is not only a key to academic success, but also an outlet for self-expression. Hadaway and colleagues (2002) put it this way: "At the same time writing allows us to reach beyond ourselves, it also furnishes a means of looking inward. Writing is an expression outlet for self-communication, a way to chronicle our personal reactions and journeys" (p. 137).

Writing is no longer viewed as a lone pursuit of the individual, but as a social construction. Rodby (1999) described case studies of ESL students who were able to draw on multiple systems of support from work, home, church, clubs, peer interactions, faculty, and social–cultural systems to revise their writing in a pre-first-year English class. These students are examples of the powerful role played by the systems in which students are immersed and that influence their literacy behavior, which in turn influences their academic potential.

The Role of Writing in Academic Literacies

Academic writing is used to help students draw on their prior knowledge in preparation for new activities (for example, stimulating students' interests through a freewrite), consolidate and review new information and experiences (using learning logs, journals, notetaking, reaction papers, summaries, and study exercises), or reformulate and extend knowledge (using formal, structured reflection assignments such as lab reports or essay exams, or impromptu writing) (Langer & Applebee, 1987).

What Do Writers Need?   Learners need time and opportunity to write regularly. They need a real reason for writing, such as a pen-pal letter exchange. They need a genuine audience—to share their writing with their classmates or others. Students need role models of people who are using writing to fulfill life purposes. A safe environment for writing is important, with voluntary sharing, one-on-one conferences, and emotional and intellectual support for the writing. Feedback is essential, blending a moderate level of error correction with a thoughtful response to the writer's ideas. Finally, writers need a sense of community with others who can collaborate and validate one another's efforts (Hadaway, et al., 2002).

Examples of authentic writing include students offering medical advice in get-well letters and giving Santa Claus directions so he can deliver a motorcycle (Edelsky, 1986). Students can write notes to one another and post these in a class mailbox. Teachers who work with students on each phase of the writing process can help students find topics that interest them and to which they can dedicate their efforts.

Dialogue journals are a means of increasing fluency and promoting interpersonal communication. These are like written conversations between a student and a teacher, and are kept in a bound notebook or on a computer disk or file. The goal is for partners to exchange ideas and information about whatever interests them, free of the concern for form and correctness. The writing is not corrected, graded, or evaluated, and is characterized by nonthreatening, high-interest, nonhierarchical exchanges.

Students like dialogue journals because the topics are student generated, the interaction emphasizes meaning rather than form, and the language input from the teacher is comprehensible, private, and supportive (Peyton, 1990). English learners reap numerous benefits, including the exchange of ideas and the practice of daily writing.

Stages of Writing Development for Young English Learners.   Young children's writing behavior reflects a series of developmental stages, starting with *scribbling and drawing* (the child tries to imitate writing); then *prephonemic* (the writer uses real letters, but the meaning stands for whole ideas); *early phonemic* (the writer uses letters to stand for words), and finally *transitional* (enroute to conventional spelling, the child uses invented or temporary spelling) (Hadaway, et al., 2002). Emergent spelling, whether it stems from first- or second-language acquisition, is a rich source of knowledge about the child's intellectual and interlanguage development. Research is scant on the stages of writing for adolescents.

Beginning English learners usually enter English in the transitional phase; the more similar their home language alphabet is to the English alphabet, the more easily their writing skills will transfer to English (Odlin, 1989). English learners at the beginning proficiency level need to learn vocabulary, using word banks on the wall or index cards that they can alphabetize, classify, or illustrate (Lipton & Hubble, 1997). Beginning students can complete simple frame sentences like "I like _____ because _____," copy words and sentences, or write and illustrate their own books (Hadaway, et al., 2002).

Intermediate English learners with increased vocabulary can attempt more complex sentences in various genres of personal and expressive writing (letter writing, notetaking, short essays, and lists). At this level, students are struggling with the correct forms of plural nouns, pronouns, verb tenses, and subject–verb agreement; they make many errors at the sentence level, such as fragments, run-ons, and collocation errors (incorrect phrasal combinations, such as "emphasize on") (Leki, 1992).

Advanced English learners can write responses to many academic assignments, such as personal or literary essays, worksheets, and essay tests. Their writing features many of the issues with which native speakers struggle, such as topic focus, parallel sentence structures, and paragraph cohesion.

The Writing Workshop

In the writing workshop, students write collaboratively, drawing on other students and the teacher as resources. The teacher's role becomes that of facilitator and listener. Students can brainstorm and share ideas, and then write these ideas in a list form that resembles poetry. Students may enjoy writing buddy journals, in which they write back and forth to each other (Bromley, 1989). The writing workshop is based on the writing process: prewriting, drafting, and feedback/editing.

With a process approach to writing, students learn that writing is a part of life, with trial-and-error experimentation. Students can emulate the style of other writers, try out various genres, and, in short, just dive in!

Prewriting.   Students use oral language experiences to develop their need and desire to write. During *prewriting*, they talk and listen about shared experiences, read literature, brainstorm, or role-play (Enright & McCloskey, 1988). Prewriting helps to generate, incubate, explore, test, and integrate ideas, and students benefit from the questions others ask as they shape and explore ideas.

Drafting.   In the early stages of writing English, fluency is a much more vital goal than accuracy. Writers use the drafting stage to capture ideas quickly, doing the best they can with vocabulary, syntax, and spelling without anxiety over the need for accuracy. This drafting is followed by revision—sharing and discussing the content and clarity of the writing so students can expand their thinking and communicate more expressively before editing perfects the form and grammar.

Self-Review.   All writers face similar problems as they draft. They have the following concerns: elaborating with enough details for the audience to understand the subject, or possibly simplifying the presentation; providing clear purpose or thesis; following the organization promised in the introduction; developing and organizing the content; defining important concepts; using clear logic; being concise; and using correct grammar and mechanics. Providing a checklist in these areas for self- and peer-review brings these concerns to the fore.

Feedback through Peer Response and Writing Conferences.   Students share feedback through formal sharing meetings in which students explain where they are to a peer, read their work aloud, and ask peers for comments; or they can use informal, student-initiated interactions. To be useful, peer responding must be part of the writing process from the beginning, so that students are aware of writing for their peers as well as for the teacher (Liu & Hansen, 2002).

Peers are most successful as respondents when they are grouped with two other writers whose topic is similar. In this way, they are more prepared to become more deeply involved in the discussion of ideas, topic development, and use of sources (Campbell, 1998). Peer response offers feedback to the writer about the content, point of view, and tone of the work, and helps students focus on the messages they intend to communicate (Leki, 1990).

The teacher can provide feedback on early drafts, mostly suggesting ideas for content by writing comments that reflect a personal response. It is important to balance positive and negative comments, to provide specific suggestions, and to reference specific text segments in the feedback (Bates, Lane, & Lange, 1993). A rubric is a helpful device for shaping the critique because it makes standards explicit.

Individual writing conferences are opportunities for the teacher to listen to each student talk about the work in progress. The teacher asks "following" questions to reflect the student's ideas about the topic, or "process" questions to help organize and focus the writing (Graves, 1983). It is important for students to restate in their own words what the instructor suggests, because this is more likely to lead to substantial revision (Goldstein & Conrad, 1990).

Editing.   If a perfected version of the writing is not necessary, students may archive their rough drafts in a portfolio without rewriting; the process itself has been useful to capture and share ideas, which is the point of writing for the purpose of communication. If, however, the writing is to be publicly shared or published, students need to be accurate in order to achieve the pride of authorship. Editing "fixes up" errors or mistakes in usage and spelling after the message is intact. Students who learn to self-edit can improve their own writing.

Error Correction.   With younger English learners and newcomers, teachers should encourage expression of ideas without correcting grammar. Writers should be rewarded for trying new formats and more complicated sentences. Error correction is a process of tactfully bringing students to enjoy perfecting their vocabulary, grammar, and usage, with two central guidelines: communication of meaning is paramount, and self-correction is most desirable. Writers can be taught to proofread one anothers' writing as part of the writing process. Thus error correction is done with tact, and individually.

Restrictive correcting means marking only a few types of errors at one time, prioritizing some for improvement (Bartram & Walton, 1994, p. 80). A grammar textbook should provide alternative sentence structures to the simple subject–verb pattern. *The Art of Styling Sentences* (Longknife & Sullivan, 2002) offers practice in making sentences more complex.

The key to error correction is to encourage the student to monitor writing with enough focus to improve but without too much anxiety (Bates, et al., 1993).

Publishing.   There are various ways to publish student writing: performing a play, making a bound book for circulation in the class library, reading poetry aloud, posting an essay on a bulletin board, or circulating a class newspaper to the community. Desktop publishing software provides simple newsletter formats. Students can master basic page layout rules: Put the most important information near the top of the page, do not put two headlines side by side, minimize the variety in type fonts on the same page, and do not make columns smaller in width than two inches. A masthead at the top of the newsletter with an artistic appearance creates a professional-looking production.

Use of Technology.   The use of technology in ELD has moved far beyond simply teaching students to use word processing. There is an almost inexhaustible number of sites useful to the teaching of literature, starting with the home pages of teaching organizations such as the National Council of Teachers of English (www.ncte.org), TESOL (www.tesol.org), and NABE (www.nabe.org). There are sites devoted to ESL (*The Internet TESL Journal,* www.iteslj.org), to reading (www.readingonline.org), and to children's literature and language arts (http://falcon.jmu.edu/~ramseyil/childlit.htm).

There are grammar tutorials online (www.englishpage.com/minitutorials), a thesaurus (http://thesaurus.reference.com), a rhyming dictionary (www.rhymezone.com), and how-to instructions for writing for newspapers and magazines (www.writesite.org). There are websites constructed *by* ESL students (http://edvista.com/claire/internet-esl.html and www. tesol.net). Voices of Youth (www.unicef.org/voy) is a site in which children from all over the world share information via live chats and e-mail messages; ePALS Classroom Exchange (http://epals.com) also links students worldwide. Greenlaw and Ebenezer (2005) feature a wealth of such electronic resources.

Conclusion: Best Principles and Practices in Oracy and Literacy

The best teaching approaches to oracy and literacy support the following principles: (1) language and content are integrated, (2) students' first language and native culture are recognized and validated, (3) materials use authentic and real-life language, (4) diversity in learning styles is encouraged, (5) an emphasis is placed on learning strategies, (6) interaction and collaborative learning are important, and (7) student learning is purposeful.

Skilled ELD teachers are able to move students level by level through ELD standards so that English development is a systematic process, not a random endeavor. Responsibility for the progress of English learners is distributed across the curriculum, but this progress is developed in a specialized way by ELD teachers who are knowledgeable in all facets of ELD. ELD practitioners need to work closely with teachers in other content domains to integrate academic instruction with ELD in all content areas.

Last, ELD teachers adhere to the principles of the teaching with integrity model as they sustain the highest expectations for their students and use intercultural communication to help students reach a solid working relationship between the first and second languages. This brings ELD to a fully professional level.

Overall, if the oracy and literacy discussed in this chapter are performed naturally in the context of rich, interesting learning, the acquisition of skills is relatively unnoticed by the learner. The state of "flow" occurs, in which life is exciting and attention is rapt. If the pressure is on, however—a test, a public performance—skills must be learned with focus and determination, labor, and sweat. Teachers with integrity recognize that both kinds of learning have their place. Teaching English learners is both toil and treat!

9

Dual-Language Development

English learners and native English speakers can support each others' language learning.

expectation

■ Prospective teachers will encourage students to express meaning in a variety of ways, including in their first language, and can manage first-language support such as para-educators, peers, and books. *(Element 7.12 of the California Teaching Performance Expectations. Reprinted by permission of the California Commission on Teacher Credentialing.)*

Bilingual Education: Rationale and Roots

How many people can say they are truly fluent in more than one language? In many parts of the world, people are schooled in multiple foreign languages. In Canada and elsewhere, the ability to communicate, read, and write in two languages is encouraged. The United States is one of the few countries in which a young person can graduate from secondary school without ever studying a second language. Yet many young people enter schooling in the United States already fluent in a primary language other than English, a proficiency that can function as a resource. Ideally, schools offer programs that help students whose families speak a language other than English to sustain fluency and develop academic competence in their heritage language while acquiring fluency and literacy in English. This is bilingual education in its best sense.

This chapter addresses program models that induct speakers of other languages into English instruction. Although most of these programs take place at the elementary level, an increasing number of students immigrate to the United States at the middle and high school levels, and programs must be designed to meet their needs as well. The program models presented in this chapter vary greatly on one key dimension—how much encouragement is offered to students to maintain their primary language and how much instructional support they receive to accomplish this.

Linguistic Multicompetence as a Goal

For the past 400 years, people living in North America have spent time and energy either settling a large continent, accommodating to that settlement, or trying to survive colonization. This has left little time to develop second-language fluency; moreover, the ideology of colonialization dictates that monolingualism become the cultural norm, to the neglect of honoring a multiplicity of languages. Thus most individuals in the mainstream culture of the United States are monolingual, and most indigenous languages are in danger of extinction. Yet millions of people around the world are *multicompetent language users* (Cook, 1999), meaning their bilingualism or trilingualism acts as an asset to them or to their society.

Multicompetency in language means that those individuals who are monolingual need to acquire one or more other languages. In the United States, this means that monolingual English speakers must learn another language, and those fluent in other languages must learn English. Thus this chapter has two focuses: bilingual education for those students who speak the language of their community (also called *heritage language*), and second-language study for monolingual English speakers. Primary-language instruction, including its companion, foreign-language instruction, is a key instructional application (see Figure 2.2, page 34). Together, content area instruction, ELD instruction, and primary-language instruction constitute the chief areas of focus for the linguistically multicompetent student.

To accomplish this three-part educational program, teachers encourage students to express meaning in a variety of ways, including in their first language. The first language is not only a means to acquire knowledge but also a goal and area of academic study in itself. A teacher with integrity sees the primary language of the students as a resource and promotes heritage-language competence with the support of para-educators, peers, books, and other educational materials.

Why Become Bilingual?

Bilingualism in the Modern World.   The term *bilingual* means an individual who can function effectively, with both oracy and literacy skills, in two languages. Many people in the world are bilingual or multilingual. In many nations, groups of individuals use other languages in addition to the national language in their everyday lives (Valdés, 2001). Many countries in today's world are officially bilingual, meaning that more than one language is used in government or education. As the world becomes progressively more global in economic, political, and cultural terms, bilingualism, and even multilingualism, has become a highly desirable trait, a career enhancement in the modern world of international commerce. As Stavans (2001) put it,

> In today's fragmented world, it is hard not to be an advocate of multilingualism: Rather than banning or stigmatizing the languages of immigrants and native Americans, we should treat them as resources that could benefit the country both culturally and economically. The most intelligent solution is to favor bilingual programs that develop children's ability to speak their mother tongues, rather than discard them through a single-minded emphasis on English. (p. 179)

Bilingual individuals experience cognitive and linguistic advantages when compared to monolinguals, performing better on tests of divergent thinking, pattern recognition, problem solving, and metalinguistic awareness (Cummins, 1976; Cenoz & Genesee, 1998; Thomas & Collier, 1997). Research on bilingual individuals does not support the fallacy that bilingualism is a detriment to cognitive functioning. In fact, Swain and Lapkin (1982), in their comprehensive review of research on Canadian immersion instruction, concluded, "There is no evidence to suggest that an early exposure to bilingual schooling results in cognitive confusion. Rather, normal intellectual growth occurs, with some indication that growth may be enhanced in an early total immersion setting" (pp. 68–69). Knowing a second language often opens doors to other cultures, leading to understanding of cultural differences and providing opportunities for intercultural communication.

Bilingualism, Identity, and Empowerment.   We cannot discuss bilingual education while ignoring issues of identity and empowerment for speakers of subordinated minority languages. Assimilation into the superordinate culture and economic system is often the engine that drives such programs. As the dominant culture constructs an assimilationist language education under the auspices of bilingual education—which it so often does, with educational specialists and policymakers drawn from the monolingual English-speaking mainstream culture—the dominant culture superimposes its value systems, customs, and behaviors on students. However, educational programs that were designed for one culture cannot simply be translated into another if we expect students to succeed. The underlying assumptions and values of two cultures must negotiate such educational efforts with mutual respect.

Too often such efforts result in students from minority cultures becoming confused over the different values, attitudes, and requirements between home and school. They may experience a loss of identity and pride in their ethnicity, a loss of cultural knowledge, and, often, academic failure. In the process of adapting to dominant mainstream culture patterns, they may internalize the feeling that their language and culture are of secondary status, and in the process lose respect for themselves, their families, and their culture.

These students may internalize the view that their **dual-language proficiency** is a "problem"—and this is tantamount to symbolic violence, a foundation for linguistic genocide (defined by Skutnabb-Kangas [2000] as systematic extermination of a minority language). Too often the understanding is lost that both minority and majority cultures have equal contributions to make to an integrated society. Bilingual education becomes the tool of a functionalist, reductionist process reduced to the message: "Learn English, move up, move on, or move out."

But schools can do much to support students as they attempt the difficult goal of linguistic multicompetence. Socioemotional and cognitive support includes full respect for minority-language students' ethnicity, respect for the resources of heritage-language speakers (Galindo, 1997), full inclusion of families in decision-making processes, and a commitment to a pluralistic society. Moreover, much research supports the claim that the cognitive skills required for academic success are acquired faster when a firm foundation in the first language is established (Molina, Hanson, & Siegel, 1997).

Advocacy for Bilingual Programs.   The National Association for Bilingual Education (NABE) is an organization that promotes educational equity for language-minority students and fosters professional development for bilingual educators. A similar organization for teachers of English learners, Teachers of English to Speakers of Other Languages (TESOL, Inc.), has taken the position that bilingual education is the best approach to the education of English learners (TESOL, 1976, 1992). The 1992 statement recommends that bilingual programs incorporate the following facets:

- Comprehensive English as a second language instruction for linguistically diverse students that prepares them to handle content area material in English.
- Instruction in the content areas that is not only academically challenging, but also tailored to the linguistic proficiency, educational background, and academic needs of students.
- Opportunities for students to further develop and/or use their first language to promote academic and social development.
- Professional development for both ELD and other classroom teachers that prepares them to facilitate the language and academic growth of linguistically and culturally different children. (p. 12)

Bilingual education, in its most basic form, incorporates three characteristics: (1) continued development of the primary language, (2) acquisition of a second language (usually English), and (3) instruction in the content areas (Ovando & Collier, 1998). A fourth characteristic is the promotion of self-esteem and pride in the primary culture. However, not all so-called bilingual education programs have as a goal or result the addition of second-language proficiency to the high level of native-language proficiency—*additive bilingualism.* Many program models actually result in *subtractive bilingualism*—second-language acquisition at the cost of loss of proficiency in the primary language. The message too often given to heritage-language speakers is, "To learn English you must forgo your home language." Teachers with integrity have clarity of vision about the importance of supporting students' heritage languages, and understand the cultural, social, and economic loss to the individual and society when a student's primary language is not honored.

The History of Bilingual Education in the United States

The Controversy over Bilingual Education.   Bilingual education is controversial because provision of educational services to immigrants in general, and Spanish-speaking immigrants in particular, is a highly contested political issue in the United States (see Crawford,

2004). This issue will expand in the future as Spanish speakers overtake African Americans as the largest minority population in the United States. Teachers of English learners cannot avoid being a part of this controversy and have a proactive role to play in advocating for bilingual services (Cazden, 1986).

Bilingual education has existed in the United States since the time of the first settlers. Over more than four centuries, it has been accepted or rejected depending on the politics of the era and the "cycles of liberalism and intolerance" (Trueba, 1989). Immigrants from all over the world have brought their languages and cultures to North America, yet periodic waves of language restrictionism and social pressures toward assimilation have coerced many children of immigrants to abandon the language of their parents and virtually eradicated the capacity of many U.S. citizens to speak a second language.

Culturally, the people of the United States have embraced bilingualism when it has been economically useful. In periods when the economic fortunes of the United States were booming, European immigrants and their languages were not forbidden (non-European immigrants, however, have long faced linguistic and cultural barriers). However, in times of recession, war, or national threat, immigrants and their cultures and languages have been seen as a threat.

For English learners, English-only schooling has often brought discrimination and cultural suppression as English has been heralded as the key to patriotism and school success. Only after legal apartheid in the United States was ended by civil rights acts in the 1960s did Congress enact the Bilingual Education Act as a means of addressing the needs of students whose first language was not English, and only in the 1970s did landmark court cases make language instruction a civil right for children with a limited command of English. Even though federal legislation has supported the right of English learners to be educated in their native language, individual states have sometimes restricted bilingual education (e.g., California's [1998] Proposition 227, Arizona's [2000] Proposition 203, and Massachusetts' [2002] "Question 2," statewide referenda that invalidated the states' bilingual education laws).

Despite the extensive evidence that bilingual education helps English learners succeed in school, bilingual education continues to be an area of contention. Many people feel that any tolerance of linguistic diversity undermines national unity. Four main arguments have been used by those who are against the use of minority languages in schools (Stavans, 2001): (1) linguistic diversity will lead to political disunity and ethnic conflict; (2) linguistic diversity will lead to political disloyalty—minorities will remain loyal to their own backgrounds and home countries, delaying assimilation; (3) state-sponsored bilingual services will reduce the incentive to learn English, and (4) the rule of English as the nationally dominant language will diminish.

Periodically throughout history, English has been proposed as the national language of the United States, yet this has never been enacted into law. Although the United States has no official language, 27 states have passed laws proclaiming English as official (U.S. English, 2005). In contrast, others uphold the view that the United States is enriched by a mixture of distinct cultures and languages and oppose the movement to declare only one language as legal.

The classrooms of the United States are increasingly diverse. The challenge to any primary-language development program is to cherish and preserve the rich cultural and linguistic heritage of the students as they acquire English. Bilingual education has been considered by many to be a teaching method, but it can also be considered a policy, a way in which instruction is organized and managed. Bilingual education in the twenty-first century has become bilingual and bicultural and is rapidly becoming multilingual and multicultural.

Bilingual Education in Colonial America.   By 1664, 18 colonial languages plus Algonquin were spoken on Manhattan Island (see Table 9.1 for a timeline of selected milestones in the history of dual-language use in the United States). Soldiers who fought for the colonists in the American Revolution spoke German, Dutch, Swedish, and Polish. Spanish was dominant in the territories settled by Spain and French in the land claimed by France. Then, as now, many in the upper classes were multilinguistically competent; for example, Benjamin Franklin spoke French and read German, and the Continental Congress published many official documents in German and French.

Throughout the early nineteenth century, schools were established to preserve the linguistic heritage of new arrivals. In 1847, Louisiana authorized instruction in French, English, or both on the request of parents. The territory of New Mexico authorized Spanish–English bilingual education in 1850, immediately after the Treaty of Guadalupe-Hidalgo in 1848 that ceded New Mexico to the United States. In 1900, more than 4 percent of the U.S. elementary school population was receiving instruction either partially or exclusively in German (Crawford, 2004).

Language Restrictionism.   Almost all Native-American languages were suppressed in early America, with one exception: In an 1828 treaty, the U.S. government recognized the language rights of the Cherokees, who eventually established a 21-school educational system that used the Cherokee syllabary to achieve a 90 percent literacy rate in the language. This support ended when Cherokees were driven off their land and forced to relocate. In 1879 the federal government forced all Native-American children to attend English-only boarding schools where they were punished for using their native language.

As large numbers of Jews, Italians, and Slavs immigrated to America, descendants of the English settlers began to resent and fear these newcomers. Mexican and Asian immigration in the West brought renewed calls for "foreign" language restriction. Imperialism led to English-only policies in public and private schools in the U.S. territories of Puerto Rico and the Philippines (Crawford, 2004).

Anti-German hysteria during World War I ended the use of the German language in all areas of public life (Cartagena, 1991). A similar hysteria ended Japanese-language schools during World War II. Until the late 1960s, using a language other than English in the public schools of Texas was a crime, and students were punished for using Spanish at school (Crawford, 2004). Bilingual instruction by the late 1930s was virtually eradicated throughout the United States, even though in 1923 the U.S. Supreme Court prohibited coercive language restriction on the part of the states. In the 1940s, *Álvarez v. Lemon Grove School District* was the first legal case to establish the illegality of school segregation based on language. Despite this ruling, educators spoke of language-minority children as being "culturally deprived" and "linguistically disabled," and on the basis of their performance on IQ tests

table 9.1   Selected Milestones in the History of Dual-Language Use in the United States*

Event	Date	Significance
North America was rich in indigenous languages.	Pre-1492	Linguistic diversity is a type of biodiversity; language encodes millennia of information about the physical and social environment.
Spain established missions in California.	16th century	Spanish rulers decreed the abolition of indigenous languages and their replacement by Spanish.
German schools operated in Philadelphia.	1694	English was not a universal language of schooling in the United States.
U.S. Articles of Confederation were written in English, French, and German.	1781	Early acknowledgment of U.S. multilingualism on the part of the Founding Fathers.
Louisiana Territory was sold to the United States.	1803	President Thomas Jefferson tried to impose English-only administration on the new territory; French-speaking residents of New Orleans came close to rebellion.
Western U.S. was settled by European Americans.	1800s	Mexicans and Native Americans were excluded from white-only schools.
Mexican territory was annexed to the United States in the Treaty of Guadalupe-Hidalgo.	1848	Citizens in the annexed areas were guaranteed the rights they already enjoyed.
The federal government forced Native-American children to attend off-reservation schools.	1879	Schools were English-only; Native Americans were punished for using their native language.
U.S. won the Spanish-American War and colonized Puerto Rico and the Philippines.	1898	English became the mandatory language of colonial schools.
Spanish was outlawed in U.S. schools, leading to "Spanish detention."	late 1800s–1960s	Students could be punished for speaking Spanish in school in every state but the territory of New Mexico.
The governor of Iowa banned the use of any foreign language in public: on the streets, in churches, or on the telephone.	1917	German speakers were the target.
Ohio passed legislation to remove all uses of German from the state's elementary schools.	1918	Mobs raided schools and burned German textbooks.

table 9.1   Selected Milestones in the History of Dual-Language Use in the United States (Continued)

Event	Date	Significance
Massive IQ testing of Puerto Ricans in New York was used to justify widespread school placement of Spanish-speaking children 2–3 years below grade level.	1936	Thousands of New York Puerto Ricans launched a campaign for bilingual education.
Japanese-language schools were closed.	1941	Japanese were incarcerated in internment camps with English-only schools.
10,000 Latinos boycotted schools in Los Angeles demanding bilingual education and more Latino teachers; boycotts spread across U.S.	1968	Leaders of Los Angeles boycott were arrested; two years later charges against them were declared unconstitutional.
ESEA Title VII offered funding for bilingual education programs.	1968	First bilingual kindergarten in New York City; first bilingual education major at Brooklyn College.
Bilingual programs reached only one out of every 40 Mexican-American students in the Southwest.	early 1970s	Based on these data, the U.S. Office of Civil Rights began enforcing compliance with judicial mandates.
Latino enrollments in U.S. professional schools of dentistry, law, medicine, and engineering were only 3 percent of students.	1985	Substandard K–12 general education culminated in poor enrollment in higher education.
Latino scholars, professors, and writers were only 3 percent of U.S. college teachers.	1990s–present	Substandard K–12 general education culminated in continued dearth of Latino professionals as academic role models.
175,000 bilingual teachers were needed in the U.S.	1993	Substandard K–12 general education culminated in continued dearth of Latino professionals as bilingual teachers.
French Americans in Maine thwarted passage of English-only bill.	1999	Maine was the first state to defeat an Unz-initiative-type English-only bill.
Antibilingual education initiatives are passed in California, Arizona, and Massachusetts.	1998–2002	Use of L1 in instruction was systematically outlawed.
English became the official language of Iowa.	2002	Iowa was the 27th state to make English the official language.

*See also Crawford (2004, pp. 96–97) for the expanded timeline titled "Linguistic Diversity in America."

Sources: Cockcroft (1995); Wiese and García (1998); Crawford (1999).

administered in English, a disproportionate number of English learners ended up in special classes for the educationally handicapped.

The Rebirth of Bilingual Education.   Cuban immigrants in Florida, fleeing the 1959 revolution, demanded bilingual schooling for their children in Florida, because, as Stavans (2001, p. 67) pointed out, "these wealthy and ideologically active émigrés" refused to allow their children to be educated solely in English. A bilingual program was begun at the Coral Way Elementary School in Dade County with the objective of fluency and literacy in both English and Spanish. As the movement for bilingual education spread, by 1974 there were 3,683 students in bilingual programs in the elementary schools and approximately 2,000 in the secondary schools (Hakuta, 1986).

After the federal government passed the Bilingual Education Act of 1968 (Title VII, an amendment to the 1965 Elementary and Secondary Education Act), the Dade-County-type focus on developmental bilingualism was altered toward a compensatory slant (Wiese & García, 1998). English learners were considered to be educationally disadvantaged, and bilingual education was geared toward providing resources to compensate for this "handicap." The focus shifted again in 1989, when developmental bilingual programs became the focus.

Contemporary Antibilingual Education Movements.   Since the mid-1980s, language loyalties have become a means of reframing racial politics. English-only movements have been funded by social conservatives in the United States, with the goals of adopting a constitutional amendment to make English the official language of the United States, repealing laws mandating multilingual voting materials, restricting bilingual funding, and enforcing English-language proficiency as a requirement for naturalization (Cartagena, 1991). Bilingual education is a subject that is bound up with identity, status, culture, power, and nationalism, and thus is more than just a "language" issue. Spending resources on dual-language instruction has become a political "hot button" (Macedo, Dendrinos, & Gounari, 2004).

Federal Law and Judicial Decisions.   The progress of bilingual education in the United States has advanced on three fronts: cultural, legislative, and judicial. Because the U.S. Constitution reserves to states the right to dictate educational policy, support for bilingual education varies from state to state. When the U.S. Congress enacted legislation to begin Title VII of the Elementary and Secondary Education Act in 1968, federal funding became available for bilingual education programs; almost simultaneously, the courts began to rule that students deprived of bilingual education must receive compensatory services.

The historical precedents, federal legislative initiatives, and judicial fiats combined to establish bilingual education in the United States. The information that follows is a chronological record combining legislation and judicial rulings. Table 9.2 presents the legislative acts that have affected bilingual education policies at federal and state levels. Cases that have been adjudicated in state and federal district courts have established much of the legal rights to a high-quality primary-language education in the United States. The cases presented in the following discussion are summarized in Table 9.3 (pp. 252–253).

The 1860 case *Plessy v. Ferguson* legitimized racial segregation in public places if the facilities were equal. Throughout the late nineteenth and early twentieth centuries, this

table 9.2 Federal, State, and Local Bilingual Education Policies

Type, Level of Mandate	Specific Policy	Date	Impact on English Learners
Federal treaty	U.S. government & Cherokee tribes	1828	The U.S. government recognized the language rights of the Cherokee tribes. Eventually, the tribes established a 21-school educational system that used an innovative syllabary to achieve a 90 percent literacy rate in Cherokee.
	Treaty of Guadalupe-Hidalgo (U.S./Mexico)	1848	Mexican residents of appropriated territory in what is now California, Arizona, New Mexico, Texas, Utah, and Nevada were promised the right to use Spanish in schools, courts of law, employment, and everyday life.
	Philippines and Puerto Rico become U.S. territories.	1895	Public and private schools were forced to use English as the language of instruction. Submersion in English was a sustained policy in Puerto Rican schools until the 1950s.
Federal legislation	Federal "Indian" boarding schools	1879	Native American children were forced to attend off-reservation, English-only schools where they were punished for using their native language.
	The Civil Rights Act: Title VI	1964	Prohibited denial of equal access to education on the basis of race, color, national origin, or limited proficiency in English in the operation of a federally assisted program. Compliance is enforced through the U.S. Office for Civil Rights.
	Bilingual Education Act (Title VII of the Elementary and Secondary Education Act)	1968	Federal recognition of the unique educational disadvantages faced by non-English-speaking students. It authorized $7.5 million to finance 76 bilingual education projects serving 27,000 children.
	The May 25 Memorandum from the Office for Civil Rights	1970	School districts with more than 5 percent national-origin minority children were told they must offer special language instruction for students with a limited command of English. Prohibited the assignment of students to classes for the disabled on the basis of their English-language skills; prohibited placing such students in vocational tracks instead of teaching them English; and mandated that administrators communicate with parents in a language they can understand.
	The Equal Education Opportunities Act (EEOA) (U.S. Congress)	1974	"No state shall deny equal educational opportunities to an individual on account of his or her race, color, sex, or national origin by the failure of an educational agency to take appropriate action to overcome language barriers that impede equal participation by its students in its instructional programs."
	Reauthorization of the Bilingual Education Act	1974	Specifically linked equal educational opportunity to bilingual education. Eliminated poverty as a requirement; allowed Native-American children to be eligible; provided for English-speaking children to enroll in bilingual education programs; and funded programs for teacher training, technical assistance for program development, and development and dissemination of instructional materials.
	Lau Remedies—guidelines from the U.S. Commissioner of Education	1975	Standardized requirements for identification, testing, and placement into bilingual programs. Districts were told how to identify and evaluate children with limited English skills, what instructional treatments to use, when to transfer children to all-English classrooms, and what professional standards teachers need to meet.

(continued)

Type, Level of Mandate	Specific Policy	Date	Impact on English Learners
	Reauthorization of the Bilingual Education Act	1978	Added to the definition of bilingual education. Instruction in English should "allow a child to achieve competence in the English language." Additionally, parents were included in program planning, and personnel in bilingual programs were to be proficient in the language of instruction and English.
	Reauthorization of the Bilingual Education Act	1988	Increased funding to state education agencies, placed a three-year limit on participation in transitional bilingual programs, and created the fellowship programs for professional training.
	Reauthorization of the Bilingual Education Act	1989	Developmental bilingual programs were expanded to maintain the native language of students.
	Reauthorization of the Bilingual Education Act	1994	Amended and reauthorized the Elementary and Secondary Education Act of 1965 within the framework of the Goals 2000.
	No Child Left Behind Act	2001	All schools are required to provide qualified teachers; all students are required to pass standardized tests.
State legislation	Louisiana authorized instruction in French, English, or both on the request of parents.	1847	Early support for bilingual education.
	The territory of New Mexico authorized Spanish–English bilingual education.	1850	Early support for bilingual education.
	The State Constitution of New Mexico "guaranteed" rights of the Treaty of Guadalupe-Hidalgo.	1912	Bilingual teachers were employed to teach Spanish-speaking students.
	Ohio passed legislation to remove all uses of German from the state's elementary schools.	1918	Subsequently, 15 states legislated English as the basic language of instruction.
	Legislative provisions for limited-English-proficient student instructional programs in various states	1999	State education codes do not necessarily include bilingual programs, but may instead specify ESL instructional programs, bilingual/dual-language instructional programs, or both.
State initiative	California's Proposition 227 (Unz Initiative)	1998	Restricted educators' use of primary language as a means of instruction.
	Arizona's Proposition 203 (Unz Initiative)	2000	Restricted educators' use of primary language as a means of instruction.
	Massachusetts's Question 2	2002	Restricted educators' use of primary language as a means of instruction.
School district policy	Dade County, Florida, began bilingual education as Cuban immigrants, fleeing the 1959 revolution, requested bilingual schooling for their children.	early 1960s	The first program at the Coral Way Elementary School was open to both English and Spanish speakers.

Sources: Cockcroft (1995); Wiese and García (1998); Crawford (1999).

ruling was used to segregate Mexican and other Latino children; in the early 1900s, fewer than one in five Mexican children in the United States attended any school (Cockcroft, 1995). In 1923, *Meyer v. Nebraska* overturned a Nebraska law that prohibited the teaching of modern foreign languages to grade school children; the ruling held that denial of access to foreign language was a violation of the Fourteenth Amendment to the Constitution.

The nation's first successful school integration lawsuit was in 1931, 23 years before *Brown v. Board of Education* declared that separate facilities were "inherently unequal." Seventy-five Mexican children in Lemon Grove, California (near San Diego), were segregated from the newly constructed Lemon Grove Grammar School and told they must attend classes in a nearby two-room barn used for cows and pigs. Irate parents boycotted the school and brought suit before a California superior court against Lemon Grove School District. A judge ruled that separation of English learners from English-speaking students was unconstitutional. It was a clear victory for desegregation; however, Mexican students and other Latinos were not to benefit from a similar federal ruling until 1973.

In 1946, in the case *Méndez et al. v. Westminister School District*, five Mexican fathers successfully sued a Southern California school district because their children were forced to attend a separate school from white children. In 1947 the Ninth Circuit Court of Appeals upheld the ruling, and Governor Earl Warren signed into law a repeal of segregated school statutes in the California Education Code. This ended school segregation in California.

The Civil Rights Act: Title VI (online at http://usinfo.state.gov/usa/infousa/laws/majorlaw.civilr19.htm) prohibited discrimination on the basis of race, color, or national origin in the operation of a federally assisted program and prohibited the denial of equal access to education because of an English learner's limited proficiency in English.

The Bilingual Education Act: Title VII of the Elementary and Secondary Education Act (1968) authorized $7.5 million to support education programs, train teachers and aides, develop and disseminate instructional materials, and involve parents. This was a part of President Lyndon Johnson's civil rights legislation.

The May 25 Memorandum from the Office for Civil Rights (1970) mandated that school districts with more than 5 percent English learners must offer them some kind of special language instruction rather than tracking them into special education or vocational classes on the basis of their English-language skills, and that administrators must communicate with parents in the parents' language.

Serna v. Portales Municipal Schools (1972) ordered instruction in native language and culture as part of a desegregation plan, the first enforcement of the educational mandates of the 1964 Civil Rights Act. *Keyes v. School District No. 1, Denver, Colorado* halted the practice of labeling Mexican-origin students as whites in desegregating black schools. In *Lau v. Nichols* (1974), the U.S. Supreme Court established the right of students to differential treatment based on their language-minority status.

The Equal Education Opportunities Act (EEOA) of 1974 (U.S. Congress) was a civil rights statute defining what constitutes a denial of equal educational opportunity: An educational agency that fails to take appropriate action to overcome language barriers that impede equal participation by its students in its instructional programs is guilty of violating the civil rights of its students (Wiese & Garcia, 1998). The U.S. Office for Civil Rights began to visit school districts with large numbers of English learners to ensure compliance.

table 9.3   Judicial Decisions Supporting Bilingual Education

Specific Case	Date	Impact on English Learners
Meyer v. Nebraska	1923	The Supreme Court banned an English-only law in a case brought by German Americans.
Del Rio Independent School District v. Salvatierra	1930	A Texas superior court found that the Del Rio Independent School District could not segregate Mexican students. This ruling was overturned because the school district argued that the segregation was necessary to teach English to Mexican students.
Alvarez v. Lemon Grove School District	1931	A State superior court ruled that school segregation was against the law in California.
Méndez et al. v. Westminster School District	1946, 1947	The U.S. Ninth District Court applied the 14th Amendment to schools, insisting "schools must be open to all children . . . regardless of lineage."
Serna v. Portales Municipal Schools	1972	This was the first federal court enforcement of Title VI of the Civil Rights Act. A federal judge ordered instruction in native language and culture as part of a desegregation plan.
Keyes v. School District No. 1, Denver, Colorado	1973	Latinos must be covered by *Brown v. Board of Education*— Mexicans cannot be labeled "white" and used to create falsely desegregated schools containing only blacks and Latinos.
Lau v. Nichols	1974	U.S. Supreme Court: "There is no equality of treatment merely by providing students with the same facilities, textbooks, teachers and curriculum, for students who do not understand English are effectively foreclosed from any meaningful education." Although this case established the right of students to differential treatment based on their language-minority status, it did not require a particular instructional approach.

Reauthorization of the Bilingual Education Act in 1974 specifically linked equal educational opportunity to bilingual education. Native American children became an eligible population for the first time. The act provided for bilingual education programs, funding for programs for teacher training, technical assistance for program development, and development and dissemination of instructional materials.

Lau Remedies (1975) were guidelines from the U.S. Commissioner of Education that told districts how to identify and evaluate children with limited English skills, what instructional treatments to use, when to transfer children to all-English classrooms, and what professional standards teachers need to meet (U.S. Office of Civil Rights, 1976).

Ríos v. Read (1977) was a federal court decision that a New York school district had violated the rights of Puerto Rican English learners by providing a bilingual program that was based mainly on ESL and that included no cultural component.

Reauthorization of the Bilingual Education Act in 1978 added to the definition of bilingual education that instruction in English should "allow a child to achieve competence

table 9.3 Judicial Decisions Supporting Bilingual Education (Continued)

Specific Case	Date	Impact on English Learners
Ríos v. Read	1977	A federal court decided that a New York school district had violated the rights of English learners by providing a bilingual program that was based mainly on ESL and that included no cultural component.
Castañeda v. Pickard	1981	The Fifth Circuit Court was the first to test the 1974 EEOA statute, outlining three criteria for programs serving EL students: District programs must be (1) based on "sound educational theory," (2) "implemented effectively" through adequately trained personnel and sufficient resources, and (3) evaluated as effective in overcoming language barriers. Qualified bilingual teachers must be employed, and children are not to be placed in special classes solely on the basis of English-language achievement tests.
Idaho Migrant Council v. Board of Education	1981	State agencies were mandated to supervise the implementation of federal EEOA requirements at the local level.
Plyler v. Doe	1982	The U.S. Supreme Court decided that a state statute that denies school enrollment to children of illegal immigrants "violates the Equal Protection Clause of the Fourteenth Amendment."
Keyes v. School District #1	1983	Due process was established for remedies of EEOA matters.
Gómez v. Illinois State Board of Education	1987	State school boards were given the power to enforce state and federal compliance with EEOA regulations. Children must not sit in classrooms where they cannot understand instruction, and districts must properly serve students who are limited in English.

Sources: Cockcroft (1995); Wiese and García (1998); Crawford (1999).

in the English language." Additionally, parents were included in program planning, and personnel in bilingual programs were to be proficient in the language of instruction and English (Wiese & García, 1998).

In *Castañeda v. Pickard* (1981), the Fifth Circuit Court emphasized that programs serving English learners must be "implemented effectively" through adequately trained personnel and sufficient resources. *Idaho Migrant Council v. Board of Education* (1981) gave state agencies the mandate to supervise the implementation of federal EEOA requirements at the local level. *Plyler v. Doe* (1982) found that a state's statute that denies school enrollment to children of illegal immigrants violates the Equal Protection Clause of the Fourteenth Amendment. *Keyes v. School District #1* (1983) established due process for remedies of EEOA matters.

Reauthorization of the Bilingual Education Act in 1984 provided for developmental as well as transitional bilingual education so that children could achieve competence in English and a second language while mastering subject matter skills. Thus, for the first time, the goal of bilingual education was competence in two languages; however, no funding was provided for these programs.

Gómez v. Illinois State Board of Education in 1987 gave state school boards the power to enforce state and federal compliance with EEOA regulations.

Reauthorization of the Bilingual Education Act in 1988 increased funding to state education agencies, placed a three-year limit on participation in transitional bilingual programs, and created fellowship programs for professional training.

Reauthorization of the Bilingual Education Act in 1994 as part of the Improving America's Schools Act (IASA) aligned the Elementary and Secondary Education Act of 1965 with the reforms of the Goals 2000: Educate America Act (1994). Bilingual education programs were reconfigured with new professional development programs, increased attention to language maintenance and foreign-language instruction, improved research and evaluation, additional funds for immigrant education, and permission for participation of some private school students. English learners became eligible for services under Chapter I (Improving America's Schools Act of 1994, www.ed.gov/legislation/ESEA/toc.html).

Thus the court system upheld the legal rights of English learners under the U.S. Constitution. The federal bilingual legislation provided program-related funds as an incentive for districts to provide bilingual programs, but the right to offer educational programs—under the U.S. Constitution—is a privilege reserved to the various states. The federal government could not mandate that states offer bilingual education programs.

State Laws.   Although federal protections of the rights of English learners continue, many states have little or no requirements regarding bilingual education. In 1998, California, with a school enrollment of approximately 1.6 million limited-English-proficient children, passed **Proposition 227,** a measure rejecting bilingual education and offering students one year to become proficient in English. The proposition stipulates that

> [A]ll children in California public schools shall be taught . . . in English . . . in English language classrooms . . . through sheltered English immersion during a temporary transition period not normally intended to exceed one year. . . . Once English learners have acquired a good working knowledge of English, they shall be transferred to English language mainstream classrooms. (www.humnet.ucla.edu/humnet/linguistics/people/grads/macsuran/unztext.htm)

Although this law permits parents to apply for waivers, the decision to grant the waiver remains in the hands of the local school board, giving local authorities effective control over implementation of bilingual policies. However, in school year 1999–2000, only 10 percent of parents in California with children eligible for a bilingual waiver actually requested one. Ortiz (2003) looked at the factors differentiating schools with a high number of waiver requests from those with a low number, and concluded that schools with high and medium numbers of waiver requests had higher rates of Hispanic administrators and teachers and had higher achievement levels as measured by California's Academic Achievement Index.

Unfortunately, laws such as this one often result in a lack of support for the education of English learners. After 35 years of legislation supporting the rights of English learners, it can only be assumed that such laws infringe on students' rights—and, as sociologists would suggest, on their life chances.

The following section provides a survey of the kinds of language programs in the United States that promote second-language acquisition. These programs can be divided into two groups: bilingual education (teaching English to speakers of other languages with variable levels of support for the primary language) and second-language acquisition for monolingual English speakers (foreign language in the elementary schools and enrichment immersion programs).

This book specifically promotes dual, or two-way, immersion programs and maintenance bilingual programs as the preferred models for educating English learners. In many local contexts, this approach may not be feasible. However, teachers who teach in other types of programs can use the two-way immersion model to compare with their own program, noting the strengths and shortcomings of each model.

Dual-Language Development Programs: Bilingualism and Biliteracy

Support for the heritage languages that students bring to school is one way for the United States to promote multicompetent language use. Two kinds of primary-language-development programs promote the acquisition of English side by side with acquisition or maintenance of other languages. These are maintenance bilingual and two-way immersion programs.

In these and other bilingual programs, support for students' primary-language skills varies. Figure 9.1 represents a continuum of support for primary language. These programs incorporate English-language development as an integral part of their curriculum, with the goal of producing students who are fluent and literate in two languages. Moreover, students in these programs may study mathematics, science, and social studies in two languages in addition to reading and language arts. These programs are distinguished from foreign-language programs, in which the target language is not used for content instruction.

Maintenance Bilingual Programs

Maintenance bilingual educational programs (MBE) (also called **late-exit bilingual** and **developmental bilingual education**) are designed to preserve and advance academic proficiency in students' heritage languages as they become proficient in English, leading to additive bilingualism. The goals of maintenance bilingual programs are full development of

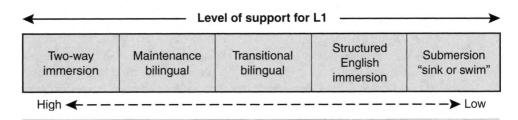

figure 9.1 Continuum of Support for Primary Languages across Types of Bilingual Programs

the student's primary language; full proficiency in all aspects of English; grade-appropriate achievement in all domains of academic study; integration into all-English classrooms; and positive identification with the cultures of both the primary- and majority-language groups (Cloud, et al., 2000).

Instruction in Maintenance Bilingual Programs.   Maintenance bilingual programs use primary-language instruction, defined as

> planned and systematic use of the primary language as both a source of and vehicle for instruction . . . which includes instruction focused on the development of the language itself (oral and literacy skills) through use of authentic written and oral literature and discourse as well as academic instruction. (Sánchez, 1989, p. 2)

Once students have a well-developed conceptual base in their primary language, they can translate into English the concepts they already know, rather than facing the far more difficult task of learning fundamental concepts in an unfamiliar language (Lessow-Hurley, 2005).

Maintenance bilingual programs first and foremost teach children to read in their first language. This is the most fundamentally important beginning for all subsequent instruction.

A wide range of material is available in students' primary language, primarily in those languages for which bilingual programs have been supported by state departments of education. Native-language literacy allows students to receive the full benefit of their own cultural heritage. Hearing and reading familiar songs, poems, folktales, and stories in the native language exposes students to literary language and various genres. Once literacy is established in the primary language, students can use these resources to create their own English texts and read English material written by others (Flores, Garcia, González, Hidalgo, Kaczmarek, & Romero, 1985).

Advantages of Maintenance Bilingual Programs.   Having literacy in the native tongue is vital for a number of reasons. First, a person's language is an important tool for processing information about the world and for organizing the way that the person feels about his or her surroundings (Vygotsky, 1978). Second, the native language is the mother tongue and retains a strong social and emotional connection to home and family. Third, achieving fluency in a second language takes six to seven years (Collier, 1987). Students must learn academic content in their first language as they spend time learning English. Fourth, speakers of multiple languages are an asset for a nation in international relations and trade as well as in cultural exchange and enrichment. Last, a sense of justice argues for the human right of each person to sustain the birth language during the educational process and to develop this language as a lifestyle choice.

The home–school connection that maintenance bilingual programs provide is essential for school success. For students to feel admiration for their languages, families, community, and home culture, they need to see these reflected in books and other materials used at school. If this does not take place, children are at risk.

> [T]he school's lack of respect for the home environment . . . result(s) in a conviction that the school culture is the "right" culture. . . . Most often in an unconscious manner, [students] begin

by feeling ashamed of their parents and their origins, rejecting their home language, anglicizing their names, and accepting the mores and attitudes that they perceive as superior.

They are often at grave risk of internalizing negative self-images of inferiority and defeat. . . . [T]hey may never feel quite comfortable in school, an environment they perceive to be alien. And so they respond in a passive manner, simply waiting the first opportunity to leave the system. (Ada, 1997, p. 161)

Gloria Anzaldúa, a Latina writer, captures this point poetically and poignantly in the statement, "If you really want to hurt me, talk badly about my language" (1999, p. 81). Students who do not receive support for their primary language often become hurt and opt to leave the system.

Two studies (Ramírez, 1992; Collier, 1987) have provided considerable support for the idea that students in MBE programs have greater academic success than students who are educated in other types of programs. Because MBE students continued to receive academic instruction in a language they could understand, they were able to keep up with English-speaking students. In contrast, students in programs with less support for their primary language over time fell further behind in academic subjects.

Slavin and Cheung (2004) reviewed many reading programs for English learners and concluded that using the first language to teach English has beneficial effects on English-language development. Oller and Eilers (2002) studied fifth-grade students in a bilingual program and found that when tested in English literacy, their scores were as high as those of comparison students in an all-English program. These and other studies confirm the efficacy of MBE (Krashen, 2004/2005).

The best approach to English-language development within the classroom is an integrated biliteracy model, with an adequate balance of support for both the native language and English. The relative relationship between oracy and literacy in the two languages, the role that both languages play in the community, and various uses of literacy in the classroom and school context work to keep this balance dynamic.

Biliteracy also entails biculturality. Table 9.4 outlines a bilingual–bicultural approach to teaching, in which the teacher helps students to acquire the linguistic and cultural knowledge needed to comprehend text and to succeed academically.

A particularly compelling use of MBE programs is in the education of Native Americans. The 74 schools operated by Native-American organizations under grants or contracts with the Bureau of Indian Affairs place a high priority on cultural and linguistic preservation, or **restorative bilingual education** (Reyhner, 1992). The attempt to increase the number of speakers of Native-American languages is crucial to the survival of these endangered languages (for more about endangered Native-American languages, see Hinton [1994]; Crawford [1995]; Southwest Educational Development Laboratory [n.d.])

Drawbacks of Maintenance Bilingual Programs.   Some of the criticism directed toward maintenance bilingual programs is that students in such programs take longer to learn English. However, an ongoing assessment of skills in both languages should ensure a consistent growth in English throughout the elementary school. If this does not happen, the specific program needs attention; we cannot criticize the program model per se if it is not well implemented.

table 9.4   A Bilingual–Bicultural Approach to Teaching: Effective Practice

Considerations That Guide Effective Practice	Description
Have high expectations regardless of language proficiency	Each student works to his or her potential in an environment that communicates the belief that all will succeed.
Use students' languages and cultural backgrounds as a tool for learning	Students read books in their second language on topics about which they have had experience. For example, Chinese students may have familiarity with the topic of the book *Everybody Cooks Rice.*
Become cultural brokers	Teachers help students to acquire knowledge and understanding of the use of the literacy skills they are acquiring, the cultural knowledge needed to comprehend text, and the structures and organization of text depending on the genre.
Engage homes and communities as partners in literacy development	Teachers work with parents to achieve a balance between languages that is useful in the home, community, and the larger culture.

Source: Adapted from Brisk and Harrington (2000).

Simultaneous Dual-Language Acquisition.   Preschool bilingual programs are pushing the age ever lower for children to learn two languages at the same time. Parents and teachers sometimes express concern for students' ability to become proficient simultaneously in two languages. What does research indicate about such a process?

Before the age of 3, children have acquired the basic elements of grammar: how words go together to make meaning. Bilingual children may sometimes mix the grammar and vocabulary of their two languages, but such errors are temporary. For example, if young speakers of Spanish are exposed to English with a standard (U.S. Midwest) accent, they will acquire that accent; however, if they learn English from speakers who speak English with a Spanish accent, they will learn English with that accent.

By the age of 5 or 6, bilingual speakers show great progress in two languages: They can use and repeat complex sentences, they have mastered 90 percent of the sound system, and they can use prepositions correctly, as well as use slang and make jokes, modify their speech if necessary to talk to younger children, and take conversational turns without being seen as interruptive or rude. These are impressive advances in language and well worth any temporary confusion along the way.

Two-Way Bilingual Education Programs

Two-way immersion (TWI) programs combine English learners from a single language background in the same classroom with approximately equal numbers of English-speaking students to provide grade-level curriculum in both languages. Students develop proficiency in both their native and second language and achieve academically through, and in, two languages (Lindholm-Leary, 2004/2005). This enhances the status of the students' primary language, promoting self-esteem and increased cultural pride for language-minority students (Lindholm, 1992), leading to increased motivation.

Almost all immersion programs involve Spanish and English, although as of 1997, immersion programs in the United States also featured Korean, Cantonese, French, Navajo, Arabic, Japanese, Portuguese, and Russian (Christian, Montone, Lindholm, & Carranza, 1997). Because Spanish is the most common second language in U.S. schools, the availability of Spanish speakers as language resources and the need to support Spanish as a language of instruction together argue for two-way education as a preferred mode of bilingual education. Most important, two-way immersion programs help to overcome the deficit model of dual-language education—the cultural myth that speaking a language other than English is a detriment to schooling, leading to academic failure, a myth that suggests linguistic minority students are culturally deficient, disadvantaged, and in need of fixing (Bartolomé, 1994).

Instruction in Two-Way Bilingual Education Programs.   In two-way immersion classrooms, Spanish is the primary language of instruction in the early grades for both English learners and native-English-speaking students, with the amount of English instruction increased each year until the academic content is taught half in English and half in Spanish by eighth grade. All students develop literacy in Spanish initially and maintain that literacy as they acquire academic English. This promotes fluency and literacy in two languages, academic achievement in two languages, and cultural appreciation and respect for both languages.

Two-way immersion bilingual education programs have been implemented in over 200 schools in the United States, with the number of schools growing yearly. Sites are located in 18 states ranging from Alaska to Florida, with the largest number in California and New York. The grade levels served are predominantly K–6, with cohorts of students beginning in kindergarten and advancing together until grade 6. Nearly all schools are Spanish–English in design, although other schools immerse students in Arabic, Cantonese, French, Japanese, Navajo, Portuguese, and Russian (with the other language in all cases being English)(see www.ncela.gwu.edu for more information).

The key to success of **dual-immersion education** is careful attention to primary-language maintenance (Veeder & Tramutt, 2000). An example of a highly successful dual-language program is that at the Valley Center–Pauma Joint Unified School District in California. Information about this program is available at www.cal.org/db/2way.

In a two-way immersion program, the primary basis of instruction is the focus on academic goals. This is not to say that language instruction is incidental. The conscious, intentional teaching and learning of language is essential for the achievement of high-level literacy and oracy skills.

Benefits of Two-Way Immersion Bilingual Education.   Why does the TWI configuration provide the most support for dual-language acquisition? Surprisingly, research has shown that two-way immersion programs are superior even to maintenance bilingual programs in sustaining and developing students' primary language. Why is this the case?

First, students' primary language is fully developed and maintained as they are given academic instruction in that language during at least part of the day. Although critics might argue that a developmental bilingual program would offer these students a far higher academic level of instruction in content areas because they would, in effect, be instructed only with other native speakers of their primary language, in reality few such programs exist and they enforce ethnic separation.

A good TWI program uses sheltered-content instruction for non-native speakers. In this way, the academic content moves forward rapidly and Spanish learners (native speakers of English) are given linguistic support. In addition, both English learners and Spanish learners are given level-appropriate ESL and Spanish-as-a-second-language (SSL) instruction and both groups are given grade-level-appropriate reading, writing, literature, and grammar instruction in their English language arts or Spanish language arts classes (Lindholm-Leary, 2004/2005).

Second, TWI programs fully support the ideal of dual-language proficiency. When majority-language speakers are expected to learn the language of the minority students, it becomes evident that a high level of proficiency in two languages is a hard-won asset. This eliminates the image of those who do not speak English as in need of remediation, a message that assumes that English learners are handicapped by their lack of English. It also exposes the fallacies that language learning is easy and submersion is effective.

Third, TWI programs reduce the segregation of primary-language speakers by integrating English learners with majority-culture students in an environment in which both groups' language skills are an asset. Last, TWI raises the status of Spanish as a second language and furthers the ideal that Americans can become fluent in more than one language.

Biliteracy.   Two-way immersion bilingual education is predicated on students' achieving grade-level literacy instruction for students in both languages. Literature and learning resources are abundant in two languages, encouraging students to write in more than one language, to share their writing with others, to help one another by speaking in both languages, and to get adults and community members who speak the primary language to assist in instruction. In this way, teachers ensure that students are receiving a challenging academic program in both languages.

Brisk and Harrington (2000) suggest considerations that guide effective practice in a two-way immersion context. First, teachers need to ensure that literacy instruction takes place in both languages. Both languages should be fully functional within the academic context. Students' primary language should be used to permit students access to core concepts; this shows respect for its value and enhances second-language acquisition.

Achieving English Proficiency in a Two-Way Program.   Cummins (2000a) argued that "a major advantage of two-way bilingual programs . . . is that they overcome segregation in a planned program that aims to enrich the learning opportunities of both minority- and majority-language students" (p. 142). However, some critics have argued that TWI delays English learning, and that these programs fail to teach English to English learners. Amselle (1999) argued that "dual immersion programs are really nothing more than Spanish immersion, with Hispanic children used as teaching tools for English-speaking children" (p. 8). Molina (2000) advised, "Without a watchful approach to the quality of two-way programs, schools will find themselves tragically exploiting the English learners they had hoped to help for the benefit of the language majority students" (p. 12).

Experts concede that the greatest challenge in two-way bilingual programs is to reduce the gap between the language abilities of the two groups, the English learners and the Spanish-language learners (SLLs). This gap appears as content classes in English are modified (slowed down) for English learners to "catch up," or as content delivery in the primary language is slowed for native English learners. One advocate of the enrichment immersion model conceded that oral communication in the second language has been found to be inadequate, because students learn to study in their second language but do not cross social lines to converse with native speakers.

Advocacy for Dual-Language Programs. Despite these criticisms, two-way immersion programs are gaining in popularity in the United States. Parents of native-English-speaking children see advantages in having their children learn academic and social skills in two languages, and parents of English learners see that the home language is valued. Strong partnerships between schools and parents are needed for these programs to continue.

One disadvantage of TWI programs is that children whose home language is not one of the two in TWI—such as Hmong speakers—must learn a third language in order to participate, without academic support for their home language. There are additional concerns often voiced by parents exploring TWI bilingual programs as an option for their children. First, parents of English learners ask if their child will be able to attain a high level of proficiency in the home language; if the identity and self-esteem of the children will be fostered and the primary culture will be maintained and transmitted; and if students will be able to converse with native speakers in both languages. Parents also wonder if the students will attain as high a level of achievement in English and the content areas as students in non-TWI programs; if the students will be able to transfer successfully to non-TWI programs after having been in the TWI program, and if they will be able to help their children with homework in a language they themselves do not understand.

Educators who teach English to speakers of other languages but are not themselves speakers of another language may hesitate to advocate for two-way immersion programs, fearing that individuals with dual-language skills will take their jobs. However, there are many ways in which monolingual teachers can demonstrate that they value students' languages and cultural experiences. Many TWI models pair a bilingual teacher with one who is not, in order to have students acquire two languages.

Sociocultural Contexts for Two-Way Bilingual Education. A TWI context is complex because the environment of the classroom and the school together influence how children learn language. Students in a TWI program do not merely acquire two languages; they do so while immersed in a sea of hidden messages communicated within the **sociocultural context of schooling** and the community (see Table 9.5).

Economics complicates the sociocultural situation. Often, too, middle-class parents who want a TWI program for their child do not support such a program if it means that their child is bused to a low-income neighborhood. Therefore it is often the home-language speakers who must bear the burden of a bus ride to a higher-income neighborhood school in order to create the language mix. This creates a hardship for the child and also lowers the mandate for upgrading schools in poor neighborhoods.

A bilingual–bicultural approach to teaching helps students to establish, maintain, and value all of their skills: the language and culture of their homes and communities, their skills in English, and even their nascent bicultural identity. Cummins (1996) argued that students' success or failure is determined largely through the process of identity negotiations between teachers and students. When students learn English and then learn by means of English, maintaining and supporting a strong sense of identity and self-esteem are important (Cummins, 2000b).

When people use language in any discourse context, the meaning is shaped and constrained by that context, whether it is interpersonal, institutional, or sociocultural. The students in a TWI program identify with socially constructed identities. For example, English learners who speak English on the playground—even when not required to—seem to be identifying with an English-speaking social identity. This identification, in turn, influences the discourse that individual produces. Taking on new language practices inevitably requires intrapersonal reconfiguration toward a bicultural identity.

Students who are supported in both languages and are able to attain a high level of scholarship can use both languages for literacy purposes as well as to create and sustain an identity that can negotiate two cultures. If teachers are able to draw from students' cultural backgrounds as a complement to the learning that goes on in the classroom, there is more potential for involving the community in a meaningful way. However, there are potential sources of tension arising from the sociocultural contexts in two-way bilingual education programs. (See Table 9.5.)

table 9.5   Sociocultural Tensions That Affect Learners in Two-Way Immersion Bilingual Education Programs

Source of Influence	Covert Message to the Learner
Social and educational discrimination that has historically existed in the attitudes toward, and treatment of, minority groups in the United States	The culture and language of the minority language are not as valuable to mainstream society as the majority language.
Tensions regarding social uses of two languages in the community of a given school	Students may learn a second language in school but are discouraged from using it outside of school.
Similarities and differences between the languages	One language is positioned as more useful for science, more valuable for college preparation, or, conversely, "easier," or more "cultural" (in a stigmatized, marked way).
Complications resulting from the different practices of literacy and learning in the distinct languages	The ways of learning one language do not work as well for the other; teachers have different styles and values.
Limitations inherent in program structure and goals	One language receives more time, materials, or advantage.

Sources: Cummins (1989); Pérez and Torres-Guzmán (2002).

Effective Curricula in Two Languages.   There are numerous examples of curricula in two languages. *Vamos a México/Let's Go to Mexico* is a 20-lesson teaching unit on the culture and traditions of Mexico developed by Christina Panzeri-Álvarez for the second grade. The unit combines Spanish and English, social studies, language arts, mathematics, art, and music. Students use a geographical atlas of Mexico to identify regions and states. They sort through travel brochures to choose favorite vacation destinations, then write a persuasive letter to their parents describing the vacation sites they have chosen and asking for permission to "travel."

Students then explore the Mexican capital, drawing and coloring a Mexican flag, and learn the "Himno nacional Mexicano" in English and Spanish. Subsequent lessons feature corn tortilla recipes, a visit to Guadalajara, mariachi orchestras, a tour of a *mercado,* a role-play bargaining experience at a Mexican market, conversion of dollars to pesos, practice with the metric system of measurement, eating *nopales* (prickly pear cactus), and making piñatas. Families who are familiar with various cities in Mexico are invited to show-and-tell. At the end of the unit, students reflect on their travels and write about their favorite places.

Transitional Bilingual Education (TBE) Programs

Early-Exit Programs

Transitional bilingual education (TBE) programs are those in which students learn English but no attempt is made to strengthen the child's first language (Molina, Hanson, & Siegel, 1997). Minimal attention is paid to the first language; although teachers may use the first language as a support for students, students are not educated in such a way that proficiency in their first language is an academic goal or outcome. Although the **transition** to English may take place within one academic year (usually third grade) in an **early-exit bilingual program,** or in other transition programs after three years of primary-language instruction, the idea that the first language will eventually disappear permeates the atmosphere of schools with transition programs.

Subtractive Bilingualism as an Outcome.   The Bilingual Education Act of 1968 (Title VII, an amendment to the 1965 Elementary and Secondary Education Act), which provided the first funding for bilingual education in the United States, was explicitly compensatory. Children who were unable to speak English were considered to be educationally disadvantaged, so federal aid to bilingual education was justified as a "remedial" program (Wiese & García, 1998) to compensate for the skills that students "lacked." The focus shifted again in 1989, when MBE programs were expanded, and maintaining and developing the native language of students became an important goal for advocates of bilingual education.

Transitional bilingual education programs support the use of students' home language in academic settings only until students are considered ready to transfer into English-only education. This supports a subtractive view of bilingualism, in effect requiring that English learners discontinue the use of their native language to become fluent in English (Nieto, 2000). In these programs, students receive initial instruction in most, if not all, content areas in their home language while they are being taught English. TBE programs are assimilationist in that bilingualism is seen as a means for acquiring English (Wong-Fillmore & Valadez, 1986). The assumption is that unless language-minority students are fluent in

English, they will not be able to become full participants in school and society. This does not support a role for heritage-language literacy (Clair, 1994).

Instruction in Early-Exit Programs.   For children to function eventually at a high level in English, cognitive academic language proficiency must be emphasized while at the same time sustaining academic content in the primary language until students are ready for an all-English curriculum (Cummins, 1979). Programs using two languages can separate these languages by time, devoting a specific time to each language. In an "alternate use" model, languages are used on alternating days: Monday, primary language; Tuesday, English; Wednesday, primary language; and so on. In a "divided day" model, students study academic subjects in their primary language in the morning and in English in the afternoon. In both these models, academic instruction occurs in both languages.

Languages can be separated by teacher, with an English-speaking teacher and a primary-language teacher sharing a team-teaching situation. In similar situation, a paraprofessional aide either teaches ELD or provides primary-language support. A caution in using this latter design is the association of the minority language with school personnel who do not have fully credentialed teaching status.

Languages can be organized by subject—primary language for mathematics, English for science, and so on. If this model is used, school personnel need to be careful to teach equally academic subjects in each language. Models in which the primary language is used only for language arts, music, and art and English is used for science and mathematics send a message about the status of the primary language.

The novice bilingual teacher may say everything twice, first in English and then in the primary language. This *concurrent translation model* has been found to be ineffective because students tune out until they hear their primary language. Another approach is *preview/review*, in which the introduction and summary are given in one language and the presentation in the other (Lessow-Hurley, 2005).

As students become more proficient in English, teachers can provide instruction in English while students, in their groups, talk and write in the home language. Bilingual teachers and students may habitually alternate between the two languages used in their community (Valdés-Fallis, 1978). This code-switching is regarded as a developmental aspect of acquiring a second language and/or a reflection of the community's language use.

Cooperative grouping in which English learners work cooperatively with native speakers of English increases students' opportunities to hear and produce English and to negotiate meaning with others. Cohen's complex instruction model (Cohen, Lotan, & Catanzarite, 1990; Cohen, 1994) encourages equal access for all students in a cooperative group by assigning well-defined roles to each group member and ensuring that these roles rotate frequently. To be most effective, grouping needs to be flexible and heterogeneous in language, gender, ability, and interest.

Experts in second-language acquisition have long debated the extent to which the first language should be used during instruction of the second language. Pedagogy such as the direct method used by language-tutoring services such as Berlitz use no primary language, whereas Lin (2001) and many other researchers amply demonstrate the multiple benefits of second-language teaching that uses, and builds on, students' L1. To some extent, many words are learned fastest when simply translated. Use of the primary language lowers stress in learning English because most learners naturally mentally map the L2 directly on to the existing L1, drawing connections, contrasting ideas, and viewing the L2 through their L1.

Use of the primary language—even if the teacher who does not speak it fluently tries to use it—demonstrates to students that making mistakes is not a big deal. By trying to learn students' L1, the teacher shows respect for students' language and culture. However, overuse of L1 can bring about dependency and loss of useful language practice if it replaces opportunities for listening and speaking practice in English (Buckmaster, 2000).

Advantages of Early-Exit Programs. Even if early-exit transitional programs are of high quality, any early advantage of learning English is outweighed by the disadvantage of little support for primary-language development. A comprehensive English-language development curriculum, if available, can be a strength of transitional bilingual education. A parent involvement component is also a necessity to ensure that parents can continue to provide academic support even when instruction switches entirely to English.

Recent studies on school reform and education for English learners all support the same findings: Students learn better when actively engaged in a nurturing environment that honors and respects their language and culture (Nelson, 1996). A TBE program can be carried out in an ambiance of respect and encouragement for both languages.

Drawbacks of Early-Exit Programs. There are numerous problems with early-exit TBE programs. They are instituted under the common misconception that two or three years is sufficient time to learn English for purposes of schooling, when in fact this is not long enough for students to build academic language skills in either their native tongue or English. As a consequence, they may not be able to carry out cognitively demanding tasks in either language. Moreover, TBE programs often segregate English learners into remedial, compensatory education, usually in **pull-out ESL instruction.**

TBE is discriminatory if learners who are in the top reading group in their primary language before being transitioned do not receive grade-level instruction in English. These students may fall behind English-only readers, who are at the same time moving forward to the next grade level in their reading. Despite their previous success, they cannot continue to learn in their heritage language—a subject to which they have devoted three years—because TBE does not offer primary-language maintenance. If the primary language is seen only as a means of learning English, respect for the L1 as an academic domain is nonexistent.

Another shortcoming of TBE is the negative effect that English-only schooling has on home-language use. When students begin speaking only English in school, they frequently switch to English as their primary language of communication. This retards rather than expedites their schooling, primarily because children and parents lose the benefit of a shared language for such purposes as homework help. For these and other reasons, TBE programs have not led to school success for many students.

Structured English Immersion (SEI) Programs

Structured English immersion (SEI) programs are those in which students are taught solely in English, supplemented with strategies designed to increase their understanding of the content, and teachers are not necessarily fluent in the L1 of the students. Many of the teaching techniques used for SEI programs were developed for use in multilingual, often urban classes where not a single primary language is shared by the learners. In the past in these classes, the use of L1 was not feasible, or was strongly discouraged because of the belief that L1 would interfere with learning English.

Instruction in Structured English Immersion Programs.   Structured English immersion (SEI) programs are designed to address the learning needs of English learners whose English is at the intermediate level of fluency or higher. Unfortunately, this approach is too often used for beginning English learners. The chief element of "structure" built into these programs is the use of specially designed academic instruction in English (SDAIE), also called **sheltered English.** SDAIE incorporates specific teaching (not language) modifications to make a lesson understandable to students (see Chapter 7).

Advantages of Structured English Immersion Programs.   Students obtain access to core curriculum subjects when the content is modified using SDAIE, and thus they can maintain parity with native-English-speaking classmates. Even literature classes can be modified with SDAIE so that English learners are not relegated to ELD programs whose course credits may not be considered college preparatory in nature. However, teachers need to be trained in SDAIE techniques.

SEI programs have one key advantage: All teachers are responsible for the education of English learners and must be knowledgeable about language development issues and techniques. Students are not linguistically segregated, which too often occurs in secondary school settings.

Drawbacks of Structured English Immersion Programs.   Although supporters of SEI programs promote increased time spent immersed in English as a way to increase classroom learning, SEI is based on an erroneous assumption: that more time spent immersed in a foreign language will somehow compensate for a lack of comprehension. Even with an elaborate set of SDAIE techniques designed to augment—in reality, substitute for—verbal explanation, few experts would agree that a student subjected to SEI achieves the same level of comprehension that the same student would achieve if taught in the primary language.

Not only is SEI predicated erroneously on the efficacy of exposure to content (whether or not the content is fully comprehensible), but also a key factor is missing in this approach—the fact that the opportunity is lost for dual-language proficiency. The same drawbacks identified in the TBE model also hold true for SEI programs: There is no development of the primary language, resulting in subtractive bilingualism. Moreover, teachers in SEI are excused from the responsibility for communicating with students in their primary languages, which lowers their integrity as educators.

Newcomer Programs

The goal of newcomer programs is to provide recent immigrants with a program that fosters rapid English learning during the period of early acculturation. Newcomer centers, such as Newcomer High School in San Francisco, are more common at the secondary level than at the elementary level. A newcomer program may be organized as a separate program at its own location or as a program within a school (Genesee, 1999).

The chief rationale for newcomer programs is that students must learn English before they can be educated in English. A second rationale is that students need social and emotional support during the time they may experience culture shock. A third rationale is that there are not enough teachers for the number of English learners, so the latter must be grouped for educational services.

Instruction in Newcomer Programs.   Programs vary in length of day; some are full day, in which students have various content courses along with ESL, whereas others are half-day or after school. The majority of newcomer programs enroll students for a year, although some can last four years and others only one semester or one summer (Genesee, 1999).

The curriculum is designed to help students move into the regular language support program as soon as possible while helping them to gain an understanding of U.S. schools and educational expectations. Techniques of sheltered instruction (SDAIE) predominate in content classes, if offered. Increasingly, however, the newcomer model is characterized by "front-loading." This means that only English-language development is offered, on an intensive basis, during the newcomer period, so students do not have access to the core academic curriculum.

Advantages of Newcomer Programs.   An intensive English-language development period, given an effective ELD curriculum, can probably bring novice learners to an advanced beginner's level within a period of months. Devoting time to this process to the exclusion of all other content may be appropriate for a very limited time—probably no more than three months—and only if the student can spare the time away from the core curricular content.

Another advantage to newcomer programs is the chance to befriend other students who may be new, practice study skills, and gain an understanding of U.S. schools and educational expectations, although in reality these goals could also be attained if students were offered these same services while they are attending a full academic program.

Drawbacks of Newcomer Programs.   The idea that students must learn English before they can be educated in English has a convincing ring, but research has cast doubt on this argument. Major disadvantages of the newcomer approach are, first, the idea that newcomers should be separated from the mainstream, English-speaking population during their period of early adjustment. The U.S. Supreme Court, in *Brown v. Board of Education* (1954), ruled that separate educational programs, however well meaning, are inherently unequal in implementation. The idea that immigrants should be educated separately—at any stage—promotes segregation (Orfield & Lee, 2005).

Second, the newcomer approach is based on subtractive bilingual education. Academic support in the primary language is seldom offered, much less primary-language development. It is probably helpful for a student to receive counseling and other assistance to help with culture shock, but no amount of socioemotional "support" in English during students' adjustment period can realistically take the place of real support—receiving mediation in the primary language.

Third, content vocabulary cannot be learned effectively in a front-loaded manner; it is an integrated part of learning content concepts. Therefore no real content-related English can be learned outside of the core academic program.

Finally, students are inevitably slowed in their educational advancement when forced to halt academic learning until their English is developed to some arbitrary point. It is not clear that students who attend such programs in high school are actually fulfilling the academic credit requirements that would make them eligible for a four-year college on graduation. Moreover, if basic interpersonal skills take two years of exposure to English to develop, and cognitive academic language takes five or more years to develop (Cummins, 1981a; Collier, 1987, Ramírez, 1992), then theoretically two to five years of "boot camp" English would be required, an inordinate time for newcomers to be segregated. Thus the newcomer model is ill-advised.

Submersion (Sink-or-Swim)

The default mode for educating English learners in U.S. classrooms is **submersion.** Even the new buzzwords, **full inclusion** and **mainstreaming,** translate to "submersion" if explicit instructional modifications are not available that support full access to the core curriculum for English learners. Submersion means that students are placed in mainstream classrooms and receive instruction in English, with English monolingualism as the goal. No provisions are made for the language and academic needs of English learners. The associated social difficulties experienced by English learners in a language-majority classroom are not addressed.

As a result of submersion, some students may survive or even succeed academically (they "swim"), but many do not have the cognitive and academic foundation in the primary language at the time of education in English and therefore do not attain success (they "sink"). "Sink" means that they eventually drop out of school; however, it is more correct to say that they are "pushed out" by instructional policies that have provided no accommodation for the fact that they entered schooling without access to the dominant language of the school and received no support for their English acquisition.

In addition to being academically disabling, submersion denies students their rights under law:

> Submersion is not a legal option for schools with non-native-English speakers; however, oversight and enforcement are lax, and many smaller schools with low populations of NNS [non-native-speaking] students are simply unaware that they are required to provide some sort of services to these students. Parents of these children, for cultural and other reasons, tend not to demand the services their children are entitled to; thus it is not uncommon to find submersion in U.S. public schools. (Roberts, 1995, pp. 80–81)

Models for dual-language education are summarized and compared in Table 9.6. From this comparison, it is evident that creating multicompetent linguists is an arduous process, yet the end result is a level of achievement to which educated people around the world aspire. Teachers with integrity strive to make this possible for their students and for themselves.

Second-Language Study for Monolingual English Speakers

Foreign Language in the Elementary School (FLES)

Foreign-language-in-the-elementary-school (FLES) programs are one way in which certain U.S. communities have approached the development of multicompetent language users,

table 9.6 Summary and Comparison of Dual-Language Education Models

Program Model	Description	Strengths	Drawbacks
Maintenance Bilingual Education (MBE) (also called *late-exit bilingual* and *developmental bilingual*)	Primary language is both a source of and vehicle for instruction; children learn to read in their first language. It includes instruction focused on the development of the language itself (oral and literacy skills) through use of authentic written and oral literature and discourse as well as academic instruction.	Native-language literacy allows students to receive the full benefit of their own cultural heritage. One's language is an important tool for processing information about the world. The mother tongue retains a strong social and emotional connection to home and family. Fluency in L2 takes 6–7 years. Students must learn academic content in their L1 and L2. Speakers of multiple languages are a national asset in international relations, trade, and cultural exchange. Each person has the right to sustain L1 during the process of maturity and education. The home–school connection that maintenance bilingual programs provide is essential for school success. Essential for restoration of endangered languages such as Native American languages.	The chief criticism of maintenance bilingual programs has been that students in such programs take longer to learn English than in other programs; however, this simply indicates poor program implementation.
Two-Way Bilingual Education (TWI)	Combines English learners from a single language background in the same classroom with approximately equal numbers of English-speaking students to provide grade-level curriculum in both languages.	Students' L1 is fully developed and maintained as they are given academic instruction in that language during at least part of the day.	English learners may be exploited as language models for majority-language students without receiving adequate ESL instruction in the process.

(continued)

table 9.6   Summary and Comparison of Dual-Language Education Models (Continued)

Program Model	Description	Strengths	Drawbacks
Two-Way Bilingual Education *(continued)*		Sheltered content is used for instructing non-native speakers—SDAIE, but in the primary/minority language (usually Spanish, making the program specially designed academic instruction in Spanish—SDAIS) to maintain grade-level content. Exposes the fallacies that language learning is easy and submersion is effective. Segregation of primary-language speakers is reduced by integrating English learners with majority-culture students in an environment in which both groups' language skills are an asset.	Children whose home language is not one of the two in TWI must learn two more languages in order to participate, without academic support for their home language. A high level of proficiency in the home language must be maintained. The identity and self-esteem of the children must be fostered and the primary culture maintained and transmitted. Parents must be able to help their children with homework in a language that they themselves may not understand.
Transitional Bilingual Education (TBE)	Students learn English while no attempt is made to strengthen their first language.	A comprehensive English language development curriculum	Subtractive bilingualism Two or three years is not sufficient time to learn English for purposes of schooling. TBE program often segregates English learners into remedial, compensatory education. TBE is discriminatory if grade-level students in the primary language do not receive grade-level English instruction. English-only schooling has a negative effect on home-language use because children and parents lose the benefit of a shared language for such purposes as homework help.

table 9.6   Summary and Comparison of Dual-Language Education Models (Continued)

Program Model	Description	Strengths	Drawbacks
Structured English Immersion (SEI)	Students are taught solely in English supplemented with SDAIE strategies designed to increase their understanding of the content.	Students obtain access to core curriculum subjects when the content is modified using SDAIE and thus can maintain parity with native-English-speaking classmates. However, teachers need to be trained in SDAIE techniques.	SEI is based on an erroneous assumption: that more time spent immersed in a foreign language will somehow compensate for a lack of comprehension. Even with an elaborate set of SDAIE techniques designed to augment—in reality, substitute for—verbal explanation, few experts would agree that a student subjected to SEI achieves the same level of comprehension that the same student would achieve if taught in the primary language.
Newcomer ("front-loaded" ELD)	Recent immigrants receive intensive ELD during the period of early acculturation on the premise that students must learn English before they can be educated in English and that students need social and emotional support during the time in which they may experience culture shock.	Intensive ELD may be appropriate for a very limited time—probably no more than three months—and only if the student can spare the time away from the core curricular content. Newcomers can befriend other students who may be new, practice study skills, and gain an understanding of U.S. schools and educational expectations.	Separate educational programs, however well-meaning, are inherently unequal in implementation. The idea that immigrants should be educated separately—at any stage—promotes segregation. The newcomer approach is based on subtractive bilingual education. Academic support in the primary language is seldom offered, much less primary-language development. Content vocabulary cannot be learned effectively in a front-loaded manner, but is instead an integrated part of learning content concepts. Students are inevitably slowed in their educational advancement (college preparatory) when forced to halt academic learning until their English is developed to some arbitrary point.

(continued)

table 9.6   Summary and Comparison of Dual-Language Education Models (Continued)

Program Model	Description	Strengths	Drawbacks
Submersion (sink-or-swim)	English learners are not given academic or linguistic support.	None	Submersion denies students their rights under the law—it is illegal.
Foreign Language in the Elementary School (FLES)	English-speaking elementary students learn a foreign language, with emphasis on enjoyment, focused on songs and cultural content.	Children before puberty have more opportunity to attain nativelike pronunciation in a foreign language. Young students have contact with a linguistic alternative to their native language, which encourages metalinguistic awareness. FLES offers exposure to another culture in a richer way than students might normally experience through social studies alone.	Without exposure to native-language speakers, students who study a second language often fail to attain communicative competence. FLES programs are usually not academically rigorous. French rather than Spanish is the preferred FLES language in many communities. Students who are already competent in a primary language are seldom those to whom FLES is afforded.
Second/Foreign Language Immersion for Language-Majority Students (enrichment education)	English-speaking students learn a foreign language as the means for acquiring academic content.	Successful only when the second language is a high-status language in which the middle-class will allow English-speaking children to be immersed for instructional purposes.	The low status of Spanish as a second language of instruction puts it at risk of eradication. Majority students, even while achieving a reading knowledge of the second language, attain low communicative competence.

beginning students in grades 4, 5, 6, or earlier in second-language study. North Carolina and Minnesota are leaders in implementing FLES programs. In addition to reading and language arts, mathematics, science, and social studies, students study a foreign language. The emphasis is usually on enjoyment, with the curriculum focused on songs and cultural content. Usually, a single teacher makes the rounds of the school as a specialist, visiting each elementary class twice a week for 40 minutes.

Advantages of Foreign Language in the Elementary School.   The great advantage of FLES programs is threefold. First, research has repeatedly documented that children before puberty have more opportunity to attain nativelike pronunciation in a foreign language.

Rather than a rapid decrease at a certain point—the so-called critical period (Lenneberg, 1967)—it is probably more accurate to think of phonological mimicry as a skill that decreases gradually from birth. That is, babies have only a slight predisposition toward phonemes in their native language from hearing it in the womb, but every year that passes narrows the possibility that the brain is exposed to other phonemes. Foreign language at the elementary level thus offers exposure to alternative phonemes at a time when the brain can still somehow hear them accurately.

Second, beyond exposure to alternative phonemes, FLES offers young students contact with a wide range of linguistic alternatives to their native language. This encourages metalinguistic awareness, the skill of looking at language flexibly, from a "meta" viewpoint— to stand outside language, in a way, to see it as a system whose rules and representations can vary. FLES may enhance students' abilities in their native language and their skill in language knowledge and usage in general.

Third, FLES offers exposure to another culture. Because language and culture are inseparable, students often enjoy a richer contact with the target culture than they might normally experience through social studies alone. This addresses the social isolation that a monolingual population suffers because of living in a linguistically homogeneous site far from contact with globalizing influences.

Drawbacks of Foreign Language in the Elementary School. Foreign-language elementary programs suffer from four major weaknesses. First, without exposure to native-language speakers, students who study a second language often fail to attain communicative competence. Having only one person—the teacher—as a foreign-language speaker limits the interaction in the foreign language to relatively brief periods during the school week (with exceptions; the diplomatic community and the wealthy elite can attain increased language contact through cosmopolitan living, frequent travel, or private tutors).

Second, only in the most exclusive schools is the FLES program academically rigorous, with a focus on extensive vocabulary acquisition, careful pronunciation, and literary content. In many countries, a high level of academic proficiency is attained at an early age in second-language instruction, and a third foreign language is introduced at the late elementary or early secondary level. Thus, compared to many other countries, the low level of attainment in only one language in most U.S. FLES programs is a minimal achievement.

Third, French rather than Spanish is the preferred FLES language in many communities because the largely upper-middle-class populace considers French a more prestigious language, despite the fact that global markets support Spanish far more than French as an economically astute choice for Americans who live in a largely Spanish-speaking Greater America. Therefore, in terms of cultural investment, FLES programs are not as useful to the economy and culture of the United States in the long run as are developmental bilingual programs—those that sustain and develop the language of those who are already fluent in a second language and live in a community that shares this language.

Fourth, those students who are already competent in a primary language are seldom those to whom FLES is afforded; they usually do not attend the schools in areas of high socioeconomic status in which FLES is a feature. Thus the very students who could make the most rapid advances in a third language—truly the mark of a multicompetent linguist—are often not given the opportunity.

In summary, for monolingual students, FLES programs are better than *no* exposure to foreign language. However, many of the features of two-way immersion programs offer advantages that address the drawbacks of FLES.

Second/Foreign–Language Immersion Programs for Language–Majority Students

Second-language immersion, also called **enrichment education (Canadian model),** provides academic and language instruction in two languages, with additive bilingualism as a goal. (This is not to be confused with two-way immersion bilingual education.) In Canada, where English and French have high language status for instructional purposes, middle-class English-speaking children are instructed in French, which is incorporated into the programs both as a subject and as a medium of instruction (Lambert, 1984). In the United States, a comparable context is the exclusive schools of the upper socioeconomic class, in which foreign languages are highly supported, as much for culture enrichment as for second-language skills.

Instruction in Second/Foreign-Language Immersion Programs.   In early immersion programs, the second/foreign language is introduced in kindergarten or grade 1. Early partial immersion uses English about 50 percent of the time rather than delivering academic instruction solely through the second language (Cloud, et al., 2000). A key difference between these models and two-way immersion programs is that there is no specific provision for native-language speakers (in the case of Canada, French-speaking students) to be schooled with the language-majority students.

Advantages of Second/Foreign-Language Immersion Programs.   The enrichment immersion model is successful only when the second language is a high-status language in which the middle class will allow English-speaking children to be immersed for instructional purposes. In the case of French, the minority language is considered high status in Canada not only because national laws mandate that the governmental functions take place in two languages, but also because French—not the local French of the relatively low-status French Canadians, but the French of France—maintains a high prestige worldwide.

Drawbacks of Second/Foreign-Language Immersion Programs.   Some educators have pointed to the academic success of language-majority speakers who are immersed in French in Canada as a model for public schools in the United States. However, in the United States, rather than being seen as a resource, the students' primary language is often at risk of suppression because it is considered low status. Because French is an accepted language of government in Canada, families of monolingual English speakers are willing for their children to spend time being educated in French. In contrast, because Spanish and other minority languages are not official languages of the United States, families of monolingual English speakers are rarely willing for their children to be educated in these languages.

Hence, in the Canadian context, French is seen as an asset for students, whereas in the United States, minority languages are seen as a deficit of students. Therefore the French-immersion programs serve as faulty model for U.S. schools. Two-way immersion programs in the United States are close to the Canadian model, but in the two-way immersion model, parental support for the minority language is not as automatic as it is in Canada given the differences in relative prestige of the minority language in the larger society.

A second drawback in the Canadian model is that majority students, even while achieving a reading knowledge of French, often fail to attain communicative competence or speaking fluency. This may be because they are not socially integrated with French-Canadian students at school or in their communities, or because speaking ability is not emphasized in their immersion experience.

It is difficult to see how public school students in the United States will be able to become multicompetent language users without a full-scale commitment on the part of society to foreign language education as an integral component of the curriculum. Moreover, the norm of monolingualism on the part of English speakers also must shift in order for more students to acquire a second or third language. Perhaps the mainstream media could promote bilingualism by featuring celebrities who are bilingual—not only Arnold Schwarzenegger, but also young actors such as Leonardo DiCaprio, who is fluent in German.

Upper-class families in the United States have the privilege of avoiding the limitations of the public schools. These families often take advantage of a simple solution to create multicompetent linguists of their children, especially in the prestige language, French, which they seem to favor. The children are schooled in a way that create academic proficiency as well as social fluency in several languages. Their solution also creates the global connections that advance their children's future careers—they send their children to boarding schools in Switzerland.

Achieving a Linguistically Multicompetent Society

Even though communities exist in many parts of the world with populations who are linguistically multicompetent, this is a vision yet to be realized in the United States. Efforts to teach foreign languages are best if they start early, as do FLES programs, or are academically rigorous, as are enrichment immersion programs. However, the real leap forward in attaining a linguistically multicompetent society is full utilization of the resources of English learners. These linguists are best supported if the primary language is a full partner in instruction.

In this effort, majority- and minority-language speakers must help one another. The only hope that native English speakers have in the United States to become multilingually competent (aside from long and frequent trips abroad) is to use the language resources of minority-language speakers. If language-minority students are mainstreamed into classes with English speakers, teachers must make every effort to let students feel full support for their language skills. Teachers who believe in a rich communicative classroom can use teacher–student relationships to draw on and encourage all students' language.

Because bilingual education is implicated in identity politics and empowerment of minorities, funding issues have often become grounds for contention among sociopolitical factions in government and society. These issues should not be allowed to dominate the effort to educate students in the best way possible. If any such complex issue can be simplified to a slogan, let it be this: Let students learn in the language that works best for them. And help them learn multiple languages!

10

The Assessment of English Learners

Teachers can use observation checklists for individual assessment.

expectation

■ Prospective teachers know how to evaluate student learning processes and products, including student errors in oral and written language, in order to understand how to plan differentiated instruction. *(Element 7.9 of the California Performance Teaching Expectations. Reprinted by permission of the California Commission on Teacher Credentialing.)*

There are as many types of assessment as flavors of ice cream at the local Baskin Robbins' 31 Flavors shop. This chapter addresses the various kinds of assessments, the different educational contexts in which assessment takes place, and how these can be used to evaluate student learning, including student errors in oral and written language. Included in this chapter are discussions of the implications of assessment for English learners and the role of teachers in the assessment process.

Assessment is an integral part of the model of teaching in Figure 2.2 (see page 34). Foundations, planning, and applications feed into assessment, which in turn cycles back to inform the previous segments. Assessment in schools is a combination of mandated, standardized tests; teacher-made assessments; and grading practices that communicate as accountability to administrators, family, and community.

Types of Assessment

Current educational reform is standards based and driven by assessments. The assessment "machine" resembles the Russian doll, with layers of assessment nested within other layers of assessment. These layers include national, state, district, school, grade-level, and teacher-made assessments, and finally the individual student's response. Embedded in all of these layers are population-specific assessments such as those that exist for English learners. This section offers a closer look at some terms that are used to label types of assessment.

Assessment Terms

The domain of assessment features a rich variety of concepts. During *performance-based assessment,* students demonstrate proficiency by doing a task while someone evaluates their success using a rubric or set of performance standards. *Alternative assessment* is frequently associated with any type of assessment that is not traditional—thus alternative—not standardized, not multiple choice, and not teacher constructed. Examples of alternative modes of assessment include observation by teacher, portfolios, essays, and short-answer responses. *Authentic assessment* is a type of alternative assessment in which the task that is done is similar to or part of some relevant real-world activity. For example, high school seniors in a health-science class might be asked to solve problems they encounter in their daily life related to health issues.

Quantitative assessment involves results that are summarized in a numerical score, whereas the results of **qualitative assessment** are described and usually use a rating scale or scores on a rubric. **Formative assessment** is usually applied during a task so that assessment can be used to improve performance. **Summative assessment** provides an evaluative summary, such as a final grade. These terms are clarified throughout this chapter (see also the glossary).

Standardized versus Less-Standardized Assessment. Methods for assessing a performance can be *standardized* (students are scored according to a predetermined value level) or *less standardized* (scoring is flexible, depending on the outcome desired). To fully evaluate student capabilities, a combination of **standardized assessment** and less-standardized assessment is often used. Teachers often design tests that are scored quickly using a scoring key, which serves as a standard. This, of course, is not "standardized" like a test that uses national norms, such as large-scale, commercially published tests. A teacher might use a structured observation checklist as a formative assessment while students are working on a task, in order to monitor specific skills such as emergent literacy skills, word identification skills, and oral reading (Miller, 1995). Using an answer key, the teacher can quickly score standardized assessments.

Open-ended assessment, on the other hand, is less standardized. Open-ended assessments may feature longer problem-solving exercises, performances or exhibitions, and/or portfolios that contain student work gathered over a period of weeks or months. Teacher-made *scoring rubrics* can be determined in advance of an assignment and assist both teacher and student by determining the basis for scoring. Even though open-ended assessment may seem more labor intensive and subjective, with effort, acceptable agreement can be achieved between a group of assessors (Maeroff, 1991).

Standardized Proficiency Tests.   Several large-scale standardized proficiency tests are used to assess progress. These are either **norm-referenced standardized tests** that compare student scores against a population of students—such as the Language Assessment Scales (LAS), a test designed to measure oral language skills in English and Spanish, and the Woodcock-Muñoz Language Assessment—or *criterion-referenced standardized tests*, used principally to find the level of language skills students have learned. The focus of criterion-referenced standardized tests is on how much of a given set of materials the students have achieved, rather than how well they have done in relation to one another or to a national sample.

Classroom Assessment

Ways to Assess.   As suggested in Chapter 5, Wiggins and McTighe's (1998) model of backward design suggests that teachers should begin their lesson planning backwards, or begin their planning with assessment. They suggest that when teachers ask themselves what in-depth knowledge they want their students to know, teachers can plan the activities and move toward those goals. The selection of assessment is highly dependent on the grade-level academic standards guiding the lesson, on the language and learning objectives of the lesson, and on the discipline.

If a middle school social studies teacher, for example, is interested in assessing content area knowledge, he or she might ask a group of students to construct a timeline of Civil War battles. If this same teacher is assessing both content area knowledge *and* oral language use, the students might be asked to prepare a presentation for the whole class describing their timeline. If this teacher is also interested in assessing whether students reached their learning objectives, he or she might ask students to make notes about the Civil War battles they used to construct the timeline.

Teachers should not hesitate to be creative in developing assessments that capture students' academic development (whether it is academic content, language, or learning strategies). Box 10.1 summarizes general means by which teachers can assess their English learners, and Table 10.1 suggests ways to assess in oral language, reading, and writing.

Box 10.2 provides examples of ways to evaluate learning in the content areas. These assessments should be guided by the grade-level standards and the goals or objectives the teacher has selected. Also, the English learner's level of English proficiency is an important factor in deciding which assessment will allow the learner to demonstrate knowledge of content area and de-emphasize language skills. O'Malley and Pierce (1996) raised an important issue about assessing content area knowledge: Reducing language demands increases the likelihood of capturing more accurately what students really know about a specific subject. Box 10.2 identifies several ways to evaluate student learning and products in academic areas.

Teachers of English learners are always concerned about growth in their students' proficiency and use several ways to evaluate growth in oral comprehension (listening and speaking), reading, and writing. The English-language development standards are useful guides

box 10.1

General Ways to Evaluate Student Learning

Teacher observation, informally and formally	Oral presentations
Standardized tests	Drawings
Criterion-referenced tests	Short responses to questions
Multiple-choice tests	Yes/no answers to questions
True/false tests	Debates
Correction tests (students find errors)	Nonverbal presentations
Cloze tests (students fill in randomized blanks)	Interviews
Completion tests	Storytelling
Problem solving	Computer assignments
Provide explanation	Role-playing
Self-assessment	Dramatization
Portfolios	Assessment of note taking
Journals and logs	Musical presentations
Essays	Small-group presentations
Hands-on projects	Student–teacher conferences

in highlighting for teachers and students the benchmarks for performance in these various dimensions of language.

Scoring Rubrics. To offer instructionally sound assessment, teachers must analyze student work and train students to do this analysis as well. Together, teachers and students need to practice self-assessment on a daily basis so that students can regularly work with the teacher to make judgments about their own progress as learners.

A **rubric** serves as a scoring guide to describe various requirements or levels of student performance. The use of rubrics helps to score student work more accurately, quickly, fairly, and reliably, and can communicate standards to teachers and students about what is consid-

table 10.1 Ways to Assess English Learners in Oral Language, Reading, and Writing

Oral Language	Reading	Writing
Greetings	Portfolios	Portfolios
Requests for information	Summaries	Writing samples
Yes/no responses	Notes	Journals
Storytelling	Cloze tests	Logs
Describing/short sentences	Vocabulary	Individualized writing conferences
Teacher observation notes		Show peer evaluation of summaries
	Pair-share	Text
		List of concepts
		Analysis of text

Note: Language and samples should be appropriate to proficiency levels and ELD standards.

box 10.2

Content Area Assessments

Content Area Assessments . . .

- Are guided by content standards and objectives
- Avoid separating language from content
- Are scaffolded by the teacher to supply help when necessary and gradually removed when no longer needed
- Feature reduced language demands to increase the likelihood of seeing what students really know
- Have oral language, reading, and writing abilities embedded in the content
- Should be selected according to students' English-language proficiency levels
- Take the following form:

Exhibits or projects	Summary of findings
Diagrams	Definitions or descriptions
Visual displays	Word associations
Tables or graphs	Vocabulary items
Organizers	Compare and contrast items
Short answers	Lists
Requests to summarize text	Clarifications
Nonverbal responses (beginners)	Evaluative exercises
Word problems	

ered a high-quality response. Rubrics give students a better idea about the level of performance their work should exhibit, and helps them to understand the meaning behind the criteria for grades. When the students are given the rubric in advance, or when they help to create it, they can self-assess their work before completion, as well as offer feedback to their peers.

To develop a rubric, first decide what criteria define "quality performance." Then assemble samples of work that demonstrate a range of quality. Attempt to separate samples of student work into levels using a three- to six-point scale. Samples of good, average, and poor work used to determine the levels can then be shown to students to help them understand the quality levels.

Some teachers work with students to analyze the standards required for the task and design rubrics together with the students. With not only the standards in mind but also the evaluative criteria, students are more likely to complete work (Perrone, 1994).

Teacher-Constructed Tests.   Teacher-constructed tests can assess skills in reading, comprehension, oral fluency, grammatical accuracy, writing proficiency, and listening. Tests can be highly convergent (one right answer required) or open-ended (many answers possible). Valid tests can be constructed using the following criteria (adapted from Canale in Cohen [1991]): (1) what is tested is what has been taught (testing should look like learning); (2) the focus is on authentic problems; and (3) tests offer group collaboration as well as individual work.

Teacher Observation and Evaluation.   Teachers often use observation to diagnose needs and document student progress. A teacher can record how members of a collaborative group interact and work together, or how students use oral language across various areas of the curriculum and interactional situations. Observations sampled at different times of the year can show student progress.

Observations can be informal or formal (as in miscue analysis), and can be based on highly structured content or on divergent and creative activities. One observation instrument is the Student Oral Language Observation Matrix (SOLOM). Using observation, the teacher rates students' proficiency in comprehension, fluency, vocabulary, pronunciation, and grammar based on descriptors ordered on a one-to-five scale.

Formative and Summative Assessment. Teachers can use formative assessment to help students maintain momentum and solve ongoing problems and to give constructive feedback during the learning process. This may involve progress checks, which help students stay on track by requiring weekly progress reports or early deadlines for outlines or rough drafts. Progress checks can improve the final product and help the student be free of the tension and frustration caused by procrastination.

Formative evaluation permits much valuable ongoing readjustment of the learning process (and instructional planning). The responsibility for this monitoring is shared between teacher and learners. Teachers can help by providing encouragement, structure, and guidelines and by making themselves available during the basic struggle to use English as a means of expression.

Summative assessment can be performance based, such as a play with other students as audience, an exhibit for parents, or a publication with a printer's deadline. Despite the satisfaction that these culminating events offer, the substance of assessment remains tied to the question, "Were the content standards achieved?" What did the project achieve? What was learned about the content? What was learned about the process? And, most exciting, what is still not known? What remains to be discovered? This summative assessment is the basis for metalearning—learning about improving learning.

Portfolio Assessment. Portfolio assessment maintains a long-term record of students' progress, provides a measure of student productivity, helps to improve students' self-esteem as a result of showing progress and accomplishment, honors diverse learning styles, and encourages students to take an active role in self-assessment (Gottlieb, 1995). Portfolios typically contain a table of contents, reflective entries that discuss the work from the student's perspective, and copies of rubrics that explain why certain works received the grades they did.

Types of Portfolios. A *selection portfolio* contains work samples; for example, what a student considers the most difficult task, or what was personally the most interesting. This is sometimes called a *best-works portfolio,* which features the works of which the student is proudest, with reflective writing or audiotaping from the student explaining why the particular works were chosen. A *process portfolio* might contain evidence of developmental work. Other portfolio contents include self-assessment, photographs and video recordings, semantic webs and concept maps, and/or teacher's notes about the student (Glaser & Brown, 1993).

Use of Portfolios with English Learners. Portfolios can be used to record students' progress in reading, beginning with an initial reading assessment and including group and individual checklists to document reading-related behaviors. Oral-assessment portfolios can be used to document the results when students are asked to invent a story, to listen or retell, and to produce spontaneous speech. Contents might include audio recording of retellings or oral think-alouds. A writing portfolio features rough drafts as well as final copies, and may include writing samples such as compositions, letters, reports, drawings, and dictations. Pierce (1998) and Wolfe-Quintero (1998) offer suggestions on planning and implementing portfolio assessment for ESL students.

Student Self-Assessment and Peer Assessment.   Students are increasingly expected to take responsibility for their own learning, combining teacher assessment with **self-assessment** and **peer assessment**. To encourage reflection on their learning, teachers can have students keep a learning log in which they evaluate their practice and make plans for future effort. Students include in their portfolios a description of their strongest and weakest areas and why, the areas in which they made the most growth, and plans for improvements in their weakest area. Students can offer themselves a grade, along with justification (McNamara, 1998b).

McNamara (1998a) recommended that teachers offer three types of feedback to student portfolios: *cheerleading* feedback (encouragement); *instructional* feedback (suggestions of strategies or materials): and *reality-check* feedback (assistance in setting more realistic goals or softening student self-criticism). Brown (1998) offers a rich source for self- and peer assessments for English learners, including assessment of group work, oral presentation, natural communication, interviews, and so forth. O'Malley and Pierce (1996) provide a useful compendium of assessments for educators, including self- and peer assessments.

Grading English Learners.   Most teachers use testing to assign grades to learners. It is not easy to assign grades to English learners, separating academic difficulties from language-acquisition challenges. Some teachers of SDAIE-enhanced content classes use a traditional A–F grading scale in accordance with grade-level expectations. Although assignments are adjusted to meet the students' language levels, performance standards are not lowered. Alternatively, a pass/fail grading scale is used to avoid comparing English learners with English-proficient classmates. A modified A–F grading scale might be used for ELD classes, with A–F grades given based on achievement, effort, and behavior, and report card grades modified by a qualifier signifying work performed above, at, or below grade level.

Achievement and Proficiency Tests

Achievement Tests.   To assess the student's learning in specific instructional content, achievement tests that are available in both English and Spanish are used. A curriculum-based achievement test is given after instruction has taken place and contains only material that was actually taught. However, many contemporary standardized achievement tests are not aligned with specific curricular content.

Competency tests are achievement tests used to provide information about whether a student should be promoted or advanced. Many school districts mandate remedial instruction between terms for students who fail to meet minimum competency standards. Such supplementary instruction must take into consideration the needs of English learners. Some states have provisions that modify or exempt testing for English learners until they are ready for competency testing. Other states offer modifications in the testing such as extended time, a separate site, small-group testing, or testing supervised by a familiar person.

Proficiency Tests.   To measure overall ability in English, **proficiency tests** are often used. These tests are sometimes divided into subskills or modes of language (speaking, listening, writing, reading, vocabulary, and grammar). These tests are often not authentic measures of language skill; they may not engage the learner's intrinsic interest by such means as providing a story or feature article from which test items are drawn, which may result in the learner being unable to assign personal meaning. Educators should be cautious about using proficiency tests to predict academic or vocational success because language is only one element among many that contribute to success.

Diagnosis and **placements tests** are proficiency tests used to determine the academic level or grade level into which students need to be placed. In addition to identifying the students who are English learners and determining the level of proficiency, placement tests can be used to monitor the progress of English learners in acquiring English and assist in transferring students to mainstream classrooms. Teachers and school administrators sometimes have a choice about which tests are used and for what purposes, but often specific tests, such as California's CELDT, are mandated by state authorities.

California English Language Development Test.   The main purpose of the California English Language Development Test (CELDT) is to identify new students who are English learners in grades K–12, to determine their level of English proficiency, and to annually assess their progress toward becoming fluent-English proficient. Districts are required to administer the test within 30 calendar days after a student first enrolls in a public school, notify parents of test results within 30 days after receiving data from the testing publisher, and administer the test annually until students are reclassified. The CELDT covers four skill areas: listening, speaking, reading, and writing. Students in kindergarten and grade 1 are assessed only in listening and speaking. Students in grades 2 though 12 are assessed in all four areas.

The CELDT contains five proficiency levels: beginning, early intermediate, intermediate, early advanced, and advanced, along the four dimensions of language (listening, speaking, reading, and writing). The results of this test are used to place students in the appropriate academic program available at the school, as well as to monitor progress and, ultimately, provide information for student reclassification into fluent-English-proficient status. Furthermore, the CELDT is aligned with the California English Language Development Standards (see Chapter 6) and closely tied to the state's language arts standards. Both prescribe specific language objectives that teachers should address in their lesson plans (see Table 6.1, page 143) and facilitate a focus on the linguistic needs of English learners.

Limitations of Assessment

Tests play a large role in placing and reclassifying (redesignating) English learners. Standardized tests, though designed to be fair, are not necessarily well suited as measures of language ability or achievement for English learners. In fact, both the testing situation and the test content may be rife with difficulties and bias. It is usually up to teachers to develop effective grading procedures and communicate assessment results to students, parents, and other educators (Ward & Murray-Ward, 1999).

Thus it is teachers who must recognize and protest unethical, illegal, and otherwise inappropriate assessment methods and hold the line on unethical uses of assessment information. Schools and teachers implement the tests; without them this entire process of testing would be impossible to administer. Needless to say, teachers with integrity understand the complexity of layers operating in this testing, the political forces driving the accountability movement, and the compromises that affect their role in implementing these tests.

Difficulties in the Testing Situation

The context in which a test is administered may affect students, causing anxiety. Lack of experience with testing materials and lack of rapport with the test administrator may cause additional difficulties for culturally and linguistically diverse students. Allowing students to take practice exams may familiarize them with the formats and reduce test anxiety. Moreover, English learners usually need time for mental translation and response formulation, and may need more time to answer individual questions. Students from other cultures do not necessarily operate under the same concept of time as do European Americans. Some students may need a time extension or should be given untimed tests.

When testers and students do not share the same language or dialect, the success of the testing may be reduced. Students who are shy or wary of the testing situation may not freely verbalize or be quick to answer questions; they may be embarrassed to volunteer a response or receive positive feedback about their performance, and they may not feel comfortable making eye contact with a test administrator. Students may be socialized in primary cultures that discourage guessing. Other students may be defensive about teachers' negative stereotypes, or resent the testing situation itself (Cloud, et al., 2000).

In California, as an example, the State Board of Education amended the regulations for one of the standardized tests, mandating that school districts provide English learners with such testing variations as flexible seating, flexible schedule, translated directions, and glossaries. Other accommodations target English learners with special needs. California's CELDT includes an extensive checklist for bilingual special education students and includes lists of alternate instruments that can be used to measure English proficiency, as well as specific modifications that can be made in administering the examination.

Test Bias

Tests, particularly achievement tests, may be inherently biased in a way that affects the performance of English learners. *Cultural bias* is present when test items derived from mainstream culture may be understood differently or not at all by English learners, or when test items feature terms used only in particular cultural or geographic regions. Many students have never experienced certain food items, sports, musical instruments, nursery rhymes, or children's stories that are prominent in European-American homes. Cultural bias can include *class bias;* for example, a "bank deposit slip" might be familiar only to middle- and upper-class students. *Language-specific bias* is created when a test developed for use with one language is translated into another language; the translation may fail to furnish equivalent vocabulary items. *Dialect bias* occurs when certain expressions are relevant only to certain dialect speakers. Skilled teachers with integrity are clear about tests and their limitations, always keeping in mind how these affect their students' performance.

Teachers therefore must be clear about what they are testing and what they want their students to be able to demonstrate. Using a variety of assessments ensures that teachers are indeed testing their students in those areas in which they want their students to demonstrate growth.

The "multiple modes of assessment" rule is used in special education placement because schools have found that using different testing instruments or measures provides a clearer picture of the student's needs and brings the stakeholders closer to making the decision that is best for the child. This is also true in reclassification of English learners (see Chapter 6). Many states, including California, mandate that multiple modes of assessment be used (including teacher observation) to determine whether the student no longer requires language support.

Technical Concepts

Validity

A test is valid if it measures what it claims to be measuring. Content validity means that a test samples the content it claims to test in some representative way. For example, if a reading curriculum includes training in reading technical documents, then a test of that curriculum would include a test of reading a technical document.

Reliability

A test is reliable if students attain similar scores when they take the same test again. Although many variables can affect a student's test score—such as fatigue, hunger, or poor lighting—these variables usually do not introduce very large score deviations. A student who scores 80 percent on a teacher-made test probably has scored 40 on one-half of the test and 40 on the other half, regardless of whether the halves are divided by odd/even items or first/last sequence. These are common ways of checking for reliability within the test itself.

Practicality

Teachers who understand the needs of English learners can help students perform at a high level whatever the nature of the assessment. They can adjust their instruction to balance lesson planning with the need to prepare students to perform well on tests, whether teacher made or standardized achievement tests. They can monitor the testing process for bias and accommodate the testing context to meet the special needs of the situation. Most of all, teachers can provide a sense of balance, putting assessment in its proper context as one means of supporting instructional quality.

Assessing English Learners with Special Needs

English learners with special needs are not exempt from assessment. The Individuals with Disabilities Education Act (IDEA) mandates inclusion of students with disabilities in general testing conducted in schools and requires that accommodations or appropriate adaptations be made, when needed. States frequently mandate the accommodations or modifications in testing procedures that can be offered to such students.

Examples of accommodations in the test setting include, for example, providing special lighting or furniture and administering the test individually by a familiar member of the school staff. Modifications that can be made in the presentation of the examination include larger bubbles in answer sheets, key words or phrases highlighted, and large print and Braille editions of tests. It is important for teachers to work collaboratively because decisions about necessary testing accommodations are better informed when multiple voices discuss the needs and best interests of the bilingual special education child.

In discussing services for English learners with special needs, Baca and Valenzuela (1994) suggested that teachers should be actively involved throughout the assessment process. Although they are referring to special education prereferral interventions, this recommendation holds true for any language-skills testing, including testing for reclassification. The special education teacher should be part of the team working closely with the English-language development specialist or designee to address language-specific student needs.

Too frequently the linguistic needs of bilingual special education students are placed on the back burner or not addressed at all. Classroom instruction may focus on academic needs exclusively, and student progress in English-language proficiency may go unmonitored and/or unaddressed. Special education teachers frequently report that in the eyes of their site administrator, special education comes before language education, and that what seems to be more important than language development is meeting the objectives of the individual education plan (IEP). This is a misplaced priority. Language education should be integrated with special education as a central component. How can achievement in specific areas improve without addressing the necessary cognitive connections provided by students' primary language? Language needs must be integrated into the instructional program because this is the only way English learners will receive input that is comprehensible and addresses their learning needs.

Student Errors in Oral and Written Language

Recognizing errors made by English learners in oral and written communication is an important skill in effective teaching. Often, students are misidentified as having learning problems and referred to special education when the linguistic errors they are making are due to second-language acquisition errors, not biology. A study conducted in 1999 in Massachusetts looked at how and why teachers recommended bilingual students for special education (Conner & Boskin, 2001). The eleven teachers in this study indicated that bilingual students were referred to special education because they exhibited errors and had difficulty with verb tenses. Also, these teachers saw bilingualism as equivalent to cognitive deficiency because they mislabeled and misdiagnosed errors that were part of the process of second-language acquisition rather than representing cognitive deficiencies. The researchers also found that these teachers lacked knowledge in language development issues and took common language errors made by language learners (e.g., difficulty conjugating verbs) to be biological or organic problems.

Errors as Indicators of Language Learning

Some important basic principles can help teachers understand and anticipate errors made by English learners. *Errors* are systematic, whereas *mistakes* tend to be random. Errors are a sign that students are acquiring language, so it is important to view errors in that light. Error is a positive feature of language learning and not a sign of abnormal speech patterns. Teachers of English learners can view errors as a window into their students' thinking. The more language is produced, the more errors are made, and the more learning can occur. The goal is to have the learner produce as much language as possible and to create awareness about the benefits of making productive errors.

Anticipating Errors

Errors are a function of language-acquisition level (ELD level). Teachers who know their students can learn to expect specific kinds of errors and then correct accordingly. The American Council on the Teaching of Foreign Languages (ACTFL) (www.actfl.org) provides guidelines that can help teachers identify systematic error-making according to ELD levels. Box 10.3 displays these descriptions.

Students' Awareness of Error

Students who are aware of the errors in their communication can bypass the risk of these errors becoming permanent, thus limiting their language growth. The teacher's role is to promote students' error awareness because the second-language learner generally does not recognize errors. In the past, error correction was usually done by giving students tests or quizzes. However, research tends to show this may not be the most effective way to correct; feedback takes time, and by the time students are made aware of their language errors, they have forgotten about them. In other words, error correction must be contextualized for it to have meaning to the learner and to have an effect on the language learner's development. Unless errors are pointed out right away, it is likely the errors will persist.

How, then, can teachers help students become aware of their errors without making them feel inferior or ashamed? First, teacher-dominated error correction is not as effective in correcting systematic errors as teachers often believe; the students' affective filter may go up and the information regarding errors may not be internalized. Therefore the teacher's role is to make students themselves aware of errors when errors occur. Once students recognize their errors themselves, they will pay more attention to forms when they produce language and be able to correct errors by themselves.

---

box 10.3

Errors According to ELD Levels

Beginner/ACTFL Level Novice:
Learners need to listen and look at language but not be required to produce it in public—mostly, errors are an embarrassment. Individual or paired practice is useful, including high-interest activities with lots of visuals, controlled vocabulary, and simple sentence structures.

Intermediate (ACTFL Level Intermediate):
High-interest activities in which errors do not impede the communication of meaning are useful. Tasks are structured to accomplish focused growth in measurable ways, balanced by language activities in which the learner is interested and at which the learner can feel success.

Advanced (ACTFL Level Advanced):
Error correction focuses on learner self-correction, balanced by targeted teacher feedback. Emphasis is equal across grammatical, strategic, sociolinguistic, and discourse functions.

Native-Speaker-Like (ACTFL Level Superior):
Still needs occasional error correction!

Note: ACTFL = American Council on the Teaching of Foreign Languages.

One way in which teachers can provide students with opportunities to notice errors is to record students' oral English. Students can then listen to themselves and analyze what they said and how they said it; in this way, they can begin to identify the frequently occurring errors. Teachers can also give their students immediate feedback in the form of appearing to misunderstand when students make errors, as the following conversation illustrates:

English learner: He drived his car.

Teacher: Sorry?

English learner: He droved, he drive, ah, he drove his car.

Another way to deliver indirect error awareness feedback is to *recast* the learner's output, focusing on the communicative content. A teacher gives feedback by reformulating an incorrect utterance, maintaining the original meaning of the utterance. Many parents do this with their children who are beginning to speak. This kind of feedback is more natural and subtle than other forms of feedback. Following are examples of how a teacher can reformulate a student's incorrect utterance:

English learner: He drived his car before.

Teacher: He drove it yesterday?

English learner: Ah, no, he drove it the day before yesterday.

English learner: Why he no want this sandwich?

Teacher: Why doesn't he want this sandwich? I don't know.

English learner: Yes! Why doesn't he want this sandwich?

Numerous studies show that giving immediate corrective feedback enhances learners' second-language acquisition. Giving immediate feedback and doing it in the right manner helps language learners become aware of their errors and enables them to self-correct errors. Again, self-correction of errors, instead of teacher correction, leads students to acquire the language form and to remember how to use it properly.

Correcting Errors

Error Correction for Speaking.   In speaking, the purpose or goal is communication—not accuracy. If meaning is communicated, errors can be ignored. If not, the listener must be patient. The role of the teacher is to rephrase and show interest. Learners should not be forced to speak in whole sentences: Native speakers seldom do, and it is not important. Pointing out errors publicly only humiliates students and runs the risk of students not wanting to speak or practice language.

Error Correction While Listening.   Errors in listening often appear as misunderstandings that can be quickly clarified. Observant teachers can read their students' body language and facial expressions, or use periodic comprehension checks to check for understanding. Teachers can then repeat, rephrase, or use other techniques to provide comprehensible input. Teachers can come back to the student who is having difficulty and double-check to see if the message was understood.

Recent language-teaching methods emphasize the interactional aspects of language. Students are no longer expected to be passive learners doing monotonous tasks, such as listening to prepared text and choosing between two given answers. Teachers can help their students develop listening skills through interactive board games such as Pictionary and Twenty Questions. Riddles, logic puzzles, and brainteasers can also be used to develop students' listening and problem-solving abilities.

Error Correction for Reading.   It is hard to recognize students' errors while they are reading silently because there is no obvious evidence of errors to be found. Therefore it is impossible to give feedback at the time students are making errors, so they may read without understanding or misunderstand the contents. Traditional error correction in reading is done by comprehension check when students finish reading a sentence, a story, or an article. However, a teacher does not need to wait until students complete their reading task. To prevent students from making errors, a teacher can give them tasks to guide their reading more effectively, such as using a thinking tree, a main idea organizer, a cause-and-effect organizer, a character map, or a concept map. By integrating these tasks, a teacher can look at students' reading process and modify it on an as-needed basis, which is more meaningful to the reader.

Reading aloud in class is one of the most difficult and stressful situations for English learners—and for students in general. This should be avoided; it is a skill rarely used in life. Miscue analysis is done privately, one-on-one. Paired reading is acceptable if both parties are enjoying it. Errors do not matter—expression counts. In sustained silent reading, errors will appear as miscomprehension.

Errors in Written Language.   Writing is an area that lends itself to user-friendly error correction; most error correction of English learners is done on written text. Error correction is personal, individualized, and private, and students benefit from positive feedback on their writing.

A teacher can also give feedback on small errors, such as the use of articles, participles, or prepositions, that are often ignored in reading and listening error correction. Again, the focus is on communication. Content and expression are more important than precision. Students should be encouraged to write and not to fear the blank page.

To enhance students' self-correction ability, a teacher can discuss with students the errors made by all readers. Making a list of these general errors in writing and having students use this list to proofread their writing is an important aspect of self-assessment. Raimes (1983) suggested 12 checkpoints of errors in proofreading. These are listed in Box 10.4.

The teacher's job is to assign writing that makes a difference in the world. The uniqueness of the learner's worldview is a priceless treasure that must be cultivated above all. The more learners write, the more errors are made—so errors are productive!

The Writing Process as Error Correction

The writing process is a useful tool for error correction for English learners. This process includes the several stages of writing—prewriting, drafting, editing/peer review, and the final product. Here teachers can target error correction and give feedback on one type of error at one time. By prioritizing and targeting errors, students are not overwhelmed or disheartened. Instead, they begin to see writing as a process of writing and rewriting, each time focusing on a different aspect of writing. This is also a useful way to demystify the process of writing so that students learn to see that it takes time to polish their craft (see Chapter 8).

Proofreading: Twelve Common Errors

1. New paragraph needed	7. Word order
2. Error in spelling	8. Word form
3. Capitalization	9. Vocabulary
4. Punctuation	10. Grammar
5. Verb form	11. Sentence structure or boundary
6. Verb tense	12. Missing letter or word

Source: Raimes (1983).

Students should be reminded that most writers do not produce a perfect product every time but instead receive feedback for improvement. Peer review is another aspect of the writing process that is useful to English learners. Have the writer read the writing aloud. A student in the role of reviewer comments on the main idea and supports that idea. The reviewer takes notes, writes up the notes, and gives these to the writer and teacher before the writer has done a rewrite.

Assessing with Integrity

Maintaining integrity in the assessment of English learners is central to ensuring that they have equitable access to academic success. Teachers with integrity have knowledge and expertise about the role of assessment in short- and long-term instructional planning. They are also cognizant of the implications of various tests in their students' academic progress and how these affect their students' life chances. Teachers with integrity avoid using only one mode of assessment to generalize about their students' achievements, and they hesitate to make important decisions about students' academic performance, language abilities, academic placement, or reclassification based on one piece of information.

Maintaining integrity in assessment includes the following:

- Clarity about the purpose and role of assessment results
- Multiple modes of assessment
- Use of authentic assessments
- Accommodation for English learners with special needs
- Balance of integration of teacher's observations with standardized testing
- Communication between student, teacher, and parents
- Collaborative and democratic decision making
- Recognition of the time- and labor-intensive quality of good assessment
- Progress monitoring as part of assessment process
- Use of assessment to support, not interrupt, student progress

Thus, assessing with integrity integrates knowledge, skills, and professional ethics. Teachers are responsible at every turn for seeing that assessment is valid, reliable, unbiased, and nonintrusive. Moreover, teachers have the professional responsibility to ensure that the results of assessment are incorporated into revised pedagogy. This closes the loop in the cycle of planning and delivery of instruction. Making sure that the community is a part of this cycle is addressed in Chapter 11.

11

Accountability to Families and Community

Community radio offers students a voice in local affairs.

expectation

■ The candidate understands how and when to collaborate with specialists, para-educators, family members, and the community to foster the formation of a learning community that supports English-language development.

In many neighborhoods in the United States, the school is a focal point of community life. School is where one goes every day, where one's fortunes are decided by the smile or frown of a teacher's approval, and the future is shaped as surely as the point on a sharpened pencil.

For English learners in U.S. schools, classrooms can be an environment in which they can "read the word and read the world"; that is, a place where instruction is understandable and meaningful, where teachers are supportive and teach with integrity, and where families are welcome. Conversely, school can be a place where peers are dismissive or worse, full of mockery; where teachers are bored and disengaged; and where parents are treated as second-class citizens. The day-by-day decisions and actions of parents and teachers create links—or create barriers—to the community that surrounds the schools.

This chapter explores the connection between the school and the community. The theme is collaboration, and the expectation is that the teacher will take the lead in establishing a cooperative climate between the students in the classroom, parents and family members, community members, community helpers in the classroom, and other members of the school staff. The collaboration is culturally responsive—it involves the culture and language of the community in a positive way.

The goal is for the members of the class to function like a close-knit family; classmates enjoy being together, work on projects that are both interesting and comprehensible, and find the world of learning exciting and fulfilling. The local community is proud of the school, and parents eagerly cooperate with teachers in the support of their children's education. This is represented in Figure 2.2 (see page 34).

The closest connection between schooling and the community is the issue of accountability. No amount of feel-good emotion that passes between school and families, for example, is valuable unless the school is performing its premier role: making high-quality education accessible to the students in that community. In each community in which schools function well, the schools exude a sense of hope—not only for the children, but also for the future of the whole community.

Educators who can create partnerships with families facilitate their participation in the schools, sending the message that the schools value the home culture and will respond to family and community concerns and aspirations.

Teaching with integrity means that teachers face the reality of culture and language differences with openness and willingness to work hard to overcome challenges of communication. Not speaking the primary language of the student is not an excuse for distancing oneself from parents, but rather should be a stimulus for learning other languages and becoming familiar with other cultures.

Becoming involved with the community is challenging. This chapter situates the education of English learners within the life of the community.

Forming a Community of Learners

Traditional classrooms are teacher-centered. Without student input, the teacher determines the educational goals, initiates and organizes learning activities, and evaluates achievement. In a learner-centered classroom, in contrast, students work together collaboratively and show self-discipline and accountability. This change from traditional to learner-centered pedagogy is accomplished largely through group collaboration (Bassano & Christison, 1995).

In a learner-centered environment, the teacher integrates the interests, values, and skills of the students into instruction. The "communal" prior knowledge that students bring represents the combined wisdom of the family and community, as well as the integral self of the "whole child." This in turn fosters synergy: Together, the whole group is more than the sum of its individual members.

Ana Díez and Leandra Marchis collaborate at Fontana High School (Fontana, California) to prepare seniors to pass the Advanced Placement test in Spanish. One group of students comprises native English speakers who have learned Spanish as a second language. A sister class comprises native-Spanish-speaking students, some of whom are recent immigrants from Mexico and Central or South America. Many of the native-English-speaking students are from Spanish-heritage families who have experienced intergenerational Spanish-language loss; the classes take part in extracurricular activities together that help to acculturate the recent immigrants to life in the United States and reacculturate English speakers to their Spanish-language heritage.

Thus the idea of a community of learners means not only a classroom in which members are tightly knit, but also a classroom connected to the families of the learners. For English learners at the K–12 level, the effect of their parents' or other family members' proactive involvement is often positive attitudes toward the school and the teacher, increased motivation to learn, and follow-through on homework. Research shows that efforts to involve families reap benefits not only for the students, but also for the teacher. Successful schools in language-minority communities have high levels of family involvement sustained by active outreach to the community.

The Classroom as a Community

In a positive classroom community, students are active in decision making and collaborative interaction. To create a sense of community is to honor students' humanity and to get to know students as persons, being open to students' creative impulses and finding ways for students to manage their own learning. In addition, the teacher who genuinely believes that students know a lot despite their L2 status will draw on students' knowledge and use this knowledge to enrich instruction.

Foremost in the formation of a classroom community is sustained use of cooperative or collaborative learning (see Chapter 5) to increase a sense of cohesion and reduce intercultural tension, as well as minimize hierarchical rankings of students (Cohen, et al., 1990). Students who work together on common goals and tasks begin to see their work as a collective responsibility (Lyons & Pinnell, 2001).

Group work gives students new responsibilities that facilitate their academic development. The teacher guides the process of student leadership and provides instruction that is responsive to students' interests within the constraints of the standards-based curriculum.

The Culture of the School and Classroom

Each school develops its own culture, a combination of the leadership of the school, the role parents play in that leadership, and the community in which the school operates. According to John Dewey (1916), education should serve democratic goals. For a school to embody these democratic principles, however, the administration and staff must be responsive to the diverse interests of the communities they serve:

> [I]t is imperative that the school culture or environment is a positive, open, accepting one that models what should be in the broader social, economic, and political culture of

society. Schools must not only be a reflection of, but should be a change agent for a more pluralistic, global, tolerant, positive society. (Brown & Kysilka, 2002, p. 165)

In schools where staff members make a conscious and determined effort to share joint activity and common goals, a sense of collective responsibility is strong. Teachers care not only for their own students, but also for the student body as a whole. Rather than following a strictly top-down leadership model, the school promotes a collegial organization, with more and varied leadership roles, including leadership roles for students. Student achievement tends to rise in this type of school, and staff members—along with parents—feel more supported and suffer less stress (Lyons & Pinnell, 2001).

Classrooms too have particular cultures. These may be highly similar in values to the culture at large; they may reflect the values of a particular subculture if the teacher and students are all members of that subculture; or they may be a cultural battleground in which the values and behaviors of teacher and students, or students and other students, are in conflict. When the values of the dominant culture conflict with that of the students, the potential for student success is diminished.

The Relation of Cultural Values and Schooling

In the United States, researchers have sought explanations for the fact that students from some cultural backgrounds succeed in school more than others. Family values play a significant role in the success of schoolchildren (Ginsburg & Hanson, 1985). The commitment the family makes to "schooling-directed efforts" (Reese, Balzano, Gallimore, & Goldenberg, 1995, p. 57) strongly affects early school adaptation and academic achievement.

Myths about Family Involvement.   Different myths about the school–home relationship have been used as explanations for the difficulty that culturally and linguistically diverse students have faced in schools. The rhetoric of the 1960s was that "disadvantage" explained the lack of school success for minorities; this justified compensatory funding for schools in low-income communities. The drawback of this approach was that compensatory funding was never enough to create full equality of schooling conditions between advantaged and disadvantaged communities. The rhetoric of the 1970s and 1980s was that "cultural mismatch" was to blame—that is, "those" families' values and behaviors did not align with the values and behaviors that created success in school. Again, this explanation avoided remediating the structural social problems such as discrimination, racism, or economic exploitation.

In the 1990s, a more subtle argument was put forth that modifies the cultural mismatch argument slightly, to the same end. In this new version of the cultural mismatch myth, it is not specific cultures that are mismatched with U.S. schooling practices, but rather "traditional agrarian" cultures in general compared to industrialized societies. In this argument, traditional/agrarian societies based on extended kinship networks in rural economies evolve moral codes

> favoring filial piety and intergenerational reciprocity, gender-specific ideals of social and spiritual values rather than specialized intellectual ones, concepts of childhood learning that emphasize the acquisition of manners and work skills without competitive evaluations, and concepts of the adult years as the prime period for significant cognitive development. (Levine & White, 1986, p. 3).

The following section examines the myth that "traditional agrarian" values are mismatched to school success.

Positive Contributions of Traditional Values.   Immigrants from Latino societies are often from rural areas in which obedience to and respect for elders are adaptive values in contexts in which family members must work closely together for survival. Do these traditional, rural values put Latino children at a disadvantage in individualistic and competitive school settings? Researchers such as Suarez-Orozco (1989) have suggested that rather than being a detriment, traditional agrarian values may be a source of emotional support and personal identity.

The Spanish word *educación* is a false cognate with the English *education*: The word in Spanish does not distinguish between schooling as academic work and upbringing as moral training. Research data (Reese, et al., 1995) document that knowing right from wrong, respecting and obeying one's parents, displaying correct behavior, and honoring one's family are a part of the concept of being well educated, or having "educación," for many Latino families. The researchers found that these values worked to the benefit of student success by reinforcing the discipline of the school and, when combined with other factors such as a strong paternal role in schooling, were positive overall.

However, despite the virtues of these values, they may be necessary but not sufficient for school success. Aggressive pursuit of educational opportunities; encouragement for students to enroll in difficult classes; and then finding academic support and resources for students' homework completion, books, and supplies may be significant factors that restrict school success to the middle and upper classes. These institutional barriers to equal opportunity must be identified and addressed.

School Practices versus Cultural Values.   The daily routines of schooling may be at odds with students' cultural values. Toohey (1998) noted three instructional practices that a teacher in a first-grade class enforced as a part of classroom management that communicated the importance of individualism over collectivism, reflecting the values of mainstream culture (in this case, of mainstream Canadian culture) but not necessarily reflecting students' cultural training. The first practice was exemplified by the maxim, "Sit at your own desk"; the second, "Use your own things"; and the third, "Use your own words and ideas."

Certain ways of seating children restricted them from conversing with peers. Students were forbidden to lend or borrow goods—even pencils—which restricted social relations based on sharing. Students were also repeatedly told, "Do your own work," which reinforced the idea that cognition is individual and not co-constructed.

The practices described in Toohey (1998) unfortunately created limitations for students rather than facilitated cooperative practices, and they denied English learners the use of peer resources. Toohey's example exemplifies the conflict of school values and students' cultural values.

Culturally Responsive Practices.   Besides teachers, schools and classrooms can also be grounded in principles of integrity. The school culture can be made more community-friendly in a number of ways. The curriculum of the school can incorporate topics, knowledge, and skills that the community deems valuable. Extracurricular clubs, field trips, even the music played at school should be inclusive and respectful toward diversity (Brown & Kysilka, 2002).

Two of the greatest barriers to success for language-minority students are elementary school programs that result either in subtractive bilingualism or language segregation, and middle or high school programs that track language-minority students into nonacademic tracks, another form of language-based segregation. This is socially divisive and damaging to the social and political fabric of the United States.

Respect for primary-language use is at the core of responsiveness toward the community's culture. In a large measure, the commitment the school makes toward additive bilingualism shapes the students' language future. Each community in which dual-language competence is a resource functions as a source of bilingual talent, strengthening the economic future of the United States.

Family Involvement in Schooling

"Strong parent involvement is one factor that research has shown time and time again to have positive effects on academic achievement and school attitudes" (Ovando & Collier, 1998). Successful program models are available that help parents and other family members work together successfully with school personnel. Teachers with integrity have clarity about how they define **family involvement** and what role teachers and family members are expected to play in sustaining the home–school connection.

Too often, teachers approach families with a deficit perspective, perhaps believing that family members are somehow not interested in their child's progress. Some teachers find it easier to educate students who resemble their own children linguistically and culturally—and have difficulty with what Delpit (1995) called "other people's children," those who speak another language and return home to a culture different from the teacher's. Bridging this cultural gap by getting to know the students' families is a vital and enriching shift in perspective.

What Is Family Involvement?

Each school and each community has its own vision of the role families should play in schooling. Some schools seem to want families to be involved only in specific ways and at times determined by the staff. The rise of nontraditional and alternative family structures has shifted the perspective on the role of the family from the term *parents* to the more inclusive term *family members.*

In the past, community members spent time with children, teaching them values and supervising and nurturing their hobbies and interests. Modern society has become complex and demanding, and many people are too busy to get to know their neighbors' children. Schools have an expanded role—an almost exclusive mandate—to do the nourishing of children that used to be done by extended families, neighbors, churches, and other community organizations.

The focus in family involvement has shifted from parents to families. Intercultural educators who make a special effort to understand and communicate with families will find many inherent strengths. Gone are the days in which teachers could assume that families do not want to be involved; many families who seem apathetic or unavailable are simply hard to reach (Davies, 1991), and schools must adapt their traditional ways of communicating.

Ways to Involve Families.   Parent education programs, home–school communication, volunteering, academic teaching and learning at home, decision making, and acting as school–community liaisons are all ways to involve families (Epstein, 1995). Family members can help with small groups of individuals in classes; assist with tutorial or remedial work; help to plan projects and field trips, serve on school committees; and participate in curriculum, budget, and other advisory capacities, including hiring of teachers and other staff members. Another helpful role is that of community liaison, that go-getter who calls other families to publicize meetings and open house activities, and helps to organize extracurricular activities.

Exemplary Parental Involvement: Migrant Education.   Migrant education in the 1980s set an exemplary standard for parent involvement, especially in states with large populations of migrant workers, such as California, Texas, Illinois, Michigan, and Wisconsin. Funding of migrant education programs was contingent on parental involvement on advisory boards and parental consent in such areas as budget allocations. One exemplary program is the Monterey County Migrant Education Parent Involvement, Education & Training Program, which offers parents CPR training and involvement in La Familia Migrant Parent Conference, Parent Outdoor Leadership and Team Building training, and a Parent Regional Advisory Council (see www.monterey.k12.ca.us/migrant-education/parent-involvement. html).

Recent research has explored the strengths of migrant families and advised school administrators and teachers to build on these strengths rather than focusing exclusively on the hardships of migrant life. A few innovative programs have addressed the structural difficulties faced by migrant families, such as the delay in transfer of school records from one site to the next and the substandard access to study areas and health care in migrant housing camps.

Families' Rights to Due Process

Court rulings and civil rights legislation have ensured that when school employees make decisions that affect children, parents have numerous rights to due process. Box 11.1 features the Declaration of Rights for Parents of English Language Learners under the No Child Left Behind Act. Rather perversely, the U.S. Department of Education website that offers this declaration requires a relatively esoteric web player to be installed on the computer of a parent who might want access to this information.

All parents have the fundamental right to the school's support for the home language. To deny access to native-language literacy exploits minorities (Cummins, 1989) and promotes linguistic racism. Teachers with integrity who are committed to the value of additive bilingualism help families understand the advantages that bilingualism provides to the individual. Family support for bilingualism helps to establish expectations for high academic performance in two languages (Molina, et al., 1997).

Issues in Family Involvement

Educators seeking to increase family involvement have encountered predictable concerns. Ovando and Collier (1998, pp. 301–309) organized these issues into five school–family issues: language differences, family structure and needs, educational background and values,

box 11.1

Declaration of Rights for Parents of English Language Learners under No Child Left Behind

Under the No Child Left Behind Act, parents of English language learners can expect:

1. To have their child receive a quality education and be taught by a highly qualified teacher.
2. To have their child learn English and other subjects such as reading and other language arts and mathematics at the same academic level as all other students.
3. To know if their child has been identified and recommended for placement in an English language acquisition program, and to accept or refuse such placement.
4. To choose a different English language acquisition program for their child, if one is available.
5. To transfer their child to another school if his or her school is identified as "in need of improvement."
6. To apply for supplemental services, such as tutoring, for their child if his or her school is identified as "in need of improvement" for two years.
7. To have their child tested annually to assess his or her progress in English language acquisition.
8. To receive information regarding their child's performance on academic tests.
9. To have their child taught with programs that are scientifically proven to work.
10. To have the opportunity for their child to reach his or her greatest academic potential.

Source: Office of English Language Acquisition (OELA) (2004).

knowledge about education and beliefs about learning, and power and status. Table 11.1 presents these concerns paired with proposed solutions.

In some communities, parents do not want their children to be educated in the home language because they think it will stigmatize the child, because they have been told that the language will slow down the child in school, or because they prefer that the home language be taught through community resources, such as Saturday schools or private tutoring.

For example, Hualapai Indian parents in Peach Springs, Arizona, reacted negatively when educators proposed that schools establish a Hualapai–English bilingual program. Many of the parents had attended English-only schools and had been repeatedly told that the native language was unimportant, so they did not believe that such instruction would benefit their children. A high-tech approach based on computer-assisted language learning for the Hualapai language was eventually successful, after parents had become convinced of its value (Watahomigie, 1995).

One issue in family involvement is parental overinvolvement. In some cases, parents do not rely on legal means to exert power in schools, but do so in more informal ways. They use personal connections that influence the behavior of school administrators, personal relationships with the teacher, gifts or expensive fundraising pledges to the school, and so forth. Some parents sign up to participate in class as volunteer aides and from this role attempt to intervene in classroom instruction by favoring their own child. From the teacher's point of view, family involvement should promote achievement but not disrupt instruction.

table 11.1   Issues in School–Family Relationships and Possible Tactics for Improvement

Component	Concern	Tactics for Teachers
Language	Educators' language confuses parents.	Translate jargon into plain English and then into home language.
	Lack of support on the part of community members for primary-language instruction	Advocate maintenance of the home language in all parent communication.
Family structure	The struggles of day-to-day survival affect families' ability to support the home–school partnership.	Arrange conferences at convenient times for working families.
	Alternative family structures affect the home–school relationship.	Speak about "families" rather than "parents." Accept the relationships that exist.
Educational background, attitudes toward schooling	School expectations may not match the parents' expectations for their children.	Discover the parents' aspirations for their children. Do everything possible to have the school and family agree on high standards.
	Educators make unwarranted assumptions about the attitudes of parents toward schooling.	Ensure that communication with school is always honest and positive.
Knowledge and beliefs about education	Parents who learn about school culture, their role in U.S. schools, and the specific methods being used in their child's classroom may not be reinforcing these methods at home.	Family education events, family literacy classes, primary-language written and oral information, formal and informal teacher–family talks, and family tutoring training are a part of the picture.
	Parents and teachers differ in the perception of the home–school relationship.	Teachers do not merely inform parents; interest and communication are fully two-way.
Power and status	The inherent inequality of the educator–layperson relationship undermines communication.	Schools have a "family space" at the school. Parents should be informed and involved in decisions.
	Programs for parents may convey a message of cultural deficiency.	The funds-of-knowledge approach affirms and respects the knowledge of the home.
	Language-minority community members are underrepresented in instructional and administrative positions in the schools.	Bilingual speakers are paid well and are considered respected assets to the school as well as to the classroom.

Source: Adapted from Ovando and Collier (1998, pp. 301–309).

Barriers in Family–School Communication

If families of English learners are not visible at parent meetings or traditional parent–school activities, teachers and school officials may think that parents are not interested in what happens in schools. Some parents report that they experience specific barriers in communicating with school authorities. These include the failure of school staff to consult with them about the type, scheduling, or location of events; feeling intimidated by school staff and awkward about approaching school personnel; feeling patronized or talked down to; and feeling suspicious or angry about specific incidents.

Some parents may feel that it is disrespectful to challenge the teachers' opinion of their child. These and other communication problems can be reduced if teachers of English learners are trained in effective communication strategies; if they are aware of, and do not believe, myths about lack of parental interest (Chavkin, 1989); and if they are aware of the particular values of the culture in regard to parent–child relationships.

Teachers with integrity are experts in their content areas, and this content includes some level of expertise in child psychology. When culturally specific interventions are needed for parental involvement, these must be specific to the developmental level of the child.

Enhancing Home–School Communication

Even if the teacher does not speak the same language as the family, nonverbal messages can convey warmth and interest to family members. Whether in informal greetings in the parking lot, at a classroom open house, or during family–teacher conferences, teachers should show respect toward family members by such courtesies as rising as guests enter the room, greeting guests at the door, and accompanying them to the door when they leave.

If notes, letters, or newsletters are sent home in the home language, they are more likely to be read (see *Reporting to Parents in English and Spanish*, www.ammieenterprises. com). However, some parents cannot read, and a community liaison should be employed by the school to facilitate parent–teacher communication in these cases.

Initial communications with parents that are parent-child-teacher-friendly and focus on positive aspects of schooling and student performance are important. In these communications, teachers are seen as people to be trusted and not always the bearers of bad news. Any program of home–school communication is first based on having established a rapport with parents in person. This is particularly important if the student is an adolescent or has a learning problem.

The most important focus for school–home notes is the improvement of academic productivity, such as the amount or quality of completed classwork or homework. When students complete work accurately, improvements in classroom conduct occur simultaneously—few children can complete their work accurately and have time to misbehave. However, simply reducing disruptiveness does not in itself cause an improvement in academic performance (Kelley, 1990).

Family–Teacher Conferences

The conscientious teacher makes careful preparation for **family–teacher conferences,** making sure that scheduled times are convenient for family members and preparing a showcase portfolio of the student's successes. One teacher recounts the course of a typical conference:

> I usually go to the door to greet each set of parents. I make sure I say their names correctly. We might begin the conference with small talk, especially if the student has told me of a recent and notable family event. Then I show the parents the student's work portfolio and

go over the high points. If the parents need to see how an average child might perform, I have a folder ready that has anonymous work that shows grade-level work—sometimes it's easier that way for parents to put their child's work in perspective.

Most of the time, parents want to talk about the child—I just listen. It helps me get a more complete view of the child. If the work really needs improvement, I recommend a set of steps to get things moving forward. Before time is up, I like to set a timeline for improvement so not too much time goes by before we get together again.

Sometimes an interpreter is needed for family–teacher conferences; this complicates the interaction but shows respect for the home language. Teachers should avoid using the student to interpret, but instead anticipate the need for an interpreter in advance and have a community member or school interpreter present. When an interpreter is part of the dialogue, the communicators talk directly to one another. The interpreter translates the exchange, trying as closely as possible to match the concepts and emotions conveyed. A teacher who can watch such nonverbal responses as facial expressions, voice intonations, and body movements can extend communication.

At the secondary school level, two or more teachers may meet with the parents as a group when a single interpreter is present. The role of the interpreter in facilitating the interchange then becomes critical in easing the strain for parents of meeting more than one teacher at a time.

Communication during family conferences is strengthened in several ways. Careful records and samples of student work document the student's progress so that the teacher can inform the parents early if the child falls behind expectations in some area. Contact with parents is recorded in an activity log, including date, subject, and parents' reactions; this provides evidence that communication efforts have been made. The teacher's positive tone of voice communicates appreciation for parents' help.

Conferences that include the student help to foster self-regulated learning. Many secondary school teachers get students involved by having them facilitate the conference and showcase a portfolio of their work. Students can show the family what has been learned, and family members have the opportunity to ask the student questions and express their ideas. Teachers act as guides by clarifying ideas and issues and responding to specific questions (Davies, Cameron, Politano, & Gregory, 1992).

This three-way conference is based on the use of a portfolio to document student learning; informal conversation by which the family can comment on the student's work; the student's maturity and preparation to participate; and teacher guidance during the event in case of misunderstanding or if a student drifts off topic. These conferences are useful in observing parent–child interaction and in drawing parents into the learning community.

How Families Can Assist in a Child's Learning

The family's support for literacy forms the foundation for school achievement. Schools who have a take-home library of print- and media-based materials encourage learning activities outside of school. In a dual-language setting, families can work with their children in either language.

Family literacy projects help children achieve in school. Ada (1989) held parent literacy nights, in which children read stories to their parents that they had written. Eventually parents wrote their own stories and read these aloud on videotapes, which circulated to great enjoyment throughout the parent community.

In a New England elementary school, a young teacher invited Puerto Rican parents to class to tell stories about their personal lives and histories (Solsken, Willett, & Wilson-Keenan, 2000). In Fresno, California, the Hmong Literacy Project was initiated by parents to help students appreciate their cultural roots, preserve oral history, and maintain their culture through written records. The program helped families develop not only literacy skills in Hmong and in English, but also skills in math and computers, which then allowed families to help their children academically (Kang, Kuehn, & Herrell, 1996). Opening up computer labs to parent–child joint activity also promotes informational literacy.

Websites are available that feature various models of family involvement (see Table 11.2). Many of these Websites link to others; even if some disappear, there is enough information on the Internet to be of assistance to families. Some of the sites offer links to primary-language materials; for example, the California Teachers Association website offers family involvement brochures in ten languages (online at www.cta.org/FamilyInvolvement/Brochures.htm).

table 11.2   Internet Resources Promoting Family Involvement

Website	Content
www.childdevelopmentinfo.com/learning/parent_teacher.shtml	How to establish a parent–teacher relationship; guidelines for parental behavior at a teacher conference; typical phrasing for questions to ask about educational concerns; follow-up reading
www.cpirc.org	Includes a bibliography of websites about parent–teacher communication and partnerships, including websites in Spanish
www.cta.org/FamilyInvolvement/FamilyInvolvement.htm	Ways that parents can help their children learn; how to improve teacher–parent conferences; how to get parents involved in the school; brochures in 11 languages
www.responsiveeducation.org/tipHelpfulHints.html	Ways to increase family involvement in the school; how to access sources of help outside the school; ways to measure the success of family–school partnerships
www.ncrel.org/sdrs/areas/issues/envrnmnt/famncomm/pa100.htm	A list of actions that schools and parents alike can take to increase involvement. Audioclips (in English) and text versions of the same are featured. Includes a link to an article on secondary school parental involvement.
www.ncrel.org/sdrs/areas/issues/envrnmnt/famncomm/pa3lk1.htm	Explanations of how to improve the school climate to encourage parental involvement
www.ncpie.org	How to help parents to understand the No Child Left Behind Act; includes lists of family–community organizations that promote home–school links
http://gseweb.harvard.edu/hfrp/projects/fine.html	Features the Family Involvement Network of Educators founded by Harvard University
www.middleweb.com/TeachFam.html	Ways that teachers can promote family involvement

A Model of Home–School Relationships

Table 11.3 offers tactics for involving parents in learning, such as providing information to parents and learning from them about their views of education. These suggestions are drawn from Jones (1991), Díaz-Rico and Weed (2002), and Díaz-Rico (2004). Rather than include a separate list of suggestions from each source, these are presented in categories.

Faltis (2001) provides a four-level sequence for home–school relationships (see Table 11.4). Although teachers may not be able to reach the highest level of parental involvement at a particular school site, the model presents an overall view of the possibilities.

Transformative School–Community Partnerships

Rather than looking at the classroom solely as a collection of individuals, educators are now aware that these learners are a part of a larger community whose goals, aspirations, struggles, and resources form the basis on which school achievement rests. School–community partnerships are fundamental to the education of English learners.

Is **empowerment** the goal of school–community partnerships? Although the goal of many such programs and relationships is to teach parents to help their children succeed academically, topics such as racism, social equality, and economic exploitation are often avoided (Valdés, 1996). It might do more good for liberal educators to channel the empowerment rhetoric into the election of officials who will enforce equal funding for low-income neighborhood schools. Nevertheless, Delgado-Gaítan (1994) defines *empowerment* as a way in which a historically underrepresented group can recognize their potential and state their goals of access to resources, and thus power. Partnerships in which both partners are mutually respectful seems a fruitful means toward this end.

Getting to Know the Community

Teachers who take the time to shop in the neighborhood, visit community centers, eat dinner or picnic with families, or attend religious services in the community often take the first step toward forming and sustaining school–community partnerships. Some schools sponsor a Grandparents' Day so that students can invite family members to class.

When investigating the daily life of the community, it is particularly valuable to look at the social practices that support learning, including such factors as social and political relations, existing oracy and literacy practices, religious beliefs, and relationship to the neighborhood, media, health institutions, and schools (Delgado-Gaítan, 1994). These influence the way in which the community uses learning as a means toward power.

Community Support for English Learners

School partnerships with community-based organizations (CBOs) can assist students' academic achievement in a variety of ways: by offering students tutoring services in their first language, helping students develop leadership skills and promoting higher education goals, and providing information and support on issues that affect families. Students can be invited to the local library to offer their stories, books, and poetry—in both English and the primary language—to other students. Teachers can recommend books, volunteer to tell stories once a month, or participate in family literacy nights.

table 11.3   Tactics for Educators to Involve Families in Schooling

Type of Involvement	Suggestions
Provide information	• Chat with parents as they pick up their child after school. • Use the telephone as an instrument of good news and send home notes when students are doing well. • Videotape programs for parents. • Operate a parent hotline. • Encourage parent-to-parent communication. • Hold parent workshops on helping their children with reading skills. • Provide bilingual handouts that describe programs available through the school. • Make available a list of parental rights. • Send home personal handwritten notes, using a translator if necessary. • Create parent–student handbooks. • Have students write classroom newsletters. • Welcome new families with packets delivered to the home.
Showcase English learners	• Enter students in art contests or exhibits sponsored by community or professional organizations. • Offer to train students in storytelling or read-aloud techniques at libraries or children's centers. • Encourage pride in dual-language proficiency.
Ways to bring parents to school	• Invite parents personally, whenever possible. • Encourage parents to come to class to make crafts with students, or to discuss culture, calligraphy, or family history. • Schedule parent conference or meetings without conflict with work schedules. • Welcome siblings at parent conferences or meetings. • Provide babysitting services for parent conferences. • Maintain a friendly school office and bilingual staff. • Establish an explicit open-door policy so parents will know they are welcome; include welcoming signs in primary language. • Suggest specific ways parents can help to promote achievement. • Help parents to obtain remedial help, if necessary, in a timely way. • Create social opportunities during meetings, with food and dramatic or musical performances if time permits. • Hold student–teacher–family breakfasts once a month. • Provide translation at schoolwide events. • Schedule primary-language speakers at school events. • Recognize parents for involvement at award ceremonies, send thank-you notes, and speak positively of parents to their child.
What teachers can learn from parents	• Ideas of better ways to communicate • A richer understanding of the student's role(s) in the family • The hopes that parents have for their son's or daughter's schooling • Student's hobbies, interests, and strengths • Use of L1 in home and with peers

table 11.3   Tactics for Educators to Involve Families in Schooling (Continued)

Type of Involvement	Suggestions
What teachers can learn from parents *(continued)*	• Academic habits in the home • Mass media consumption • Cultural aspects of health and nutrition
Homework tips for parents (adapted from Jones [1991])	• Set aside a family quiet time when each person has homework or other activities to do that demand concentration. • Have a regular means for finding out what assignments to expect. • Make sure there is a place set aside for homework; provide paper, pencils, adequate lighting, etc. • Check with the child to see if they understand the assignment. If needed, work through a problem. Have someone available call for help if necessary. • Check the completed assignment with the child. • Praise the work or offer constructive improvements.
Workshops and parent support groups (adapted from Jones [1991])	• Make-it-and-take-it workshops to construct home learning materials; for example, Family Math • Family learning center, school library, or computer center open several nights a week with learning activities for all ages • Learning fairs, single-topic sessions held in the evening • Parent support groups hosted by community members • Family room—a room at school set aside for families to drop in and participate in informal activities, play with toys, and talk with other parents • Workshops on child and adolescent development • Special topic workshops on reading, math, study skills, self-esteem, health, family communication, etc. • College admission workshops • Adult education (computer literacy, family literacy) • Conflict resolution and violence in the community
Tactics for teachers to involve parents in policy decisions	• Ask representative parent committees to advise and consent on practices that involve culturally and linguistically diverse students. • Talk with parents before and after school to encourage them to get involved in school issues. • Make school facilities available for meetings of community groups. • Draw on parents' expertise in such areas as finance, school improvement, and personnel issues. • Honor the integrity of parents and families by respecting what they know and recognizing their strengths.

Source: Diaz-Rico (2004).

table 11.4   Four Levels of Parent–School Involvement

Level of Involvement	Description of Activity
I. Teacher–parent contact	The teacher initiates positive home–school contact and dialogue by chatting, making home visits, talking with community workers, and arranging for after-school homework help or tutoring to promote students' success.
II. Sharing information in the home about schooling	The teacher uses student-produced newsletters, personal notes, telephone calls, and other notices (in the home language if possible) to keep families informed about school events and meetings, changes in school schedules, help available from community-based organizations, and sources of academic support.
III. Participation at home and school	Parents, caregivers, and other concerned adults are encouraged to visit and assist in the classroom and attend school meetings and social events. Students may be assigned to find out about knowledge their families have about planting, medicine, etc., and then teachers can find a way to use and elaborate on this information in class.
IV. Parental empowerment in curricular decisions	Teachers support parents who become involved as colleagues in professional activities and decisions; parents initiate advisory committees and community tutoring centers and find multiple means to influence school policy and support academic learning outside of the classroom.

Source: Faltis (2001).

Teachers can speak at meetings of community service organizations such as Rotary and Kiwanis with current information about multicultural and linguistic issues. Articles in local newspapers about students' school achievements, prizes they have won, or their college and career goals show community support for ESOL programs.

Educators who are most successful are connected with the community—they treat families and community members as partners. When the community acts in close harmony and partnership with the school, students take initiative and responsibility in community activities and social action (Auerbach, 2002). This is the real meaning of a community of learners grounded in a context of integrity.

Working with Para-Educators

Teachers of English learners often work with **para-educators:** instructional aides, volunteers from the parent community, tutors from other grades, or other community volunteers. The classroom teacher must plan lessons carefully in order to use the extra help effectively, maintain high-quality instruction, and ensure that assistants in the classroom feel valued.

To obtain assistants in the classroom, the teacher can team with another classroom to find older students to volunteer as cross-age tutors or classroom buddies. Parents can be recruited through invitations sent home with students or through personal contacts at open house activities, student conferences, or home visits. The local high school and university may be able to provide a list of outreach organizations and names of contact people.

The strongest skills and dispositions that an aide can bring to the classroom are good language skills, the ability to work with students in a reliable way, a working knowledge of classroom management, and an understanding of the students' culture as well as the culture of the classroom. Although it is certainly desirable for the volunteer to have good English-language skills, those who do not speak English well but have good primary-language skills, for example, can preteach necessary subject matter vocabulary and concepts that will subsequently be taught by the teacher in English.

Planning That Includes Assistants

Para-educators can assist in preparing materials, perform assessments, tutor or supervise small groups of students, or provide whole-class instruction with teacher supervision. Some teacher aides deliver primary-language or ELD instruction. No matter what the duties of the assistant, the teacher is responsible for seeing that instructional quality is maintained, that the aide is effective in promoting student achievement, and that students receive instruction from the aide that is as rich as it would be from the teacher.

Teachers who value the help provided by assistants must be willing to invest time in both planning and supervising in order for such individuals to be employed effectively. Moreover, student achievement should not be evaluated solely by the assistant, but rather with the supervision or participation of the classroom teacher.

Aides need classroom space for their tutoring, group work, or clerical tasks. The number of students for which an aide is responsible may vary from one-to-one tutoring to supervising the entire class while the teacher is involved in conferences or individual student contact. Planning for assistance always includes a backup plan so that the day's activities can be modified in case the aide is unavailable.

Co-planning—sharing responsibility for designing the day's activities—enhances the assistant's sense of ownership, acceptance, and value that makes the role rewarding and helps the aide feel part of the instructional team.

Instructional Roles of Para-Educators

To enhance teamwork, the assistants need to be given clear directions and understand not only what is expected of them, but also what is expected of the students. Para-educators are also a source of valuable feedback to the teacher on students' needs and accomplishments. Instruction provided by the aide is valid and important and should be considered as such by the students.

Often teacher assistants who are brought into the classroom to offer primary-language instruction share the students' cultural background. These individuals can provide valuable linguistic and emotional support for students as they learn English. On the other hand, such aides may subtly modify the teacher's educational intentions.

Hye-Lim Park, an international graduate student at a local university, was placed for a fieldwork assignment in the school that her young child attended. Ms. Reicher, a second-grade teacher in a bilingual classroom, accepted her help in the role of assistant. While working on cooperative projects, the students were expected to exchange ideas and information as well as compose and deliver group reports. Ms. Reicher asked Ms. Park to work with one group.

In observing Ms. Park interact with these students, the teacher noticed that students were silent as they worked individually on the project. She found that Ms. Park had asked the students to speak only English in the group so that she could understand what they were saying to one another. However, students were silenced by this requirement, and the silent work did not encourage group interaction. A compromise had to be negotiated with Ms. Park that would encourage students to develop speaking proficiency in English while retaining the comfort level they enjoyed by speaking Spanish with one another. (LTD-R)

For their efforts, paraprofessionals deserve appreciation, whether it is a spoken "thank you" and a pat on the back or an occasional gift or token of esteem. Box 11.2 provides guidelines for teachers who are working with a para-educator.

Educators with integrity are aware that although they are the instructional leaders, the successful classroom is one in which all participants have a stake in the outcome. Students, family members, and community helpers all play a role in the learning community. When the ambience in the classroom is cooperative and welcoming, students feel constructive, knowing their goals are shared and supported. This is the optimum partnership of school and community.

box 11.2 Guidelines for Working with and Supervising a Para-Educator

- Develop a daily schedule of activities.
- Inform your para-educator about your expectations of him or her.
- Demonstrate and verbally explain specific teaching tactics to be used for particular lessons and students.
- Be sure that the para-educator is fully informed about every aspect of classroom activity. Maintain full communication.
- Be open to suggestions from the para-educator.
- Take time to observe the aide's performance.
- Provide praise or corrective feedback for specific actions.
- Determine who evaluates the para-educator's performance and try to do so in writing on a regular basis (at least monthly). Make sure someone reviews the evaluation with him or her.
- Provide remedial attention for any documented weak areas and keep a record of effort spent working on these areas.
- Do not criticize the para-educator in front of the students. When corrective feedback is necessary, make it constructive and private.
- Deal immediately with any problems that may arise.

Source: Adapted from Westling and Koorland (1988).

12

Analyzing an Instructional Plan and Adapting It for English Learners

Teachers are best evaluated in the context of the classroom.

Prospective teachers are increasingly being assessed before certification. In California, these assessments take the form of the **Teaching Performance Assessment (TPA),** which comprises four required tasks that allow teacher candidates to demonstrate what has been learned in preservice education. The following mini-lesson is intended to integrate the concepts that have been presented in this book. It reflects the knowledge required by a prospective teacher in lesson adaptation to meet the needs of English learners. This is not, however, intended to model task 1 of the TPA.

Expectations for Adapting Instruction

A teacher's primary responsibility is to ensure that each student learns the knowledge and skills required at the specific grade level. Learners have a developmental achievement range of about five years on any given skill; that is, one 7-year-old may color with crayons at the level of a child 9.5 years of age, whereas in the same class, another 7-year-old may have the coloring skills of a child aged 4.5 years. Multiply this age range by 30 students on the many cognitive and sensorimotor skills required for school success, and the 30 students transform into a web of complexity for the classroom teacher—without adding special needs students, who provide a completely different set of challenges.

The presence of English learners complicates the classroom situation. In fact, one could calculate that teaching an English learner is really like teaching two students. The first is the primary-language-speaking student, equipped with native speaker skills in the first language, complete with the culturally learned habits of mind and experience. The second is the same student as he or she functions in English, equipped with tentative skills in a new language and acquiring a developmental set of learning skills and habits that are used in the new culture.

Thus, instruction must not only be appropriate to the age-level developmental readiness of the learner, but instruction must also be adapted to communicate academic content to English learners; they, like learners of other skills, have at least a five-year developmental range in their English skills, as well as variation in the previous time they have spent learning English, variation in their primary-language skills, variation in their prior L1 and L2 instruction, variation in the amount of English used at home, and so forth.

Analyzing the Lesson with the Needs of the English Learner in Mind

This chapter first presents a typical instructional plan, written for a mainstream class (one without English learners or special needs students). For English learners to participate and achieve success, the lesson must be adapted to meet the needs of these learners. These adaptations take into consideration the English-language skills of the individual learner (as represented by scores on the CELDT, for example) as well as the general developmental needs of the learner at the age given.

About the English Learner

Box 12.1 presents the information gathered about Silvia, a fourth-grade English learner, using the English Learner Profile provided by administering the questionnaire in Box 3.1 (see page 42). This information is the basis for the subsequent exercise in adapting instruction.

From the information gathered, it appears that Silvia is a serious student with conscientious work habits. She relies on reading for information, and her Spanish literacy is an asset in this regard. Her reading skills in English, in fact, are more advanced than her listening, speaking, and writing. Her teacher is supportive of her primary language and culture, although the structured English immersion model that the school uses does not feature Spanish as an academic subject.

Example of the Learner's Language Skills

Boxes 12.2 and 12.3 present samples of oral and written responses collected as evidence of the learner's English proficiency.

box 12.1

Learner Profile

Silvia is a 9-year-old in the fourth grade. She attended kindergarten through second grade in Mexico, speaks Spanish, and enjoys reading books in Spanish. Upon her arrival last year, her parents requested placement in a primary-language classroom, where she began learning English. She has been a successful student, likes school, and is seldom absent.

Silvia approaches learning with a reflective, precise, detail-oriented style. She prefers to work alone. Her predominant learning strategies involve reading, following written directions carefully, and asking for help from the teacher when she does not understand, as well as returning to the teacher to check whether she has understood correctly after completing a few steps of an assignment. She is anxious to please and is well behaved and quiet, speaking only when spoken to in class and seldom volunteering answers in English. She has a best friend in a different class and gets along with the other students in a shy, reserved manner. Her family consists of an older sister and younger brother. Family life takes place in Spanish, and she lives in a largely Spanish-speaking neighborhood where little English is spoken.

Silvia's teacher encourages English learners to use Spanish atlases, encyclopedias, and dictionaries as reference materials. Although the teacher is not bilingual, she has "Spanish time" once a day after lunch in which students take turns bringing her books, music disks, and magazine articles in Spanish to share with the class. However, there is no instruction in Spanish available at Silvia's grade level.

Her CELDT scores in English-language development indicate that she is a beginner in speaking and listening, an early intermediate in writing, and an intermediate in reading.

box 12.2

Example of the Learner's Written Language Skills: Response to the Prompt "What Friendship Means to Me"

I don't be friend with only people like me, I have Africa Amercan and white to. I like to learn different culture and people. My friend Alena, we get along pretty well. Some times we help each others homework. I know a kid don't have friend, because he is mean, he cheat in games, and he took my snack. My friends are helpful. I miss my friend Carmen in Mexico. I like Carmen because she is always very loveing and careing. Carmen I love and miss you a lot and I want you to be my best friend too forever and be happy together.

box 12.3

Example of the Learner's Oral Language Skills: Response to the Prompt "Tell Me about Your Family"

My family is my father, my mother, and my brother and sister, and my … abuelo and abuelita in Mexico and my other abuela and my … aunts and uncles and … cousins. They are in Mexico. We make a trip to see them at Christmas and they are happy to see me. My abuelita cry and kiss me. I want to stay there but I like it here too.

Analyzing the Example of the Learner's Language Skills

The example of the student's language skills provides evidence that Silvia's writing is a fluent representation of her speech. When she writes, she is able to stay on topic and develop a range of ideas in response to the prompt. The sentence structure shows well-formed sentences containing subjects and verbs, combined with several run-on sentences. Grammatically, there are some problems with verb forms representing tense and number—her verbs lack the past-tense form. Spelling shows about 95 percent accuracy.

Orally, Silvia can respond with adequate content in situations requiring personal information. Her vocabulary is, in general, adequate for purposes of communication, although she switches to Spanish when the correct form in English is unavailable to her. Her verbs lack past-tense forms, showing confusion between the single past event and the ongoing, or habitual, present tense. What form of adaptation is needed for the instruction of this learner?

Analysis of the Lesson Plan

A sample lesson plan is provided that involves content objectives in life science (see Box 12.4). The lesson is designed for the fourth grade.

A structured procedure is used to analyze the instructional plan to test its applicability for English learners. First, what are the lesson objectives? Do they include a clear description of the content objectives, the language objectives, and the learning strategy objectives?

Second, in what activities do the learners participate to achieve the lesson objectives? To complete these activities, what skill levels are required of the learner in English-language reading, writing, speaking, and listening?

Third, how will the learner be assessed? Are the lesson activities the basis for assessment, or will there be a test or other instrument to evaluate the learner's performance?

Instructional Adaptations

As the teacher contemplates the lesson, several questions come to mind. These are presented in the following list, and are summarized in Box 12.5, with the idea that prospective teachers will use these questions to structure their answers.

- What are the learning needs of this student, and what would be a challenge to this student?
- What adaptations would make the content more accessible to the student, and why?
- Given the student's language skills and the content area, what assessment strategies would be appropriate?

Adaptations to the Lesson Objectives

The Content Objective.   In this lesson, the content objective is "to identify and describe the planets in the solar system." The advantage to the native English speaker in this objective is that the words *Mars, Venus, Jupiter,* and other names of the planets may be a part of the prior knowledge of children growing up in mainstream American culture; it is doubtful that the learners are hearing these terms for the first time. An English learner may have

box 12.4

Sample Instructional Plan

Lesson topic: The Solar System

Grade level: 4

Class composition: 19 native English speakers, 14 English learners (L1 is Spanish; CELDT levels of learners are Beginning in speaking and listening, Early Intermediate in writing, and Intermediate in reading); 18 boys, 15 girls

Materials: Visual and factual charts in English about the planets and their composition; encyclopedias, books about planets, pictures of the planets; PowerPoint lecture and handouts, worksheet handout

Performance objective: Students will learn that the solar system consists of the sun and nine planets. They will participate in the class lecture and a research activity about their given planet. They will then create a travel brochure of that planet.

Content objective: To identify and describe the planets in the solar system.

Language objective: Use newly acquired vocabulary words about the solar system.

Learning-strategy objective: To collate research from a variety of sources to write a research report

Warm-up: Students will take a tour past a bulletin board display of the sun and nine planets. When they return to their seat, students will raise their hands and share with the class what they know about one of the planets.

Activity 1: Class lecture

Students will listen to a PowerPoint lecture in English about the solar system.

Activity 2: Vocabulary

Students will volunteer vocabulary words from the lecture as the teacher writes the words on the overhead projector. Students will then work in pairs to write the vocabulary words along with the definitions.

Activity 3: Choosing a planet

Students draw a number (1–33) from a jar representing the order in which they can choose the planet they want to "visit." The same number of names of planets is on the bulletin board. The student who has #1 chooses first and so forth until all planets have been chosen. Students choosing the same planet will work in teams.

Activity 4: Creating a travel brochure about a planet

Students will research information about their planet and design a travel brochure. The teacher will hand out a rubric indicating what information should be included in the brochure. Each student will present his or her final product to the class.

Final assessment: The travel brochures are scored by the teacher according to a rubric.

box 12.5

Analysis of Instructional Plan

Using the learner profile provided in Box 12.1, combined with the example of student work in Boxes 12.2 and 12.3, study the instructional plan provided in Box 12.4. Inferring the learner's needs from the example of student language skills and the student profile, complete the activities below.

1. *Identify* two specific learning needs of the English learner (Sylvia).
2. *Examine* the components of the plan that could be challenging for this student and *explain* why these components might be difficult.
3. How would you *adapt* the lesson component to make the content more accessible to Sylvia?

heard these terms in the native language and have to relearn the terms in English, as well as the pronunciation. This makes the content objective harder for the English learner.

The Language Objective.   It should be evident that the language objective, "Use newly acquired vocabulary words about the solar system," is not phrased in terms of the ELD standards. According to the California ELD standards, in grades 3 through 5 the challenge for an English learner at the early intermediate ELD level and intermediate levels should be to "apply knowledge of content-related vocabulary to discussions and reading." How will the English learner acquire the vocabulary words in order to use them in discussions and reading? Will the English learner find these words easy to acquire from the context of the readings, or will special help be needed?

The Learning-Strategy Objective.   In this lesson, the learning-strategy objective is "to collate research from a variety of sources to write a research report." Again, inherent in this objective is the understanding that learning to collate data into a report would be a challenge for all fourth-grade students; however, writing the report is an additional hurdle for the English learner, who may not have the writing skills to support that activity. Moreover, reading the original texts from which the information is to be collated is an additional challenge that fourth-grade native speakers of English may be able to take for granted, but that would be difficult for an English learner.

It is evident, therefore, that the objectives of the lesson contain hidden subobjectives that may undermine the success of the English learner. The objectives need to be modified.

Adaptations to the Lesson Activities

The instructional plan features a set of four activities: a class lecture, vocabulary work, selection of focus planet, and creation of a travel brochure about the planet. Each one of these activities has certain features that may be problematic for the English learner.

Activity 1: Class Lecture.   In the first activity, students will listen to a PowerPoint lecture about the solar system. Sylvia needs comprehensible input during the teacher's talk; this may be provided if the teacher incorporates pictures, charts, and other means for describing the solar system. Sylvia's listening abilities are at the level of beginner. Therefore listening to a long verbal explanation, even when accompanied by visuals, may be taxing. Reading a lot of words displayed on a wall might be difficult, and it may be hard for her to acquire the vocabulary in context.

A movie about the solar system would be more dramatic. Something could be rented from the local library. The ratio of words to visuals would be lower. Students could receive a sheet of vocabulary words taken from the film and circle the words as they heard them. Then teams of two students could act out each word in "solar system charades."

Activity 2: Vocabulary. In the second activity, students will volunteer vocabulary words from the lecture as the teacher writes the words on the overhead projector, and then work in pairs to write the vocabulary words along with the definitions.

Activity 3: Choosing a Planet. As students choose a planet and are thus grouped, the language skills of the other students become an issue. Although the choice of planets appears to be fair, students *could* opt to select planets that had been chosen by their friends, and thus could result groups that were composed of all native-English-speaking students or all English learners. The groups would not, then, be heterogeneous, and the resulting efforts of an all-native-English-speaking group would be relatively advantaged by the language skills of the group. It would be better if the teacher composed the groups in advance at random to create mixed-language skills, and then had each group draw a number and choose a planet after the groups had been composed.

Activity 4: Creating a Travel Brochure about a Planet. In this culminating activity, students in groups will research information about their planet and design a travel brochure. The teacher will hand out a rubric indicating what information should be included in the brochure. Each student will present his or her final product.

The workload in this activity requires the ability to read quickly in order to skim and scan science materials for information, to take notes, and then to write a summary report. This is a challenge for the average fourth-grade student, and for an English learner would require far better language skills than those of the early intermediate or intermediate level. Adaptations would be for the English learner to work in a cooperative group, perhaps with the task of finding suitable photos for the final (group) project and writing the captions for these photos. From the report, a section could be chosen for the English learner to read aloud to the group as it proofreads the assignment.

In this activity, a structured cooperative learning process will enable Sylvia to participate with other learners during the research process. Her participation is designed to challenge but not to overtax her English development.

Adaptations to the Lesson Assessments

The lesson assessment is excellent, with formative assessment provided by the teacher in modeling the use of the rubric to self-assess the contents of the brochure, and students use the rubric to check their own work. The oral language provided by these discussions should make use of specially designed academic instruction in English (SDAIE). (See Chapter 5.) Sylvia's vocabulary acquisition from this lesson should be assessed using the ELD standards, as is indicated by the ELD-based language objective for an English learner with intermediate fluency.

Box 12.6 presents one way in which this lesson can be adapted for English learners. A skilled teacher might recognize other possible adaptations.

The lesson plan as it stands is well suited for fourth-grade learners, in line with the fourth-grade science standards and featuring activities that will challenge their listening, speaking, reading, and writing skills. With suitable adaptation, it can also be a successful experience for an English learner with reading skills of intermediate fluency and oral skills at the level of advanced beginner.

Conclusion: Reflections on the Success of the Adapted Lesson

An important element of the teaching model used in this book is the practice of a critical stance, incorporating reflective teaching. This critical perspective examines the strengths and weaknesses of the lesson, including its adaptations for specific learners such as English learners. After planning and implementing a lesson, teachers can reflect by asking the following questions:

- What are the strengths of the lesson plan in general?
- How effectively were content, language, and learning-strategy objectives connected?
- Were needs of English learners effectively and clearly identified, including challenges they may face in this particular lesson?
- How did adaptations address those challenges?
- How did the English learner perform in this lesson?
- What evidence is there that learning has taken place?

Many chapters of this book contain useful suggestions for adapting instruction to meet the needs of the English learner. Lesson adaptation to meet the needs of the English learner is the daily task of a teacher with integrity.

box 12.6

Instructional Plan with Adaptations for English Learners

Lesson topic: The Solar System

Grade level: 4

Class composition: 19 native English speakers, 14 English learners (L1 is Spanish; CELDT levels of learning are Beginning in speaking and listening, Early Intermediate in writing, and Intermediate in reading); 18 boys, 15 girls

Materials: Visual and factual charts in English and Spanish about the planets and their composition; encyclopedias, books about planets, pictures of the planets; PowerPoint lecture with embedded visuals accompanied by handouts; worksheet handout in L1 and L2

Performance objective: Students will learn that the solar system consists of the sun and nine planets. They will watch an informative film and play a vocabulary-acquisition game. They will then create a travel brochure of a specific planet.

Content objective: To identify and describe the planets in the solar system.

Language objective: Use newly acquired vocabulary words about the solar system

Learning-strategy objective: To collate research from a variety of sources and design an alternative information display format.

Warm-up: Students will take a tour past a bulletin board display of the sun and nine planets. When they return to their seat, students will raise their hands and share with the class what they know about one of the planets.

Activity 1: Class lecture

Students will watch a movie about the solar system. During the movie, students use a sheet of vocabulary words taken from the film and circle the words as they hear them. Then teams of two students act out each word in "solar system charades."

Activity 2: Choosing a planet

Students are grouped in heterogeneous groups. Each team draws a number, and after consulting with one another, selects a planet when their number is called. As a team-building activity, students choose a team name and "success handshake." Students work in a structured format with assigned roles to ensure that each student has the opportunity to contribute information to the group.

Activity 3: Creating a travel brochure about a planet

Students will research information about their planet and design a travel brochure. The teacher will explain the concept of travel brochures and provide a model. The teacher will hand out a rubric indicating what information should be included in the brochure. Each student will present his or her final product. The teacher asks each student to make a practice presentation privately with the teacher.

Formative assessment: The teacher models using the rubric to self-assess the contents of the brochure, and students use the rubric to check their own work.

Final assessment: The travel brochures are scored by learners, peers, and the teacher according to the rubric.

Glossary

academic content standards (*see* content standard)

acculturation the process of adapting to the mainstream culture without giving up one's first culture

acquisition learning a language, whether consciously or unconsciously (In Krashen and Terrell's Natural Approach, internalizing language by using authentic communication rather than by explicit teaching of rules and forms)

adaptation for English learners changes made by the teacher to lesson or assessment components considering the language levels of the English learner(s) that allow students to participate more successfully; examples: SDAIE, assistance from another student or adult, additional time, etc.

additive bilingualism English learners' proficiency in the heritage language is advanced

anxiety (in second-language learning) feelings of self-consciousness and fear of making mistakes

assessment collecting evidence, analyzing, evaluating, and communicating about student progress (*see also* authentic assessment; formative assessment; norm-referenced standardized test; peer assessment; performance-based assessment, placement test; portfolio; proficiency test; qualitative assessment; quantitative assessment; rubric; self-assessment; standardized assessment; summative assessment)

attitudes (of learners in language learning) beliefs about the self as a learner, the role of English, the primary language, the teacher, or schooling

authentic assessment assessment that is similar to, or embedded in, relevant real-world activities, such as debugging a computer program or providing community service; assessment consistent with classroom goals, curricula, and instruction

basic interpersonal communication skills (BICS) the language used to communicate basic needs or to share informal social interactions with peers, with a focus on getting across a message

behaviorism a system of teaching and learning based on principles of reward and punishment

BICS (*see* basic interpersonal communication skills)

bilingualism proficiency in two or more languages

biliteracy reading and writing in two languages

California Commission on Teacher Credentialing (CCTC) the state professional board that is responsible for setting and monitoring standards for teacher licensing

California English Language Development Test (CELDT) a statewide, standardized proficiency test used to measure attainment in English acquisition

CALP (*see* cognitive academic language proficiency)

clarity of vision the process by which individuals achieve a deepening awareness of the sociopolitical and economic realities that shape their lives

code-switching a language use strategy involving alteration between the first and second language during oral language use

cognitive academic language learning approach (CALLA) an approach to content instruction that integrates academic language development, content area instruction, and explicit instruction in learning strategies

cognitive academic language proficiency (CALP) language used to succeed in school, useful for higher-order thinking

cognitive learning strategies the use of critical thinking skills, learning strategies, and other types of conscious mental functioning to acquire and retain knowledge

common underlying proficiency (CUP) the hypothesis that the primary and second languages

318

have a shared foundation, and that knowledge of the primary language facilitates second-language acquisition

communicative competence the ability to use grammatical, sociolinguistic, discourse, and strategic language skills

comprehensible input the hypothesis that the learner acquires language by means of messages that have meaning (*see also* monitor model)

content area an academic discipline such as English language arts, mathematics, science, or history/social studies

content objective, in an instructional plan a lesson plan objective that stipulates a desired knowledge or skill to be gained in a content area

content standard a description of a desired goal for individual student knowledge and skills in a subject area such as mathematics, English language arts, or social studies based on specific criteria established by national, state, or local governments or professional organizations

critical pedagogy Paulo Freire's program of adult native-language literacy built on the themes and actions identified in everyday life, in which students learn to criticize and act on their conditions and seize ownership of the written code in order to change their lives and social circumstances

critical perspective the ability to look at broad social issues of dual-language proficiency and language policy in order to develop a deeper understanding of the effects of culture and language on the success—or disenfranchisement—of minority students

critical thinking the ability to perform acts of critical reasoning, such as analyzing ideas, separating fact from opinion, drawing inferences, and thinking for oneself. In Paulo Freire's terms, critical thinking suggests an awareness or consciousness of oneself as an agent in learning and transforming one's reality.

cultural congruence the relative advantage enjoyed by students in schools in the United States who are from families with cultural values similar to those of the Anglo-western European culture

cultural deficit model the explanation that poor school performance of minorities is due to inferior cultural environments; this explanation overlooks the relationship between discrimination and school failure

culturally responsive pedagogy also referred to as *culturally compatible, culturally relevant,* or *culturally sensitive teaching;* the ways in which a teacher can make accommodations for students whose classroom behavior and approach to learning differ from those that are congruent with the culture of the school

cultural mismatch the explanation that poor school performance of minorities is due to differences between students' approach to learning and the culture of the school; this explanation overlooks the relationship between discrimination and school failure

culture explicit and implicit patterns for living; the dynamic system of commonly agreed-on symbols and meanings, knowledge, belief, art, morals, law, customs, behaviors, traditions and/or habits that are shared and make up the total way of life of a people, as negotiated by individuals in the process of constructing a personal identity

culture shock the frustration, loss of self-esteem, depression, anger, or withdrawal a newcomer to a culture may feel when disoriented by cultural cues from the new culture

developmental bilingual education program also called *late-exit bilingual* and *primary-language maintenance bilingual education* (*MBE*); program whose goal is for students to preserve and advance academic proficiency in their heritage language as they become proficient in English

dialect a way of speaking or writing that individuals have developed within the context of a special group of speakers, based on such factors as geographic isolation or a sense of class, cultural, or age-specific solidarity

direct teaching a method of instruction that is teacher-centered, with an emphasis on learning of facts, sequenced steps, or rules

discourse, classroom language used in the classroom for teaching and learning, as well as other social functions such as regulatory language and interpersonal exchanges

discrimination the process by which people representing certain groups are treated unfairly

diversity the wide range of cultural and linguistic backgrounds; behavioral, learning, and communication styles; socioeconomic backgrounds; beliefs; needs; desires; and customs found in society

dominant culture a culture that has political and/or economic control and prevails over others

dominant ideology   a body of ideas held and circulated by cultural groups in power that are used to control or secure advantage over others economically, politically, or socially

dual-immersion education   (*see* immersion bilingual education program, two-way)

dual-language proficiency   being proficient in more then one language

early-exit bilingual program   (*see* transitional bilingual education program)

ELL   English-language learner (*see* English learner)

emergent literacy   a philosophy about learning to read that encourages reading teachers to build on students' exposure to print in the culture at large and various informal kinds of reading in which prereaders may have engaged in order to "grow" them into reading and writing behaviors

empowerment   to help students develop the knowledge, skills, and values needed to become social critics who can make reflective decisions and implement their decisions in effective personal, social, political, and economic action

English as a second language (ESL)   instruction that takes place with learners whose primary language is not English, yet who live in places where English has some sort of special status or public availability

English-language development (ELD)   instruction designed and structured specifically for English learners to develop skills in listening, speaking, reading, and writing

English Language Arts (ELA) Standards (California)   a set of standard expectations (K–12) for learners' skills and knowledge in reading, writing, and listening/speaking

English Language Development (ELD) Standards (California)   a set of standard expectations for English learners' skills and knowledge in reading, writing, and listening/speaking; the ELD categories parallel those of the ELA standards

English learner   a student with a primary language other than English who is developing proficiency in English

enrichment education (Canadian model)   a model for additive bilingual education that uses L1 and L2 as the media of instruction and focuses on learning the target language through content teaching; L1 and L2 are both majority languages, equally prestigious and valued by the community

ethnographic study   an inquiry process that seeks to provide cultural explanations for behavior and attitudes using rich description from an insider's point of view, as the researcher becomes not only an observer of the target culture but also an active participant

expectations, academic   the level of performance anticipated of students by teachers

family involvement   the role played by parents and other family members in the academic life of a student

family–teacher conference   a structured discussion of a student's academic performance that takes place at fixed intervals throughout the school year, with participation by the teacher and family members, usually parents

first language (L1)   also called *mother tongue* or *primary, native, home, or heritage language;* the language learned at home from the primary caregivers

formative assessment   monitoring of student performance during instruction to determine whether students are progressing adequately toward achieving the specific objective(s), so that instruction can be adjusted accordingly

funds of knowledge   expertise available in the community that can be drawn on to make curriculum and instruction relevant to the daily lives of students

grammar, teaching   teaching students to pay particular attention to the form and structure of language; explicit instruction in the rules of usage or correctness

graphic organizer   a visual frame used to represent and organize information; a diagram showing how concepts are related

hegemony   a condition in which the discourse of the dominant group in society propagates itself through society, creating an unspoken unity in which the interests of the dominant group come to represent the interests of the subordinated groups as well. Rather than relying on openly coercive means, the dominant discourse gains the consent of the dominated

heritage language   the language spoken by an indigenous or immigrant group when compared to the dominant language of the mainstream culture

Hispanic   (*see* Latino)

home language survey   a questionnaire given to a student (or family member on behalf of the student) to determine the student's primary language

ideology (*see* dominant ideology)

identification procedures for English learners the means for determining, when students enroll in school, whether they need ELD services

immersion bilingual education (*see* enrichment education; structured English immersion; two-way immersion program)

institutional racism the curriculum, communication practices, or rules of an institution that systematically discriminate against one group or race

instructional plan a set of decisions made by the teacher during planning that outlines the sequence and organization of an instructional experience

intercultural communication exchange that takes place between individuals of different cultures

interlanguage the interim form of language constructed by the learner of a second language based on a combination of knowledge of L1; approximation of systems, rules, and forms of L2; and unconscious internalized universal language rules

L1 first (primary, native) language

L2 second language (any language learned after the primary language)

language-acquisition device (LAD) the hypothesis that a mental language processor unconsciously acquires grammar rules

language-majority student a native speaker of English in the United States

language-minority student a student who speaks a non-English language in a mainstream classroom (this may be a misleading term, because in many English learner classrooms, the primary language that is not English *is* the majority language)

language objective, in an instructional plan the desired language skill to be gained in some facet of instruction

late-exit bilingual education (*see* developmental bilingual education program)

Latino a term used to denote an individual whose lineage derives from Mexico, Spain, Central America, South America, or the Caribbean

learning strategy a mental procedure used by a learner to think, study, monitor, and evaluate while doing academic work

learning-strategy objective, in lesson plan the cognitive, metacognitive, and/or social–affective skills targeted by the instructional plan

learning style a consistent tendency or preference within an individual student for thinking, relating to others, types of classroom environments, and learning experiences

linguistic racism derogatory treatment of, or negative attitude toward, individuals because of the language they speak, including the use of a non-prestige dialect

mainstream culture the culture that is the most prevalent in a society

maintenance bilingual education (MBE) program (*see* developmental bilingual education program)

mastery learning a teaching approach in which students must learn one unit and pass a test at a specified level before moving on to the next unit

mediation the process of intervening by a person or psychological tool between the learner and object or concept that is to be learned in order to provide assistance

meritocracy an educational or social system in which people believe that advancement is due to ability rather than prior social advantage

metacognition the ability to plan, monitor, and evaluate one's learning or to learn about one's own learning styles and strategies

metacognitive learning strategy a systematic approach used during learning to direct, plan, monitor, or evaluate learning or to advance self-knowledge

monitor model Krashen's theory of second language acquisition

multicompetent language use proficiency in more than one language

multicultural education the study of effective education practices for multiethnic classrooms, grounded in social justice and based on critical pedagogy; addresses ethnocentrism and ethnic supremacy; confronts individual biases, attitudes, and behaviors of educators as well as school policies and social practices

native culture the culture in which the primary language is acquired along with primary socialization

native language (*see* first language)

natural approach Krashen and Terrell's teaching method based on children's acquisition of a second language in ways similar to the acquisition of the first language

"No Child Left Behind" (NCLB) Education Act reauthorization of the Elementary and

Secondary Education Act (ESEA), passed by the U.S. Congress in 2001

norm-referenced standardized test   evaluation that compares a student's test performance to that of other students, with results usually reported in percentile rankings

oracy   pertaining to that which is communicated by speaking and listening

para-educator   an instructional assistant, usually one who is not a credentialed teacher

parent–teacher conference   (*see* family-teacher conference)

pedagogy   the art, practice, or profession of teaching

peer assessment   evaluation that takes place among students who are trained to identify and correct errors or be of other assistance

performance-based assessment   evaluation that consists of students' exhibiting how well they have achieved an objective by doing it; this is a measure of whether and to what degree students have achieved the standards

performance-based instruction   a type of instructional design in which the objectives are chosen to match the specific skill that students will demonstrate as evidence of learning

phonemic awareness   the understanding that sounds correspond to symbols; a prerequisite to reading

phonics   a reading strategy in which the learner explicitly constructs a sound–symbol connection

placement test   proficiency evaluation to determine the appropriate level of subsequent instruction

portfolio   a collection of student products that shows progress and/or reflects the extent to which a student has attained instructional goals

praxis   the relationship between clarity of vision and action that seeks to transform society into a more equitable and just environment

prejudice   a negative prejudgment made about another person based on stereotypes

primary-language   (*see* first language)

primary-language literacy   the ability to read and write in the primary language

primary-language maintenance program   (*see* developmental bilingual education program)

prior knowledge   the schemata that learners bring to the learning task based on previous experience and learning

proficiency test   a test that determines a student's level in English, usually defined independently of any particular instructional program

proposition 227, in California   a successful ballot initiative that severely limited access to bilingual education

pull-out ESL instruction   an instructional approach that removes English learners from the mainstream classroom for compensatory ELD activities

qualitative assessment   assessment that features descriptions or rating categories (such as scoring rubrics)

quantitative assessment   assessment that features a numerical score

racism   the belief that one race is superior to another; the practice of committing or participating in acts of discrimination against individuals of another race

reclassification   sometimes referred to as *redesignation;* the process by which an English learner qualifies for "graduation" from transitional bilingual education services by achieving a criterion level of test score

redesignation   (*see* reclassification)

reflective teaching   the act of evaluating instructional practices before, during, and after a teaching situation that allows a teacher to improve decision making

restorative bilingual education   the attempt to increase the number of speakers of a heritage language that is in danger of extinction

rubric   a scoring chart with predetermined levels of evaluation that describes degrees of competency

scaffold   a temporary framework or mediation used to increase a learner's success on a task

schema (pl. schemata)   a mental structure or unit of understanding used to store knowledge

SDAIE   (*see* specially designed academic instruction in English)

second language (L2)   any language (whether second or twentieth) that is learned after the first language

second-language acquisition (SLA)   learning any language (whether second or twentieth)—in school or in some other way—after the first language

self-assessment   self-monitoring and evaluating for purposes of self-improvement and academic progress

self-esteem   positive self-concept or evaluation of oneself

separate underlying proficiency (SUP)   the assumption that content and skills learned through the primary language do not transfer to English, or that the primary language is a handicap that interferes with and delays second-language acquisition

sheltered English (*see* specially designed academic instruction in English)

social–affective learning strategies the use of emotions or social relations to enhance learning

social functions of language the uses that language serves in society

sociocultural context of schooling the interactive environment that students and other members of the school community share in the classroom and school surroundings, including the beliefs, values, and behaviors that are enacted

socioeconomic status a general designation of social standing, as measured by income or wealth, but also such variables as power, lifestyle, associates, leisure activities, place of residence, educational background, etc.

specially designed academic instruction in English (SDAIE) instruction that combines second-language acquisition principles with those elements of quality teaching that make a lesson understandable to students

stance, critical a transformative, reflective practice in which an individual chooses a particular challenge to face and attempts to assert influence within an institution by using a given tactic, thus creating a critical incident that is later evaluated

standardized assessment a test on which the student is scored according to predetermined criteria; for example, a teacher's use of an answer key to grade a test. The term *standardized* is commonly used for large-scale, commercially published tests in which a student's score is compared to national norms

standards (*see* content standard)

standards-based instruction teaching and learning guided by specific criteria that are grade and content specific

stereotype a mental picture or schema that is held in common about members of a group and represents an oversimplified opinion

strategy techniques used by the learner (and mediated by the teacher) that promote the acquisition of knowledge

structured English immersion (SEI) a form of English-only education in which the program objective is proficiency in English based on a subtractive model without development of L1 literacy; students are expected to gain proficiency enough to enter mainstream classes in one year; L2 is the medium of instruction, with a focus on learning the target language through content teaching; L1 may be denigrated and relegated to inferior status

submersion English learners are placed with native speakers in classrooms where teachers have no training in language-teaching pedagogy or sheltered content (SDAIE) practices

subtractive bilingualism English learners' proficiency in the native language is deemphasized and lost

summative assessment an evaluation that measures the extent of mastery of lesson objectives

teaching performance assessment (TPA), in California an assessment that measures aspects of the Teaching Performance Expectations (TPEs) that describe what teachers need to know and do before receiving a basic teaching credential

Teaching Performance Expectations (TPEs) what teachers need to know and do before receiving a basic credential

tracking grouping students by ability level, language usage, or career choice; under conditions of institutional discrimination, it is based more on students' social status than real ability

transition a phase of schooling when students prepare to receive all their instruction in English, without second-language support

transitional bilingual education program a subtractive model of bilingual education in which students are given instruction in their first language only until they can be transferred to all-English instruction, at which point support or instruction in the first language is discontinued

two-way immersion (TWI) program that groups English learners from a single language background in the same classroom with approximately equal numbers of English-speaking students, with grade-level-approximate curriculum provided in both languages

Bibliography

Abramson, S., Seda, I., & Johnson, C. (1990). Literacy development in a multilingual kindergarten classroom. *Childhood Education, 67*(2), 68–72.

Ada, A. (1989). Los libros mágicos. *California Tomorrow,* 42–44.

Ada, A. F. (1997). Mother-tongue literacy as a bridge between home and school cultures. In J. V. Tinajero & A. F. Ada (Eds.), *The power of two languages: Literacy and biliteracy for Spanish-speaking students* (pp. 158–177). New York: Macmillan/McGraw-Hill.

Adamson, H. D. (1993). *Academic competence.* New York: Longman.

Agne, K. J. (1992). Caring: The expert teacher's edge. *Educational Horizons, 70*(3), 120–124.

Alder, N. (2000). Teaching diverse students. *Multicultural Perspectives, 2*(2), 28–31.

Allen, E., & Vallette, R. (1977). *Classroom techniques. Foreign languages and English as a second language.* San Diego, CA: Harcourt Brace Jovanovich.

Amery, H. (1979). *The first thousand words: A picture word book.* London: Usborne.

Amery, H., & Milá, R. (1979). *The first thousand words in Spanish.* London: Usborne.

Amselle, J. (1999). Dual immersion delays English. *American Language Review, 3*(5), 8.

Anderson, J., & Gunderson, L. (2004). "You don't *read* a science book, you *study* it": An exploration of cultural concepts of reading. Online at www.readingonline. org/electronic/elec_index.asp?HREF=anderson/index. html.

Anzaldúa, G. (1999). *Borderlands/La frontera: The new mestizos* (2nd ed.). San Francisco: Aunt Lute Books.

Aoki, E. (1992). Turning the page: Asian Pacific American children's literature. In V. J. Harris (Ed.), *Teaching multicultural literature in grades K–8.* Norwood, MA: Christopher-Gordon Publishers.

Asher, J. (1982). *Learning another language through actions: The complete teachers' guidebook.* Los Gatos, CA: Sky Oaks.

Asian Americans in Children's Books. (1976). *Interracial Books for Children Bulletin, 7*(2).

Asian Pacific Fund (2003, Fall/Winter). *Asian outlook: Bay area people in need.* Online at www.asianpacificfund. org/resources.

Association for Supervision and Curriculum Development [ASCD] Improving Student Achievement Research Panel. (1995). *Educating everybody's children—Diverse teaching strategies for diverse learners: What research and practice say about improving achievement* (R. W. Cole, Ed.). Alexandria, VA: Association for Supervision and Curriculum Development.

Attinasi, J. (1994). Racism, language variety, and urban U.S. minorities: Issues in bilingualism and bidialectalism. In S. Gregory and R. Sanjek (Eds.), *Race* (pp. 319–347). Rutgers, NJ: Rutgers University Press.

Auerbach, E. R. (1991). Toward a social-contextual approach to family literacy. In M. Minami & B. P. Kennedy (Eds.), *Language issues in literacy and bilingual/multicultural education* (pp. 391–408). *Harvard Educational Review* Reprint Series No. 22. Cambridge, MA: Harvard Educational Review.

Auerbach, E. R. (2002). *Case studies in community partnership.* Alexandria, VA: Teachers of English to Speakers of Other Languages.

Baca, L., & Valenzuela, H. (1994). *Reconstructing the bilingual special education interface.* National Clearinghouse for Bilingual Education Program Information Guide Series, 20. Washington, DC: National Clearinghouse for Bilingual Education.

Bahr, C. M., & Rieth, H. J. (1989). The effects of instructional computer games and drill and practice software of learning disabled students' mathematics achievment. *Computers in the Schools, 6*(3–4), 87–101.

Balderrama, M. V. (2001). The (mis)preparation of teachers in the Proposition 227 era: Humanizing teacher roles and their practice. *The Urban Review, 33*(3), 255–267.

Bandlow, R. (2002). Suburban bigotry: A descent into racism & struggle for redemption. In F. Schultz (Ed.), *Annual editions: Multicultural education 2002–2003* (pp. 90–93). Guilford, CT: McGraw-Hill/Dushkin.

Bangert-Drowns, R. L., Kulik, J. A., & Kulik, C. C. (1985). Effectiveness of computer-based education in secondary schools. *Journal of Computer-Based Instruction, 12*(3), 59–68.

Barr, R., & Johnson, B. (1997). *Teaching reading and writing in elementary classrooms* (2nd ed.). New York: Longman.

Bartolomé, L. I. (1994). Beyond the methods fetish: Toward a humanizing pedagogy. *Harvard Educational Review, 64*(2), 173–194.

Bartolomé, L. I., & Balderrama, M. V. (2001). The need for educators with political and ideological clarity: Providing our children with "The Best." In M. de la Luz Reyes & J. J. Halcón (Eds.), *The best for our children: Critical perspectives on literacy for Latino students* (pp. 48–64). New York: Teachers College Press.

Bartram, M., & Walton, R. (1994). *Correction: A positive approach to language mistakes.* Hove, UK: Language Teaching Publications.

Bassano, S., & Christison, M. A. (1995). *Community spirit: A practical guide to collaborative language learning.* San Francisco: Alta Book Center.

Bates, L., Lane, J., & Lange, E. (1993). *Writing clearly: Responding to ESL compositions.* Boston: Heinle & Heinle.

Batey, A. (1986). Building a case for computers in elementary classrooms: A summary of what the researchers and the practitioners are saying. Paper presented at the Second Leadership in Computer Education Seminar, Seattle, WA.

Beane, J. A. (1991). Sorting out the self-esteem controversy. *Educational Leadership, 49*(1), 25–30.

Beatty, P. (2000). *Lupita mañana.* New York: Harper-Collins.

Bell, D. (1977). On meritocracy and equality. In J. Karabel & A. H. Halsey, (Eds.), *Power and ideology in education* (pp. 607–635). New York: Oxford University Press.

Belmont, J. M. (1989). Cognitive strategies and strategic learning: The socioinstructional approach. *American Psychologist 44*, 142–148.

Bennett, C. (2003). *Comprehensive multicultural education: Theory and practice* (5th edition). Boston: Allyn & Bacon.

Bennett, J. M. (1998). Transition shock: Putting culture shock in perspective. In M. J. Bennett (Ed.), *Basic concepts of intercultural communication* (pp. 215–223). Yarmouth, ME: Intercultural Press.

Berk, L. (1994, November). Why children talk to themselves. *Scientific American*, 78–83.

Berk, L. E., & Winsler, A. (1995). *Scaffolding children's learning: Vygotsky and early childhood education.* Washington, DC: National Association for the Education of Young Children.

Berman, E. H. (1984). State hegemony and the school process. *Journal of Education, 166*, 239–253.

Bialo, E., & Sivin, J. (1990). *Report on the effectiveness of microcomputers in schools.* Washington, DC: Software Publishers Association.

Bilinguals brainier than monolingual counterparts. (2004). *The Journal of Communication & Education: Language Magazine, 4*(3), 13.

Bloom, B. (Ed.). (1956). *A Taxonomy of Educational Objectives: Handbook I. Cognitive Domain.* New York: Mckay.

Bodinger-deUriarte, C. (1991). Hate crime: The rise of hate crime on school campuses. *Research Bulletin, Phi Delta Kappa, 10*, 1–6.

Bourdieu, P. (1977). *Reproduction in society, education, and culture* (with J. Passeron). Los Angeles: Sage.

Boydston, J. A. (Ed.). (1967–1991). *The collected works of John Dewey* (37 volumes). Carbondale: Southern Illinois University Press.

Brantlinger, E. (1994). *The politics of social class in a secondary school: View of affluent and impoverished youth.* New York: Teachers College Press.

Brisk, M. E., & Harrington, M. M. (2000). *Literacy and bilingualism.* Mahwah, NJ: Erlbaum.

Brisk, M., Burgos, A., & Hamerla, S. (2004). *The situational context of education: A window into the world of bilingual learners.* Mahwah, NJ: Erlbaum.

Bromley, K. D. (1989). Buddy journals make the reading-writing connection. *The Reading Teacher, 43*(2), 122–129.

Brooks, J., & Brooks, M. (1993). *In search of understanding: The case for constructivist classrooms.* Alexandria, VA: Association for Supervision and Curriculum Development.

Brophy, J. (1983). Research on the self-fulfilling prophecy and teacher expectations. *Journal of Educational Psychology, 75*, 631–661.

Brophy, J. (1988). On motivating students. In D. Berliner & B. Rosenshine (Eds.), *Talks to teachers* (pp. 201–245). New York: Random House.

Brophy, J., & Good, T. L. (1986). Teacher behavior and student achievement. In M. Wittrock (Ed.), *Handbook of research on teaching* (3rd ed.). New York: Macmillan.

Brown, G., & Yule, G. (1983). *Teaching the spoken language.* Cambridge: Cambridge University Press.

Brown, J. D. (Ed.). (1998). *New ways in classroom assessment.* Alexandria, VA: Teachers of English to Speakers of Other Languages.

Brown, R. (1973). *A first language: The early stages.* Cambridge, MA: Harvard University Press.

Brown, S. C., & Kysilka, M. L. (2002). *Applying multicultural and global concepts in the classroom and beyond.* Boston: Allyn & Bacon.

Bruner, J. (1983). *Child's talk.* Oxford: Oxford University Press.

Bruner, J. (1986). *Actual minds, possible worlds.* Cambridge, MA: Harvard University Press.

Brutt-Griffler, J., & Samimy, K. K. (1999). Revisiting the colonial in the postcolonial: Critical praxis for the non-native-English-speaking teachers in a TESOL program. *TESOL Quarterly, 33*(3), 413–431.

Buber, M. (1991). *I and thou.* New York: Touchstone

Buckmaster, R. (2000, June 22–28). First and second languages do battle for the classroom. *(Manchester) Guardian Weekly: Learning English* supplement, 3.

Burbules, N. C., & Bruce, B. C. (2001). Theory and research on teaching as dialogue. In V. Richardson (Ed.), *Handbook of research on teaching* (4th ed., pp. 1102–1121). Washington, DC: American Educational Research Association.

Byrd, P., & Benson, B. (1994). *Problem–solution: A reference for ESL writers.* Boston: Heinle & Heinle.

Caine, R., & Caine, G. (1997). *Education at the edge of possibility.* Alexandria, VA: Association for Supervision and Curriculum Development.

California Commission on Teacher Credentialing. (n.d). *California Teaching Performance Assessment field review guidebook.* Sacramento: Author.

California Commission on Teacher Credentialing. (1997). *California standards for the teaching profession.* Sacramento: Authors.

California Department of Education (CDE). (1995). *Every child a reader: The report of the California Reading Task Force.* Sacramento: Author.

California Department of Education (CDE). (1999a). *English-language development standards for California public schools, kindergarten through grade twelve.* Online at www.cde.ca.gov/re/pn/fd/documents/englangdev-stnd.pdf.

California Department of Education (CDE). (1999b). *Mathematics framework for California public schools.* Sacramento: Author.

California Department of Education (CDE). (1999c). *Reading/language arts framework for California public schools, kindergarten through grade twelve.* Online at www.cde.ca.gov/sp/se/sr/documents/cntnt-ela.pdf.

California Department of Education (CDE). (1999d). *Social sciences framework for California public schools.* Sacramento: Author.

California Department of Education (CDE). (2000a). *Science framework for California public schools in grades kindergarten through twelve.* Sacramento: Author.

California Department of Education (CDE). (2000b). *Strategic teaching and learning: Standards-based instruction to promote content literacy in grades four through twelve.* Sacramento: Author.

California Department of Education (CDE). (2004a). *California English Language Development Test (CELDT). A communications assistance packet for school districts/schools.* Sacramento: Author.

California Department of Education. (2004b). *Numbers of English learners by language.* Online at http://data1.cde.ca.gov/dataquest/LEPbyLang1.asp.

California Department of Education (CDE). (2004c, April 14). *Standards and assessment notes.* Sacramento: Author.

Campbell, C. (1998). *Teaching second language writing: Interacting with text.* Pacific Grove, CA: Heinle & Heinle.

Canale, M. (1983). From communicative competence to communicative language pedagogy. In J. Richards & R. Schmidt (Eds.), *Language and communication* (pp. 2–27). New York: Longman.

Capper, J., & Copple, C. (1985). *Computer use in education: Research review and instructional implications.* Washington, DC: Center for Research into Practice.

Cartagena, J. (1991). English only in the 1980s: A product of myths, phobias, and bias. In S. Benesch (Ed.), *ESL in America: Myths and possibilities.* Portsmouth, NH: Boynton/Cook.

Cazden, C. (1986). ESL teachers as language advocates for children. In P. Rigg & V. Allen (Eds.), *When they don't all speak English* (pp. 9–21). Urbana, IL: National Council of Teachers of English.

Cenoz, J., & Genesee, F. (1998). Psycholinguistic perspectives on multilingualism and multilingual education. In J. Cenoz & F. Genesee (Eds.), *Beyond bilingualism: Multilingualism and multilingual education* (pp. 16–34). Clevedon, UK: Multilingual Matters.

Center for Applied Research in Educational Technology. Questions and answers; Summary and review. Online at http://caret.iste.org/index.cfm.

Center for Teaching Excellence–Searle. (2005). Online at http://teach.northwestern.edu.

Chamot, A. U. (1987). The learning strategies of ESL students. In A. Wenden & J. Rubin (Eds.), *Learner strategies in language learning.* Englewood Cliffs, NJ: Prentice Hall.

Chamot, A. U., & O'Malley, J. (1987). The Cognitive Academic Language Learning Approach: A bridge to the mainstream. *TESOL Quarterly, 21*(2), 227–249.

Chamot, A. U., & O'Malley, J. (1994). *The CALLA handbook: Implementing the cognitive academic language learning approach.* Boston: Addison-Wesley.

Chan, L. (2004). The inexorable rise in demand for qualified ESL teachers. *Language, 3*(6), 30–31.

Chandler, D. (2004a). *Semiotics: The basics.* Online at www.aber.ac.uk/media/Documents/S4B.

Chandler, D. (2004b). *Semiotics for beginners.* Online at www.aber.ac.uk/media/Documents/S4B.

Chavkin, N. F. (1989, Summer). Debunking the myth about minority parents. *Educational Horizons,* 119–123.

Chomsky, N. (1959). Review of B. F. Skinner "Verbal Behavior." *Language, 35,* 26–58.

Christian, D., Montone, C., Lindholm, K. J., & Carranza, I. (1997). *Profiles in two-way bilingual education.* Washington, D.C.: ERIC Clearinghouse.

Christie, J., Enz, B., & Vukelich, C. (Eds.). (1997). *Teaching language and literacy.* New York: Longman.

Clair, N. (1994). Informed choices: Articulating assumptions behind programs for language minority students. *ERIC/CLL News Bulletin, 18*(1), 1, 5–8.

Clark, A. (1993). *Associative engines: Connectionism, concepts, and representational change.* Cambridge: Cambridge University Press.

Cloud, N., Genesee, F., & Hamayan, E. (2000). *Dual language instruction.* Boston: Heinle & Heinle.

Cockcroft, J. D. (1995). *Latinos in the struggle for equal education.* Danbury, CT: Franklin Watts.

Coghlan, N. (2004). The stories from 2004. Online at www.esl-lounge.com/tales-04.shtml.

Cohen, A. (1991). Second language testing. In M. Celce-Murcia (Ed.), *Teaching English as a second or foreign language* (2nd ed, pp. 486–506). New York: Newbury House.

Cohen, A. D. (2004). Researching the effect of styles, strategies, and motivation on language learning tasks. Presentation at the Teachers of English to Speakers of Other Languages annual meeting, Long Beach, CA.

Cohen, E. (1994). *Designing groupwork: Strategies for the heterogeneous classroom.* New York: Teachers College Press.

Cohen, E., Lotan, R., & Catanzarite, L. (1990). Treating status problems in the cooperative classroom. In S. Sharon (Ed.), *Cooperative learning: Theory and research* (pp. 203–229). New York: Praeger.

Cole, K. (2003, March). *Negotiating intersubjectivity in the classroom: Mutual socialization to classroom conversations.* Presentation at the American Association for Applied Linguistics annual conference, Arlington, VA.

Cole, M. (1998). *Cultural psychology: Can it help us think about diversity?* Presentation at the American Educational Research Association annual meeting, San Diego, CA.

Collie, J., & Slater, S. (1987). *Literature in the language classroom.* Cambridge: Cambridge University Press.

Collier, V. (1987). Age and rate of acquisition of second language for academic purposes. *TESOL Quarterly, 21*(4), 617–641.

Collins, J. L., & Sommers, E. A. (Eds.). (1984). *Writing online: Using computers in the teaching of writing.* Montclair, NJ: Boynton/Cook.

Conner, M. H., & Boskin, J. (2001). Overrepresentation of bilingual poor children in special education classes: A continuing problem. *Journal of Children and Poverty, 7*(1), 23–32.

Cook, G. (2001). Old dogmas, new direction. *TESOL Teacher Education Interest Section, 16*(2), 1, 3–4, 10.

Cook, V. (1999). Going beyond the native speaker in language teaching. *TESOL Quarterly, 33*(2), 185–209.

Corbeil, J.-C., & Archambault, A. (2004). *The Firefly five language visual dictionary: English, Spanish, French, German, Italian.* Richmond Hill, Can.: Firefly Books.

Cotton, K. (1991). *Computer assisted instruction.* San Francisco: Northwest Regional Educational Laboratory.

Crawford, J. (1995). Endangered Native American languages: What is to be done, and why? *The Bilingual Research Journal, 19*(1), 17–38.

Crawford, J. (1999). *Bilingual education: History, politics, theory, and practice* (4th ed.). Los Angeles: Bilingual Educational Services.

Crawford, J. (2004). *Educating English learners: Language diversity in the classroom* (5th ed.) (formerly titled *Bilingual education: History, politics, theory, and practice*). Los Angeles: Bilingual Educational Services, Inc.

Crystal, D. (1987). *The Cambridge encyclopedia of language.* Cambridge: Cambridge University Press.

Cullinan, B. A. (1987). *Children's literature in the reading program.* Newark, DE: International Reading Association.

Cummins, J. (1976). The influence of bilingualism on cognitive growth: A synthesis of research findings and explanatory hypothesis. *Working Papers on Bilingualism, 9*, 1–43.

Cummins, J. (1979). Linguistic interdependence and the educational development of bilingual children. *Review of Educational Research, 49*(2), 222–251.

Cummins, J. (1980). The cross-lingual dimensions of language proficiency. Implications for bilingual education and the optimal age issue. *TESOL Quarterly, 14*(2), 175–187.

Cummins, J. (1981a). Age on arrival and immigrant second language learning in Canada: A reassessment. *Applied Linguistics, 2*(2), 132–149.

Cummins, J. (1981b). The role of primary language development in promoting educational success for language minority students. In *Schooling and language minority students: A theoretical framework* (pp. 3–49). Sacramento: California State Department of Education.

Cummins, J. (1984). *Bilingualism and special education: Issues in assessment and pedagogy.* San Diego, CA: College-Hill.

Cummins, J. (1989). *Empowering minority students.* Sacramento: California Association for Bilingual Education.

Cummins, J. (1996) *Negotiating identities: Education for empowerment in a diverse society.* Los Angeles: California Association for Bilingual Education.

Cummins, J. (2000a). Beyond adversarial discourse: Searching for common ground in the education of bilingual students. In P. McLaren & C. J. Ovando (Eds.), *The politics of multiculturalism and bilingual education* (pp. 126–147). Boston: McGraw-Hill.

Cummins, J. (2000b). Negotiating intercultural identities in the multilingual classroom. *CATESOL Journal, 12*(1), 163–178.

Cummins, J., & Sayers, D. (1997). *Brave new schools: Challenging cultural illiteracy.* New York: St. Martin's Press.

Curran, M. E. (2003). Linguistic diversity and classroom management. *Theory into Practice, 42*(4), 334–340.

Dale, P., & Wolf, J. C. (1988). *Speech communication for international students.* Englewood Cliffs, NJ: Prentice Hall Regents.

Dale, T., & Cuevas, G. (1987). Integrating language and mathematics learning. In J. Crandall (Ed.), *ESL through content-area instruction: Mathematics, science, social studies.* Englewood Cliffs, NJ: Prentice Hall/ Regents.

Dale, T., & Cuevas, G. (1992). Integrating mathematics and language learning. In P. Richard-Amato & M. Snow (Eds.), *The multicultural classroom* (pp. 330–348). White Plains, NY: Longman.

D'Arcangelo, M. (1998). The brains behind brain. *Educational Leadership, 56*(3), 68–71.

Davies, D. (1991). Schools reaching out: Family, school and community partnerships for student success. *Phi Delta Kappan, 72*(5), 376–382.

Davies, A., Cameron, C., Politano, C., & Gregory, K. (1992). *Together is better: Collaborative assessment, evaluation, and reporting.* Winnepeg, Can.: Peguis.

Day, F. A. (1994). *Multicultural voices in contemporary literature: A resource for teachers.* Portsmouth, NH: Heinemann.

Day, F. A. (1997). *Latina and Latino voices in literature for children and teenagers.* Portsmouth, NH: Heinemann.

Day, F. A. (2003). *Latina and Latino voices in literature: Lives and works.* Westport, CT: Greenwood Publishers.

De Avila, E. A., & Duncan, S. E. (1980). *Finding out/ Descubrimiento.* Corte Madera: Linguametrics Group.

Delgado-Gaítan, C. (1994). Sociocultural change through literacy: Toward the empowerment of families. In B. M. Ferdman, R-M. Weber, & A. G. Ramírez (Eds.), *Literacy across languages and cultures* (pp. 143–169). Albany: State University of New York Press.

Delgado-Gaítan, C., & Trueba, H. (1991). *Crossing cultural borders: Education for immigrant families in America.* New York: Falmer Press.

Delpit, L. (1995). *Other people's children: Cultural conflict in the classroom.* New York: New Press.

Dewey, J. (1916). *Democracy and education: An introduction to the philosophy of education.* New York: Macmillan.

Dewey, J. (1963). *Experience and education.* New York: Free Press. (Original work published 1938)

Díaz, R. (1983). Thought and two languages: The impact of bilingualism on cognitive development. *Review of Research in Education, 10,* 23–34.

Díaz-Rico, L. T. (2000). Intercultural communication in teacher education: The knowledge base for CLAD teacher credential programs. *CATESOL Journal, 12*(1), 145–161.

Díaz-Rico, L. T. (2004). *Teaching English learners: Strategies and methods.* Boston: Allyn & Bacon.

Díaz-Rico, L. T., & Weed, K. Z. (2002). *Crosscultural, language, and academic development handbook.* Boston: Allyn & Bacon.

Dicker, S. (2003). *Languages in America* (2nd ed.). Clevedon, UK: Multilingual Matters.

Dickinson, D. K. (1986). Cooperation, collaboration and a computer: Integrating a computer into a first-second-grade writing program. *Research in the Teaching of English, 20*(4), 357–378.

Dudley-Marling, C., & Searle, D. (1991). *When students have time to talk.* Portsmouth, NH: Heinemann.

Duncan, S., & DeAvila, E. (1979). Bilingualism and cognition: Some recent findings. *NABE Journal, 4*(1), 15–50.

Earle, R. S. (1992). *The use of instructional design skills in the mental and written planning process of teachers.* Paper presented at the convention of the Association for Educational Communications and Technology, Iowa (ERIC document ED347 987).

Early, M. (1990). Enabling first and second language learners in the classroom. *Language Arts, 67*(6), 567–574.

Echevarria, J., Vogt, M. E., & Short, D. (2000). *Making content comprehensible for English language learners: The SIOP model.* Boston: Allyn & Bacon.

Edelsky, C. (1986). *Writing in a bilingual program: Habia una vez.* Norwood, NJ: Ablex.

Education Trust, The. (1998). *Education watch: The Education Trust 1998 state and national data book.* Washington, DC: Author.

Enright, D., & McCloskey, M. (1988). *Integrating English: Developing English language and literacy in the multilingual classroom.* Reading, MA: Addison-Wesley.

Epstein, J. L. (1995). School/family/community partnerships: Caring for the children we share. *Phi Delta Kappan, 76*(9), 701–712.

Evertson, C. M., & Emmer, E. T. (1982). Effective management at the beginning of the school year in junior high classes. *Journal of Educational Psychology, 74,* 485–498.

Faltis, C. (2001). *Joinfostering* (3rd ed.). Upper Saddle River, NJ: Prentice Hall.

Fields, S. (1997). Making sense of alphabet soup. *CATESOL News, 29*(1), 5.

Flores, A., & Gage-Serio, O. (2003). The kids from Mexico who don't speak Spanish. Presentation at the California Teachers of English to Speakers of Other Languages annual conference, Pasadena.

Flores, B., Garcia, E., González, S., Hidalgo, G., Kaczmarek, K., & Romero, T. (1985). *Bilingual instructional strategies.* Chandler, AZ: Exito.

Fogarty, R. (1991). *How to integrate the curriculum.* Arlington, IL: IRI Skylight.

Foucault, M. (1980). *Power/knowledge: Selected interviews and other writings 1971–1977.* New York: Pantheon Books.

Fox, M. (1987). *Teaching drama to young children.* Portsmouth, NH: Heinemann.

Frank, C. (1999). *Ethnographic eyes: A teacher's guide to classroom observation.* Portsmouth, NH: Heinemann.

Freire, P. (1970). *Pedagogy of the oppressed.* New York: Seabury Press.

Freire, P., & Macedo, D. (1987). *Literacy: Reading the world and the world.* South Hadley, MA: Bergin & Garvey.

Fuller, B. (2003). Education policy under cultural pluralism. *Educational Researcher, 32*(9), 15–24.

Galambos, S., & Goldin-Meadow, S. (1990). The effects of learning two languages on metalinguistic development. *Cognition, 34,* 1–56.

Galindo, R. (1997). Language wars: The ideological dimensions of the debates on bilingual education. *Bilingual Research Journal, 21* (2 & 3). Online at http://brj.asu.edu/archives/23v21/articles/art5.html#issues.

Gallegos-Nava, R. (2001). *Holistic education: Pedagogy of universal love.* Brandon, VT: Foundation for Educational Renewal.

Gardner, H. (1983). *Frames of mind: The theory of multiple intelligences.* New York: Basic Books.

Gardner, H. (1993). *Multiple intelligences: The theory in practice.* New York: Basic Books, 1993.

Genesee, F. (Ed.). (1999). *Program alternatives for linguistically diverse students.* Santa Cruz, CA: Center for Research on Education, Diversity and Excellence. Online at www.cal.org/crede/pubs/edpractice/Epr1.pdf.

Gibbons, P. (2003). Mediating language learning: Teacher interactions with ESL students in a content-based classroom. *TESOL Quarterly, 37*(2), 247–273.

Gibson, M. (1987). Punjabi immigrants in an American high school. In G. & L. Spindler (Eds.), *Interpretive ethnography of education: At home and abroad* (pp. 281–310). Hillsdale, NJ: Erlbaum.

Gillen, J. (2003). *The language of children.* New York: Routledge.

Ginsburg, A., & Hanson, S. (1985). *Values and educational success among disadvantaged students.* Washington, DC: U.S. Department of Education. (ERIC ED268 068)

Giroux, H. A. (1988). *Teachers as intellectuals: Toward a pedagogy of critical learning.* New York: Bergin & Garvey.

Giroux, H. A., & McLaren, P. (1996). Teacher education and the politics of engagement: The case for democratic schooling. In P. Leistyna, A. Woodrum, & S. A. Sherblom (Eds.), *Breaking free: The transformative power of critical pedagogy* (pp. 301–331). *Harvard Educational Review* Reprint Series #27. Cambridge, MA: Harvard University Press.

Glaser, S., & Brown, C. (1993). *Portfolios and beyond: Collaborative assessment in reading and writing.* Norwood, MA: Christopher-Gordon.

Goldenberg, C., & Gallimore, R. (1991). Changing teaching takes more than a one-shot workshop. *Educational Leadership, 49*(3), 69–72.

Goldstein, L. M., & Conrad, S. M. (1990). Student input and negotiation of meaning in ESL writing conferences. *TESOL Quarterly, 24,* 441–460.

Gollnick, D. M., & Chinn, P. C. (2001). *Multicultural education in a pluralistic society* (6th ed.). Upper Saddle River, NJ: Merrill/Prentice Hall.

Gómez, R. A. (1991). *Teaching with a multicultural perspective.* Urbana, IL: ERIC Clearinghouse on Elementary and Early Childhood Education. Online at http://ceep.crc.uiuc.edu/eecearchive/digests/1991/gomez91.html.

Gonzáles, L. N., & Watson, D. (1986). *S.E.T.: Sheltered English teaching handbook.* San Marcos, CA: AM Graphics & Printing.

González, R. (2002, July). The No Child Left Behind Act: Implications for local educators and advocates for Latino students, families and communities. *National Council of La Raza, 8,* 1–15.

Gottlieb, M. (1995). Nurturing student learning through portfolios. *TESOL Journal, 5*(1), 12–14.

Graham, S. (1991). A review of attribution theory in achievement contexts. *Educational Psychology Review, 3,* 5–39.

Gramsci, A. (1971). *Selections from the prison notebooks of Antonio Gramsci* (Trans. & Ed. Q. Hoare & G. N. Smith). New York: International Publishers.

Grant, C. A., & Sleeter, C. (1986). *After the school bell rings.* Philadelphia: Falmer Press.

Grasha, A. F. (1990). Using traditional versus naturalistic approaches to assess learning styles in college teaching. *Journal on Excellence in College Teaching, 1,* 23–38.

Grasha, T. (1996). *Your teaching style.* Pittsburgh, PA: International Alliance of Teacher Scholars.

Graves, D. (1983). *Writing: Teachers and children at work.* Portsmouth, NH: Heinemann.

Graves, K. (1996). Teaching opposites through music: Lesson plan. Online at www.lessonplanspage.com/MusicOpposites.htm.

Greenlaw, J., & Ebenezer, J. V. (2005). *English language arts and reading on the Internet.* Upper Saddle River, NJ: Pearson.

Griggs, S. A. (1991). Learning styles counseling (ERIC Digest ED341890). Online at www.ericdigests.org/1992–4/styles.htm.

Grimes, D. M. (1977). *Computers for learning: The use of computer-assisted instruction (CAI) in California public schools.* Sacramento: California State Department of Education.

Groisser, P. (1964). *How to use the fine art of questioning.* Englewood Cliffs, NJ: Teacher's Practical Press/Prentice Hall.

Groves, M. (2001, August 20). "Direct instruction" paying off. *Los Angeles Times,* B1, B8.

Gunning, T. G. (1996). *Creating reading instruction for all children* (2nd ed.). Boston: Allyn & Bacon.

Hadaway, N. L., Vardell, S. M., & Young, T. A. (2002). *Literature-based instruction with English language learners, K–12.* Boston: Allyn & Bacon.

Hakuta, K. (1986). *Mirror of language.* New York: Basic Books.

Hakuta, K., Butler, Y. G., & Witt, D. (2000). *How long does it take English learners to attain proficiency?* Santa

Barbara: University of California Linguistic Minority Research Institute Policy Report 2000–1.

Halliday, M. A. K. (1978). *Language as a social semiotic.* Baltimore: University Park Press.

Hamayan, E. (1994). Language development of low-literacy students. In F. Genesee (Ed.), *Educating second language children* (pp. 278–300). Cambridge: Cambridge University Press.

Hamers, J. F., & Blanc, M. A. H. (1989). *Bilinguality and bilingualism.* Cambridge: Cambridge University Press.

Harel, Y. (1992). Teacher talk in the cooperative learning classroom. In C. Kessler (Ed.), *Cooperative language learning* (pp. 153–162). Englewood Cliffs, NJ: Prentice Hall.

Harris, V. (1997). *Teaching multicultural literature in grades K–8.* Norwood, MA: Christopher-Gordon.

Hart, L. (1983). *Human brain, human learning.* New York: Longman.

Harvard Civil Rights Project. (2002). *Race in American public schools: Rapidly resegregating school districts.* Cambridge, MA: Author. Online at www.researchmatters. harvard.edu/story.php?article_id=485.

Hatfield, M. M., Edwards, M. T., Bitter, G., & Morrow, J. (2004). *Mathematics methods for elementary and middle school teachers.* Hoboken, NJ: John Wiley & Sons.

Hawkins, M. (2004). Researching English language and literacy development in schools. *Educational Researcher, 33*(3), 14–25.

Haycock, K., Jerald, C., & Huang, S. (2001). *Thinking K–16, closing the gap: Done in a decade.* Washington, DC: The Education Trust.

Heimlich, J. E., & Pittelman, S. D. (1986). *Semantic mapping: Classroom applications.* Newark, DE: International Reading Association.

Heinig, R. B., & Stillwell, L. (1974). *Creative dramatics for the classroom teacher.* Englewood Cliffs, NJ: Prentice Hall.

Heinle & Heinle. (2002). *Launch into Reading L1—A reading intervention program.* Boston: Author.

Helmer, S., & Eddy, C. (2003). *Look at me when I talk to you: ESL learners in non-ESL classrooms.* Toronto: Pippin.

Henwood, D. (1997). Trash-o-nomics. In M. Wray, M. Newitz, & A. Newitz, (Eds.), *White trash: Race and class in America* (pp. 177–191). New York: Routledge.

Hess, N. (2001). *Teaching large multilevel classes.* Cambridge: Cambridge University Press.

Hinton, L. (1994). *Flutes of fire: Essays on California Indian languages.* Berkeley, CA: Heyday Books.

Holz, A. (1996). *Walking the tightrope: Maintaining balance for student achievement in mathematics.* San Luis Obispo, CA: California Polytechnic State University, Central Coast Mathematics Project.

Hoover, J. J., & Collier, C. (1986). *Classroom management through curricular adaptations.* Lindale, TX: Hamilton Publications.

Horwitz, E., Horwitz, M., & Cope, J. (1991). Foreign language classroom anxiety. In E. Horwitz & D. Young (Eds.), *Language anxiety: From theory and research to classroom implications* (pp. 27–36). Englewood Cliffs, NJ: Prentice Hall.

Houtchens, B. (2001) Teaching English learners: A critical perspective. In M. de la Luz Reyes & J. J. Halcón (Eds.), *The best for our children: Critical perspectives on literacy for Latino students* (pp. 198–212). New York: Teachers College Press.

Hruska-Riechmann, S., & Grasha, A. F. (1982). The Grasha-Riechmann Student Learning Scales: Research findings and applications. In J. Keefe (Ed.), *Student learning styles and brain behavior* (pp. 81–86). Reston, VA: NASSP.

Hymes, D. (1972). On communicative competence. In J. Pride & J. Holmes (Eds.), *Sociolinguistics* (pp. 269–293). Harmondsworth, UK: Penguin.

Hymes, D. (1974). *Foundations of sociolinguistics.* Philadelphia: University of Pennsylvania Press.

Jacoby, B., & Associates (1996). *Service learning in higher education. Concepts and practices.* San Francisco: Jossey-Bass.

Jensen, E. (1998). *Teaching with the brain in mind.* Alexandria, VA: Association for Supervision and Curriculum Development.

Johnson, B. (1996). *The performance assessment handbook: Volume 1, Portfolios and Socratic seminars.* Larchmont, NY: Eye on Education.

Jones, J. M. (1972). *Prejudice and racism.* Reading, MA: Addison Wesley.

Jones, L. T. (1991). *Strategies for involving parents in their children's education.* Bloomington, IN: Phi Delta Kappa Educational Foundation.

Joyce, B., & Weil, M., & Calhoun, E. (2003). *Models of teaching* (7th ed.). Boston: Allyn & Bacon.

Jussim, L. (1986). Self-fulfilling prophecies: A theoretical and integrative review. *Psychological Review, 93,* 429–445.

Kang, H.-W., Kuehn, P., & Herrell, A. (1996, Summer). The Hmong literacy project: Parents working to preserve the past and ensure the future. *The Journal of Educational Issues of Language Minority Students, 16.* Online at www.ncela.gwu.edu/pubs/jeilms/vol6/jeilms 1602.htm.

Keefe, M. W. (1987). *Learning style theory and practice.* Reston, VA: National Association of Secondary School Principals.

Kelley, M. L. (1990). *School–home notes: Promoting children's classroom success.* New York: Guilford Press.

Kessler, C., Quinn, M., & Fathman, A. (1992). Science and cooperative learning for LEP students. In C. Kessler (Ed.), *Cooperative language learning* (pp. 65–83). Englewood Cliffs, NJ: Regents/Prentice Hall.

Kinnaman, D. E. (1990). What's the research telling us? *Classroom Computer Learning, 10*(6), 31–39.

Koch, A., & Terrell, T. (1991). Affective reactions of foreign language students to natural approach activities and teaching techniques. In E. Horwitz & D. Young (Eds.), *Language anxiety: From theory and research to classroom implications.* Englewood Cliffs, NJ: Prentice-Hall.

Kottler, J. A., & Kottler, E. (1993). *Teacher as counselor: Developing the helping skills you need.* Newbury Park, CA: Corwin Press.

Kozulin, A. (1998). *Psychological tools: A sociocultural approach to education.* Cambridge, MA: Harvard University Press.

Krashen, S. (1981). Bilingual education and second language acquisition theory. In *Schooling and language minority students: A theoretical framework* (pp. 51–79). Los Angeles, CA: Evaluation, Dissemination and Assessment Center, California State University, Los Angeles.

Krashen, S. (1982). *Principles and practice in second language acquisition.* Oxford: Pergamon Press.

Krashen, S. (2004/2005). Skyrocketing scores: An urban legend. *Educational Leadership, 62*(4), 37–39.

Krashen, S., Long, M., & Scarcella, R. (1979). Age, rate, and eventual attainment in second language acquisition. *TESOL Quarterly, 13*(4), 573–582.

Krashen, S., & Terrell, T. (1983). *The natural approach: Language acquisition in the classroom.* Oxford: Pergamon Press.

Kress, J. E. (1993). *The ESL teacher's book of lists.* New York: The Center for Applied Research in Education.

Lambert, W. (1984). An overview of issues in immersion education. In California Department of Education, *Studies on immersion education* (pp. 8–30). Sacramento: California Department of Education.

Lane, D. A. (1989). Bullying in school. *School Psychology International, 13,* 5–16.

Langer, J. A., & Applebee, A. N. (1987). *How writing shapes thinking.* Urbana, IL: National Council of Teachers of English.

Larrivee, B. (1999). *Authentic classroom management. Creating a community of learners.* Boston: Allyn & Bacon.

Lave, J., & Wenger, E. (1991). *Situated learning: Legitimate peripheral participation.* New York: Cambridge University Press.

Leistyna, P., Woodrum, A., & Sherblom, S. (Eds.). (1996). Glossary. In P. Leistyna, A. Woodrum, & S. A. Sherblom (Eds.), *Breaking free: The transformative power of critical pedagogy* (pp. 301–331). *Harvard Educational Review* Reprint Series #27. Cambridge, MA: Harvard University Press.

Leki, I. (1990, November). Potential problems with peer responding in ESL writing classes. *The CATESOL Journal, 3,* 5–19.

Leki, I. (1992). *Understanding ESL writers.* Portsmouth, NH: Boynton/Cook.

Leki, I. (1995). Coping strategies of ESL students in writing tasks across the curriculum. *TESOL Quarterly, 29* (2), 235–260.

Lenneberg, E. (1967). *Biological foundations of language.* New York: Wiley.

Lessow-Hurley, J. (2005). *The foundations of dual language instruction* (4th ed.). Boston: Allyn & Bacon.

Levine, R., & White, M. (1986). *Human conditions: The cultural basis of educational development.* New York: Routledge & Kegan Paul.

Levine, T., & Long, R. (1981). *Effective instruction.* Washington, DC: Association for Supervision and Curriculum Development.

Lin, A. M. Y. (2001). Doing-English-lessons in the reproduction or transformation of social worlds? In C. N. Candlin & N. Mercer (Eds.), *English language teaching in its social context* (pp. 271–286). New York: Routledge.

Lindholm, K. (1992). Two-way bilingual/immersion education: Theory, conceptual issues and pedagogical implications. In R. Padilla & A. Benavides (Eds.), *Critical perspectives in bilingual education research* (pp. 195–220). Tucson, AZ: Bilingual Review/Press.

Lindholm-Leary, K. J. (2004/2005). The rich promise of two-way immersion. *Educational Leadership, 62*(4), 56–59.

Lipton, L., & Hubble, D. (1997). *More than 50 ways to learner-centered literacy.* Arlington Heights, IL: Skylight Professional Development.

Little, L. W., & Greenberg, I. W. (1991). *Problem solving: Critical thinking and communication skills.* White Plains, NY: Longman.

Liu, J., & Hansen, J. G. (2002). *Peer response in second language writing classrooms.* Ann Arbor: University of Michigan Press.

Long, M. H. (1987). Listening comprehension: Approach, design, procedure. In M. H. Long and J. C. Richards (Eds.), *Methodology in TESOL: A book of readings* (pp. 161–176). New York: Newbury House.

Longknife, A., & Sullivan, K. D. (2002). *The art of styling sentences* (4th ed.). Hauppauge, NY: Barron's.

Lyons, C. A., & Pinnell, G. S. (2001). *Systems for change in literacy education.* Portsmouth, NH: Heinemann.

Macedo, D., Dendrinos, B., & Gounari, P. (2004). *Hegemony of English.* Boulder, CO: Paradigm.

Macedo, D., & Freire, A. M. A. (1998). Foreword. In P. Freire, *Teachers as cultural workers* (pp. ix–xix). Boulder, CO: Westview Press.

Maeroff, G. (1991, December). Assessing alternative assessment. *Phi Delta Kappan, 73*(4), 272–281.

Mahoney, D. (1999). Stress clapping. In N. Shameem & M. Tickoo (Eds.), *New ways in using communicative games* (pp. 20–21). Alexandria, VA: Teachers of English to Speakers of Other Languages.

Malavé, L. (1991). Conceptual framework to design a programme intervention for culturally and linguistically different handicapped students. In L. Malavé & G. Duquette (Eds.), *Language, culture and cognition* (pp. 176–189). Clevedon, UK: Multilingual Matters.

Malkina, N. (1998). Fun with storytelling. In V. Whiteson (Ed.), *New ways of using drama and literature in language teaching* (pp. 41–42). Alexandria, VA: Teachers of English to Speakers of Other Languages.

Manning, M. L., & Baruth, L. G. (2003). *Multicultural education of children and adolescents.* Boston: Allyn & Bacon.

Marinova-Todd, S., Marshall, D., & Snow, C. (2000). Three misconceptions about age and L2 learning. *TESOL Quarterly, 34*(1), 9–34.

Marlowe, B. A., & Page, M. L. (1999). Making the most of the classroom mosaic: A constructivist perspective. *Multicultural Education, 6*(4), 19–21.

Marshall, B. (1999a). Making learning happen—Whose responsibility is it? (Part 1). *CATESOL News, 30*(5), 11, 12, 14, 16.

Marshall, B. (1999b). Making learning happen—Whose responsibility is it? (Part 2). *CATESOL News, 31*(1), 11, 12–14, 25.

Marzano, R. J., & Kendall, J. S. (1996). *A comprehensive guide to designing standards-based districts, schools, and classrooms.* Alexandria, VA: Association for Supervision and Curriculum Development.

May, F. B., & Rizzardi, L. (2002). *Reading as communication* (6th ed.). Upper Saddle River, NJ: Merrill/Prentice Hall.

McCaleb, S. P. (1994). *Building communities of learners.* New York: St. Martin's Press.

McCaslin, N. (2000). *Creative drama in the classroom and beyond.* New York: Longman.

McDermott, R., & Gospodinoff, K. (1981). Social contexts for ethnic borders and school failure. In H. Trueba, G. Guthrie, & K. Au (Eds.), *Culture and the bilingual classroom: Studies in classroom ethnography* (pp. 212–230). Rowley, MA: Newbury House.

McGriff, S. J. (2005). *Learning styles: A brief overview of differences in human learning characteristics.* Online at www2.sjsu.edu/depts/it/edit226/learner/lrngstyl.pdf.

McIntyre, B. M. (1974). *Creative drama in the elementary school.* Itasca, IL: F. E. Peacock.

McKeon, D. (1994). When meeting common standards is uncommonly difficult. *Educational Leadership, 51*(8), 45–49.

McLaren, P. L. (1987). On ideology and education: Critical pedagogy and the politics of empowerment. *Social Text, 7,* 153–186.

McLaughlin, B. (1992). *Myths and misconceptions about second language learning: What every teacher needs to know.* Santa Cruz, CA: National Center for Research on Cultural Diversity and Second Language Learning.

McNamara, M. J. (1998a). Self-assessment: Keeping a language learning log. In J. D. Brown (Ed.), *New ways in classroom assessment* (pp. 38–41). Alexandria, VA: Teachers of English to Speakers of Other Languages.

McNamara, M. J. (1998b). Self-assessment: Preparing an English portfolio. In J. D. Brown (Ed.), *New ways in classroom assessment* (pp. 15–17). Alexandria, VA: Teachers of English to Speakers of Other Languages.

Mestel, R. (2001, April 25). Childhood bullying is common, study finds. *Los Angeles Times,* A10.

Mestel, R., & Groves, M. (2001, April 3). When push comes to shove. *Los Angeles Times,* E1, E3.

Miller, W. H. (1995). *Alternative assessment techniques for reading and writing.* West Nyack, NJ: The Center for Applied Research in Education.

Mirich, D. (1998). You gotta have heart—Reaching LEP students in the mainstream classroom. *NABE News, 22*(3), 19–20, 22.

Molina, H., Hanson, R. A., & Siegel, D. F. (1997). *Empowering the second-language classroom: Putting the parts together.* San Francisco: Caddo Gap Press.

Molina, R. (2000). Building equitable two-way programs. In N. Cloud, F. Genesee, & E. Hamayan (Eds.), *Dual language instruction* (pp. 11–12). Boston: Heinle and Heinle.

Moll, L. (2001). The diversity of schooling: A cultural–historical perspective. In M. L. Reyes & J. J. Halcon (Eds.), *The best for our children. Critical perspectives on literacy for Latino students* (pp. 13–28). New York: Teachers College Press.

Moll, L., & González, N. (1997). Teachers as social scientists: Learning about culture from household research. In P. M. Hall (Ed.), *Race, ethnicity and multiculturalism* (pp. 89–114). New York: Garland.

Monroe, S. (1999). Multicultural children's literature: Canon of the future. In I. A. Heath & C. Serrano (Eds.), *Annual editions 99/00: Teaching English as a second language.* Guilford, CT: Dushkin/McGraw-Hill.

Montana Office of Public Instruction. (2000). Montana standards for arts. Online at www.opi.state.mt.us/PDF/standards/ContStds-Arts.pdf.

Morgan, R. (1992). Distinctive voices—Developing oral language in multilingual classrooms. In P. Pinsent (Ed.), *Language, culture, and young children* (pp. 37–46). London: David Fulton.

Morine, G. (1976). *A study of teaching planning: Beginning teacher education study.* (Tech. Rep. No. 76-3-1). San Francisco: Far West Laboratory for Educational Research and Development.

Natheson-Mejia, S. (1989). Writing in a second language. *Language Arts, 66*(5), 516–526.

National Association for Music Education, The. (2005). National standards for music education. Online at www.menc.org/publication/books/standards.htm.

National Association for Sport and Physical Education (NASPE). (2005). *National standards.* Online at www.

aahperd.org/naspe/template.cfm?template=ns_index. html.

National Board for Professional Teaching Standards. (2005). Online at www.nbpts.org/standards/stds.cfm.

National Center for Education Statistics (NCES). (2000). *NAEP 1999 trends in academic progress: Three decades of student performance*. Washington, DC: U.S. Department of Education.

National Center for Education Statistics (NCES). (2003a). *Status and trends in the education of Hispanics* (Indicator 7.b). Online at http://nces.ed.gov/pubs 2003/hispanics.

National Center for Education Statistics. (2003b). *College enrollment and enrollment rates of recent high school completers, by race/ethnicity: 1960 to 2001*. Online at http://nces.ed.gov/programs/digest/d03/tables/dt185.asp.

National Center for Education Statistics (NCES). (2004). Public elementary and secondary school districts in the United States 2000–2001. Online at http://nces.ed.gov/pubs2002/100_largest/table_15_1.asp.

National Clearinghouse for English Language Acquisition and Language Instruction Educational Programs (NCELA). (2003). *The growing numbers of limited English proficient students 1991/1992–2001/02*. Washington, DC: Author.

National Commission on Excellence in Education. (1983). *A nation at risk*. Washington, DC: U.S. Department of Education.

National Commission on Teaching and America's Future. (2002). *Teacher shortage question unraveled: NCTAF challenges the nation to address the teacher retention crisis.* Washington, DC: Author.

National Council for the Social Studies. (1994). *Charting the course: Social studies for the 21st century*. Washington, DC: Author.

National Council of Teachers of Mathematics (NCTM). (1989). *Curriculum and evaluation standards for school mathematics*. Reston, VA: Author.

National Council of Teachers of Mathematics (NCTM). (2000). *Principles and standards for mathematics*. Reston, VA: Author.

National Education Association (NEA). (1975). *Code of ethics of the education profession*. Washington, DC: Author.

National Education Goals Panel (NEGP). (1991). *The national educational goals report: Building a nation of learners*. Online at www.ncrel.org/sdrs/areas/issues/envrnmnt/go/go4negp.htm.

National Society for Experiential Education. (n.d.). Online at www.nsee.org.

Nelson, B. (1996). *Learning English: How school reform fosters language acquisition and development for limited English proficient elementary school students*. Online at www.nceala.gwu.edu/pubs/ncrcdsll/epr16.htm.

Nero, S. J. (2005). My visit to Australia. *International Black professionals & Friends in TESOL Caucus, 7*(1), 1.

Newman, J. M. (1985). What about reading? In J. M. Newman (Ed.), *Whole language: Theory in use* (pp. 99–100). Portsmouth, NH: Heinemann.

Nieto, S. (2002). *Language, culture and teaching: Critical perspectives for a new century*. Mahwah, NJ: Erlbaum.

Nieto, S. (2003). *Affirming diversity* (4th ed.). New York: Longman.

No Child Left Behind (NCLB). (2001). Title III, Part A, Sec. 3102. Purposes (1). Online at www.ncela.gwu.edu/about/lieps/5_ellnclb.html.

Nunan, D. (1989). *Designing tasks for the communicative classroom*. Cambridge: Cambridge University Press.

Odlin, T. (1989). *Language transfer: Cross-linguistic influence in language learning*. Cambridge: Cambridge University Press.

Office of English Language Acquisition (OELA). (2004). *Declaration of rights for parents of English language learners under No Child Left Behind*. Washington, DC: Author.

Ogbu, J. (1978). *Minority education and caste: The American system in crosscultural perspective*. New York: Academic Press.

Ogbu, J., & Matute-Bianchi, M. (1986). Understanding sociocultural factors: Knowledge, identity, and school adjustment. In *Beyond language: Social and cultural factors in schooling language minority students* (pp. 73–142). Los Angeles: Evaluation, Dissemination and Assessment Center, California State University, Los Angeles.

O'Grady, C. R., & Chappell, B. (2000). With, not for: The politics of service learning in multicultural communities. In P. McLaren & C. J. Ovando (Eds.), *The politics of multiculturalism and bilingual education* (pp. 208–224). Boston: McGraw-Hill.

Oller, K., & Eilers, R. (Eds.). (2002). *Language and literacy in bilingual children*. Clevendon, UK: Multilingual Matters.

Olmedo, I. M. (1993, Summer). Junior historians: Doing oral history with ESL and bilingual students. *TESOL Journal, 2*(4), 7–9.

O'Malley, J. M., & Pierce, L. V. (1996). *Authentic assessment for English language learners*. Menlo Park, CA: Addison-Wesley.

Orfield, G., & Lee, C. (2005). *Why segregation matters: Poverty and educational inequality*. Online at www.civilrightsproject.harvard.edu/research/deseg/deseg05.php.

Ortiz, F. (1988). Hispanic-American children's experiences in classrooms: A comparison between Hispanic and non-Hispanic children. In L. Weis (Ed.), *Class, race, and gender in American education* (pp. 63–86). Albany: State University of New York Press.

Ortiz, G. (2003). Waivering hopes. *Language, 3*(2), 18–21.

Ovando, C., & Collier, V. (1998). *Bilingual and ESL classrooms: Teaching in multicultural contexts*. Boston: McGraw-Hill.

Oxford, R. (1990). *Language learning strategies: What every teacher should know.* Boston: Allyn & Bacon.

Oyama, S. (1976). A sensitive period for the acquisition of nonnative phonological system. *Journal of Psycholinguistic Research, 5,* 261–284.

Page, R. (1991). *Lower-track classrooms: A curricular and cultural perspective.* New York: Teachers College Press.

Palinscar, A. S., & Brown, A. L. (1984). Reciprocal teaching of comprehension-fostering and comprehension-monitoring activities. *Cognition and Instruction, 1,* 117–175.

Pappas, C. C., Kiefer, B. Z., & Levstik, L. S. (2006). *An integrated language perspective in the elementary school: An action approach.* Boston: Allyn & Bacon.

Payne, C. (1977). A rationale for including multicultural education and its implementation in the daily lesson plan. *Journal of Research and Development in Education, 11*(1), 33–45.

Peal, E., & Lambert, W. (1962). The relation of bilingualism to intelligence. *Psychological Monographs, 76*(546), 1–23.

Pedrosa, E. C. (1990, August). Talking in the new land. *New England Monthly,* 34–81.

Peñalosa, F. (1980). *Chicano sociolinguistics: A brief introduction.* Rowley, MA: Newbury House.

Peregoy, S. F., & Boyle, O. F. (2001). *Reading, writing, and learning in ESL* (3rd ed.). New York: Addison Wesley Longman.

Peregoy, S. F., & Boyle, O. F. (2004). *Reading, writing, and learning in ESL* (4th ed.). New York: Addison Wesley Longman.

Pérez, B., & Torres-Guzmán, M. (2002). *Learning in two worlds* (3rd ed.). New York: Longman.

Perrone, V. (1994). How to engage students in learning. *Educational Researcher, 51*(5), 11–13.

Peyton, J. K. (1990). Dialogue journal writing and the acquisition of English grammatical morphology. In J. K. Peyton (Ed.), *Students and teachers writing together: Perspectives on journal writing* (pp. 67–97). Alexandria, VA: Teachers of English to Speakers of Other Languages.

Philips, S. (1972). Participant structures and communicative competence: Warm Springs children in community and classroom. In C. Cazden, V. John, & D. Hymes (Eds.), *Functions of language in the classroom* (pp. 370–394). New York: Teachers College Press.

Pierce, B. N. (1995). Social identity, investment, and language learning. *TESOL Quarterly, 29*(1), 9–31.

Pierce, L. V. (1998). Planning portfolios. In J. D. Brown (Ed.), *New ways in classroom assessment* (pp. 6–10). Alexandria, VA: Teachers of English to Speakers of Other Languages.

Pierce, L. V. (2003). Accountability and equity: Compatible goals of high stakes testing? *TESOL Matters, 13*(2), 1, 6.

Popham, W. J. (2001). *The truth about testing: An educator's call to action.* Alexandria, VA: Association for Supervision and Curriculum Development.

Poplin, M., & Weeres, J. (1992). *Voices from the inside: A report on schooling from inside the classroom.* Claremont, CA: Claremont Graduate School, Institute for Education in Transformation.

Prabhu, N. S. (1990). There is no best method—Why? *TESOL Quarterly, 24*(2), 161–176.

Probst, R. E. (1988). *Response and analysis: Teaching literature in junior and senior high school.* Portsmouth, NH: Heinemann.

Raimes, A. (1983). *Techniques in teaching writing: Teaching techniques in English as a second language.* Oxford: Oxford University Press.

Ramírez, J. (1992, winter/spring). Executive summary, final report: Longitudinal study of structured English immersion strategy, early-exit and late-exit transitional bilingual education programs for language-minority children. *Bilingual Research Journal, 16* (1 & 2), 1–62.

Rao, Z. (2004). Matching teaching styles with learning styles in East Asian contexts. Online at http://iteslj.org/techniques/Zhenhui-TeachingStyles.html.

Raphael, T. E. (1986). Teaching question answer relationships, revisited. *The Reading Teacher, 39,* 516–523.

Ratey, J. J. (2001). *User's guide to the brain: Perception, attention, and the four theaters of the brain.* New York: Pantheon Books.

Ravitch, D. (1995). *National standards in American education: A citizen's guide.* Washington, DC: Brookings Institution Press.

Ray, B., & Seely, C. (1997). *Fluency through TPR storytelling.* Berkeley, CA: Command Performance Institute.

Reese, L., Balzano, S., Gallimore, R., & Goldenberg, C. (1995). The concept of *educación:* Latino family values and American schooling. *International Journal of Educational Research, 23*(1), 57–81.

Reid, D. (1992). Linguistic diversity and equality. In P. Pinsent (Ed.), *Language, culture and young children: Developing English in the multi-ethnic nursery and infant school* (pp. 16–26). London: David Fulton.

Reid, J. M. (1995). *Learning styles in the ESL/EFL classroom.* Boston: Heinle & Heinle.

Reimer, K. M. (1992). Multiethnic literature: Holding fast to dreams. *Language Arts, 69*(1), 14–20.

Reyhner, J. (1992). American Indian bilingual education: The White House conference on Indian education and the tribal college movement. *NABE News, 15*(7), 7, 18.

Reynolds, F. (1988). Reading conferences. In C. Gilles, M. Bixby, P. Corwley, S. R. Crenshaw, M. Henrichs, F. E. Reynolds, & D. Pyle (Eds.), *Whole language strategies for secondary students* (pp. 138–140). New York: Richard C. Owen.

Rist, R. (1970). Student social class and teacher expectations: The self-fulfilling prophecy of ghetto education. *Harvard Educational Review, 40*(3), 70–110.

Roberts, C. (1995, summer/fall). Bilingual education program models. *Bilingual Research Journal, 19* (3 & 4). Reprinted in L. Orozco (Ed.) (1998), *Perspectives: Educating diverse populations,* Bilingual education program models: A framework for understanding (pp. 79–83). Boulder, CO: Coursewise Publishing.

Rodby, J. (1999). Contingent literacy: The social construction of writing for nonnative English-speaking college freshmen. In L. Harklau, K. M. Losey, & M. Siegal (Eds.), *Generation 1.5 meets college composition: Issues in the teaching of writing to U.S.-educated learners of ESL* (pp. 45–60). Mahwah, NJ: Erlbaum.

Rodríguez, D., & Rodríguez, J. J. (1986). *Teaching writing with a word processor, grades 7–13.* Urbana, IL: ERIC Clearinghouse on Reading and Communication Skills and National Council of Teachers of English.

Rodríguez, R., Prieto, A., & Rueda, R. (1984). Issues in bilingual/multicultural special education. *Journal of the National Association for Bilingual Education, 8*(3), 55–65.

Rose, D. (2001). Acronymonia. *CATESOL News, 33*(1), 8–9.

Rosenblatt, L. (1978). *The reader, the text, the poem: The transactional theory of the literary work.* Carbondale: Southern Illinois University.

Rosenthal, L., & Rowland, S. B. (1986). *Academic reading and study skills for international students.* Englewood Cliffs, NJ: Regents Prentice Hall.

Rosenthal, R., & Jacobson, L. (1968). *Pygmalion in the classroom.* New York: Holt, Rinehart & Winston.

Rowe, M. B. (1974). Wait time and rewards as instructional variables: Their influence on language, logic, and fate control. Part I: Wait time. *Journal of Research in Science Teaching, 11,* 81–94.

Rueda, R. (1987). Social and communicative aspects of language proficiency in low-achieving language minority students. In H. Trueba (Ed.), *Success of failure? Learning and the language minority student* (pp. 185–197). New York: Newbury House.

Sadker, D., & Sadker, M. (2003). Questioning skills. In J. Cooper (Ed.), *Classroom teaching skills* (7th ed., pp. 101–147). Boston: Houghton-Mifflin.

Salovey, P., & Mayer, J. D. (1990). Emotional intelligence. *Imagination, Cognition, and Personality, 9*(3), 185–211.

Samway, K. D., & McKeon, D. (1999). *Myths and realities: Best practices for language minority students.* Portsmouth, NH: Heinemann.

Sánchez, F. (1989). *What is primary language instruction?* Hayward, CA: Alameda County Office of Education.

Santa Ana, O. (2004). Giving voice to the silenced. *Language, 3*(8), 15–17.

Sasser, L. (1992). Teaching literature to language minority students. In P. Richard-Amato & M. Snow (Eds.), *The multicultural classroom* (pp. 300–315). White Plains, NY: Longman.

Scharer, P. L. (1992). Teachers in transition: An exploration of changes in teachers and classrooms during implementation of literature-based reading instruction. *Research in the Teaching of English, 26*(4), 408–445.

Schifini, A., Short, D. J., & Tinajero, J. V. (2002). *High point.* Carmel, CA: Hampton-Brown.

Schroeder, J. E. (1998). Consuming representation: A visual approach to consumer research. In B. B. Stern (Ed.), *Representing consumers: Voices, views and visions* (pp. 193–230). London: Routledge.

Schumann, J. (1978). The acculturation model for second-language acquisition. In R. Gringas (Ed.), *Second language acquisition and foreign language teaching* (pp. 27–50). Washington, DC: Center for Applied Linguistics.

Selinker, L. (1972). Interlanguage. *IRAL, 10*(3), 209–231.

Selinker, L. (1991). Along the way: Interlanguage systems in second language acquisition. In L. Malavé & G. Duquette (Eds.), *Language, culture and cognition* (pp. 23–35). Clevedon, UK: Multilingual Matters.

Shannon, G. (1988). Making a home of one's own: The young in cross-cultural fiction. *English Journal, 77*(5), 14–19.

Sheffield, L. J., & Cruikshank, D. E. (2005). *Teaching and learning mathematics: Pre-kindergarten through middle school.* Hoboken, NJ: John Wiley & Sons.

Shepard, A. (1994). From script to stage: Tips for readers theatre. *The English Teacher, 48*(2), 184–190.

Shoemaker, C., & Polycarpou, S. (1993). *Write ideas: A beginning writing text.* Boston: Heinle & Heinle.

Short, D., & Echevarria, J. (2004/2005). Teacher skills to support English language learners. *Educational Leadership, 62*(4), 8–13.

Short, D., & Echevarria, J., & Vogt, M. (2003). *Making content comprehensible for English learners: The SIOP model* (2nd ed.). Boston: Allyn & Bacon.

Short, K. G. (2001). Why do educators need a political agenda on gender? In S. Lehr (Ed.), *Beauty, brawns, and brain: The construction of gender in children's literature* (pp. 186–192). Portsmouth, NH: Heinemann.

Sim, S., & Van Loon, B. (2005). *Introducing critical theory.* Duxford, UK: Icon Books.

Skiba, R. (1997). Code switching as a countenance of language interference. *The Internet TESL Journal, 3*(10), n.p. Online at http://iteslj.org/Articles/Skiba-Code Switching.html.

Skinner, B. (1957). *Verbal behavior.* New York: Appleton, Century, Crofts.

Skutnabb-Kangas, T. (1981). *Bilingualism or not: The education of minorities* (L. Malmberg & D. Crane, Trans.). Clevedon, UK: Multilingual Matters.

Skutnabb-Kangas, T. (2000). *Linguistic genocide in education—Or worldwide diversity and human rights?* Mahwah, NJ: Erlbaum.

Slavin, R., & Cheung, A. (2004). *Effective reading programs for English language learners: A best-evidence synthesis.* Online at www.csos.jhu.edu/crespar/techreports/Report66.pdf.

Slee, P. T. (1994). Situational and interpersonal correlates of anxiety associated with peer victimization. *Child Psychology and Human Development, 25,* 97–107.

Sloyer, S. (1982). *Readers theatre: Story dramatization in the classroom.* Urbana, IL: National Council of Teachers of English.

Smith, S. L., Paige, R. M., & Steglitz, I. (1998). Theoretical foundations of intercultural training and applications to the teaching of culture. In D. L. Lange, C. A. Klee, R. M. Paige, & Y. A. Yershova (Eds.), *Culture as the core: Interdisciplinary perspectives on culture teaching and learning in the language curriculum* (pp. 53–91). Minneapolis: Center for Advanced Research on Language Acquisition, University of Minnesota.

Snow, C., & Hoefnagel-Hoehle, M. (1978). The critical period for language acquisition: Evidence from second language learning. *Child Development, 49,* 1114–1118.

Soe, K., (2000). Effect of computer assisted instruction (CAI) on reading achievement: A meta-analysis. Online at www.prel.org/products.

Solé, D. (1998). Poetry for pronunciation, pronunciation for poetry. In V. Whiteson (Ed.), *New ways of using drama and literature in language teaching* (pp. 84–85). Alexandria, VA: Teachers of English to Speakers of Other Languages.

Soloman, B. A., & Felder, R. M. (2005). Index of Learning Styles Questionnaire. Online at www.engr.ncsu.edu/learningstyles/ilsweb.html.

Solsken, J., Willett, J., & Wilson-Keenan, J. (2000). Cultivating hybrid texts in multicultural classrooms: Promise and challenge. *Research in the Teaching of English, 35,* 179–212.

Sonbuchner, G. M. (1991). *How to take advantage of your learning styles.* Syracuse, NY: New Readers Press.

Soto, G. (1992). *Pacific crossing.* San Diego, CA: Harcourt Brace.

Southwest Educational Development Laboratory. (n.d.). Profiles of native language development programs. Online at www.sedl.org/pubs/lc05/appendix_c.html.

Spindler, G. (1982). *Doing the ethnography of schooling.* New York: College Publishing.

Spindler, G., & Spindler, L. (1963). *Education culture: Anthropological approaches.* New York: Holt, Rinehart & Winston.

Stauffer, R. G. (1970). *The language-experience approach to the teaching of reading.* New York: Harper & Row.

Stavans, I. (2001). *The Hispanic condition: The power of a people* (2nd ed.). New York: HarperCollins.

Suarez-Orozco, M. (1989). Psychosocial aspects of achievement among recent Hispanic immigrants. In H. Trueba and L. Spindler (Eds.), *What do anthropologists have to say about dropouts?* (pp. 99–116). New York: Falmer Press.

Suid, M., & Lincoln, W. (1992). *Ten-minute whole language warm-ups.* Palo Alto, CA: Monday Morning Books.

Sulzby, E. (1986). Writing and reading: Signs of oral and written language organization in the young child. In W. H. Teale & E. Sulzby (Eds.), *Emergent literacy: Writing and reading* (pp. 50–89). Norwood, NJ: Ablex.

Sumaryono, K., & Ortiz, F. W. (2004). Preserving the cultural identity of the English language learner. *Voices from the Middle, 11*(4), 16–19.

Sunal, C. S., & Haas, M. E. (2005). *Social studies for elementary and middle grades: A constructivist approach.* Boston: Allyn & Bacon.

Swain, M., & Lapkin, S. (1982). *Evaluating bilingual education: A Canadian case study.* Clevendon, UK: Multilingual Matters 2. (Eric Doc. ED225345).

Swerdlow, J. L. (2001). Changing America. *National Geographic Magazine, 200*(3), 42–61.

Sylwester, R., & Cho, J.-Y. (1992/1993). What brain research says about paying attention. *Educational Leadership, 50*(4), 71–75.

Teachers of English to Speakers of Other Languages (TESOL). (1976). *Position paper on the role of English as a second language in bilingual education.* Alexandria, VA: Author.

Teachers of English to Speakers of Other Languages (TESOL). (1992). *TESOL statement on the role of bilingual education in the education of children in the United States.* Alexandria, VA: Author.

Teachers of English to Speakers of Other Languages (TESOL). (1997). *ESL standards for pre-K–12 students.* Alexandria, VA: Author.

Tharp, R. (1989). Psychocultural variables and constants: Effects on teaching and learning in schools. *American Psychologist, 44*(2), 349–359.

Thernstrom, A., & Thernstrom, S. (2003). *No excuses: Closing the racial gap in learning.* New York: Simon & Schuster.

Thomas, W., & Collier, V. (1997). *School effectiveness for language minority students.* Alexandria, VA: National Clearinghouse for Bilingual Education. Online at www.ncela.gwu.edu/pubs/resource/effectiveness.

Thonis, E. W. (1981). Reading instruction for language minority students. In California State Department of Education (Ed.), *Schooling and language minority students: A theoretical framework* (pp. 147–181). Sacramento: Office of Bilingual Education.

Thornton, S. (1991). Teacher as curricular-instructional gatekeeper in social studies. In J. Shaver (Ed.), *Hand-*

book of research on teaching and learning in the social studies. New York: Macmillan.

Tikunoff, W. J. (1988). Mediation of instruction to obtain quality of effectivesness. In S. Fradd & W. J. Tikunoff (Eds.), *Bilingual education and bilingual special education: A guide for administrators* (pp. 99–132). Boston: Little, Brown.

Tompkins, G. (2002). *Literacy for the 21st century: A balanced approach* (3rd ed.). Upper Saddle River, NJ: Merrill.

Toohey, K. (1998). "Breaking them up, taking them away": ESL students in grade 1. *TESOL Quarterly, 32*(1), 61–84.

Townsend, J. S., & Fu, D. (1998). A Chinese boy's joyful initiation into American literacy. *Language Arts, 75*(3), 193–201.

Trivizas, E. (1993). *The three little wolves and the big bad pig.* New York: Simon & Schuster.

Trueba, H. (1989). *Raising silent voices: Educating the linguistic minorities for the 21st century.* New York: Newbury House.

Tucker, G. R. (1990). Brief note—Benefits of bilinguality. *NABE News, 13*(5&6), 5, 17–18.

Tunnell, M. O., & Jacobs, J. S. (2000). *Children's literature, briefly* (2nd ed.). Upper Saddle River, NJ: Merrill/Prentice Hall.

University of California at Berkeley. (2005). Equals and Family Math. Online at www.lawrencehallofscience.org/equals.

U.S. Census Bureau. (2000). *Hispanic population in the United States (2000 March CPS).* Online at www.census.gov/population/www/socdemo/hispanic/ho00.html.

U.S. Census Bureau. (2001a). *The Asian and Pacific Islander population in the United States: March 1999* (Update) (PPL-131). Online at www.census.gov/population/www/socdemo/race/api99.html.

U.S. Census Bureau. (2001b). *Census 2000 supplementary survey.* Washington, DC: Author.

U.S. Census Bureau. (2003). *Language use and English-speaking ability: 2000.* Online at www.census.gov/population/www/cen2000/phc-t20.html.

U.S. Department of Education. (1998). *Fall staff survey.* Online at http://nces.ed.gov/pubs2000.

U.S. Department of Education (2004). *U.S. Department of Education joins faith-based leaders in San Antonio to kick off informational initiative for parents.* Online at www.ed.gov/news/pressreleases/2004/04/04072004.html.

U.S. English. (2005). *States with official English laws.* Online at http://www.us-english.org/inc/official/states.asp.

U.S. Office for Civil Rights. (1970). *May 25 memorandum (DHEW memo regarding language minority children).* Online at www.ed.gov/about/offices/list/ocr/docs/lau1970.html.

U.S. Office for Civil Rights. (1976). *Lau remedies.* Online at www.ksde.org/sfp/esol/lauremedies.htm.

U.S. Office of Elementary and Secondary Education. (2002). *Strategies for making adequate yearly progress, using curriculum based-measurement for progress monitoring.* Online at www.ed.gov/admins/lead/account/aypstr/edlite-slide054.html.

Valdés, G. (1996). *Con respeto: Bridging the distance between culturally diverse families and schools: An ethnographic portrait.* New York: Teachers College Press.

Valdés, G. (2001). Multilingualism. In Lingustic Society of America, "Fields of Linguistics." Online at www.lsadc.org/web2/fldcont.html.

Valdés-Fallis, G. (1978). *Code switching and the classroom teacher.* Washington, DC: Center for Applied Linguistics.

Valenzuela, J. S., & Baca, L. (2004). Procedures and techniques for assessing the bilingual exceptional child. In L. M. Baca & H. T. Cervantes (Eds.), *The bilingual special education interface* (4th ed., pp. 184–203). Upper Saddle River, NJ: Pearson Merrill/Prentice Hall.

Veeder, K., & Tramutt, J. (2000). Strengthening literacy in both languages. In N. Cloud, F. Genesee, & E. Hamayan (Eds.), *Dual language instruction* (p. 91). Boston: Heinle and Heinle.

Vonnegut, Jr., K. (1974). Afterword. In F. Klagsbrun (Ed.), *Free to be . . . you and me.* New York: McGraw-Hill.

Vygotsky, L. (1978). *Mind in society.* Cambridge, MA: Harvard University Press.

Vygotsky, L. (1981). The genesis of higher mental functions. In J. V. Wertsch (Ed. & Trans.), *The concept of activity in Soviet psychology* (pp. 144–188). Armonk, NY: Sharpe.

Vygotsky, L. (1986). *Thought and language* (Rev. ed.). Cambridge, MA: MIT Press. (Original work published 1934)

Wallraff, B. (2000). What global language? *The Atlantic Monthly, 286*(5), 52–66.

Ward, A. W., & Murray-Ward, M. (1999). *Assessment in the classroom.* Belmont, CA: Wadsworth.

Warren, L. (1998–1999). Class in the classroom. *Teaching Excellence, 10*(2). Athens, GA: Professional and Organizational Development Network in Higher Education.

Watahomigie, L. (1995). The power of American Indian parents and communities. *Bilingual Research Journal, 19*(1), 99–115.

Weaver, S. J., & Cohen, A. D. (1997). *Strategies-based instruction: A teacher training manual.* CARLA Working Paper Series #7. Minneapolis: University of Minnesota Press.

Weinberg, M. (1990). *Racism in the United States: A comprehensive classified bibliography.* New York: Greenwood Press.

Weinstein, C. E. (1988). Assessment and training of student learning strategies. In R. R. Schmeck (Ed.),

Learning strategies and learning styles (pp. 291–313). New York: Plenum Press.

Wellman, H. M. (1985). The origins of metacognition. In D. L. Forrest-Pressley, G. E. Mackinnon, & T. G. Waller (Eds.), *Metacognition, cognition, and human performance* (pp. 1–31). Orlando, FL: Academic Press.

Wells, C. G. (1981). *Learning through interaction: The study of language development.* Cambridge: Cambridge University Press.

Wells, G., & Chang-Wells, G. L. (1992). *Constructing knowledge together: Classrooms as centers of inquiry and literacy.* Portsmouth, NH: Heinemann.

Westling, D. L., & Koorland, M. A. (1988). *The special educator's handbook.* Boston: Allyn & Bacon.

Whitney, I., & Smith, P. K. (1993). Bullying in schools: Mainstream and special needs. *Support for Learning, 7,* 3–7.

Wiese, A. M., & García, E. E. (1998). The Bilingual Education Act: Language minority students and equal educational opportunity. *Bilingual Research Journal, 22*(1). Online at http://brj.asu.edu/v221/articles/art1.html.

Wiggins, G. P., & McTighe, J. (1998). *Understanding by design.* Alexandria, VA: Association for Supervision and Curriculum Development.

Wilen, W., Ishler, M., Hutchison, J., & Kindsvatter, R. (2000). *Dynamics of effective teaching* (4th ed.). New York: Addison Wesley Longman.

Wink, J. (2000). *Critical pedagogy: Notes from the real world.* New York: Addison Wesley.

Wirt, F. M., & Kirst, M. W. (1997). *The political dynamics of American education.* Berkeley, CA: McCutchan.

Wold, S. A. (1993). What's in a name? Labels and literacy in readers theatre. *The Reading Teacher, 46*(7), 540–545.

Wolf, D. P., & Pinstone, N. (1991). *Taking full measure: Rethinking assessment through the arts.* New York: College Entrance Examination Board.

Wolfe-Quintero, K. (1998). ESL language portfolios: How do they work? In J. D. Brown (Ed.), *New ways in classroom assessment* (pp. 11–14). Alexandria, VA: Teachers of English to Speakers of Other Languages.

Wolfram, W. (1991). *Dialects and American English.* Englewood Cliffs, NJ: Prentice Hall.

Wong-Fillmore, L. (with L. Meyer). (1990). The classroom as a social setting for language learning. Presentation at the Celebrating Diversity Conference, Oakland, CA.

Wong-Fillmore, L., & Valadez, C. (1986). Teaching bilingual learners. In W. C. Wittrock (Ed.), *Handbook of research on teaching.* New York: Macmillan.

Woolfolk, A. (2004). *Educational psychology* (9th ed.). Boston: Allyn & Bacon.

Yaden, D., & Templeton, S. (1986). Introduction: Metalinguistic awareness—An etymology. In D. Yaden & S. Templeton (Eds.), *Metalinguistic awareness and beginning literacy: Conceptualizing what it means to read and write* (pp. 3–10). Portsmouth, NH: Heinemann.

Young, T. A., & Vardell, S. (1993). Weaving readers theatre and nonfiction into the curriculum. *The Reading Teacher, 46*(5), 396–406.

Zanger, V. V. (1994). "Not joined in": The social context of English literacy development for Hispanic youth. In B. M. Ferdman, R-M. Weber, & A. G. Ramírez (Eds.), *Literacy across languages and cultures* (pp. 171–198). Albany: State University of New York Press.

Author Index

Subject Index

Note: Bold numbers indicate pages on which topics are discussed as key terms.